CONSIDERING CHILDREN'S LITERATURE

D0063983

Where does it [our soul] go when we die?
Maybe it will join infinity!

CONSIDERING CHILDREN'S LITERATURE
A READER

edited by
ANDREA SCHWENKE WYILE
and
TEYA ROSENBERG

broadview press

Library and Archives Canada Cataloguing in Publication

Considering children's literature : a reader / edited by Andrea Schwenke Wyile and Teya Rosenberg.

Includes bibliographical references and index.
ISBN 978-1-55111-604-4

1. Children's literature—History and criticism. I. Rosenberg, Teya, 1962– II. Schwenke Wyile, Andrea, 1964–

PN1009.A1C66 2008   809′.89282   C2007-907126-0

Broadview Press is an independent, international publishing house, incorporated in 1985. Broadview believes in shared ownership, both with its employees and with the general public; since the year 2000 Broadview shares have traded publicly on the Toronto Venture Exchange under the symbol BDP.

We welcome comments and suggestions regarding any aspect of our publications— please feel free to contact us at the addresses below or at broadview@broadviewpress.com.

North America
Post Office Box 1243, Peterborough, Ontario, Canada K9J 7H5
2215 Kenmore Ave., Buffalo, NY, USA 14207
Tel: (705) 743-8990; Fax: (705) 743-8353.
email: customerservice@broadviewpress.com

UK, Ireland, and continental Europe
NBN International, Eastover Road, Plymouth, UK PL6 7PY
Tel: 44 (0) 1752 202301   Fax: 44 (0) 1752 202331
Fax Order Line: 44 (0) 1752 202333
email: enquiries@nbninternational.com

Australia and New Zealand
UNIREPS, University of New South Wales
Sydney, NSW, Australia 2052
Tel: 61 2 9664 0999; Fax: 61 2 9664 5420
email: info.press@unsw.edu.au

www.broadviewpress.com

Broadview Press acknowledges the financial support of the Government of Canada through the Book Publishing Industry Development Program (BPIDP) for our publishing activities.

Copy-edited by Catherine Dorton.

Typesetting and assembly: True to Type Inc., Claremont, Canada.

This book is printed on paper containing 100% post-consumer fibre.

PRINTED IN CANADA

For our mentors and our students

CONTENTS

Chapter IX: Theoretical Explorations and Practical Issues / 297

ACKNOWLEDGEMENTS

For their invaluable assistance: Miranda Deyarmond and Hannah Wyile. For their permissions and generosity: the authors and their publishers.

PREFACE

In selecting the material to include in this reader, an almost impossibly large number of criteria governed our ideal. The key factor we considered when making our selection is that this collection is meant to be a starting place for the study of the many facets of children's literature, not a comprehensive compendium. We introduce nine areas of consideration—introductory ideas, historical books, picturebooks, nursery rhymes and poetry, fairy tales and fantasy, young adult literature, drama and theatre, film adaptations, and practical issues and theoretical explorations—in as broad and complementary a fashion as we can within the confines of this book. Rather than compiling nine books on specialized branches, we've pruned and grafted, with the idea that this book could be used to support and supplement the study of children's literature in a variety of courses and contexts. Most of the selected scholarship dates from the past 25 years, which coincides with the rise of children's literature as an academic discipline; a couple of older selections provide some sense of the continuity of discussions about children's literature. We've attempted to provide a range of perspectives, from generally accessible pieces to more complex applications and theoretical analyses, including a sampling of insights into typically under-represented forms—poetry, theatre, and film adaptations—and their impact as cultural capital. While we also wanted to address the tendencies toward Anglocentrism and Eurocentrism in children's literature studies, the dearth of available translations and the limitations of working solely in English made this goal one of the biggest challenges.

Each chapter begins with a few quotations from works that complement our selections of previously published articles and book chapters; these excerpts can be used to initiate discussion either individually or in conjunction with other contributions. In addition to the leads for further research provided by each article that has a Works Cited, we have appended a brief list of suggested further readings. We've persuaded a few authors to contribute a postscript to their piece, commenting on their current views about their topic, which demonstrates that while a piece of writing may be unchanging, writers are not.

Our hope is that this eclectic collection will provide pathways into the ever-expanding field of children's literature scholarship and criticism, a field with plenty of room for new scholars and advocates.

What about me—do I have an imagination?

I

INTRODUCING THE STUDY OF CHILDREN'S LITERATURE

I am convinced of the importance of children discovering things for themselves. However tactfully an adult may push them towards discoveries in literature, these do not have quite the treasure trove value of the books picked up wholly by accident ... in the process they will learn the art of comparison and subconsciously acquire critical standard.... They may even argue about this with their friends and so make the beginning of an effort at rationalizing their appreciation or dislike of cultural objects. (8-9)

—Peter Dickinson, "A Defense of Rubbish" (1970)

Fast food appeals to the appetites of the young. It may be synthetic, but it is tasty in a bland way. It is cheap, easily available, and requires no effort. Fast food is reliable and consistent; if you have ever eaten a Big Mac, you know exactly what your next Big Mac is going to taste like.

[Twinkie] books have similar attributes. They can be read quickly and require minimal mental effort. Everything is spelled out for you—there is no need to read between the lines, or analyze, or even concentrate. If you have read one book in a series, you can feel confident about what the next book is going to be like. And when you have finished, you can give it away, or trade it with a friend for another book in the series. (50-51)

—Marilyn Kaye, "The Twinkie Collection: Books That Have No Apparent Redeeming Value but Belong in the Library Anyway" (1990)

In the past, educators and librarians who worked with children and their books were inclined to leave most editorial, production, and advertising decisions to publishers and book editors. It was recognized that along with the jewels of children's books came a certain proportion of trash and even more of mediocrity, but there was also a tacit assurance that the jewels in the long run would survive. Today the trash and the mediocre are more threatening. The sheer economic need of publishers to push things into, through, and out the other end of the pipeline means that the best is less visible and consequently is often remaindered and disappears. Because of these publishing conditions it is more necessary than ever for professionals dealing with children and their books to take responsibility for seeking and purchasing the best books with children, reviewing them, and enjoying them with young readers and so helping keep them in print. (392-93)

—Sheila Egoff and Wendy Sutton, "Epilogue: Some Thoughts on Connecting" (1996)

When I read with inexperienced readers I find that their difficulties lie not in the words, but in understanding something that lies behind the words, embedded in the sense. It's usually an oblique reference to something the writer takes for granted that the reader will understand, so that the new text will mean more than it says. Imagine a smart detective standing over a corpse and remarking "Curiouser and curiouser," where a phrase from *Alice in Wonderland* is set into another book as if to say "This is a well-read detective," or in order to draw a parallel with Alice. It's a very ancient habit to make texts polysemic. With Chaucer and Shakespeare it wasn't plagiarism or showing off but a form of tribute or flattery. With modern novelists it might be anything from crossword puzzles to irony. Readers sometimes feel they are really rewriting the story as they read it. Barthes calls some of this "writerly" text. To read writerly text you have to do at least half of the work. (20-21)

—Margaret Meek, "Clubs, Networks and Spies" (1988)

As we become more experienced in reading so we can become less and not more skilled. In some ways we even make one kind of reading do for all. I mean this in two ways: first, about the way we read only what we find comfortable, rushing through novels to finish the story and then going on to another one. Then, if we are reading teachers or teachers of literature, we may adopt too easily patterns of work which don't encourage us to inspect what we do. Habitual readers can become less adventurous than their skills allow. It's like driving in second gear in a high-powered car. (35)

—Margaret Meek, "Adult Lessons" (1988)

Introduction

The study of children's literature is not just about children and the books said to be for them; it is also about the societies and cultures from which the literature comes, and it is about the assumptions and ideas we hold about children and childhood. For adults, reading children's literature is ultimately both an act of nostalgia and of self-examination. When we consider children's literature, we must include ourselves in the equation: What kinds of readers are we? How do we relate to books and stories? To what degree should we impose our experience upon others? Reading children's literature actively can lead to all kinds of remarkable (and sometimes unsettling) revelations about ourselves and our society.

Consider Aidan Chambers's distinction between flat-earth readers and intergalactic readers:

Repetitious reading of any kind of book, of any one author, is flat-earth reading. It may not know about, or worse still may not acknowledge, that the world is round, plural, disparate, many-faceted. Flat-earth readers resist any invitation to explore beyond the boundaries of their familiar territory because of the fearsome dangers that are sure to lie in wait at the edge of their world. One of these dangers is called boredom, another is called difficulty. A third is fear of exhaustion ... (139)

The aim of *Considering Children's Literature* is to provide an initial framework of topics and critical material on the subject and to assist readers in becoming "critically appreciative (galactic) readers" (Chambers 141). This journey will take readers through some surprising terrain!

The first questions to consider in the study of children's literature are inevitably, what limits our understanding of children? and how are our views on literature altered when thinking about literature in relation to children? These are questions that quickly lead some adults to be very sure of themselves, particularly if they haven't spent much time around children lately. The typical view is that children are under twelve years of age, innocent, and must be protected from the corrupt world. Looking carefully at the literature itself and at what educators, librarians, and literary analysts say about the literature suggests broadening this typical perspective. Although we've called the book *Considering Children's Literature*, the essays collected here apply to the full range of books of interest to children of all ages, some of whom prefer to be called teenagers or young adults, and some of whom are indeed "grown-up" in size or interest but have not "grown out of" the wonders that are found in books and literature of all shapes and sizes. As Margaret Meek reminds us in "Adult Lessons," more experience doesn't necessarily make us better readers. Our expectations often blind us to what a story has to offer and sometimes make us see things that aren't even there. The common adult desire to ensure that children have appropriate morals and models also often negatively affects the conception, production, and reception of books.

The four essays in the first chapter provide wide-ranging insights on the fundamental questions that underlie the study of children's literature and suggest that literature is indeed a powerful force. The stories we read as children shape our understanding of ourselves and others, of literature and its possibilities, and of the world as a whole. Aidan Chambers and Natalie Babbitt focus more particularly on issues related to literature and reading. Hazel Rochman and Naser Yusefi provide critical reminders and insights on the inevitable politics that shape the production, reception, and distribution of books. The factors they discuss suggest that part of the reason it can be difficult to become an intergalactic reader is because of societal laws of gravity (all puns intended), which often lead to the very limitations Chambers notes of flat-earth readers. The study of children's literature is full of paradoxes, and therein exists its fascination as a topic of scholarly study.

Works Cited

Chambers, Aidan. *Booktalk.* London: Bodley, 1985.

Dickinson, Peter. "A Defense of Rubbish." *Children's Literature in Education 3* (November 1970): 7-10.

Egoff, Sheila and Wendy Sutton. "Epilogue: Some Thoughts on Connecting." *Only Connect: Readings on Children's Literature.* 3rd ed. Sheila Egoff et al., eds. Toronto: Oxford UP, 1996. 377-94.

Kaye, Marilyn. "The Twinkie Collection: Books That Have No Apparent Redeeming Value but Belong in the Library Anyway." *Lands of Pleasure: Essays on Lillian H. Smith and the Development of Children's Libraries.* Adele M. Fasick, Margaret Johnston, Ruth Osler, eds. Metuchen, NJ: Scarecrow P, 1990. 49-61.

Meek, Margaret. "Adult Lessons." *How Texts Teach What Readers Learn.* Stroud, Glos.: Thimble P, 1988. 35-37.

——. "Clubs, Networks and Spies." *How Texts Teach What Readers Learn.* Stroud, Glos.: Thimble P, 1988. 20-22.

Happy Endings? Of Course, and Also Joy (1970)
Natalie Babbitt

What in the world is a children's story anyway? What makes it different from a story for adults? Why does one writer choose to write for children and another for adults; or, if you will, what quality makes one writer's work appropriate for children while the work of another points in the other direction?

P.L. Travers has said, "There is no such thing as a children's book. There are simply books of many kinds and some of them children read. I would deny, however, that [they were] written for children." Well, perhaps. Sometimes. But someone must have the child in mind even if the author doesn't. Someone, editor or critic, must head a story in the right direction. As a rule, it isn't an especially difficult direction to find. Everyone can tell a child's book from one for adults, just as everyone knows hot water from cold. The difficulty lies in trying to define the essential nature of the difference.

The most common assumption, at least on the part of people who have had little to do with children's literature, is that books for adults are serious in intent while books for children are designed to amuse. But this is only an assumption and nothing more. There are indeed many serious stories for adults and truckloads of children's stories intended only for pleasure, but the reverse is just as true. Fluff, be it trivial or memorable, predominates in both worlds. However, you would be doing both an injustice if you tried to define their separate natures on the basis of fluff. There are no answers to be had by contrasting Jeeves to Winnie-the-Pooh, Hercule Poirot to Nancy Drew, Rhett Butler to the Grinch, or even the Yankee from Connecticut to Dorothy from Kansas. Dear friends all, each in his own place and time, but all members of the same unsubtle family. This leaves in each world an armful of books that are sometimes called classics (make your own list). These are both serious in intent *and* entertaining, as all good stories should be; and it is only in these that any real definition can be found, if in fact it exists at all.

Well, then, perhaps you will say that the difference is still obvious, fluff or no, because adult books deal with adult emotions: love, pride, grief, fear of death, violence, the yearning for success, and so on. But why do we so often forget that children are not emotional beggars? They understand these feelings every bit as well as we do, and are torn by them as often. There is, in point of fact, no such thing as an exclusively adult emotion, and children's literature deals with them all. As for love, "Sleeping Beauty" and her sisters are nothing if not love stories of one kind, while *The Wind in the Willows* is another, and *Heidi* and *Hans Brinker* yet others.

Pride? Where is pride more gleefully exposed than in Toad of Toad Hall? For grief unsurpassed, try the closing chapters of *The Yearling*. Fear of death begins in childhood and is dealt with supremely well in *Charlotte's Web*, while its other side, the quest for immortality, is dealt with just as well in *Peter Pan*. When it comes to violence, Ali Baba, Jack the Giant Killer, and the brave little tailor are only three of hundreds of inventive and bloody examples. And the yearning for success is a thread so common to all stories that I wonder why I even bothered to bring it up.

There is really no difference where emotional themes are concerned. There are only the subtleties, the nuances, the small ironies, of which adult fiction has made far more use but which are equally available to children's fiction, where their fitness is dictated exclusively by the writer's style and his attitude toward the perceptivity of his readers.

No difference in emotional themes? No—I will correct myself. There is one emotion which is found only in children's literature these years and for many years past, and that emotion is joy.

Next you will perhaps turn to range or scope or whatever you wish to call it. But even here, only at first glance does this appear to be genuine ground for defining a difference. While there was a time when the best adult fiction was timeless in nature and dealt at the core with Everyman, that is no longer true. Decade by decade, new books for adults have become more personal, more singular. It is a long and narrowing road from *Moby Dick* to *Portnoy's Complaint*. More and more often we find ourselves making do with what Isaac Bashevis Singer has called "muddy streams of consciousness which often reveal nothing but a writer's boring and selfish personality."

Everyman has gone out of fashion for adults. What separates us has come to seem more pertinent than what draws us together. But Everyman is present still in the best children's stories, just as he always has been. All children can identify with and learn from characters like Peter Rabbit and Sendak's Max, in spite of the years between their creation; but many adults have trouble finding common coin with Henry Miller's Mona the way they could with Tolstoy's Natasha.

Content? Barring only graphic sex and other routine adult preoccupations (many of these dull to begin with), there is little difference. War, disability, poverty, cruelty, all the harshest aspects of life are present in children's literature. Daily banalities are there too, and the more subtle stuff of boredom, prejudice and spite. Where did we get the idea that a children's book is gentle and sweet? The only ones that are are those written by people who have been deluded by isolation or a faulty memory into thinking that children themselves are gentle and sweet.

A children's book is peopled with talking animals and other such fantastics? Sometimes, but by no means always. And anyway, adults are just as prone to attributing human characteristics to non-human things as children are, in life if not in their fiction. You need only mention the family dog or cat at a dinner party to find this out. And as for the dark world, children did not invent Martians, poltergeists, the séance or the Devil, or, I might add, the id and the ego, those goblins that out-goblin anything in the Brothers Grimm. If fantasy is absent from adult fiction, it is absent only because adults are too pompous to admit they still have a taste and a need for it.

A children's book uses simple vocabulary geared to the untrained mind? Compare a little Kipling to a little Hemingway and think again. Opening sentence of *A Farewell to Arms*: "Now in the fall the trees were all bare and the roads were muddy." Opening sentence of *How the Rhinoceros Got His Skin*: "Once upon a time, on an uninhabited island on the shores of the Red Sea, there lived a Parsee from whose hat the rays of the sun were reflected in more-than-oriental splendour." So much for that!

You might in desperation do something with size of type, seeing that children's books are usually printed in larger typeface; but this is really only because they shrewdly refuse to be bothered by anything less. Their eyes, after all, are by and large 20-20 per cent better than ours. You might also be reduced to bringing up length—children's books are usually shorter. However, I question whether, having said this, you have said much.

Not one of the above proposals will stand up. They are too arbitrary, too trivial, too riddled with exceptions. Perhaps it is possible only to settle for knowing the difference between the two literatures without being able to articulate it. And there are just enough stories that fall somewhere in between to cloud the issue further. Scrooge, Bilbo Baggins, Alice, Huck Finn, even Charlie Brown—for whom were these created? Ichabod Crane, William Baxter, Jason and Medea—on whose shelf do they belong? Perhaps P.L. Travers was right after all. Perhaps there is no such thing as a children's book once we are blessedly beyond the forgettable.

And yet it seems to me that there is a tangible difference when you apply one rather simple sieve to the mass. It does not work for every children's story, but perhaps it does apply to all that we remember longest and love best and will keep reading aloud to our children and our children's children as a last remaining kind of oral history, a history of the essence of our own childhood. I am referring, of course, to The Happy Ending.

Not, please, to a simple "happily ever after," or to the kind of contrived final sugar coating that seems tacked on primarily to spare the child any glimpse of what really would have happened had the author not been vigilant; not these, but to something which goes much deeper, something which turns a story ultimately toward hope rather than resignation and contains within it a difference not only between the two literatures but also between youth and age.

What, in the very simplest terms, is a child, after all, but an unrepressed adult? What is maturity, that supposed nirvana we seem never fully to achieve, but total emotional control learned from confrontation with that old apocalypt, experience, which teaches us the necessity for compromise? When one learns to compromise, one learns to abandon the happy ending as a pipe dream, or—a children's story.

When we envy our children, we envy them this first of all: "Oh," we say, "they have their whole lives ahead of them," and we believe with them and for them what we no longer believe for ourselves—that anything is possible. We believe that they may grow up to be another Sarah Bernhardt, a Madame Curie, a Jefferson, a Dickens—pick whichever giant you like. We believe that they may grow up happy, fulfilled, beyond pain. And when we pity our children, we pity them for this: "Oh," we say, "I wouldn't be young and have to go through all that again for anything."

By "all that" we really mean that we remember all too well the first hard lessons in compromise, the abandonment of the primary and then the secondary dream, and so on and on down to what we have at last settled on as possible. Alas, we have arrived and we are not unique after all. We are not beautiful, nor clever, nor even very good; and, no matter how well we do what we do, there is always someone who can do it better. The white house on the hill is lost to us forever, and all of our sweet tomorrows are rapidly becoming yesterdays which were almost (if we were lucky) but not quite.

But for the children, no matter how unpromising their circumstances, it is not too late. And we who write for them, or, if you must, we whose work seems appropriate for them, are perhaps those who, far from being glum, have a particularly tenacious view of life as an experiment in possibility without compromise. If we are not clever nor unique, we can at least recall without remorse how it felt to believe that we might be someday; probably despite plain and discouraging evidence, we are still not totally without hope; and so, in our stories—since, like it or not, every story comes out of the psyche of its author—Wilbur can escape an early death, Cinderella can be Queen, Bilbo can outwit the dragon, and the ugly duckling can become a swan. Not without pain, not without violence, not without grief; but in the end, somehow, everything will always be all right.

To be sure, there are stories for adults which end happily; but it is, in the stories that have lasted, a qualified happiness only, the quiet happiness of characters who have made their peace with their own compromises. So Natasha, at the end of *War and Peace* "had grown stouter and broader ... her features ... wore an expression of calm softness and serenity. Only on rare occasions now the old fire glowed in her again."

Not so with Ratty and Mole and Toad. Their story ends this way: "The ... animals continued to live their lives ... In great joy and contentment. Sometimes, in the course of long summer evenings, the friends would take a stroll together ... and it was pleasing to see how respectfully they were greeted ... : 'There goes the great Mr. Toad! And that's the gallant Water Rat ... and yonder comes the famous Mr. Mole!'" Beauty established, nobility achieved, all obstacles overcome. A pipe dream, or—a children's story.

Axes for Frozen Seas (1985)
Aidan Chambers

The Woodfield Lecture is arranged annually by the Department of Library and Information Studies at Loughborough University under the sponsorship of Woodfield and Stanley Ltd., library suppliers and publishers of *Junior Bookshelf*, in honour of H.J.B. Woodfield, founder of the firm and the journal. "Axes for Frozen Seas" was the fourth lecture, given in 1982. One of the more useful results of being asked to give a formal talk on a subject of your own choice is the chance to concentrate on topics of particular personal concern.

During the 1960s I had argued that more attention should be paid to children's immediate reading interests, that we should respect their views and taste, that we should publish more books that spoke directly to them. I had written *The Reluctant Reader* to support this line of thought in relation to fiction for teenagers, and had become general editor of the Topliners series in an attempt to do something about providing a publishing opportunity.

By the middle of the 1970s, however, I was sometimes dismayed by the turn the argument had taken. I had been saying that we needed the best of all kinds of literature and that some kinds were missing or were only done ineffectually. In other words I was arguing for a healthy, egalitarian pluralism. By the mid 1970s some people seemed to be suggesting that the only literature that mattered was whatever young people immediately liked. The litmus test was no longer the judgement of a particular group of adults from a literary background—whether they had anything to do with children or not (the group I had often criticized for their exclusive control over children's book publishing)—and was quickly shifting to the judgement of groups of adults with other special interests (to do with, for instance, racism, politics, sexism, commercial bookselling and like preoccupations), who always claimed to be working on behalf of children's own opinions and "rights." These care-takers often made a near-fetish of selecting books according to two criteria: first, whether the book met the demands of their own specialist point of view (if it was "positive" in its depiction of, say, sex roles, or would sell in large quantities if book-ownership was the aim); and, second, whether on an untutored reading children instantly liked the book.

The pendulum had swung from an élitist to an equally narrow, populist extreme. Underlying this shift was a changed assumption about the role of the teacher, expressed in slogans like "The teacher should not impose his/her own tastes on children." The modish word was "intervention." Should the teacher ever intervene between children and their reading was a seriously asked question. The old-fashioned attitude held that children learned to be discriminating readers by being given only the best of great literature and being shown by discriminating teachers how to read it. The new view was that children became discriminating readers by reading anything and everything they wanted to and so learned to decide for themselves what they preferred, the terms "good" and "bad" literature being suspect.

I found myself in agreement with neither extreme. I saw books of extraordinary character being ignored by influential adults simply because of their oddity or difference from some popular norm and therefore never finding their way to children, who, as a result, got no chance at all to decide whether they liked them or not. While the important question of how a teacher helps children enjoy what at first sight seem 'difficult' books was seldom discussed or was dismissed as irrelevant.

All this came to a head for me when *The Stone Book* by Alan Garner was published in 1976. In the next few years I grew tired of being told by teachers that children didn't like it, that they didn't think it was a children's book at all. I knew from my own experience that, given some help, children could find it one of the most stimulating books available. Other teachers worked with me in bringing it to young readers, often confirming my own findings, and helping in the discovery of how to read this exceptional work and how to present it to our pupils.

When the invitation came to give the Woodfield Lecture, therefore, I knew what I wanted to do. I wanted to say something about what I had come to think of as "transformational" writing. I meant quite simply literature which, if read creatively, reader and author making the story together, had the effect of transforming us as readers and as people. I had already tried to explore this from a critical point of view in "The Reader in the Book" (34). Now I wanted to demonstrate it through the words of other teachers and their pupils as they reported such readings to me.

The version given here has been slightly edited and begins after the pleasantries customary on such an occasion.

* * *

Before I tell you about the passage from which my title comes, I must try your patience with an autobiographical tidbit. It is twenty-five years this academic year since I began work bringing literature and children together. In all that time some thoughts have remained constant, some aims primary. Forgive me for stating them again; I'll be brief.

First, it is my conviction, strengthening as the years go by, that literary reading is the single most important cultural and educational activity we all—adults and children—engage in. Second, literary reading begins where the reader is and goes on from there. Unless you find yourself in books you have a hard time finding anybody else. Third, the presence of plenty of books, wide-ranging in story and treatment, the chance to browse among them frequently, to hear them read aloud, and being given time to read them for oneself, are all central to children's literary development. Fourth, we learn more and more certainly every year that the mediation of literature to children by a literate, sympathetic adult is the single most important factor in the creation of a desire among children to read, and to read adventurously—a point I shall come back to later.

I repeat all this here because I am conscious that what I want to say in the rest of this talk might easily be misunderstood. So let me reinforce the point. I belong to the demotic tradition; I believe literature belongs to all the people all the time, that it ought to be cheaply and easily available, that it ought to be fun to read as well as challenging, subversive, comforting, and all the other qualities we claim for it. Finally, I hold that in literature we find the best expression of the human imagination, and the most useful means by which we come to grips with our ideas about ourselves and what we are.

Which brings me to those frozen seas. The phrase comes from a letter written by Franz Kafka when he was twenty years old to his friend Oskar Pollack. They were debating the ancient argument about whether literature is simply a diversion, a way of spending time happily, or whether it has some greater value. This is what Kafka wrote:

It seems to me that one should only read books which bite and sting one. If the book we are reading does not wake us up with a blow on the head, what's the point of reading? To make us happy, as you write to me? Good God, we would be just as happy without books, and books which make us happy, we can at a pinch write them for ourselves. On the other hand we have need of books which act upon us like a misfortune from which we would suffer terribly, like the death of someone we are fonder of than ourselves ... a book must be the axe which smashes the frozen sea within us. That's what I think. (*Briefe, 1902-24*. qtd. in Josipovici 12)

Kafka's images are bleak, and for my part I must say at once that I can't for the life of me see why we shouldn't have what both men want. I don't want just some kinds of literature; I want it all. On the other hand, I do have to say that in the end Kafka is right. If literature doesn't do for us what he wants, it isn't worth bothering about. Indeed, if all I am looking for is diversion I can always get it with far less effort than reading costs from television and films, or, best of all, from doing nothing. I am not very interested—and never have been— in bringing up children as diversionary readers. I have always assumed that the idea was to bring children into their literary heritage, and to enable them in the act of the deepest possible and most avidly desired literary reading.

I must admit that recently I've begun to feel that if most people responsible for bringing literature and children together used to think that this was the central aim, a great many think it is the case no longer. An admired and popular poet for children told me the other day that he doesn't regard himself as a poet—which is entirely his affair of course—and that he didn't think it mattered whether or not children ever read any of the poets from our past. Onc rathcr stark example of what I mean. Another, I note with some depression, is that a number of publishers have cut almost to nothing their production of children's novels, except for the predictably popular, and have increased the kind of non-literary publishing they do: the pop-up toys which are books only because they are bound between covers; the gimmick books, the obvious example of which must be *Masquerade* (an admirably apt title in the circumstances); and the promotion of routine adventure stories, thin in every sense, as something virtuous because they are, as the saying goes, what children want.

In fact, the thing that now worries me most is an attitude not just visible but, to use the word of the stockmarket and one which is again apt in the circumstances, bullish. It is fashionable just now to assume—not to argue or suggest but to assume—that what children want are books which have an immediate undifferentiated appeal, that they must be either funny or pertinent, by which is usually meant, the subject must be one that is a preoccupation of the adult concerned. Complexity, multi-layering, richness of language, the kind of book which demands that the reader match the author in an act of creation that costs thought and energy: these are out-of-date.

Before I go on—a last attempt to keep my balance in your ears—let me say that I too look for books that have immediate appeal, that amuse me, and that deal with subjects I want to hear about. And I am *not* someone who claims that the *children* in children's literature don't matter. On the contrary. It is because they matter so much that Kafka's demand for literature that trans-forms—if I may use that word to contain the ideas behind what he was saying and what I'm trying to say too—currently needs reasserting and indeed reassessing in our thinking about literature and children.

Perhaps I should try and identify more closely the sort of book I have in mind when I talk about transformation. Books that transform me as I read, and go on working in me afterwards when they have become part of me, often refresh and reinvigorate the language. At the very least they attend to it. Words are what an author uses. In one sense they are all s/he uses. Thus literature is, among other things, about words, about language. Whether you are like Philippa Pearce, who wants to write in such a way that the reader feels s/he can reach through the book like reaching through a window and touch what is on the other side—an aim George Orwell owned as well—or whether you are like James Joyce, who clearly wanted his readers to feel the weight and quality of his language on the page, you cannot escape language either as an author or as a reader.

Then the transforming books are ones which, as W.H. Auden says in his marvellously lucid essay, "Reading," "can be read in a number of different ways. Vice versa, the proof that pornography has no literary value is that, if one attempts to read it in any other way than as a sexual stimulus, to read it, say, as a psychological case-history of the author's sexual fantasies, one is bored to tears."

Transformational books enrich in some degree our image of the world and its being; they help illuminate me, and others for me, and the society I live in, as well as the societies that other people live in.

To try and boil all that down: the transforming books are multi-layered, multi-thematic, linguistically conscious, dense. The opposite sort of writing is—to use another catch-all word for convenience' sake—reductionist. By which I mean it limits what we read to a narrow range of the familiar, the obvi-ous, the immediately appealing, and concentrates on subjects and treatments confined to the bland and well-tried.

All of which sounds excessively ponderous and solemn, as if I think trans-formational books are always likely to be obscure and difficult. On the con-trary, as I hope to demonstrate in a minute.

Before that, two more points. First, happily there are signs in more and more schools that we are beginning to take seriously the idea that children are quite as capable as adults of critical reading—in the literary sense—and that we need to understand more about how to engage with them in critical responses. Second, we are perhaps beginning to appreciate also that creating literary readers is a matter of raising expectations in the reader that match the demands of the book in question. I have, for example, heard adults tell children that Lucy Boston's *Children of Green Knowe* is a ghost story. That is a case of raising the wrong expectations and there can be no wonder that children find the book boring or confusing and don't finish reading it, if that is what they are led to expect.

These points in mind, let me go on to some books, beginning with *The Crane* by Reiner Zimnik. It has had a chequered history. First published by Brockhampton Press (now Hodder) in 1969 in a translation from the original German by Marion Koenig, it had what is usually described as a modest success. In other words, no one paid much attention. Later, it appeared in a Puffin edition using the US translation published by Harper and Row, which cuts out significant elements. I doubt if that version fared any better. My attention was drawn to the book when Nancy published in the September 1971 issue of *Signal* an article by Nina Danischewsky, which did for me what I hope to find all the time in critical writing. Let me list what I mainly look for in criticism. I hope critics will:

1. Introduce me to authors or works of which I was hitherto unaware.
2. Convince me that I have undervalued an author or work because I had not read them carefully enough.
3. Show me relations between works of different ages and cultures which I could never have seen for myself because I do not know enough and never shall.
4. Give a "reading" of a work which increases my understanding of it.
5. Throw light upon the process of artistic "Making."
6. Throw light upon the relation of art to life, to science, economics, ethics, religion, etc.

Of course I did not compile this list; you'll find it in the essay by W.H. Auden I referred to earlier, which is included in *The Dyer's Hand* (8). Danischewsky's article covered numbers 1 to 4. Pretty good going in one piece. I'm still grateful to her for that service, and expect to remain so. Zimnik's work is, in my view, one of the small masterpieces of children's literature.

The Crane is deceptively direct in tone, plain and simple in the folktale manner, but I began to realize with Danischewskian hindsight that it is also laden with challenges and the features I described earlier as belonging to transformational work. Child characters enter the story only incidentally. The protagonist is, at the beginning, a young workman who wears a feather in his blue cap. He is given the job of driving the town's new crane—the tallest in the country—climbs to the cabin and there remains, attended from below by his friend, the dreamer Lektro, who drives an electric delivery truck.

During the story, as episodic events are related to us, weeks pass and years; even, one sometimes feels, social epochs. Certainly we witness a war, an elemental flood, a repopulation of the earth. But through it all the crane driver stays at his post, a survivor, a witness, a prophetic figure, and a fool in the classic sense. The variety of interpretive possibilities, Zimnik's textual manner, the absence of child characters, and the unapologetic refusal of the text to hide its indeterminacies behind a façade of persuasive explanatory detail have confused, even disturbed, so many adult readers that the book has often been judged "unsuitable" for children, too difficult, too strange.

The fiction is all the more opaque for these readers because of other devices also. Zimnik's omniscient narrator will, for instance, enter the story from time to time, moving from the third person to the first. "I have drawn the town councillors flat on purpose" he suddenly announces on the story's fourth page, and if you look at the illustration you see has indeed done just that. This text detail was one of those cut out of the American version, even though it is a crucial element in the success of the narrative. The line drawings that share the book half-and-half with the words similarly play about with point of view, with the openly fictional set against a pretence of the realistic. They include, for instance, documentary realia like the facsimile of a telegram sent to the crane driver and drawings of fish with holes in their bodies swimming happily about.

In words and drawings, between which there is a subtle and generative relationship, for both are needed to make the Text, the images are placed one after another without specific linking by way of connections suggested by the narrator, or the usual conventions of story logic. So, from readers with closed minds about how narrative should work, the book gets short shrift.

But Zimnik is not trying for the kind of narrative consistency familiar in most children's stories. What he is doing is closer to dream narrative. As in dream, the images present themselves as entirely inevitable. We must first accept them like that, as individual images each with its own meaning, and not struggle to find a logic connecting one to the next. Zimnik helps us by employing an oral storyteller's style: concrete, uncluttered, simple in diction and syntax (or at least that is how the translation is and we must suppose it is true to the original). Not only does this style produce the naturalistic surface Zimnik wants, but it also connects with children. He can be fairly sure that children, if they know any narrative modes at all, are most likely to be familiar with the folk-fairy tale. He can therefore hope to draw child readers in, getting them on his side, by the comfortable familiarity of his narrative's codes and language. Here is a sample:

> The crane grew taller every day and the men working at the top strapped themselves on with safety-belts. Every afternoon, after five o'clock, crowds came out of the town to stroll past the structure and they all said:
> "It's going to be a marvellous crane," and the children—and most of the men—were very proud of the crane.

There was one workman who loved the crane more than anybody else did. He was young and had a feather in his blue cap and he loved the crane so much that they all said: "He's out of his mind." He hammered and riveted three times faster than the other men and when they went home at the end of the day, he climbed around at the top of the crane polishing all the screws with his handkerchief until they shone. Every night he slept under the crane. And every morning he jumped in and out of its shadow while all the others said: "That man with the feather in his blue cap is out of his mind." (14, 15)

In this beguiling way we are offered scenes, episodes, the structural point being not that they make step-by-step sense in the way that naturalistic convention dictates, but that each presents a possible meaning in itself, which, when taken with the possible meanings of each of the other scenes in the book, build up to a sequence of related meanings rather than a sequence of related events leading to a conclusive meaning. Besides this, or along the way, we get scenes of comic extravagance, of poignance, of almost Kafka-esque bleakness and loss. The effect is emotional in quality, not intellectual. If you try thinking about the story as you go along, it becomes impossibly obscure. Afterwards is the time for sorting it out. Another problem, this, for many English readers, whose training has taught them to read with their heads and to naturalize every page as they go along. But I'd suggest that the kind of reading *The Crane* calls for is much closer to a naïve child's way of reading than it is to the trained adult's, which rejects *The Crane* as too puzzling or too difficult.

There is some interesting evidence to support that view. Robert Wintle, a teacher in a Bristol comprehensive school, works with twelve- and thirteen-year-olds who need remedial help. This is what he wrote to me about his children's response to *The Crane*:

When I started reading aloud—without any introduction or explanation—they became extremely attentive. Next day they were anxious for the story to be continued. I was also asked to "just read the story and not stop to explain anything"—such as difficult words. I was fortunate in being able to use the last lesson of most afternoons to read to the class. A further bonus was that the room was a newly converted cloakroom, which, having a concrete floor, had been carpeted wall to wall, as the cheapest form of floor covering. The class of sixteen children soon developed a routine of their own. The desks and chairs were arranged around me so that each child was able to sit comfortably in the semicircle. Some sat on the floor and some sat beside me so that they could see the pictures. Although this is accepted as a norm in primary schools, it was very unusual behaviour for a whole class of children of this age in my school.

At suitable places in the text I held up the book and showed it around the group—quickly, so that the relevant pictures and passages could be matched. The group were extremely attentive, and they were obviously listening with quiet enjoyment. There was an almost tangible rapport with the class when reading to them, which made the experience mutually pleasurable.

When the story was finished, I was surprised that they requested me to read it again. The same ritual with the furniture again took place, but this time they requested a good look at certain pictures which they apparently felt were important for an understanding or interpretation. There was also some discussion on the nature of the town councillors, for example, and also what the children thought was really happening in the story. Naturally enough, they rapidly picked up the points giving insight into human nature or behaviour, although the deeper layers of meaning in the story were not obviously apparent to them. Nevertheless, the mystical and surrealistic elements evoked the greatest enjoyment—for example, the passages about the silver lion, and the eagle. These were the passages which they enjoyed hearing and which seemed to touch a chord—evoke the greatest response—although naturally enough it was not possible for them to put their feelings into words.

The interest in the book was maintained for some weeks, with intense pleasure.

I find Robert's account both moving and impressive. Anyone who has done "remedial" work with children of pubescent age will know how alienated from literature of any but the most immediately enjoyable kind they have been made, how short a span of concentration their stamina can sustain. Yet here is a group whose interest *The Crane* stimulated for "some weeks," and there are features one wants to note. The way, for example, the environment helped—the carpet, Bob's allowing the group to adopt a natural and comfortable physical relation to himself, the book, and each other. (When will we learn that what is true in the early years is just as true right through secondary school where reading is concerned?) The fact that he began without raising any expectations at all is interesting: the adult *not* getting in the way beforehand, for once. Maybe we try too hard too often, and don't trust the book to do its own work.

Nor is Bob Wintle's experience rare. I've heard from a teacher of a class of mixed-ability top juniors, for example, who listened to a serial reading with the same attention as Bob's thirteen-year-olds and who, at the end, stood up and cheered in a spontaneous outburst of applause the teacher told me he had never before witnessed in a classroom. Yet another teacher experienced just the opposite: a total silence she dared not break because it was the silence of an emotion too fragile to speak about.

Yet the continuing history of this book is far from what these reports would lead one to expect. Because I saw it disappearing into the land of O.P., from which few volumes ever return, I persuaded Macmillan to publish the Hodder translation in M Books, the fiction list of educational editions which I edit. From the beginning *The Crane* has been one of the very few poor sellers. Given the experience of teachers like Bob Wintle, one wonders, a little gloomily, why this is so.

Partly, I think, it has to do with the mediating adults raising the wrong expectations, or—much more likely—not themselves being able to sort out what a book possesses. Charles Keeping's work is another case in point. I rushed into one of my local children's libraries recently needing a Keeping picture book for some work I was doing. The librarian said, "Oh yes, we've got it of course, and it will be on the shelf. Keeping isn't very popular." Confident of her words, she took me to the stacks. Not one copy of any Keeping was there. "Typical!" she said. And indeed that sort of thing does happen just when you least expect it. But I fancy she was unconsciously parading the received opinion about Keeping's subtler picture books: that they aren't children's books because their artwork is too sophisticated. This isn't a view held by Jill Hopes, a teacher of infants in a Swindon school. She wrote to me:

> When I consider the hundred or more picture books I have in my room ... in most of them the author/artist's intentions are quite clear-cut. But Keeping leaves gaps for the imagination to fill in a very definite way and in a manner which infants do not often experience ... Keeping uses colour actually to set the scene for strong emotions ... His books usually carry obscure meanings, which children have to be encouraged to find. He makes no concessions to age, and one of the strongest features of his books—and, I believe, an invaluable one—is the depth of the texts. They are usually sparsely worded but with an extension of language which is unusual in picture books. A general criticism made of Keeping seems to be that children will not understand his books. Young children understand more than we give them credit for.

I asked Jill to show me somehow the truth of that. What I got back was not another letter but a book, called *A Book All about Books*, made for me by her six-year-olds, and all about Keeping, accompanied by a cassette of the children talking about their reading of *Charley, Charlotte and the Golden Canary*, of *Joseph's Yard* and the rest. Jill says in her covering note: "After a fortnight of almost pure Charles Keeping, I did wonder yesterday whether I had overdone it, as when talking of the recent assassination attempt in America [against President Reagan], I asked for the name of the president. It was not forthcoming, so I said, 'Come on, who is one of the most powerful and important men in the world?' Lee answered immediately and with great confidence, 'Charles Keeping.'"

Here are just two of the children's responses to Keeping from their book about him, sentences extracted from surprisingly long accounts, considering the ages of the children:

CHRISTOPHER: The pictures look like when I dream because they are scribbly and you can see the shape but they do not look really real.

LEE: When Charley found Charlotte with the golden canary, I felt happy and I don't like losing my friends because Craig was my friend and he has gone to the Isle of Wight and I miss him and feel sad.

On and on through this lovely book: six-year-olds as critics, and enjoying themselves enormously. Open, intelligent, their experience of reading books some say are too difficult for them captured in their own words and drawings. Would that adult critics and reviewers could be so direct, so honest, and so ready to allow a book to shape their lives. I cherish especially one sentence heard on Jill's tape. One of the girls was talking of losing her friend Kevin; she finished by saying with sudden brightness, "But I've still got Kevin in my head." Surely this is a transformation, a coming to conscious understanding of experience, that has resulted from her reading of Keeping's fiction about *Charley, Charlotte and the Golden Canary.* An axe for a frozen sea all right!

There is a critical path to be followed in all our reading, and in our work with children, if the ice is to be broken at all. In reading we pass through a sequence of time-space warps. If we aren't allowed to, the books always remain one surface, one time. We never then discover the narrative layers and the pleasure we get in finding them. To do that we have to stay in the time-space capsule long enough.

Here is another teacher, Irene Suter, head of a junior school in Wiltshire, doing just that with her children—letting them travel for long enough. Rene has converted her office into a mini-library. Every afternoon she has children with her in groups numbering up to eight, never more, for twenty minutes to half an hour each group. This way she sees every child in the school once every three weeks or so and, in that environment, reads and talks informally with them. She has been watching especially what happens to Anthony Browne's books, and has recorded for me the spontaneous comments made by these five- to eleven-year olds when she showed them *A Walk in the Park* for the first time, and then showed them it again later. Rene wrote:

The first stage always seems to be like a detective game—a puzzle-solving: How many absurdities can you find? Already, though, more profound questions are emerging, questions that relate to layers of meaning, inner meaning, pictorial jokes, pictorial representation of ideas, or social implications, or emotional differences, styles of living, the narrow dividing line between reality and fantasy, and the disturbing notion that not all experiences can be accounted for logically. Those more profound questionings seem to be more obvious at a second reading.

I think that books like Anthony Browne's engage children in exploring, from a very early age, ideas such as:

a. there may be other meanings in a text than are at first apparent—layers of meaning;
b. there may be additional parts of a story, not contained in the text, which are apparent only in illustrations;
c. that illustrations themselves can have several layers of meaning;
d. that you can have a practical joke [in a book];
e. that humour may be found in a joke that uses both words and a picture, when the latter has an essential part to play, not merely to illustrate a text;
f. that question-posing, arising from the text or illustrations, can lead to the discovery of additional meanings;
g. that speculation aroused by apparent incongruity can lead to exploration of response beyond the anecdotal or character-exploring stages;
h. that books demand a contribution from the reader;
i. that meaning in a text or picture is not always self-evident, or so simplistic as to be unarguable, and that each meaning is derived only by an individual response, and can be different from one individual to another.

Typical of the first-reading comments Rene recorded are these:

"That flower's got a face!"
"Hey, look at that hedge. It's her! It's the lady—Mrs. Smythe."
"There's an apple on the top there—is it real?"
"What's funny here? It's the trees—look, that's getting thicker—like a tree coming into leaf."

During the second reading the conversation is more like this:

"What's that Mickey Mouse? Is he real?"
"No, he's just a toy."
"He could be waving goodbye to them."
"Not if he isn't real."
"Anyway, what is a real Mickey Mouse?"
"I think that Smudge is just thinking about him."

"It's a funny park! It's all dark in the wood. It's not like a real park at all."
"I think it's a dream."
"It must be a dream—nobody takes pigs for a walk!"
"You could—I suppose."

"Not likely. Anyway, you'd never see Tarzan and Father Christmas togeth-
er—not even on TV."
"You might in a story."
"Yes, but this is a story—already!"
"Yes, I know—I mean, I could write a story with them both in."
"But this story—the words—don't say anything about them."

I hope you'll accept these samples from what Rene Suter claims for
Browne's book and its effect on children. As well, her recording shows what
can be done, where the talk can go, provided two things: that the opportunities are created for such talk; and that books which generate such response
are put before young readers. Another point: as Rene herself is discovering
and saying, we haven't begun to tackle the possibilities there are in talking
with children about literature because we haven't studied carefully enough
how to handle what children say about what they read. At least Rene is taking
the first crucial step: she is listening carefully to what they say and is letting
those cues guide her work.

Before I move on, though, let me quote another snatch of these children's
conversations. "I see a rainbow," one child said. "It's not a rainbow. It's like
my painted one," said her friend. "What's it doing there anyway?" said the first
child. "Well," said the other, "rainbows is happy things. That's why it's there."

Rene's work is admirable. So too was a project reported to me by Barbara
Telford, a young teacher who works in a junior school in Swindon. She read
The Stone Book by Alan Garner and found, she wrote, that

I have never been involved with any written material before which raised
quite as many emotive reactions [in myself]. The family aspects drew me in.
It is now seven years since I finally left my parents' home to build a life of
my own. This summer was the first time that I returned by myself as a daughter not as a daughter and wife. I found myself thinking about the effect my
"roots" have had on my present life and status. I actually stayed at my grandmother's house and helped in a major redecorating scheme which obliter-
ated many of the visual images left from my childhood staying at my house.
The sense of destroying evidence from the past was very strong as the character of half the house was changed beyond recognition. Looking at a photograph of my great-grandparents that fell off the wall, I saw them for the
first time as being ancestors of mine, and not just my mother's ancestors. I
did not believe it possible that I should be secretly perturbed by a modern-
ization scheme. This heightened awareness of the past has emerged in other
situations. I have never been interested in history. I have always regarded
antique bric-à-brac as rubbish. Old furniture has always been ugly and dirty,
in my view. Now I find old things more attractive, as I try to place them with
the people that may have used them ...

The Stone Book has certainly been an axe smashing a frozen sea in the life of that young teacher. And, what is best, she knows it, and is prepared to say so. Under that personally transforming impetus, she took the four books of *The Stone Book* quartet to her class of eight- and nine-year-olds. Her comments acknowledge the difficulties she faced. Her children's appreciation of literature was, as she put it, embryonic. And at the time she was gripped by *The Stone Book*, the general professional opinion was that children wouldn't and didn't like it. Not a children's book at all, some said forcefully.

Barbara's very long record of what happened next is full of insights into what it means to bring transformational literature to children. Here is a flavour of this impressive teaching:

> By having the confidence to allow the children a free hand in a class discussion, aspects of the narrative had to be thrashed out and understood by the group. They were not always given the answers on a plate and very often the children introduced interpretations that I have not previously realized. As a teacher, this is a lesson that I must bear in mind, as I tend to oversteer and restrict channels of thought and imagination ... Yet another warning to me to concentrate more on *what the children say* and less on what *I* am going to say next to keep the group on my own train of thought.

Barbara writes as if she alone made these mistakes, needing to learn these lessons. If she could read a number of transcripts of class discussions of books, and sit, as I have to quite often, and listen to adults talk with children about books, she would realize that what she is discovering is what most of us still need to be aware of.

Most impressive of all to me is Barbara's range of approaches. She sorted out what the book asks of a reader who wants to enter into it to the fullest possible extent, and found child-appropriate ways of making those connections with her children. They climbed their local church tower, for example, to compare their experience with Mary's in *The Stone Book*. (She had to resist a demand that they climb the tower, like Mary, on the outside!) They devised a family tree for the characters in the quartet and then made their own family trees—with, I might add, amusing results in the relationships they discovered among their class. They brought into school treasured family objects—those items of bric-à-brac rubbish Barbara once despised—and found themselves making an exhibition of quite startling variety and interest, the artefacts grouping themselves primarily around First World War mementoes and stuff brought back from the old British Empire in the days when Britannia spread her red across the map: unexpectedly tangible evidence of the deep-seated influence of those two threads in British life still active in the homes of ordinary folk in an English industrial town. They wrote, drew, played games stimulated by Garner's story; and in doing all this, experienced *The Stone Book* itself in at least two full readings, as well as a recording of the author reading it himself, and a viewing of his TV *Writer's Workshop* programme on the background to the writing of the story.

Ending her account, Barbara says, "I did not feel bored once ... never once did I drag my feet on the way back to the classroom after break. On the contrary, trying to work through this project caused me many anxious moments as the time available became more and more curtailed as we approached the end of term. This left timing of the reading sessions rather awkward." She had, she writes, underestimated "the length of time needed and the quantity of content in the quartet. 'I never knew there was so much in it,'" she joked, quoting a *TV Times* advertisement of that year, concluding, "We did, after all, spend six weeks on only four relatively short texts."

Of course there were moments when her children felt weary, moments when they said this was a boring bit. But instead of running for cover, wanting only immediate success and the sense of achievement a teacher can get from the easy business of making children roll about in laughter, she stuck by her enthusiasm, her belief in the worth of the book she was handling, and the value of the time spent, and indeed a belief that in the end her children would thank her for it. They did thank her for it, and there can be little doubting that, in the six summer weeks of this experience, their approach to a work of literature was itself transformed.

Of the books I've mentioned so far, *The Stone Book* best exemplifies the features I began by outlining. Its consciousness of language, the layered density of the narrative, the freshness of its approach to people and events, its structuring, its simplicity, and (the most subtle, least discussed aspect, even among people like myself who admire the book greatly) the fact that it is not the straightforward, sequentially controlled and naturalistic story it pretends to be: all these things make it a touchstone by which to redefine the limits and possibilities of literature for the young.

Of course Garner's reputation guaranteed considerable attention for the quartet, whatever the judgements reached when it came out. Quoting Auden again:

We cannot read an author for the first time in the same way that we read the latest book by an established author. In a new author, we tend to see either only his virtues or only his defects and, even if we do see both, we cannot see the relation between them. In the case of an established author, if we can still read him at all, we know that we cannot enjoy the virtues without tolerating the defects we deplore. Moreover, our judgement of an established author is never simply an aesthetic judgement. In addition to any literary merit it may have, a new book by him has a historic interest for us as the act of a person in whom we have long been interested. He is not only a poet or a novelist; he is also a character in our biography. (4)

This being so, we should examine carefully how we arrive at our decisions about the books we bring to children, and the features of those books to which we direct children's attention. Let me, therefore, tell you the plot of my own reading.

The first question I ask is *not,* "Will children like this book?" The first question, it seems to me, should be, "What happens to me as I read this book?"

I am still surprised at how difficult it is for most children's-book professionals to disengage from an immediate attempt, as soon as they pick up a book, to put some representative child in front of them as they read. All this does is act as a barrier to their own understanding, and therefore to their assessment.

So first, read; and as I read I am, to use a crude image, tape-recording my response as I go. This sounds terribly self-conscious and wearying, but it isn't, once you're used to it.

My responses fall into two categories. First, there are those caused by some feature or other in the book calling up my history as a person. Thus, for example, any domestic death scene inevitably conjures numerous memories of my childhood spent as an undertaker's son. And this colours my reading; it has to be allowed for, set against what the book may be trying to evoke. And part of this personally based reaction is the response caused by my history as a reader. In other words, to some extent all books are made out of other books; and all reading is made or marred by our previous reading. These elements must be sorted out too. Sometimes an author will deliberately be playing on them, as, to take an obvious example, the Ahlbergs do with nursery tales and characters in *Each Peach Pear Plum,* and as Jane Austen makes use of her teenage reading of Gothic novels in *Northanger Abbey.* Sometimes a book cannot escape its literary antecedents whether it wants to or not, as is the case with David Storey's *Saville,* which cannot escape D.H. Lawrence's *Sons and Lovers.*

Already, then, there is the book I read as I was reading it for the first time, and a second book that results from my contemplation of that experience. Now we find a third book, the one that answers the question, "How did the author make this book?" This is the sort of reading many of us were taught in secondary- and college-level English Lit. Some of us dislike it because of that drilling. I happen to have been taught by someone who made literary detective work enormously invigorating, so I still enjoy doing it. And it does help one understand what an author wants readers to meet in her/her work.

That done—and it sounds too pat and schematic; in fact, everything goes on in one's mind at once—the next question is, "What does this book call for from a reader if s/he is to enjoy what it offers and to discover the book's potentialities?" It is at this point that talking with other readers makes the most sense. If you like, our talking begins with a sharing of enthusiasms. I like this bit, I didn't like that bit, how surprising that you noticed that and not this

... and so on. It moves on to a sharing of problems. Why do you think the author did this? What does that mean? Why aren't we told about such-and-such? But at the heart of the exchange is always an attempt to discover the book the author was trying to make. So now we have a fourth book: the one that grows out of sharing experience and understanding.

While all this is going on we begin to see what we will need to do with children if they are to match themselves and this particular book, as Barbara Telford did with *The Stone Book*. We also find out the reference points a reader needs. Some may be too obscure for our children and then we'll know it might be better to lead up to this book through others that prepare the way—as, say, *Flat Stanley* happens to prepare the way for *The Shrinking of Treehorn*: they lie on the same track of narrative manner. We begin, in other words, to set the book up against the children, begin to answer the question, not "Will children like this book?" but 1) Is this book worth children's time and attention? If so, 2) How do I best help them engage in it, and so enjoy it? We decide, from our understanding of the book, what expectations to raise in children about it, and how best to raise those expectations in the children who face us. We might here recall Robert Wintle's wisdom in letting the book do its own work sometimes, without the adult raising any expectations at all but simply acting as an enabler: the person who provides time, the right kind of reading environment, the books themselves, and the atmosphere in which to read them.

In the end, if literature for children is to act like axes smashing frozen seas, the hands that best wield those axes will belong to sympathetic and knowledgeable adults who wield for themselves, with enormous pleasure and skill, axes of their own size and weight.

Works Cited

Ahlberg, Janet and Allan Ahlberg. *Each Peach Pear Plum*. London: Kestral, 1978.

Auden, W.H. "Reading." *The Dyer's Hand and Other Essays*. London: Faber & Faber, 1963.

Brown, Jeff. *Flat Stanley*. London: Methuen, 1968.

Browne, Anthony. *A Walk in the Park*. London: Hamish Hamilton, 1977.

Chambers, Aidan. "The Reader in the Book." *Booktalk*. London: Bodley, 1985. 34-58.

Danischewsky, Nina. "Re-Viewing Reiner Zimnik or 'Don't Mind Me! I'm Happy!'" *Signal 6* (September 1971): 115-25.

Garner, Alan. *The Stone Book*. London: Collins, 1976.

Heide, Florence Parry. *The Shrinking of Treehorn*. London: Kestral, 1975.

Josipovici, Gabriel, ed. *The Modern English Novel: The Reader, the Writer and the Work*. London: Open Books, 1976.

Keeping, Charles. *Charley, Charlotte and the Golden Canary*. Oxford: Oxford UP, 1967.

Zimnik, Reiner. *The Crane*. Leicester: Brockhampton, 1969.

Postscript (2005)

After a quick glance through, the thing that strikes me now is that there are various topics touched on which I later turned into books or separate pieces. For example, the thinking that became *Tell Me* is in embryo.

I have to say that, for me, the best of my pieces of this kind is "Anne Frank's Pen" in *Reading Talk*—with "The Future of the Book" as an addition (the two were originally a two-part lecture). "Axes" is a kind of beginning. "Anne Frank" and "The Future" are a kind of summation.

Introduction: Beyond Political Correctness (1993)
Hazel Rochman

> ... the merely human
> is denied me still
> and I am now no longer beast
> but saint.
> —Lucille Clifton

Multiculturalism is a trendy word, trumpeted by the politically correct with a stridency that has provoked a sneering backlash. There are P.C. watchdogs eager to strip from the library shelves anything that presents a group as less than perfect. The ethnic "character" must always be strong, dignified, courageous, loving, sensitive, wise. Then there are those who watch for authenticity: how dare a white write about blacks? What's a Gentile doing writing about a Jewish old lady and her African American neighbours? The chilling effect of this is a kind of censorship and a reinforcement of apartheid.

It's easy to laugh at the lunatic fringe. According to P.C. labelling, I should change my name to Hazel Rochperson. They comfort me that I am vertically challenged (short), my husband is differently hirsute (bald), my mother is chronologically gifted (old), my brother differently abled (brain-injured), and some of my best friends are people of size (fat). Not at all comforting are the same kind of euphemisms from the corporate world: words like downsizing (firing workers). Then there's ethically different (corrupt) and caloric insufficiency (hunger), or a new one for hunger, misnourishment.

But the greatest danger from the politically correct bullies is that they create a backlash, and that backlash is often self-righteous support for the way things are. Whether we are weary or indignant, we wish the whiners would just go away. Or we focus on the absurd and on the names, and then we can ignore the real issues of prejudice and hatred that keep people apart. Ethnic cleansing is the current euphemism: it's an attack on multiculturalism, and it isn't funny at all.

In promoting books with young people, we have to resist the extremes: the mindless conformity to the P.C. of multiculturalism but also the backlash. As with that other current fad, whole language, the pretentious jargon is only now catching up with what we've been doing all along—teaching and sharing great books from everywhere, stories that grab us and extend our view of ourselves.

Growing up in South Africa, I didn't think that anyone could write a good story about where I lived. I was an avid reader, but books were about English girls in boarding school or lovers running wild on the windy moors. My romantic dreams came from Hollywood. Gangsters were in Chicago, and poor people were noble heroes struggling far away in the Dust Bowl in Oklahoma. I certainly didn't think that there could be an interesting story about blacks where I lived. They were servants, not individuals like me with complex feelings and difficult moral choices, not like my family and friends, or people in books.

Apartheid didn't seem to have much to do with me. I grew up in a liberal home. I wasn't allowed to make racist remarks. I thought I was a good person. I didn't see what was going on around me. I took it all for granted. I never noticed that there were no black kids my age in my neighbourhood; not one black student in my school. I just accepted that the woman who cooked and cleaned for us lived in a room in the backyard. We knew only her first name or referred to her as the "girl"; I never thought that her children lived far away or that she was forced to leave them in order to come and look after me. I remember vaguely that one of her children died. I never asked her about her life. Read a story about her? From her point of view? What point of view?

As editor of *Somehow Tenderness Survives: Stories of Southern Africa*, I included Doris Lessing's "The Old Chief Mshlanga," a story very close to my experience of growing up white and privileged and apart. In the story, the teenage girl calls black people "natives," a derogatory term in Africa, with racist overtones of primitive, uncivilized. The natives were "as remote as the trees and rocks" (25). They were "an amorphous, black mass," and, of course, their language was "uncouth" and "ridiculous" (26). It's as if the white girl is asleep or blind. Then she meets a black man, the old Chief Mshlanga; he once owned the whole district before the whites came and "opened it up" (30). She sees him as a person, not just a native, and that starts her waking up to the world around her. First, it seems quite easy: Why can't they all live together, black and white, without elbowing each other out of the way? But she discovers that you can't just set things right with "an easy gush of feeling, saying: I could not help it. I am also a victim" (41).

She comes of age—as I did under apartheid—with the shocking awareness that the universe you've always taken for granted is evil.

Another story in the collection is from Mark Mathabane's autobiography *Kaffir Boy: The True Story of a Black Youth's Coming of Age in Apartheid South Africa.* Mathabane grew up in the ghetto of Alexandra Township, barely 10 miles from where I lived on a tree-lined Johannesburg city street. But it was another universe, unimaginable to me when I was growing up. Like the overwhelming majority of whites, I never set foot there, and I blocked out any awareness of its daily life.

Until two or three years ago, Mathabane's book was banned in South Africa. You can see why. Not only does he describe the cruel oppression, he makes us see that black child as an individual, like me. Mathabane's family are people. They aren't amorphous saintly victims, nor are they wild savages. They're definitely not the innocent, mysterious primitives in the popular safari-adventure stories of dark Africa. Racism dehumanizes, but a good story defeats the stereotype. It makes us imagine that boy's life in all its complexity and connects it to ours.

It's not just South Africa. Just as I, a white child in Johannesburg, saw the blacks around me as undifferentiated "natives," so Maya Angelou, growing up in segregated Stamps, Arkansas, couldn't see whites as individuals: "People were those who lived on my side of town. I didn't like them all, or, in fact, any of them very much, but they were people. These others, the strange pale creatures that lived in their alien unlife, weren't considered folks. They were whitefolks" (21).

They all look alike. *We* are the individuals.

A good book can help to break down those barriers. Books can make a difference in dispelling prejudice and building community: not with role models and literal recipes, not with noble messages about the human family, but with enthralling stories that make us imagine the lives of others. A good story lets you know people as individuals in all their particularity and conflict; and once you see someone as a person—flawed, complex, striving—then you've reached beyond stereotype. Stories, writing them, telling them, sharing them, transforming them, enrich us and connect us and help us to know each other.

But it's insulting to say that a book is good *because* it's multicultural. Betsy Hearne, editor of the *Bulletin of the Center for Children's Books,* was appalled at a recent conference to hear people recommend a book only because it was multicultural, as if no further evaluation were needed.

And Yet ... Beyond Recipes and Role Models

How do you evaluate books across cultures? Are there special criteria? What are the pitfalls? And in a time of declining book budgets in libraries and school media centres, when librarians do have to select very carefully, how do you balance all the demands of literary quality and popular appeal and intellectual freedom and curriculum support and multiculturalism? And how do you make kids want to read?

Of course, these issues aren't new, and there are no simple answers. As the arguments about political correctness reach a crescendo, I find myself agreeing and disagreeing with everybody. If there's one thing I've learned in this whole multicultural debate, it's not to trust absolutes. I say something and then immediately qualify it with "And yet ..." And it's usually because I find a book that upsets all my neat categories. That's what good books do: they unsettle us, make us ask questions about what we thought was certain. They don't just reaffirm everything we already know.

Underlying much of the P.C. debate is the demand that each book must do it all. Let's face it, a lot of kids don't read much for fun, especially as they get older. They don't have time. They get their stories, their dreams, their escape entertainment, without effort from TV and video and commercials. For many students, reading isn't a need and a pleasure. It's a drag. Something you do for a grade, if you have to.

The poet Katha Pollitt says that it's because young people read so little that there's such furious debate about the canon. If they read all kinds of books all the time, particular books wouldn't matter so much. If you think that the book you're promoting is the only one kids are ever going to read on a subject—about pioneers or about Columbus or about the Holocaust or about apartheid—then there's intense pressure to choose the "right" book with the "right" message. If we don't watch out, reading becomes only therapy, only medicine. We start to recommend books because they give us the *right* role models, depending on what's considered "right" in the current political climate.

Censors think that readers treat a story like a recipe or a self-help manual with directions to follow, so that you go out and do literally what you're reading about. I'm not sure what happens when we read. It's mysterious. A story grabs us; a phrase sings and won't let us be; a street or a room gives us a view; the conflict in a character startles us into seeing ourselves in a new way.

The paradox is that if we give young people didactic tracts, or stories so bland that they offend nobody, we're going to make them read even less. For books to give pleasure there has to be tension and personality, laughter and passionate conflict. That's what will grab kids and touch them deeply—and make them want to read.

A good story is rich with ambiguity. You sympathize with people of all kinds. Read Anne Fine's funny YA novels, like *My War with Goggle-Eyes*, and you get swept up into furious family quarrels about relationships and about ideas, where neither side wins. The best books glory in conflict. This is especially so with political themes, where everything can degenerate into propaganda if the characters become mouthpieces for worthy ideas. Susan Sontag uses a wonderful expression: "Literature is a party," she says, "even as disseminators of indignation, writers are givers of pleasure" (xviii).

The novelist E.L. Doctorow says that one of the things he most admires about George Bernard Shaw is that "he gave the best speeches to the people he disagreed with.... You have to allow the ambiguity. You have to allow for something to be itself and its opposite at the same time" (90).

Censors on the left and the right can't allow for ambiguity. One of their constant mistakes is to take what the narrator says, or what one character says, as the voice of the author. The Canadian novelist Margaret Atwood complains, "It's amazing the extent to which readers will think that everything anybody in any of your books says is an expression of your own opinion. Literature just doesn't work like that" (qtd. in Sumrall 76). If you judge every character to be the author, then you can never allow debate in a book, never have a protagonist who has an ugly or erroneous thought, never have a narrator who's less than perfect—perfect, that is, according to the current fashion.

A library collection does have to satisfy all kinds of requirements. But each book can't do it all. When Walter Dean Myers spoke at the Columbia Children's Literature Institute in 1990, someone in the audience asked him why he wrote a book about black kids playing basketball—it's such a stereotype, why was he feeding it? "Every book I write," he replied, "can't take on the whole African American experience." He said he had written other books in which kids did other things. But, he said, he likes basketball; lots of African American kids like basketball; and this one book is about that world.

One book doesn't carry the whole ethnic group experience. In Sook Nyul Choi's *Year of Impossible Goodbyes*, chosen as an ALA Best Book for Young Adults, the Japanese occupiers of North Korea during World War II, as seen through the eyes of a young Korean girl, are cruel and oppressive enemies. Japan-bashing is a problem in the US now, but that doesn't affect the truth of this story. You could read that book with Yoko Kawashima Watkins' *So Far from the Bamboo Grove*, about a Japanese girl on the run from cruel Koreans after World War II. Or with Yoshiko Uchida's fiction and autobiography about how Japanese Americans were treated here during World War II.

What's more, one writer is not the representative of a whole ethnic group. Maxine Hong Kingston, who wrote the classic memoir *The Woman Warrior*, complains about "the expectation among readers and critics that I should represent the race. Each artist has a unique voice. Many readers don't understand that. What I look forward to is the time when many of us are published and then we will be able to see the range of viewpoints, of visions, of what it is to be Chinese American" (qtd. in Sumrall 77). Nor does one reviewer speak for a whole ethnic group. Phoebe Yeh, a children's book editor at Scholastic, says that she is a reader before she is Chinese. I'm a Jew, but I can't speak for all Jews. Nor for all South Africans; nor even for all South Africans who are anti-apartheid.

And every time an artist or writer does something, it doesn't have to be about her race. Sheila Hamanaka's book *The Journey* is based on her five-panel mural painting. It shows the World War II experience of Japanese Americans, including her own family, who were herded up and sent to concentration camps. It's a story of prejudice and injustice, personal and official, and Hamanaka is passionate about what happened to her people. But some of Hamanaka's books aren't focused on the Japanese American experience at all. *A Visit to Amy-Claire* is a picture book about a family, about sibling rivalry, and the family happens to be Asian American. Recently, Hamanaka illustrated a delightful picture book, *Sofie's Role* by Amy Heath, about a family bakery, and there are no Asian characters at all.

Accuracy and Authenticity

Now, there are people who say that Hamanaka should stick to stories about Asians. Or that Lloyd Alexander's *The Remarkable Journey of Prince Jen* (*Booklist*'s Top of the List winner for fiction in 1991) can't be any good because Alexander can't really know the Chinese tradition. Or that Chinese American Ed Young can't illustrate African American folklore because he can't really know the culture. One of the most violent debates swirling around the issue of multicultural literature relates to accuracy and authenticity.

Of course accuracy matters. You can get a lot of things wrong as a writer, an artist, or a reviewer when you don't know a place or a culture. Junko Yokota Lewis, who's from Japan, has pointed out some important errors in Japanese costume and custom in pictures books published in the US. For example, she shows that one illustration has characters wearing their kimonos in a style that only dead people are dressed in, another shows characters with chopsticks in their hair; a third depicts food in a manner appropriate only when served to deceased ancestors. I'm from South Africa, so I know that culture better than the average American does, and reviewing a book about apartheid I might find things that others might miss.

And yet ... that isn't the whole story. Sometimes I worry that I know too much, that I can't see the forest for the trees, that steeped as I am in the South African culture, I can't always know what an American teenager doesn't know. Would an American reader be confused by something that I take for granted? One of the things that does help me is that I no longer live in South Africa, so to some extent I can see things from outside as well as in—from both sides of the border.

So what about those who say that an American can never write about Japan, that men can't write about women? In fact, some take it further. Only Indians can really judge books about Indians, Jews must review books about Jews. And further still, you get the ultimate extreme, blacks should only read about blacks, Latinos about Latinos, locking us into smaller and tighter boxes.

What I hear echoing in that sort of talk is the mad drumbeat of apartheid-speak. Apartheid made laws on the basis of so-called immutable differences.

Not only should whites and blacks be kept absolutely apart and educated separately, but among blacks, each "tribe" should be kept separate, so that Zulus should live only with Zulus and be taught in Zulu about Zulus to do things that only Zulus do. The apartheid planners said that the only work blacks could do was simple manual labour, that science and abstract thinking weren't part of their culture, and that their training should prepare them to be good servants. It's so absurd that it's hard to believe how much of it was carried out, and with untold suffering to millions.

When I went back to South Africa in 1990, I interviewed Nadine Gordimer for *Booklist* at her home in Johannesburg. I asked her if she felt that as a white she could write about black experience, and how she answered those who said she was using black suffering. She got angry. "How does a writer write from the point of view of a child?" she said. "Or from the point of view of an old person when you are 17 years old? How does a writer change sex? How could the famous soliloquy of Molly Bloom have been written by James Joyce? Has any woman ever written anything as incredibly intimate? I mean, how did Joyce know how a woman feels before she's going to get her period?" (101).

Then, in 1992, I interviewed Virginia Hamilton. She spoke about her frustration in not being allowed to write *outside* the black experience. "People won't allow it; critics won't allow it," she said. "If I would do a book that didn't have blacks, people would say, 'Oh, what is Virginia Hamilton doing?' I feel the limitation," she explained. "I'm always running up against it and knocking it down in different ways, whichever way I can. But I know that it's there and will always be there. I mean, there were people who said in the middle of my career, 'Now Virginia Hamilton has finally faced who she is.' Well, how dare they?" (1021).

In a wonderful article called "What Mean We, White Man?" Roger Sutton sums it up this way: "Literature—language— ... is a way to jump out of our own skins. If we cannot reach beyond the bounds of race, ethnicity, sex, sexual orientation, and class, literature is useless, leaving writers few options beyond Joni Mitchell-style confessional lyrics" (156).

And yet ... only gifted writers can do it, write beyond their own cultures. Fiction and nonfiction are full of people who don't get beyond stereotype because the writer cannot imagine them as individuals. Traveling to foreign places—or reading about them—isn't necessarily broadening. Many tourists return from their experience with the same smug stereotypes about "us" and "them." Too many books *about* other countries, written without knowledge or passion, take the "tourist" approach, stressing the exotic, or presenting a static society with simple categories. Some writers who try to tackle a country's complex political and social issues seem to think that in a book for young people it's fine to do a bit of background reading and then drop into a country for a few weeks, take some glossy pictures, and go home and write a book about it.

There's nothing wrong with writing a book about travel, about how it feels to be in a foreign place, even about finding a foreign place exotic. But don't pretend you're writing about the place or the people there. If the book takes a tourist approach, just touching down from the cruise ship for some local shopping, then you get the kind of nonfiction photo-essay so common in children's literature, where the pictures are arranged so that the child—usually attired in national dress—goes on a "journey," a journey that allows the book to include some colourful scenery and local customs.

Yes, authenticity matters, but there is no formula for how you acquire it. Anybody can write about anything—if they're good enough. There will always be inauthentic or inaccurate books, and defining authenticity on some exclusionary basis or other won't change a thing. The only way is to combat inaccuracy with accuracy—not with pedigrees.

Saints, Role Models, and Stereotypes

The savage savage is a stereotype, but the noble savage is, too. Both are designed to set up borders, to keep "them" far away from "us."

Michael Dorris, who acted as a consultant for the Native American list in this book, said in a *New York Times* article about the depiction of Indians in the movie *Dances with Wolves*: "Readers and viewers of such sagas are left with a predominant emotion of regret for a golden age now but a faint memory. In the imaginary mass media world of neat beginnings, middles and ends, American Indian society, whatever its virtues and fascinations as an arena for Eur-American consciousness raising, is definitely past tense" (E17). Doris Seale and Beverly Slapin in *Through Indian Eyes: The Native Experience in Children's Books*, show how often Indians are presented as whooping savages in paint or feathers, or as cute, make-believe figures for kids to playact in costume, or as noble savages, generic and distant, as in dusty museum panoramas.

Lionel Trilling said that James Agee's text for *Let Us Now Praise Famous Men*, published in the early 1940s, about poor tenant families in the South, was the most realistic and the most important moral effort of his generation. Even so, Trilling pointed out "a failure of moral realism" in the book: "It lies in Agee's inability to see these people as anything but good.... he writes of his people as if there were no human unregenerateness in them, no flicker of malice or meanness, no darkness or wildness of feeling, only a sure and simple virtue, the growth, we must suppose, of their hard, unlovely poverty. He shuts out, that is, what is part of the moral job to take in. What creates this falsification is guilt—the observer's guilt at his own relative freedom" (qtd. in Hersey xxxii).

When I was compiling the stories about apartheid for *Somehow Tenderness Survives*, I struggled at first with that kind of reverential, patronizing guilt. I looked for stories that had the right line—brave, good, strong, beautiful people succeeding in the fight for freedom—and I felt a great deal of pressure to include role-model stories.

But several things stopped me from choosing that kind of propaganda. First, reviewing the books on South Africa for *Booklist*, I had seen too many politically correct anthologies with the right balance and the reverential attitudes, that just weren't being read. You can't harangue people into reading, however worthy the cause. There has to be the pleasure of story, character, passionate conflict, and language if you're going to grab readers and make them want to read on.

Second, I listened to Nadine Gordimer when she came to speak in Chicago. She is politically militant, unequivocally committed to Nelson Mandela and the struggle against racism. But she is just as adamant that the correct attitude doesn't make a good story. She writes about betrayal, as well as courage. About people.

Ethnicity, Universals, and a Sense of Place

Of course it's great to read about your own culture and recognize yourself in a book, especially if you have felt marginalized and demonized. The writer Jamaica Kincaid, who grew up in Antigua, talks about the joy she felt when she first read the books of fellow Caribbean Derek Walcott (the 1992 winner of the Nobel Prize for Literature): "I thought we were just the riffraff of the British Empire until I read this man and thought: 'Oh yes, that is me. That is us'" (qtd. in Rule C30). Katha Pollitt says that, however much she hates the "self-esteem" argument, she has to admit that it meant something to her when she was growing up to find a female poet in an anthology (205).

But it isn't always as direct as that. Mark Mathabane remembers reading a battered copy of *Treasure Island* and realizing that there were other possibilities beyond his ghetto township (193). Similarly, Richard Wright, in *Black Boy*, describes how books gave him "new ways of looking and seeing," offering him hope that there was a world beyond the one in which he was trapped. "It was not a matter of believing or disbelieving what I read, but of feeling something new, of being affected by something that made the look of the world different" (272-73). I love the Yiddish idiom and the shtetl setting in the stories of Isaac Bashevis Singer: he makes me laugh; he makes me remember my mother's stories and her love of Singer; and he gives me a sense of my family and who I am. But I also get immense pleasure and the shock of recognition when I read Sandra Cisneros' stories in *The House on Mango Street*, about a young Chicana girl, Esperanza, coming of age in Chicago. Esperanza says her great-grandmother "looked out of the window her whole life, the way so many women sit their sadness on an elbow" (10-11). That image makes me catch my breath. It makes me think of so many women trapped at home. I remember my mother-in-law, an immigrant from Lithuania, well-educated, spirited, but a stranger, who got stuck in the rigid role prescribed for her in Cape Town's Jewish community. She used to sit like that, chin in her hands, elbows on the table, angrily watching us eat the food she'd cooked. And just as I love Cisneros, so non-Jews can find themselves in the humour and humanity of Singer's shtetl stories.

Amy Tan's *The Joy Luck Club* does give you an idea of what it's like to grow up Chinese American, and that is a good reason to read it. It's important for Asian Americans to read about themselves in books, and it's important for everybody else to read good books about them. It does show women struggling for independence, and that does give me pleasure. But it isn't reverential; the people aren't always wise and admirable. The extraordinary success of *The Joy Luck Club* has little to do with our need to know about "other" cultures. This book is a best-seller because, rooted as it is in the Chinese American experience, it explores the complexity and conflict, the love and anger, between mothers and daughters everywhere.

I was on the committee that selected Virginia Hamilton as the 1992 US nominee for the international Hans Christian Andersen Award. When the nomination was announced, some people said that she didn't have a chance or world recognition because foreigners wouldn't understand her, wouldn't read her, wouldn't translate her. She was too idiomatic, too difficult, too local, they said. They were wrong. She won. And, in fact, her books have been widely read in countries like Japan for years.

We're too quick to say, "kids won't read this." We each live in a small world and talk to people like ourselves and reinforce each other, and we think everyone agrees with us. If you choose good stories and if you promote them, it's not true that books in translation or about foreign cultures are only for the "gifted," that young people won't read books with a strong sense of a foreign place. Singer says that the opposite is true, that the more a story is connected with a group, the more specific it is, the better. In an opening note to *When Shlemiel Went to Warsaw*, he says: "In our time, literature is losing its address" (opening note). That's such a wonderful pun—losing its sense of place, its identity, and because of that, losing its ability to speak, to address an audience. (It's interesting that for him place isn't so much a landscape or a physical environment—"in a village somewhere in Ukraine"—it's really that idiom, that individual voice, rooted in a particular group and their way of life.) Singer says that in writing for children, he's not concerned with using only words that the child will understand. "Unknown words don't stop the child," he says. "But a boring story will" (16). E.B. White said the same about *Charlotte's Web*. "Children are game for anything," he said. "I throw them hard words and they backhand them over the net. They love words that give them a hard time" (qtd. in Gherman 93).

It's obvious that for mainstream young people, books about "other" cultures are not as easy to pick up as *YM* magazine, or as easy to watch as "Beverly Hills 90210." And, in fact, they shouldn't be. We don't want a homogenized culture. If you're a kid in New York, then reading about a refugee in North Korea, or a teenager in the bush in Africa, or a Mormon in Utah, involves some effort, some imagination, some opening up of who you are. In talking about books with kids, I always start with a story set where they are, here and now. Then once they're listening, I move to other cultures, in this country and across the world and back again.

Stories about foreign places risk two extremes: either they can overwhelm the reader with reverential details of idiom, background, and custom; or they can homogenize the culture and turn all the characters into mall babies. There's always that tension between the particular and the universal, between making the character and experience and culture too special, and making them too much the same. On the one hand, we don't want to be bogged down in reverential details about the way of life and the deep mystical meaning of everything the protagonist sees; we don't want to wade through thickets of idiom, background, and culture before we can get to the story. And yet … on the other hand, the pleasures of a good story emerge most forcibly from a vividly evoked, particularized setting. Details make a world. Take *Shabanu: Daughter of the Wind* by Suzanne Fisher Staples, about a young Muslim girl living with her nomadic family in the desert of Pakistan. Shabanu has spirit and intelligence and that's dangerous in a girl, especially when at the age of 12 she's promised in marriage to an old man. As we get to care for Shabanu and what happens to her, we imagine what it must be like to be her. At the same time the story is rooted in the particulars of her culture, and the sense of her place is deeply felt. The important thing is that there's no sense of the exotic; the desert is very much there but not as scenery or travelogue. This book is remarkable in showing a sense of individual personality within a tight structure.

Glossaries and Names

When I was compiling *Somehow Tenderness Survives*, both my editor, Charlotte Zolotow, and I were reluctant to have a glossary. We felt that readers would get the meaning of strange words from context. If you know there's a glossary, if makes you stiff and wary, instead of allowing you to give yourselves over to the world of the story. What persuaded us that we did need a glossary was the fact that the racist categories and racist insults needed clarification. Americans didn't know that kaffir was the worst insult, the equivalent of *nigger* here; they didn't know that *native* is derogatory. In fact, it's a sign of the shame of apartheid that it has spawned such an exact list of racial names.

This chapter started with a joke about names. And yet ... what you call people does matter, especially in a society where groups are angry and divided. When Malcolm Little dropped the last name that had been given to his family by slave owners and took on X to stand for the "true African family name that he never could know," he was making a powerful statement about his identity (199). His renaming was like a rebirth: he was freeing himself from the self-hatred that kept him enslaved. To call a man a "boy" as many whites do in South Africa, is a vicious racist insult. If servants are nameless, they aren't people.

Sensationalism and Sentimentality

Books about apartheid, about slavery, about the Holocaust, can be grim. Do you give young people books about racial oppression and mass suffering? How do you evaluate such books?

Young people want to know about these things, and it is important that they know. But, whether it's fiction or nonfiction, the account shouldn't exploit the violence; it shouldn't grab attention by dwelling on sensational detail. Nor should it offer slick comfort, the Holocaust did not have a happy ending. Nor should it fall back on exhortation and rhetoric; after a while, worlds like *horror, atrocity*, and *terrible* cease to mean anything.

The best stories tell it from the point of view of ordinary people like Anne Frank, like us. Holocaust accounts like Ida Vos's *Hide and Seek* or Isabella Leitner's *The Big Lie* succeed through understatement, allowing the facts to speak for themselves, true to the Jewish child's bewildered point of view (Why must she wear a star? What does it mean, going into hiding?). There are no gimmicks like time travel or easy escape; no rhetoric, no tears, no hand-wringing about *atrocity* and *horror*. Stories like these defeat stereotype. They overcome the evil institution, not by making the character a heroic role model or a proud representative of the race, not by haranguing us with a worthy cause, but by making the individual a person.

Against Borders

I have tried to take all these criteria into account in this book. At first I felt overwhelmed by the demands of political correctness. How was I going to choose the "right" books for the essays and resource lists? The watchdogs from right, left and center would pounce: How could you put that in? How could you leave that out? Even with my great editors and wise advisers and consultants, there were going to be so many *problems.*

My husband is a long-time apartheid fighter. "Not *problems,*" he said. "*Riches.*"

And that's really the point about the whole multicultural debate. When I lived under apartheid, I thought I was privileged—and compared with the physical suffering of black people I was immeasurably well-off—but my life was impoverished. I was blind, and I was frightened. I was shut in. And I was denied access to the stories and music of the world. Groups like Ladysmith Black Mambazo were making music right there, and I couldn't hear them. I didn't know that in the streets of Soweto there were people like Nelson Mandela with a vision of nonracial democracy that would change my life. I was ignorant, and I didn't know I was ignorant. I thought I was better than someone like Mark Mathabane's mother because she spoke English with an accent; I didn't know that she and others like her were fluent in multiple languages. I didn't know anything about most of the people around me. And because of that I didn't know what *I* could be.

Borders shut us in, in Johannesburg, in Los Angeles and Chicago, in Eastern Europe, in our own imaginations.

Works Cited

Alexander, Lloyd. *The Remarkable Journey of Prince Jen.* New York: Dutton, 1991.

Angelou, Maya. *I Know Why the Caged Bird Sings.* New York: Random, 1970.

Beard, Henry and Christopher Cerf. *The Official Politically Correct Dictionary and Handbook.* New York: Villard, 1993.

Choi, Sook Nyul. *Year of Impossible Goodbyes.* Boston: Houghton, 1991.

Cisneros, Sandra. "My Name." *The House on Mango Street.* New York: Vintage, 1991. 10-11.

Clifton, Lucille. "note to my self." *Quilting.* Brockport, NY: BOA Editions, 1991. 8.

Doctorow, E.L. Interview. *World of Ideas: Conversations with Thoughtful Men and Women about American Life Today and the Ideas Shaping Our Future.* By Bill Moyers. New York: Doubleday, 1989. 83-95.

Dorris, Michael. "Indians in Aspic." *New York Times* 24 Feb. 1991: E17.

Fine, Anne. *My War with Goggle-eyes.* Boston: Joy Street/Little Brown, 1989.

Gherman, Beverly. *E.B. White: Some Writer!* New York: Atheneum, 1992.

Gordimar, Nadine. Interview. *Booklist* 87.2 (15 Sept. 1990): 100-01.

Hamanaka, Sheila. *The Journey: Japanese-Americans, Racism and Renewal.* New York: Orchard, 1990.

Hamilton, Virginia. Interview. *Booklist* 88.11 (1 Feb. 1992): 1020-21.

Heath, Amy. *Sofie's Role.* Illus. Sheila Hamanaka. New York: Four Winds, 1992.

Hersey, John. Introduction. *Let Us Now Praise Famous Men.* James Agee. Boston: Houghton, 1988. v-xl.

Kingston, Maxine Hong. *The Woman Warrior.* New York: Knopf, 1976.

Leitner, Isabella. *The Big Lie: A True Story.* New York: Scholastic, 1992.

Lewis, Junko Yokota. "Looking Beyond Literary and Visual Images to Raise the Level of Cultural Consciousness." Chicago Children's Reading Round Table Conference. 12 Sept. 1992.

——. "Reading the World: Japan." *Book Links* (Mar. 1992): 24-26.

Mathabane, Mark. *Kaffir Boy: The Story of a Black Youth's Coming of Age in Apartheid South Africa.* New York: NAL/Dutton, 1986.

Mills, Claudia. *A Visit to Amy-Claire.* Illus. Sheila Hamanaka. New York: Macmillan, 1992.

New York Times. "Whether It's Hunger or 'Misnourishment,' It's a National Problem." 27 Dec. 1992, sec. 4:2.

Pollitt, Katha. "Why We Read: Canon to the Right...." *The Nation.* 23 Sept. 1991: 328-32. Rpt. in *Debating P.C.: The Controversy Over Political Correctness on College Campuses.* Ed. Paul Berman. New York: Laurel/Dell, 1992. 201-11.

Rochman, Hazel. *Somehow Tenderness Survives: Stories of Southern Africa.* New York: HarperCollins/Charlotte Zolotow, 1988.

Rule, Sheila. "Walcott, Poet of the Caribbean, is Awarded the Nobel Prize." *New York Times* 9 Oct. 1992: A1+.

Singer, Isaac Beshavis. "Isaac Bashevis Singer on Writing for Children." *Children's Literature* 6 (1977): 9-16.

——. *When Schlmiel Went to Warsaw.* New York: Farrar, 1968.

Slapin, Beverly and Doris Seale. *Through Indian Eyes: The Native Experience in Books for Children.* 3rd ed. Philadelphia, PA: New Society, 1992.

Sontag, Susan. Introduction. *Best American Essays.* Ed. Susan Sontag. New York: Ticknor and Fields, 1992.

Staples, Suzanne Fisher. *Shabanu: Daughter of the Wind.* New York: Knopf, 1989.

Sumrall, Amber Coverdale. *Write to the Heart: Wit and Wisdom of Women Writers.* Freedom, CA: Crossing P, 1992.

Sutton, Roger. "What Mean We, White Man?" *Voya* 15.3 (Aug. 1992): 155-58.

Tan, Amy. *The Joy Luck Club.* New York: Putnam, 1989.

Vos, Ida. *Hide and Seek.* Trans. Terese Edelstein and Inez Smidt. New York: Houghton, 1991.

Watkins, Yoko Kawashima. *So Far from the Bamboo Grove.* New York: Lothrop, 1986.

Wright, Richard. *Black Boy.* New York: HarperCollins, 1945.

X, Malcolm and Alex Haley. *The Autobiography of Malcolm X.* New York: Ballantine, 1965.

Good Books, Bad Books—and Who Decides Why (1995)
Naser Yusefi

Parents, instructors, and teachers need to know how to select books for children, which books are good and which ones should be kept out of their reach. This is the policy. In keeping with it, children's literature institutes, centres, and publishers set standards, then make and distribute lists of books recommended for children and young people. On the one hand, this can be considered praiseworthy. Piles of books are sifted through, "good" ones appear in the lists and "bad" ones are set aside. Adults appear to have no problem making these choices and selecting what they think is suitable for children.

This, however, is only one side of the coin. Making lists of "good" books is, among other things, a process of negative selection, since de facto or explicitly, it creates a list of books that had better not be read or recommended. This raises the question of the boundaries separating "good" and "bad" books. Should books be evaluated and assigned to one extreme or the other? By what standards? And why are certain books selected by one group and rejected by another?

Today in Iran, at least six centers publish annual lists of books considered fit for children and adolescents, and very often one finds books that have been approved and awarded prizes by one center, only to be censured by another. There is nothing wrong with such divergent judgments if we heed human rights and respect freedom of thought and ideas.

But the fact is that reality goes far beyond these differences in judgment. Children's literature organizations supported by the government have considerable power and simply take advantage of their position to set strict principles and standards for evaluating children's books. These institutes not only apply these principles to themselves, but impose them on nongovernmental agencies as well. There can be no doubt that such a process paves the way for the growth of narrow-mindedness. Imagine writers and their audiences: children exposed to no conflicting thoughts and opinions, no freedom of speech, and no right to make choices. How can creative literature for children and young adults grow in a society such as this?

The self-assuredness of some adults in distinguishing between right and wrong has led many of them, even when unfamiliar with the world of children, to dare to make decisions and choices for children and even dictate what they should or should not do. They neglect children's rights just as they neglect the importance of considering children's individual differences in developing their minds and revealing their talents. Surely children raised under these circumstances cannot catch up with the developing world.

The division of books into "good" and "bad" is rooted in feudalism and leads to the suppression of children's right to think and decide for themselves what to choose and what to avoid. My experience in this part of the world points to a bitter yet undeniable truth about these extremes. They represent severe obstacles in the way of introducing literature to creative minds. Different books stand for different thoughts, different opinions, different truths. Let us respect these differences so that we do not deprive children and adolescents of their right to browse freely among them, comparing them with one another, and making their own choices.

In fact, the solution to the problem is to provide facilities for children and adolescents where they can enjoy browsing books of all sorts and varieties, sit in discussion groups and debate their reasons for choosing this or rejecting that. The role of adults (parents, librarians, and teachers) in this environment is to act as coordinators and assure the children that they are available whenever needed. Only in this way can adults make it possible for children to share the numerous experiences that contribute to developing self-confidence, furthering mental and emotional growth, greater moral sensitivity, knowledge, creativity, and eventually the improvement of their lives and the paving of the way to peace. Adherence to a belief in the extremes of "good" and "bad" will do nothing but prepare young people to welcome everlasting dictatorship.

Translated from the Persian by Mansooreh Rai.

II

HISTORICAL
CHILDREN'S LITERATURE

By "children's books" I mean printed works produced ostensibly to give children spontaneous pleasure, and not primarily to teach them, nor solely to make them good, not to keep them *profitably* quiet. I shall therefore exclude from this history, as a general rule, all schoolbooks, all purely moral or didactic treatises, all reflective or adult-minded descriptions of child-life, and almost all alphabets, primers, and spelling-books; though some works in each category will be mentioned because they purposely gave much latitude to amusement, or because they contained elements which have passed into a less austere legacy. The definition is given as a broad principle liable to perpetual exception.

Roughly speaking, under its terms, there were no children's books in England before the seventeenth century, and very few even then. There are plenty of schoolbooks and guides to conduct, but none which would openly allow a child to enjoy himself with no thought of duty nor fear of wrong. Children's books did not stand out by themselves as a clear but subordinate branch of English literature until the middle of the eighteenth century.... Because an arbitrary date is a convenience, and for no other reason, I will say that that commencement took place in 1744, when John Newbery, the most authentic founder of this traffic in minor literature, published his first children's book. (1)

—F.J. Harvey Darton,
Children's Books in England: Five Centuries of Social Life (1932)

When reading a text from the past, and particularly one which is specifically concerned with child-rearing (and so is explicitly interested in integrating young people into society), it is often easier to recognize its ideological biases than it is with texts from our own period, but it is important to remember that all texts are ideological—the products of particular historical circumstances and opinions. If we fail to notice the ideological stance of a contemporary text, it is because its messages are in accordance with our own point of view and therefore seem natural. Strange though it may seem to us now, the attitudes and lessons which characterize Mrs. Sherwood's text also seemed natural and like commonsense to most of her readers. The change in our response to *The Fairchild Family* usefully illustrates the point that ideology is not just something that is done to us, but it is also part of us. (9-10)

—Kimberly Reynolds, "Forever Young: Fantasies of Childhood" (1994)

Introduction

The study of the history of children's literature is multi-faceted and includes within its parameters not only discussions of specific works of literature and authors from different times and places, but also the question of what constitutes children's literature in the past and the value of studying such literature today. Since the articles and books examining works and authors of the past are too numerous to cover adequately in this book, the focus is on the latter two elements: how we identify and understand children's literature of the past and what value such studies might have.

The question of when children's literature began is problematic, with conflicting answers. As Gillian Adams's article "Medieval Children's Literature" indicates, definitions of children and childhood as well as definitions of literature affect the perception of what constitutes children's literature, in the past as much as today. Adams provides an overview of scholarship about childhood and children's literature. She points out that one has to pay attention to details within a work to detect whether it is children's literature—a point that is true for contemporary works as well. She also challenges F.J. Harvey Darton's definition of children's literature as that which only entertains, asking us to remember that one generation's enjoyable text is another's tedium.

Unlike Adams's position that children's literature does exist in the past and is important to examine, Peter Hunt's "Passing On the Past" supports Darton's definition. The piece is meant to be inflammatory, a lit match in the canon, as it were. His argument that the study of current children, childhood, and children's books should be the main focus of the study of children's literature has not been entirely successful in undermining the status of the historical study of children's literature, but as a provocative piece of criticism, it was extraordinarily effective. There have been many replies to Hunt's argument, as he notes in his postscript.

Susan Gannon's piece "Report from Limbo" is one such response to Hunt. She uses his dismissal of the study of historical children's literature as the starting point for an overview of important developments in that area of study and how such inquiry is relevant to the study of contemporary childhood, education, and literature.

Whether or not one is interested in particular historical texts or the history of children's literature in general, the fact is that children's literature of today has grown from that of the past. The study of children's literature, in its relative newness, still has plenty of room for new studies and discussions of just how its past, present, and future connect.

Works Cited

Darton, F.J. Harvey. *Children's Books in England: Five Centuries of Social Life.* Cambridge: Cambridge UP, 1932. 1.

Reynolds, Kimberly. "Forever Young: Fantasies of Childhood." *Children's Literature in the 1890s and 1990s.* Plymouth: Northcote House, 1994. 1-17.

Medieval Children's Literature: Its Possibility and Actuality (1998)

Gillian Adams

An earlier version of this essay was read at the Second Biennial Conference on Modern Critical Approaches to Children's Literature, Nashville, Tennessee, April 10-12, 1997. I wish to thank Claudia Nelson and Marilynn Olson for their ideas for clarifications, transitions, and rephrasings; Ruth Bottigheimer and Elizabeth Scala for their bibliographical suggestions; and my two anonymous readers for further assistance. All translations in this essay are my own.

Years ago, while taking a graduate course in medieval Latin, I was struck by the wide disparity in the difficulty of the works that were assigned, a disparity that often did not coincide with other variables such as the historical period or the author's social class, profession, or region. In that course it was assumed that all the texts we addressed, whatever their degree of difficulty, were written for adults. I concluded at the time that there must have been a substantial number of adult readers with literacy skills below the third-grade level. I have since become convinced that some of the works we were looking at were written not only or even initially for semiliterate adults, a group often equated with children in the earlier periods, but for children.[1] In order to support my claim that such works should be considered children's literature I draw on evidence provided by cultural and literary historians to dispute two widely held convictions that have hampered previous critical and theoretical studies. The first is the nonspecialist belief that there can be no medieval children's literature because a conception of childhood as we know it did not exist in the Middle Ages. The second is the specialist assertion, typified by the medievalist Bennett Brockman, that "the Middle Ages made no provision for a separate literature for children, apart from pedagogical texts designed to teach them to read, to write, to cipher, and to behave civilly" ("Juvenile" 18). Finally, I discuss the ways in which some medieval works and their contexts indicate a child audience and why such works warrant further exploration as children's literature.

I

First it is necessary to dispose of the myths about medieval children that have prevented scholars from seriously considering that a literature for them might exist. There are three initial barriers, primarily hypothetical, to recognizing medieval children's literature. To begin with, there is the still-widespread belief in the "Ariès thesis," in brief that childhood was "discovered" in the seventeenth century (according to Philippe Ariès) or the eighteenth century (according to some other researchers). Ariès, as he admits in his introduction to *Centuries of Childhood,* was not a specialist in the periods for which he claims that "the idea of [*sentiment,* a separate feeling about] childhood did not exist" (128), and in fact, if his book is deconstructed, it is evident that there was a cognizance of childhood throughout those earlier periods. What his thesis amounts to is that previous centuries thought quite differently about children than did seventeenth-century France. A statement of this nature is true for any time and for any region even today: for example, the conception of childhood is different for the first half of the twentieth century and the second; for the rich, the urban poor, and the comfortable, usually suburban, middle class; and most notably for Americans and those who live in countries where poor children go to work in factories at six or seven and parents sell children into prostitution and even slavery.[2] Nevertheless, Ariès's insistence on the social construction of childhood and on not naively reading the past in terms of the present is an essential contribution to the study of past children's literatures. His work has informed many subsequent critical and historical studies and has given rise to the examination of specific works within a wide-ranging sociohistorical context that includes nonliterary texts.

It was not long after the Ariès book appeared (in 1960 in France and in 1962 in English translation) that specialists in the medieval and early modern periods began to point out what was wrong with its ideas and with the data used to support them. As early as 1975 Meradith McMunn wrote in *Children's Literature,* on the basis of her examination of the description of children in French medieval literature, that Ariès's claims are "not supported by a close look at medieval literature" ("Children" 54). She was followed by C.H. Talbot, who asserted in *Children's Literature* in 1977 that "anyone who is at all conversant with the biographies of the saints; with the lives of abbots, monks, and nuns; or with the chronicles of monasteries and cathedral churches written between the eighth and the twelfth century will realize that such a theory [as Ariès's] is untenable" (17). Books criticizing Ariès soon followed: recent works accessible to nonspecialists and available in paperback are John Boswell's *The Kindness of Strangers* (1988, see particularly 36-38), Shulamith Shahar's *Childhood in the Middle Ages* (1990), and Barbara A. Hanawalt's *Growing up in Medieval London* (1993).[3] By 1995, Hugh Cunningham can comment in *Children and Childhood in Western Society Since 1500* that disproving Ariès is "an easy goal" and that what is needed is greater attention to "the contradictions and changes over time and place in medieval thought and practice" (40). In short, medieval and early modern scholars are unanimous in discarding the Ariès thesis, in spite of the interest of many of his observations; it is time for children's literature scholars to do the same.

Ariès's claim that childhood as we now think of it did not exist before the seventeenth or the eighteenth century as well as his chapters on the ages of life, the discovery of childhood (in art), and children's dress have resulted in two additional barriers to locating medieval children's literature. The first is the idea that parents did not love (or were afraid to love) their children because infant and child mortality was so high. One finds this claim made, in spite of ample evidence to the contrary, for periods ranging from antiquity through the eighteenth century. Such a claim is logically absurd; for the greater part of human existence, life for most has been nasty, brutish, and short. Death rates have often been almost as high for adults as for children, particularly in the case of childbearing women and warriors, yet there is no lack of early literature about love. In fact, a high value was placed on children and on parental love (see Boswell, Hanawalt, Shahar, and Talbot passim), although often on a sliding scale: some children—for example, male heirs of the wealthy and powerful—were more valuable than others, and a separate literature for them was more likely to develop and to survive.

The second and more damaging idea, as far as children's literature studies is concerned, is based primarily on Ariès's discussion of medieval dress and art and his claim that children were viewed as "miniature adults." Ariès was not an art historian, and his interpretation of the evidence he presents is flawed, given that for the period he discusses artists were not interested in realism as we conceive of it. There is other medieval art, notably sculpture and manuscript illustration, that better represents the child as distinct from the adult. In Ariès's day, in contrast to the present, European children and sometimes adolescents were strongly differentiated by their clothing (for example, short pants and school smocks), so it would be natural for him to be struck by the similarity of adults' and children's clothing in medieval art. Moreover, Ariès's claim that childhood was not viewed as a separate stage of life is not supported by the ample evidence of the interest shown during the Middle Ages in discussing and defining the ages and characteristics of *infantia* (birth to six or seven years), *pueritia* (seven to twelve for girls, to fourteen for boys), *adolescentia* (the period between biological and social puberty and legal and social majority), and *juventus* (see, for example, Shahar 22 and notes; Hanawalt, passim).

Nevertheless, these myths about medieval children persist. For example, in the most recent edition of *The Pleasures of Children's Literature* (1996), although Perry Nodelman cites Pollock's and Shahar's studies, he continues to assert that in the earlier periods "a *different* conception of childhood operated, [and] that conception required no special literature for children" (70, emphasis in original).[4] If we contend that a society whose conception of childhood is alien to our own is incapable of developing children's literature, we should also argue that there could have been no children's literature in the eighteenth and nineteenth centuries in England and the United States either, since the ideas operative then about the "innocent" child and about family structure, clothing, age- and gender-appropriate activities, and social status are not identical to today's. In fact, there is no logical reason why societies with constructions of childhood that differ widely from our own (for example, China) should not develop literature for children, whether or not they actually do. To assert that only *our* conception of childhood can result in children's literature, a literature that only we are able to judge as literature in terms of its literary value (which for some reason must include "entertainment"), is the kind of cultural imperialism and ideological colonialism that modern critics, Nodelman among them, often seek to avoid (see Nodelman's often-cited essay "The Other: Orientalism, Colonialism, and Children's Literature").

II

Even if we admit, then, that the period roughly from the sack of Rome (410) to the invention of printing had different conceptions of childhood from those current in most of Europe and America today, such conceptions do not logically preclude the possibility of a literature for children. More problematic is the narrowness of vision of those who do recognize and write about medieval and early modern texts for children and youth as exemplified by the quotation from Brockman with which I began this chapter. Brockman makes two claims: first, that there is literature but that it is "pedagogical," and second, that apart from this literature there is no separate literature for children (i.e., that it was a part of adult literature that children shared with adults). Brockman is not alone; on the basis of the scholarship that I have seen to date, the only medieval texts recognized as exclusively for children are considered nonfiction: instruction manuals and courtesy books. The idea that this sort of work is all that exists is fostered by bibliographies, collections of excerpts such as that edited by Patricia Demers and Gordon Moyles, and the early chapters of F.J. Harvey Darton's *Children's Books in England*.[5]

Like Brockman, most children's literature specialists who are also medievalists address themselves to a shared literature whose content or circumstances may indicate a child audience, or they tell us how good or poor a job modern children's literature does in portraying the medieval period. I find particularly distressing the essays on medieval children's literature in volume 1 of *Children's Literature*.[6] Although Hugh Keenan's piece on Old English children's literature is suggestive, mentioning not only Aelfric's *Colloquy* (ca. 1000) but also the Exeter and Cotton gnomes, the McMunns' essay, in spite of some excellent citations, writes off the fourteenth-century French *Book of the Knight of La Tour-Landry* (translated into English in the fifteenth century) as "an encyclopedic catalogue of anecdotes, each with a very explicit moral" (23); Brockman terms its stories "crudely manipulative" ("Medieval" 40). Anyone who has read this work knows that it contains fascinating narratives of some length, some readily accessible to students today. Nothing has changed in volume 4 of *Children's Literature*, where William McMunn asserts in his introduction to the four papers from the MLA panel "Children and the Middle Ages" that "all of us on the panel agree that 'children's literature' did not exist in the Middle Ages" ("Literacy" 36).

Why will these scholars not consider as children's literature "the pedagogical texts designed to teach [children] to read, to write, to cipher, and to behave civilly" (Brockman, "Juvenile" 18) or the "entertaining stories (that) were used in programs of instruction" (McMunn and McMunn, "Children's" 22)? I believe that there are two reasons, and the case of the McMunns' and Brockman's condemnation of *The Book of the Knight of La Tour-Landry* provides a clue to the first. It seems to be the belief in the romantic notion, based on Darton's 1932 definition of children's literature, that didactic works do not count, are not truly "literature": "By 'children's books' I mean printed works produced ostensibly to give children spontaneous pleasure, and not primarily to teach them, nor solely to make them good, nor to keep them *profitably quiet*" (1, emphasis in original). Such a narrow definition of literature has been repudiated by a number of scholars, ably led for some years now by the new historicist Mitzi Myers, whose groundbreaking review of Geoffrey Summerfield castigates his book for its "presentism" and espousal of "Romantic values" (108). Brockman's essay on medieval poetry, in spite of valuable observations on lullabies and on different types of medieval didacticism, is a sad example of such "presentism." Recently Patricia Demers in *Heaven upon Earth: The Form of Moral and Religious Children's Literature, to 1850*, which begins its study of children's literature with Erasmus's 1540 *Sermon of the Chylde Jesus*, has provided a telling critique of Darton's antididactic position.

In fact, in certain countries and periods, among them medieval Europe, didacticism has been highly valued (as it is by many education students today); typical is the classical poet Horace's proclamation in his *Ars Poetica* (often part of the medieval curriculum) that *Scribendi recte sapere est et principium et fons* [The source and first principle of good writing is wisdom] (1.310). In a dictum often referred to by medieval theorists, Horace adds, *omne tulit punctum qui miscuit utile dulci / lectorem delectando pariterque monendo* [he has won the day who has mixed the useful with the pleasurable / equally delighting the reader and instructing him] (11.343-44). In Horace's own work the needle was closer to *dulci* on the continuum between *utile* and *dulci*; in most medieval literature, it tended to be closer to *utile*. Thus the works of the great literary figures of the High Middle Ages, for example, Dante and Chaucer, are explicit about the lessons to be drawn from their fictions. Yet their situation as stars of the literary canon—along with that supremely didactic work, the Bible—has never been denied. Of course, as Marxist and other ideological critics often remind us, all literature has an agenda, however carefully disguised.

I suspect that the second reason for refusing to believe that anything connected with pedagogy could be literature has to do with the need perceived by many American academic children's literature specialists to divorce themselves from the fields of education and library science. Nevertheless, from its beginnings in the ancient world, children's literature has been intimately related to pedagogics and remains so today (see Adams). European scholars appear much more comfortable with the connection than we do, on the evidence of Maria Nikolajeva's introduction to the essays in *Aspects and Issues in the History of Children's Literature* and many of the essays themselves. There is no logical reason why texts used for educational purposes should not also qualify as literature, whether they appeal to us or not. The history of education demonstrates that poetry, drama, and narrative have been used to supplement nonfiction in the schools from their beginning, whether adult material used and sometimes adapted for children or material created especially for them and whether used in ways that seem familiar to us or alien. To investigate fully the possibilities of medieval children's literature, then, we must begin with medieval education and the texts used within or as supplements to the curriculum.

III

Once we have disposed of the mythologies and prejudices that have prevented specialists and nonspecialists alike from admitting that medieval children's literature may exist, two important barriers to an accurate, scholarly assessment of that literature remain, and they have to do with the nature of medieval education. The first concerns what was once thought to be the low percentage of the population for whom literacy was deemed necessary or even desirable, the second the admittedly high price of codices. Of late, scholars have been revising literacy figures upward, led by Rosamond McKitterick for the earlier periods; for the later periods see the historical studies mentioned at the beginning of this essay. The Middle Ages are not monolithic, and certain groups of people placed a high value on literacy: the Jews (the people of the book), whose males were required by religious law to be literate enough to read the Scriptures;[7] the church (monks, nuns, and the secular clergy); royalty and the high nobility (and the clerks and legal experts who served them); and, beginning with the twelfth century, those engaged in commerce. Of course, the situation in urban areas was different from that in the countryside, and some regions were more learned and literate than others. For example, many parts of Italy, particularly the regions under Arab and Byzantine influence, never lost a respect for learning. Once most of Spain came under Muslim domination, high culture flourished. Southern France was ahead of northern France until the Renaissance of the twelfth century; there were pockets of culture in Germany; and England tended to lag behind, even with respect to Ireland. But because of the high value placed on books—both as objects sometimes worth enough to hold for ransom and as containers of text that was also highly esteemed—they, and the ability to read them, were indicators of power and status. Literacy was not only useful but necessary for upward mobility.[8]

But it is exactly the high value of a book before the invention of printing, and even for a time afterwards, that most scholars assume makes it unlikely that any but a child from a wealthy family would actually have possessed a book of his or (even more rarely) her own; if there were books for children in a household or school, they would be shared and as likely to be heard as read. There obviously could be no children's book trade in the modern sense, although there is plenty of evidence of the buying and selling of codices: as early as the eighth century certain ecclesiastical establishments depended on the money they gained from copying (see McKitterick, "Nuns' Scriptoria"; *Carolingians* ch. 4), and books for children must have been part of this trade.

Nevertheless, some children did learn how to read, whether taught in schools run by monks and nuns or by the secular clergy, at home by parents, or at court by tutors. Exactly how this teaching was done is detailed by Suzanne Reynolds in *Medieval Reading: Grammar, Rhetoric, and the Classical Text*. Although her account is based on a description in a twelfth-century English text by Alexander Neckham, *Sacerdos ad altare accessurus*, scholars agree that the general shape of the curriculum as Neckham describes it is characteristic of the whole medieval period. The student began with the alphabet, perhaps inscribed on an object in daily use such as a bowl or a belt (8), and went on to the proper pronunciation of Latin syllables by memorizing the Paternoster, the Creed, and perhaps parts of the Psalter. Much of this learning would be done by rote at a level of "uncomprehending reiteration" (10).[9] Texts were also written on parchment attached to wooden paddles or in large letters glued to a wooden board (Shahar 189). Many institutions had extremely large service books that could be seen at a distance by a number of readers, and books were often chained to bookstands so that they could be read seriatim.

Reynolds emphasizes the orality of education, arguing that students

> do not read (in our sense of the term) the text at all, for it remains at all moments and in all senses in the teacher's hands.... This is a communal reading, communicated orally ... Reasons of economy and availability make it very unlikely that individual students, even if they could write, would have had access to copies of the text. If they did write, it was probably on wax tablets.... [And] the wax tablet of *memoria* is fundamental in medieval literacy. (29)

On the other hand, in her studies of the Carolingian period, McKitterick emphasizes the dominance of the written text and of writing from the earliest periods. Talbot (22) and R.H. and M.A. Rouse describe the slates framed in wood and the wax-covered wooden *tabellae* on which students did their first writing exercises (4-5), usually, according to Reynolds, short or long paraphrases (21). It seems probable that the balance between memorized and written text varied according to time, place, the institution and its resources, and the status of its pupils.

The next text in the learning sequence was a grammar book, usually the Donatus *Ars Minor* or part of the *Ars Maior*, with local variants, which was used from the fourth until at least the fifteenth century;[10] its question-and-answer format is characteristic of other medieval master-pupil dialogues specifically designed for children. At least one child owned his own copy of Donatus, a ninth-century schoolboy named Sado, "who wrote in a mixture of rather straggling capitals and minuscule ... with a notably shaky command of grammar" across the top of the page: "*Sadoniis iste liber est sua mater dedit illi Magnum ona illa sit qui dedit hunc librum*" [this book is Sados his mother gave it to him may she be greatly honored who gave him this book] (McKitterick, "Ninth" 228). In her study of this manuscript, which is "rather inferior quality vellum" and gives other indications of an attempt at economy (for example, leaves erased and reused), McKitterick details the ways in which it has been prepared for "a learner's eye:" it has clearly punctuated sentences, section headings in "rustic capitals," and "extravagantly wide margins" (227), some of which have been ruled with narrow lines for the "annotations of the struggling student who has written (incorrectly) on one of them, *stultissimo grammatica* [extremely stupid grammar]" (228). McKitterick concludes, "Phillips 16308 in fact contradicts a frequent assumption that books in the early Middle Ages were too costly and scarce to be owned by the ordinary schoolboy" (228). The multiple copies of Donatus in the library lists of monasteries known to have flourishing schools, and the many copies that still survive, are further confirmation of McKitterick's claim.

A second work found in multiple copies, falsely attributed to the Roman philosopher Cato and universally coupled with Donatus in the elementary curriculum, is the *Catonis Disticha* [Cato's distichs]. It is a third-century collection of 152 moral couplets in four books, prefaced by a short introductory epistle and about fifty-four very short sentences, some as little as two words. The introduction addresses a child, "Cato"'s son: *Nunc te, fili karissime, docebo quo pacto morem animi tui componas* [Now I will teach you, dearest son, how you can put your mind in order] (T. Hunt 9). The work ends with *Hic finit Cato dans castigamina nato / ostendens quare mundum non debet amare* [Here Cato finishes admonishing his son / showing how he ought not to love this world].[11] From the tenth century onward "Cato" was the first item in an elementary reading book, the *Liber Catonianus*. Tony Hunt gives a full account of how the selections in this reading book varied according to location and period, but three items in addition to "Cato" were constant. First there were fables, usually Avianus's expansion of those by Babrius; then something about the Trojan war—in the earlier period the *Ilias Latina,* a shortened version of the *Iliad* from A.D. 65, which was later replaced by the medieval version of Statius's *Achilleis,* valued for its account of how Achilles obeyed his mother Thetis, her concern for him, and his upbringing by Chiron (Hunt 69). The third item was usually the *Eclogues* of the tenth-century author Theodolus, a debate between Truth and Falsehood about Christianity and paganism that owes much to Virgil's third and seventh eclogues and that was viewed as preparatory to his study. None of the works Hunt mentions, aside from "Cato" and Avianus, was originally composed for children; rather, all were appropriated (and glossed, often heavily) for and by them. Donatus, "Cato," the fables, and some of the other texts exist in multiple versions and variants with interpolations and excisions; I cannot emphasize their fluidity too strongly.

It was at this point, before the serious student went on to Virgil's *Eclogues* and the fixed texts of the classical and late Latin *auctores* (Cicero, Horace, Ovid, Lucan, Terence, and others), that according to Alexander Neckham, he was to read "*quibusdam libellis informationi rudium necessariis*" [certain shorter works necessary for the instruction of the unlearned] (Reynolds 7).[12] And, I would argue, it is at this point that we should find, between the elementary texts and the medieval equivalent of Shakespeare and other works in today's high-school canon, the optional material in a curriculum otherwise dominated by classical and late Latin texts: the poems, fables, and stories adapted or specially written for children, the "separate literature" that, according to Brockman and others, does not exist in the Middle Ages.

IV

Now that I have established that there is no reason why medieval children's literature—even material with an agenda covert enough for critics such as Brockman to accept as literature—should not exist, and that there is a place in the curriculum for such works, I would like to name a few candidates and the genres in which they occur. Most of the examples that I describe below happen to be in Latin; I am convinced that further material is available not only in Latin but in the vernaculars. Because there are medievalists who have no interest in children as an audience, indeed to whom the idea of children as a potential audience might seem utterly foreign, it is important to find as many indications as possible that a text has a connection with child readers or auditors. To discover features that indicate a child audience, absent the kind of smoking gun that McKitterick finds in Sado's grammar book, I ask the following questions: in terms of the text itself (internal evidence), is there a dedication to a named child or introductory material indicating that the work is intended for children or younger students? What is the language like—is it very simple or simpler and more direct than that in other works by the same

author clearly directed at adults, and is the language in the prefatory material more complex than the language in the body of the text? Is a child directly addressed or portrayed as a major character? How is he or she presented?
What is the appearance of the manuscript or manuscripts of the text? Are
there explanatory glosses directed at inexpert readers, as in the case of Sado's
grammar and the *Liber Catonianus*? Does the calligraphy of some versions
indicate inexpert copyists? If there are illustrations, what do they reveal about
an implied audience, keeping in mind that the primary audience for illustrated material was an adult one? Are the manuscripts inexpensively produced, or are they so lavish that they imply a princely owner?

In terms of external evidence, what is the nature of the scriptoria from
which the earliest examples come? What establishments owned the manuscripts? Are they also the sites of schools? What do we know about the author,
whether actual or ascribed (for example, "Cato" or "Aesop")? How popular is
the text and how fluid? Does it exist in multiple versions, or in Latin and the
vernaculars? With what other works is it bound? (For example, works bound
with "Cato" or the popular grammars are more likely to be directed at children). What is the historical and cultural context of the work, its period and
location? Do selections from it appear in *florilegia*, collections of excerpts for
use in the schools? Is it referred to in other texts as somehow connected with
children or with education?

I have already mentioned that fables, usually about animals, were a curriculum standard for young readers. They were often grouped with *aenigma-
ta* (riddles) by Symphosius, Aldhelm, and others, also used in the schools
from an early period (see Ziolkowski 40-46). The best-known fables are found
in collections such as "Aesop" and those by Babrius and Phaedrus in versions
known as Avianus and Romulus (see Ben Edwin Perry for an extended discussion of various versions and their use). On the basis of what has survived,
apart from classical fable material, narratives containing speaking animals
begin with ninth-century animal poems by Alcuin of York and others who
were members of Charlemagne's palace school; Alcuin's poem "The Cock
and the Wolf" is the earliest known analogue of Chaucer's "Nun's Priest's
Tale."[13]

These and other short poems are followed by *The Ecbasis Captivi*, an
eleventh-century Latin frame tale intended on one level to serve as a warning
to young novices against attempting escape from the monastery (a major
problem, according to Boswell). The inner story is about a calf (*vitulus*), a
common term for a novice, who is imprisoned by a wolf, rescued by a fox, and
taken to the court of the lion king. The work is a cento; that is, it is made up
of multiple short quotations, which may be intended as embellishment, parody, or a kind of contextual gloss, from the set texts that children would have
encountered in their studies. It is bound with school texts in the two surviving manuscripts. The *Ecbasis* is followed in turn by animal epics such as the

twelfth-century *Ysengrimus* (attributed to "Nivardus"), which is the first fully worked-out version of the Reynard the Fox material. On the basis of its complex structure, difficult language, learned jokes, and inclusion of a smutty passage, it was probably intended for an audience of ecclesiastics. The questionable passage, however, was early removed for a presumably younger audience in a version of the manuscript that comes from a teaching establishment, and selections from the *Ysengrimus* found their way into *chrestomathies* and *florilegia* bound together with grammatical and other teaching texts.[14]

Although nonspecialists will be familiar with the medieval Reynard cycle and its offshoots only from modern versions, the association of medieval children with drama, both as actors and as part of the audience, should be common knowledge (see, for example, Brockman, "Children"; Hanks; and M. and W. McMunn). In the second half of the tenth century Froumund of Tegernsee refers to using props and animal masks to get the attention of his pupils; Ziolkowski suggests that some animal poems "were perhaps scripts for schoolroom performances in which pupils donned animal masks" (5, see also 147-52). But I know only one dramatic corpus specifically written for children: the plays of Hrotswitha of Gandersheim, a late-tenth-century nun who taught in an establishment limited to female children of the German royal family and important nobility. Her series of playlets, written in simple Latin with short, snappy, often amusing dialogue and some slapstick, celebrates the victories of prepubescent girls—the major characters—over threats to their chastity and integrity. The language of the plays is totally unlike the grandiose rhetoric of works by Hrotswitha dedicated to the king and to other important adults, and there are additional internal and external features that indicate a youthful audience. The plays are still performed today, primarily in academic situations.[15]

In the later periods there appear didactic works intended for the young containing fictional narratives among their moral precepts; a prime example is the *Fecunda ratis* of Egbert of Liège. An early-eleventh-century collection of Latin verse texts of varying lengths and degrees of difficulty written and compiled for Egbert's young pupils, it is a "gallimaufry of proverbs, fables, fairy-tales, and anecdotes" (Ziolkowski 42-43). Among its treasures is the first known version of "Little Red Riding Hood," complete with moral (see Berlioz; Lontzen).

Whereas Egbert, to my knowledge, has not been translated into English, a medieval best-seller, the *Disciplina Clericalis*, has two fine translations. It is by Petrus Alfonsi, a Spanish Jew who converted to Christianity in 1106. Written in very simple Latin at a time when the language often reflected Ciceronian splendours, this collection of stories primarily from Semitic and Arab sources, is, on the evidence of Alfonsi's ornate preface and an addressee in the text ("a little boy like you"), especially intended for young students. Termed "the oldest story book of the Middle Ages" (Beeson 84), its tales are usually short, as are its easy sentences; there is much dialogue, and the anecdotes are far less didactic than one would expect given both the agenda the author promotes in the preface and the genre: wisdom literature.[16] From slightly later in the same period comes a frame tale enclosing similar stories, Johannes de Alta Silva's *Dolopathos*, or *The King and the Seven Wise Men*.[17] Versions of Alfonsi's stories appear in the *Gesta Romanorum*, Marguerite of Navarre's *Heptameron*, Boccacio's *Decameron*, and other later collections; both his and Alta Silva's tales are quite familiar to folklorists.

Jonathan Nicholls sees the *Dolopathos* and *Disciplina Clericalis* as forerunners of the somewhat later courtesy books, observing that the teaching of courtesy as a part of the grammar course began in the twelfth century, when these works were written and when the nobility became more universally literate (58). Courtesy books are the one medieval genre that has been recognized as primarily directed at children or adolescents by children's literature scholars. But readers of the McMunns' "Children's Literature in the Middle Ages" or Ann Hildebrand's helpful study of the relation between courtesy books and the *Babar* stories would be ignorant of the fact that courtesy manuals contain more than just short, basic precepts of table etiquette. The narrative material they include may be part of the reason for their wide popularity; it certainly bears further investigation.[18] Allied to the courtesy books are the "mirrors for princes," handbooks for those expected to be in positions of power, for example, the manual that Dhuoda wrote for her sixteen-year-old son, arguably an adult by Carolingian standards, when he set out for Charlemagne's court (see McKitterick, *Carolingians* 223-25).

Religious texts are another popular medieval genre that scholars who write about children's literature seem reluctant to include as true children's literature, probably because they are didactic and thus presumably not entertaining. But when Chaucer's Prioress begins her sad tale of Little Hugh of Lincoln she is embarking on a topic, if not an actual story, no doubt well known to and enjoyed by most of her audience from their childhoods. Stories about exemplary children abound throughout the history of children's literature, and stories about child saints in simple language, especially when bound with school texts, would repay close examination. In a letter of 25 February 1997, Ruth Bottigheimer suggests for consideration as children's texts the narratives taken from the Vulgate by Peter Comestor, the author of the best-selling twelfth-century *Historia Scholastica* (see Bottigheimer, *Bible* 14-23). The stories in John the Monk's fourteenth-century *Liber de Miraculis* are another possibility. And Milla B. Riggio notes that in the fifth century Claudius Marius Victor's paraphrase of Genesis, *Alethia*, was "expressly written to train the young" (48).

Neither space nor the limits of my investigations to date permit addressing the possibility of medieval children's literature in the vernaculars. Geoffrey Chaucer's *Treatise on the Astrolabe*, written for his ten-year-old son Lewis, is an obvious example of nonfiction (see T. and K. Jambeck). On the basis of manuscript evidence, Mary Shaner has discussed the ways in which a medieval romance was revised for a child reader, and Brockman argues that *Sir Orfeo* is an example of shared, or family, literature because of its internal accessibility for children and the content of the codices in which the three surviving manuscripts of it are contained ("Juvenile"). Brockman has also examined how the Robin Hood narratives were transformed from an entertainment shared by adults and children into one exclusively for children, and Harriet Spiegel has looked at the way Marie of France's *Fables* work as shared literature since "[they] not only seem well suited to children but directly address them or their well-being," and "some present a child actually being taught by a parent" (29). More work needs to be done along these lines, and perhaps in the course of scholarly explorations, more compelling evidence on the order of Shaner's discoveries will be found to connect vernacular fiction directly with children. It seems likely that examples of cross-written or threshold literature—for example, the *Morall Fabillis* of Master Robert Henryson or *Aucassin and Nicolette*—will be more frequent in the vernaculars because of their less intimate connection with education.

Thus the works that I have argued are clearly children's literature are in Latin, although there came to be vernacular versions of some of them (for example, the stories in Petrus Alfonsi, the Reynard the Fox stories, and most of the fables). This is because most education was conducted in Latin throughout the European Middle Ages, and if a text is associated with a church or a secular school, there is a strong likelihood that it was used for its pupils. The fact that the extant translations are often in extremely stilted, even pretentious, English has helped to disguise the true nature of these works. Moreover, the little excerpts of medieval Latin published for Latin students in textbooks such as *Fons Perennis* tend to lead to the conclusion that medieval Latin is a simple language—thus a simple text is just as likely to be for adults as for children. But in actuality medieval Latin comes in a wide variety of styles and complexities. It has its Dr. Seusses, Virginia Woolfs, and James Joyces, just as other languages do. If a text is short and in very simple Latin, it is proper to ask why this is so. What evidence exists that it is written for semiliterate adults as opposed to children learning how to read? Is there, for example, a more difficult, perhaps more "adult" version extant?

If we wish to certify such texts as children's literature, however, we must examine their use of language, the local meaning of terms such as *infans* (infant or child), *puer* (boy), and *puella* (girl), the literary and legal evidence for what constituted a child at that time, location, and situation, other possible audiences, and the textual criteria that I mentioned at the beginning of this section. All of these matters, one might object, are just old-fashioned philology and not a legitimate literary pursuit. But philology is no longer old-fashioned; the "new philology," according to Leah Marcus, constitutes the new frontier of modern literary studies *(Renaissance* 22-30, passim).[19] What the new philological approaches add to the old philology is a greater interest in and ease with textual instability in its material context, just as new historicism has brought a special appreciation of literary works within their cultural context. Such methodologies should help us strip away as much as possible our preconceptions, in this case of what a child and children's literature *ought* to be, and take a look at what fiction was actually written for children and what they actually read. It is a good bet that the works that I have cited above were both valued and enjoyed, because if such had not been the case, the costly material on which they were written would have been erased and used again.

I hope that younger scholars who do not suffer from misconceptions about children as unloved and as miniature adults or participate in the presentism of earlier critics will join me in the exciting search for medieval children's literature. We need fresh eyes, better scholarship, more lively translations, and new children's books reworking the old texts. In addition, I hope to begin a process whereby the many books and articles about children's literature that are operating on incorrect assumptions or that are simply wrong will be changed in subsequent editions. We also need to avoid in the future theoretical constructs built on inaccurate information such as Zohar Shavit's attempt at a historical model for the development of children's literature.

And finally, I hope to counter the current wave of ahistoricism among some children's literature scholars. They seem blind to the fact that, like readers at the end of the Middle Ages, we face a radical transformation in both the way that words are transmitted and, according to some observers, the way that children are constructed (see Cunningham 179-90). At the children's literature conference in Charlotte in 1996, a critic with a distinguished publication record asked me why the existence or nonexistence of medieval children's literature should matter. "It is so long ago," he said. Peter Hunt has written several pieces recently along similar lines; for example, in his column "Passing on the Past: The Problem of Books That Are for Children and That Were for Children," he distinguishes between "live" books and "dead" books, which he claims concern no one except historians. He challenges the view that all books for children are connected and that "we in the present can learn from the past about books and children" (200). Although Hunt claims that "different skills" are required to read books from earlier periods (202), no different skills are needed for the imaginative works that I have mentioned when they are well translated.

Moreover, such works are not "dead." I would argue, on the contrary, that, with the exception of Hrotswitha and apart from the nonfiction, most of the material in the texts that I cite in the last part of this essay is an integral part of "the sea of stories" and continues to be found in the modern period in works now generally agreed to be children's literature. The *Ecbasis Captivi* and the *Ysengrimus* were discovered and copied by Jacob Grimm in the Bibliothèque Nationale during his researches there in the 1830s; material from them is alive today in various versions of Reynard the Fox and in some of Joel Chandler Harris's Uncle Remus stories. At the same time, Grimm copied shorter medieval texts that he included in his *Kinder-und Hausmärchen* and that are now classed as fairy tales (for example, in the Jack Zipes translation, nos. 73 and 146). Grimm could recognize a fine story when he saw one, and some of the originals he transcribed continue to be a good read. We need to recognize similar medieval narratives, plays, and poems for what they originally were: fictions provided to children, most probably initially for educational purposes. But they are a far cry from *Fun with Dick and Jane*. They are children's literature.

Notes

1 For the semiliterate adult-child equation see, among others, Ruth Bottigheimer's "The Child-Reader of Children's Bibles" (45). Children's literature is not a tidy genre: the boundary between it and adult literature is indeterminate, as the Perry Nodelman-Michael Steig exchange in the *Children's Literature Association Quarterly* (Spring 1993) makes clear. All children's literature is shared with adults (if only parents and teachers) to a greater or lesser degree; some works read by children remain popular with adults; some adult literature has become children's literature (often in special versions for them); some literature is marketed simultaneously to adults and to children with the same text presented in different formats (see Sandra Beckett) or with a different target audience in another country (*Watership Down*); a work marketed as children's literature may be claimed by adults (*The Adventures of Huckleberry Finn*); some children's literature is "cross-written" (see the 1997 special volume of *Children's Literature*); some authors claim that they let their editors decide whether their work is for children or for adults; and even picture books, once thought to be for children only, are now enjoyed by and used for teaching young adults and adults. For the purposes of this essay, I am defining children's literature as texts that, on the basis of internal or external evidence, are written with a child audience in mind or for which a child audience actually existed.

2 Readers of the international journal *Bookbird: World of Children's Books* and its reports on the state of children's literature in non-Western countries are familiar with the often striking differences between Western and non-Western constructions of children and the impact of these differences on the literature to which those who are literate are exposed. Rosamond McKitterick notes the similarities between the situation of the medieval Carolingians and that of contemporary multilingual countries seeking to develop a literature apart from that of their former English or French colonizers (*Carolingians* passim).

3 Also important are the first chapter of new historicist Leah Marcus's *Childhood and Cultural Despair* (1978), Linda Pollock's *Forgotten Children* (1983), and most recently, the first two chapters of James A. Schultz's *The Knowledge of Childhood in the German Middle Ages* (1995). The bibliographies and footnotes of these works cite numerous studies in learned journals critiquing Ariès's theories, however much their interests and conclusions may differ. Talbot offers tantalizing leads to potential children's literature, but his references are so sketchy that it is impossible to follow them up. Shahar concentrates on the central and late Middle Ages (roughly from the twelfth century on) and devotes the second half of her book to education in "the second stage" (*pueritia*), roughly ages seven to fourteen. Although Hanawalt occasionally draws in material from other countries and periods, she divides her book according to the stages of childhood and provides a picture of each stage on the basis of evidence found in court records, wills, and other archival, as well as literary, sources from fourteenth- and fifteenth-century London. Schultz bases his study on the way aristocratic children are portrayed in Middle High German texts by poets who sought to please the German aristocracy and would thus be conservative in their views; he is closer to Ariès, concluding that these children are viewed as separate from adults but "deficient" and that their attempts to play adult roles are deemed inadequate. There is a split between scholars who emphasize the biological (nature) and those who emphasize the cultural (nurture); for example, Schultz criticizes Shahar's book for its "confident sentimentality" and the too-easy identification of medieval with modern children (6). Nevertheless Schultz agrees that medieval society saw childhood as a separate stage and that medieval children were loved.

4 I mention Nodelman's book in particular, although there are many similar examples, because it is arguably the best of the general books likely to be used by students and graduate students in children's literature studies. Roderick McGillis in *The Nimble Reader* (1996) is more judicious: "As nearly all the handbooks and histories of children's literature state, literature for children as we know it—a distinct body of works written and published for the edification and enjoyment of children—only came into being in an organized way in the eighteenth century" (52). But McGillis, like many others, is by implication defining children's literature in terms of its commodification; the idea that its very existence as a separate entity is tied to commercial interests was pointed out by Francelia Butler long ago in her introduction to *Children's Literature 1*. Nevertheless, the researches of scholars such as Gillian Avery and Margaret Kinnell into the children's literature of the early modern period in England have already established the existence of "a distinct body of works" prior to the eighteenth century. German scholars have pushed even further back, as Theodor Brüggemann and Otto Brunken's bibliography of 484 books and broadsides intended for children with accompanying essays and commentary demonstrates; it begins with Ulrich Boner's 1461 *Der Edelstein*.

5 Jane Bingham and Grayce Scholt's annotated bibliography, limited to England,

includes works for adults by Boethius, Bede, Geoffrey of Monmouth, and others, appropriated in whole or in part, they argue, for children. Among such works they list *Beowulf*, which, according to David Howlett, was originally children's literature: "I see *Beowulf* as Boethius for babies, teaching the young king [Aethelstan] how to behave in a time of extreme danger ... But the establishment will resist the idea that the national epic was written for a little boy" (qtd. Dugdale 51).

6   For example, in his essay on *Aesopica*, Robert G. Miner Jr. claims that "none of these editions [of Aesop] were for children (children, of course, were not invented until the seventeenth century)" (10). That fables and fable collections were associated with children throughout the classical and medieval periods is well known. For a recent discussion of the use of fable texts in the education of children during that time span see Jan M. Ziolkowski's *Talking Animals* (21-24). For Caxton's *Aesop* and later fable versions see the special issue of the *Children's Literature Association Quarterly* 9.2 (Summer 1984).

7   For an introduction to the topic of Jewish literacy see Stefan Reif, particularly 149-55. For those with the linguistic skills, the topic of medieval Jewish children and any material that may have been written for them would be a rich, and apparently uninvestigated, field.

8   McKitterick claims that an esteem for books and their contents—and a literacy level much higher than originally thought for the laity as well as the church— are as characteristic of the so-called Dark Ages as the High Middle Ages; see particularly her *Carolingians and the Written Word*. William McMunn also argues for a higher literacy rate than was once thought ("Literacy"). In her fourth chapter, "The Production and Possession of Books," McKitterick details the high cost of the many skins, the binding, and the pigments used for an illuminated book (*Carolingians*).

9   Reynolds emphasizes that even at this early stage, learning to read is learning to read in a foreign language, Latin, and it is the Latin pronunciation of the alphabet that is learned. McKitterick argues, however, that in the Frankish regions, through the Carolingian period and even extending beyond it, students were learning the learned version of their own language (perhaps on the order of standard English and "ebonics"); this practice was even more widespread in Spain and Italy (*Carolingians* passim).

10 McKitterick notes the shortcomings for elementary educational purposes of the original "Donatus" (by a fourth-century Roman grammarian), which dealt only with the parts of speech. She discusses some of the additions, variants, and substitutes made for it, even as early as the Carolingian period, in order to meet local needs (*Carolingians* 13-20).

11 The short phrases at the beginning commence with *Itaque deo supplica* [And so pray to God], *Parentes ama* [Love your parents], and *cognatos cole* [honour your relatives] (i, nos. 1-3). The longer couplets in the second section are along the lines of *Plus vigila semper nec somno deditus esto / nam diuturna quies vitiis alimenta*

ministrat [Always devote yourself more to waking than sleeping / since long repose gives nourishment to the vices] (ii, no. 2). Jonathan Nicholls comments that "such was the popularity of the original idea that, in translation and paraphrase, [Cato] reached an enormous public in every country in Europe" (64). The distichs were still popular enough in the early modern period for Benedict Burgh's fifteenth-century English paraphrase to be one of Caxton's earlier productions, *Cato*, in 1477; it went into a second edition within a year and a third in 1481 (Childs 176). For the most accessible original and translation see [Cato]. After the second half of the twelfth century the anonymous *Facetus*, "a disorganized collection of precepts that dealt with moral welfare, points of etiquette, and semi-proverbial wisdom," is often found together with the distichs (Nicholls 182).

12 For the many shifts in the upper-division classical curriculum in the medieval period, see Ernst Robert Curtius's chapter "Curriculum Authors" (48-54). He notes that "medieval reverence for the *auctores* was so great that every source [of their texts] was held to be good. The historical and the critical sense were both lacking" (52).

13 Ziolkowski provides a detailed analysis of this poem (48-53). Alcuin spent the first half of his adult life in York and was head of the cathedral school there. At the International Research Society for Children's Literature conference at York in August 1997 I presented a paper on Alcuin and his writing for children in which I argued that his poem was an example of a work "cross-written" for a dual audience of children and adults.

14 It is a shame that Zeydel's English translation of the *Ecbasis Captivi* is so unreadable; for an analysis that emphasizes the work's religious symbolism and connection to Easter, see Ziolkwoski 153-97. Mann's prose translation of the *Ysengrimus*, on the other hand, is clear and direct and has excellent notes. For the most recent work on medieval animal literature in general see Ziolkowski's authoritative book, which is sensitive throughout to the possibility of a child audience and mentions when the works he addresses are bound with school texts.

15 Hrotswitha has not been well served by the English translations, which obscure the vividness and immediacy of her text. The two most recent ones I have seen, by Larissa Bonfante (1979) and Katharina Wilson (1989), are no exception; Bonfante's is slightly preferable.

16 I presented a paper on this text, "A Medieval Storybook: The Urban Tales of Petrus Alfonsi," at the Children's Literature Association Conference in Omaha, Nebraska, in June 1997.

17 The original audience for *Dolopathos* is not easily specified because there is only one manuscript from a time (about 1200) and location close to the author; the other five that the editor Alfons Hilka cites are from the fifteenth century (vii-x). There are also later vernacular variants. Although it is dedicated to Bertrand, the bishop of Metz, I believe that this work had a youthful audience. The framing story is a rousing account of how a fourteen-year-old pagan, Lucinius, is saved from the lust of his wicked stepmother and from being burned to death by a

series of tales told by seven wise men; the secular frame concludes with a tedious account of Lucinius's conversion to Christianity later in life, added no doubt to get the bishop's approval. *Dolopathos* has been well translated by Brady B. Gilleland and is an excellent read.

18 For a detailed description of each of these medieval courtesy books in Latin, Anglo-Norman, and English with all known texts and preferred editions, see Nicholls, Appendix B (179-97).

19 The introductory chapter to Marcus's study of problematic early modern texts, *Unediting the Renaissance*, applies to critical approaches to literary works of all periods and should be required reading for graduate students who plan to deal with the material text as a network or force field linked to a wider historical and cultural matrix.

Works Cited

Adams, Gillian. "The First Children's Literature? The Case for Sumer." *Children's Literature* 14 (1986): 1-30.

Alfonsi, Petrus. *Die Disciplina Clericalis des Petrus Alfonsi (das älteste Novellenbuch des Mittelalters)*. Ed. Alfons Hilka and Werner Söderhjelm. Shorter edition. Heidelberg: Carl Winter, 1911. Trans. Joseph Ramon Jones and John Esten Keller as *The Scholar's Guide: A Translation of the Twelfth-Century Disciplina Clericalis of Pedro Alfonso*. Toronto: Pontifical Institute, 1969, and P.R. Quarrie as *The Disciplina Clericalis of Petrus Alfonsi*. Berkeley: U of California P, 1977.

Alta Silva, Johannes de. *Dolopathos sive De rege et septem sapientibus*. Ed. Alfons Hilka. Heidelberg: Carl Winter, 1913. Trans. Brady B. Gilleland. *Johannes de Alta Silva: Dolopathos, or The King and the Seven Wise Men*. Binghamton, NY: Center for Medieval and Early Renaissance Studies, 1981.

Ariès, Philippe. *Centuries of Childhood: A Social History of Family Life*. 1960. Trans. Robert Baldick. New York: Vintage, 1962.

Beckett, Sandra. "Crosswriting Child and Adult: Henri Bosco's *L'Enfant et la rivière*." *Children's Literature Association Quarterly* 21, no. 4 (Winter 1996-97): 189-99.

Beeson, Charles H. *A Primer of Medieval Latin: An Anthology of Prose and Poetry*. Chicago: Scott, Foresman, 1925.

Berlioz, Jacques. "Un petit chaperon rouge médiéval? 'La petite fille épargnée par les loups' dans la *Fecunda ratis* d'Egbert de Liège (début du XIe siècle)." *Merveilles & Contes* 55.2 (December 1991): 246-63.

Bingham, Jane and Grayce Scholt. *Fifteen Centuries of Children's Literature: An Annotated Chronology of British and American Works in Historical Context*. Westport, CT: Greenwood, 1980.

Boswell, John. *The Kindness of Strangers*. 1988. New York: Vintage, 1990.

Bottigheimer, Ruth B. *The Bible for Children: From the Age of Gutenberg to the Present*. New Haven: Yale UP, 1996.

———. "The Child-Reader of Children's Bibles, 1656-1753." In *Infant Tongues: The Voice of the Child in Children's Literature.* Ed. Elizabeth Goodenough et al. Detroit: Wayne State UP, 1994. 44-56.

———. Letter to the author. 25 February 1997.

Brockman, Bennett A. "Children and Literature in Late Medieval England." *Children's Literature* 4 (1975): 58-63.

———. "The Juvenile Audiences of Sir Orfeo." *Children's Literature Association Quarterly* 10.1 (Spring 1985): 18-20.

———. "Medieval Songs of Innocence and Experience." *Children's Literature* 2 (1973): 40-49.

———. "Robin Hood and the Invention of Children's Literature." *Children's Literature* 10 (1982): 1-17.

Brügemann, Theodor, with Otto Brunken. *Handbuch zur Kinder- und Jugendliteratur vom Beginn des Buchdrucks bis 1570.* Stuttgart: Metzler, 1987.

Butler, Francelia. "From the Editor's High Chair." *Children's Literature* 1 (1972): 7-8.

[Cato]. "'Dicta Catonis': Introduction to *Disticha.* Text." In *Minor Latin Poets* vol. 2. Ed. and trans. J.Wight Duff and Arnold M. Duff. 1934. Loeb Classical Library. 1982. 585-621.

Childs, Edmund. *William Caxton: A Portrait in a Background.* London: Northwood, 1976.

Comestor, Petrus. *Historia Scholastica Excellens Opus. Editio altera post Beneventam anni MDCIC. Accessit Index locupletissimus.* Venice: Antonius Bortolus, 1729.

Cunningham, Hugh. *Children and Childhood in Western Society Since 1500.* London and New York: Longman, 1995.

Curtius, Ernst Robert. *European Literature and the Latin Middle Ages.* 1948. Trans. Willard Trask. Bollingen Series no. 36. New York: Pantheon, 1953.

Darton, Harvey F.J. *Children's Books in England.* 1932. 3d rev. ed. Ed. Brian Alderson. Cambridge: Cambridge UP, 1982.

Demers, Patricia. *Heaven upon Earth: The Form of Moral and Religious Children's Literature, to 1850.* Knoxville: U of Tennessee P, 1993.

Demers, Patricia and Gordon Moyles. *From Instruction to Delight: An Anthology of Children's Literature to 1850.* Toronto: Oxford UP, 1982.

Dhuoda. *A Handbook for William: A Carolingian Woman's Counsel for Her Son.* Trans. Carol Neel. Regents Studies in Medieval Culture. Lincoln: U of Nebraska P, 1991.

Dugdale, John. "Who's Afraid of *Beowulf?*" *The New Yorker,* 23 and 30 December 1996: 50-51.

Ecbasis Cuiusdam Captivi per Tropologiam (Escape of a Certain Captive Told in a Figurative Manner: An Eleventh-Century Beast Epic). Ed. and trans. Edwin H. Zeydel. University of North Carolina Studies in the Germanic Languages and Literatures 46. Chapel Hill: U of North Carolina P, 1964.

Egbert of Liège. *Fecunda ratis Egberts von Lüttich.* Ed. Ernst Voigt. Halle: Max Niemeyer, 1889.

Gordon, E.V., ed. *Pearl.* 1953. Oxford: Clarendon, 1974.

Grimm, Jacob and Wilhelm Grimm. *The Complete Fairy Tales of the Brothers Grimm.* 1812-1857. Trans. and Intro. by Jack Zipes. New York: Bantam, 1987.

Hanawalt, Barbara A. *Growing up in Medieval London: The Experience of Childhood in History.* New York: Oxford UP, 1993.

Hanks, D. Thomas, Jr. "Not for Adults Only: The English Corpus Christi Plays." *Children's Literature Association Quarterly* 10.1 (Spring 1985): 21-22.

Hildebrand, Ann M. "Jean de Brunhoff's Advice to Youth: The *Babar* Books as Books of Courtesy." *Children's Literature* 11 (1983): 76-95.

Horace. *Satires, Epistles, and Ars Poetica,* with English trans. by H. Rushton Fairclough. Loeb Classical Library. 1926. Revised 1929.

Hrotswitha of Gandersheim. *The Plays of Hrotsvit of Gandersheim.* Trans. Katharina Wilson. Garland Library of Medieval Literature 62, Series B. New York: Garland, 1989.

———. *The Plays of Hrotswitha of Gandersheim.* Trans. Larissa Bonfante. New York: New York UP, 1979.

Hunt, Peter. "Passing on the Past: The Problem of Books That Are for Children and That Were for Children." *Children's Literature Association Quarterly* 21.4 (Winter 1996-97): 200-02.

Hunt, Tony. *Teaching and Learning Latin in 13th-Century England.* Vol. 1, *Texts.* Cambridge, UK: Brewer, 1991.

Jambeck, Thomas J. and Karen K. Jambeck. "Chaucer's *Treatise on the Astrolabe:* A Handbook for the Medieval Child." *Children's Literature* 3 (1974): 117-22.

Lontzen, Günter. "Das Gedicht 'De Puella A Lupellis Servata' von Egbert von Lüttich—eine Parabel zum Thema der Taufe." *Merveilles & Contes* 6.1 (May 1992): 20-44.

Marcus, Leah Sinanoglou. *Childhood and Cultural Despair: A Theme and Variation in Seventeenth-Century Literature.* Pittsburgh: U of Pittsburgh P, 1978.

———. *Unediting the Renaissance: Shakespeare, Marlowe, Milton.* London and New York: Routledge, 1996.

McGillis, Roderick. *The Nimble Reader: Literary Theory and Children's Literature.* New York: Twayne, 1996.

McKitterick, Rosamond. *The Carolingians and the Written Word.* Cambridge: Cambridge UP, 1989.

———. "A Ninth-Century Schoolbook from the Loire Valley: Phillipps MS 16308." In *Books, Scribes, and Learning in the Frankish Kingdoms, 6th-9th Centuries.* Aldershot: Variorum, 1994. 225-31.

———. "Nuns' Scriptoria in England and Francia in the Eighth Century." In *Books, Scribes, and Learning in the Frankish Kingdoms, 6th-9th Centuries.* Aldershot: Variorum, 1994. 1-35.

McKitterick, Rosamond, ed. *The Uses of Literacy in Early Medieval Europe.* Cambridge: Cambridge UP, 1990.

McMunn, Meradith Tilbury. "Children and Literature in Medieval France." *Children's Literature* 4 (1975): 51-58.

McMunn, Meradith Tilbury and William Robert McMunn. "Children's Literature in the Middle Ages." *Children's Literature* 1 (1972): 21-29.

McMunn, William Robert. "The Literacy of Medieval Children." *Children's Literature* 4 (1975): 36-41.

Miner, Robert G., Jr. "Aesop as Litmus: The Acid Test of Children's Literature." *Children's Literature* 1 (1972): 9-15.

Morris, Sidney. *Fons Perennis: An Anthology of Medieval Latin for Schools.* London: Harrap, 1962.

Myers, Mitzi. "Wise Child, Wise Peasant, Wise Guy: Geoffrey Summerfield's Case Against the Eighteenth Century." *Children's Literature Association Quarterly* 12.2 (Summer 1987): 107-10.

Nicholls, Jonathan. *The Matter of Courtesy: Medieval Courtesy Books and the Gawain-Poet.* Woodbridge, Suffolk: D.S. Brewer, 1985.

Nikolajeva, Maria, ed. *Aspects and Issues in the History of Children's Literature.* Westport, CT and London: Greenwood, 1995.

[Nivardus]. *Ysengrimus.* Ed. and trans. Jill Mann. Mittellateinische Studien und Texte 12 Leiden: Brill, 1987.

Nodelman, Perry. "The Other: Orientalism, Colonialism, and Children's Literature." *Children's Literature Association Quarterly* 17.1 (Spring 1992): 29-35.

———. *The Pleasures of Children's Literature.* 1992. Rev. ed. White Plains, NY: Longman, 1996.

Nodelman, Perry, ed. "Literary Theory and Children's Literature." *Children's Literature Association Quarterly* 18.1 (Spring 1993): 36-46.

Perry, Ben Edwin. *Babrius and Phaedrus.* Newly Edited and Translated into English, Together with an Historical Introduction and a Comprehensive Survey of Greek and Latin Fables in the Aesopic Tradition. Loeb Classical Library. 1965.

Pollock, Linda A. *Forgotten Children: Parent-Child Relations from 1500 to 1900.* Cambridge: Cambridge UP, 1983.

Reif, Stefan C. "Aspects of Medieval Jewish Literacy." In *The Uses of Literacy in the Early Medieval Period.* Cambridge: Cambridge UP, 1990. 134-55.

Reynolds, Suzanne. *Medieval Reading: Grammar, Rhetoric and the Classical Text.* Cambridge: Cambridge UP, 1996.

Riggio, Milla B. "The Schooling of the Poet: Christian Influences and Latin Rhetoric in the Early Middle Ages." *Children's Literature* 4 (1975): 44-51.

Rouse, R.H. and M.A. Rouse. "The Vocabulary of Wax Tablets." *Harvard Library Bulletin* n.s., 1.3 (Fall 1990): 2-19.

Schultz, James A. *The Knowledge of Childhood in the German Middle Ages, 1100-1350.* Philadelphia: U of Pennsylvania P, 1995.

Shahar, Shulamith. *Childhood in the Middle Ages.* 1990. London and New York: Routledge, 1992.

Shaner, Mary. "Instruction and Delight: Medieval Romances as Children's Literature." *Poetics Today* 31 (1992): 5-15.

Shavit, Zohar. "The Historical Model of the Development of Children's Literature."

In *Aspects and Issues in the History of Children's Literature*. Westport, CT and London: Greenwood, 1995. 27-38.

Smith, Elva Sophronia. *The History of Children's Literature: A Syllabus with Selected Bibliographies*. 1937. Rev. ed. Ed. Margaret Hodges and Susan Stein. Chicago: ALA, 1980.

Spiegel, Harriet. "Instructing the Children: Advice from the Twelfth-Century *Fables* of Marie of France." *Children's Literature* 17 (1989): 25-46.

Talbot, C.H. "Children in the Middle Ages." *Children's Literature* 6 (1977): 17-33.

Victor, Claudius Marius. *Alethia*. Ed. C. Schenkl. *Corpus Scriptorum Ecclesiasticorum Latinorum* 16. Vienna, 1888.

Wright, Thomas, ed. *The Book of the Knight of La Tour-Landry: Compiled for the Instruction of His Daughters*. Early English Text Society orig. ser. 33, 1906. London: Kegan Paul, 1968.

Ziolkowski, Jan M. *Talking Animals: Medieval Latin Beast Poetry, 750-1150*. Philadelphia: U of Pennsylvania P, 1993.

Passing on the Past: The Problem of Books That Are for Children and That Were for Children (1996)
Peter Hunt

It doesn't do to be disrespectful about the past. In *Criticism, Theory and Children's Literature*, I made what I thought was a necessary distinction:

> There are "live" books and "dead" books, books which no longer concern their primary audience (and [which] concern no-one else except historians) ... Concepts of childhood change so rapidly that there is a sense in which books no longer applicable to childhood must fall into a limbo in which they are the preserve of the bibliographer, since they are of no interest to the current ... child.... The history of the children's book may be interesting to the adult, but not for the child, and it is this dichotomy which is central [to defining children's books]. (61-62)

In *An Introduction to Children's Literature*, I elaborated this view:

> Reading a text "for children" from the eighteenth century is roughly equivalent to reading Middle English poetry in the original: it may be rewarding for the specialist, but unless it is translated and modernized, it has little to offer the general reader. All children, I would submit, are in the position of being "general readers." The division between books that *were* for chil-

dren and which *are* for children is, as I have suggested, a very useful one. (28)

Not necessarily.

Perry Nodelman, in a highly professional review of the first book, took me to task. My approach, he observed,

> not only generalizes wildly about the historical interests of children but also, presumably in the interests of practicality, closes off the sort of analysis of alternate versions of childhood that [Hunt] might have been able to explore, and that therefore might well have enriched his understanding of how books children *do* currently read work to construct highly specific forms of childhood subjectivity. (39)

Well, it might, and that's a view worth discussing—rather more than a scurrilous and unprofessional review of the second book, which accused me of being "out of sympathy" with the past and therefore, by implication consigned me to the Yahoo camp (Avery iv).

But I would like to make, or re-make, the case that within the ambit of the subject of "Children's Literature" there are two quite different studies operating, with different assumptions and different methodologies and ideologies: the study of books that *are* for children, and the study of books that *were* for children. This is not always acknowledged—indeed, it is resisted—because literary and historical studies have generally had the higher academic status, and "Children's Literature" has generally found it necessary to attach itself to the "respectable" in order to survive. Equally, it is assumed that there is a flow, a stream of history, that connects all books written for children, and that we in the present can learn from the past about books and children.

Both those views seem to me to be worth challenging.

To challenge the second is perhaps the more contentious. I must hasten to say that I am not out of sympathy with the past: I am out of sympathy with a view that venerates it, and holds its books to be more valuable than those of the present. (We might view the sorting process that is "literature" as simply an admission of our failure to cope with the vast variety of texts.) But I think that we should recognize that the idea of a continuum of literature, in which subject matter or mode shifts along with childhood—and which is therefore related to, and useful for, the modem study/child/academic—is suspect. The idea of a literary continuum assumes some continuity of readership and some continuity of medium: in the case of children and books, these continua only *appear* to exist. Nodelman is obviously right that books at various times past did very different things, but whether what they did (supposing that it were knowable) can actually inform our present practice is another thing. History is marked by fractures, chasms, which readers cannot in the natural way of things cross, and this is particularly true of the history of children's literature and reading.

Childhood is the most elusive of concepts: it differs virtually from house to house and from day to day; our grasp of *historical* childhoods is—for obvious socio-historical reasons—very flimsy indeed. So much so, in fact, that we tend to deduce the characteristics of childhood from the literature written *for* it— which is a very questionable process, given the adult-child power-relationship. We can be fairly sure, though, that there have been huge changes in "childhood" between 1590, 1690, 1790, 1890, and 1990.

And, of course, books have changed too, and I do not mean simply in terms of form. Let's take an example: the dichotomy between the study of books that *were* for children and that *are* for children is perhaps best represented by the chapbooks. They are the subject of fascinated and (to some) fascinating academic study; their bibliographic, historical, and socio-cultural potential has hardly been touched. But to the current child (and here I am constructing a generalization with some confidence) they are inaccessible—that is, they are crude to the point of imbecility, in both form and content. That much is obvious, but what is not so obvious is that much the same applies well into the nineteenth century—and perhaps later: for all that the books seem to look like the books of today, and have stories that seem not too far from those of today, they were different phenomena in a different cultural context.

And this is where the discontinuities of literary and social history meet. It is difficult to imagine the impact of a chapbook on a child four hundred years ago; was it the equivalent of the impact of a virtual-reality CD hologram on the child of today? Similarly, the novel of the eighteenth or nineteenth century addresses not only a concept of childhood that is very different from ours, but also a concept of reading/interacting/of the book/of the medium that is very different from ours. Now, that circumstance may be interesting historically, just as, say, the typefaces of the chapbooks are interesting for the history of typefaces. But that complex and challenging study has much less to tell the practitioners of today than is commonly assumed.

In short, while books of the more recent past may seem superficially to address modern childhood, they do not actually do so. One only has to glance at the wholesale reinterpretations by film producers of *The Secret Garden* or *A Little Princess*, or at virtually anything by Walt Disney, to see that this is so. Similarly, literary traditions manifested in the generic characteristics and expectations that so condition the reading of books by experienced adult readers are virtually inoperable for less experienced readers. Consequently, if we could regard books that *were* for and *are* for children as distinct, we might see that there are two quite different value-systems at work, and two quite different critical and theoretical methodologies appropriate to them.

You may say that there are many borderline cases, neither dead nor alive, enjoyed by some children and sustained by adults: *Uncle Remus*, the *Alice* books, *The Wind in the Willows*, *The Water Babies*, and folk tales in general. These are perhaps the most interesting, but they make my point in that they are now being directed *at* childhood, rather than being *of* childhood. (Fairy tales, the majority of which have to be severely bowdlerized, make the same point.) Can, say, the excellent Oxford edition of *The Princess and the Goblin* be said to have anything to do with a contemporary child?

At this point, I feel that I should defend myself against the accusation of "presentism." Presentism—the devaluing of history—implies that we lose our culture, and we repeat the mistakes of the past; if the teaching of history is virtually nonexistent, for example, it is possible for people to deny that the Holocaust actually happened—with horrific implications. Not only would I deplore the idea of ignoring history, but I would say that I am a fervent traditionalist—I would argue that the best children's book of the century may well be *The Stone Book Quartet*, in which Alan Garner celebrates the presence of the past. But, equally, I believe in the preservation of *all* cultures, rather than *the* "culture"; after all, books are generally burned by people whose own cultures have been degraded.

Consequently, I do not take a romantic view of the past (which is, of course, a rampant and endemic feature of those children's books which adults are inclined to valorize). My mother and father were, respectively, on the edge of the urban and rural working class, and my own memory of rural life in the 1940s (which had scarcely changed in two hundred years) was that it was oppressive and oppressing, hard, damp, cold, and smelly; those who survived were tough in a way it is hard to imagine now. All the men I knew could do almost anything, but the fact that they could do so was a matter of survival rather than of love, and the favourite verb (this is south Leicestershire) was "to mackle up," which is a little better than "botch," and implies a good deal of expediency and ingenuity, and not a lot of craft or pride.

Similarly, I do not take a romantic or reverential view of books from the past. Certainly the books, the objects, should be preserved (even, perhaps, treasured), but to accord them some superior status simply because of their age or supposed historical significance seems to me to be a serious error. Equally, to regard bibliographers and historians as the custodians of the foundations of the subject, and as "real" rather than "speculative" researchers, obscures our understanding of books, childhood and the meanings generated between them (see Hunt, "Researching"; "Scholars").

I would argue, then, that the study of past books requires and implies different skills from the study of books currently read by live children. Of course, it might at first sight seem that this division is already manifest: books that *are* for children are studied in education schools, books that *were* for children are studied in literature departments. (Or, to put it another way, *children's children's books* are studied in education, and *adult's children's books* in literature departments.) But this is precisely the problem: the philosophy and methodology of the higher status literature departments have dominated, even though they are often more concerned with the book than the interaction; are wedded to concepts of canon and to certain value systems (male, white, adult); and are essentially adultist and universalist. Those who work with books and children find themselves always in the shadow of "the classic" or "the great"—terms implying values that, like the concept of "literature" itself, are inappropriate to the subject (see Hunt, "Criticism").

In order to survive academically, "Children's Literature"—with its conferences and journals and papers and theory—has played the adult game, valuing history above the new challenges of literary interaction. It has, consequently, equipped us with some sterile and inappropriate attitudes. We should think seriously of turning the present situation around—to say that the study of books that *are* for children is the primary, interdisciplinary, intercultural, intellectually challenging, innovative, and unselfconscious centre of our study. We may draw on that historical and historico-socio-critical matrix that is the study of *past* children's books, but *that* study, far from being the root or the foundation of our work, is in fact a subdivision of historical and literary studies, and has little connection with our study of *today*.

History = literature = respectable (precisely because it does not relate to that very childish thing, childhood—that is, a *real, individual* childhood); literature is an adult province, of libraries, rare and expensive *untouchable* books; it is the province of the academic and the collector interested in the sociology of childhood, or the development of printing techniques, or the development of literary trends; it is, essentially, abstract and inward looking; it looks to the minutiae of books, and universals of culture, and although historicists may disagree, that history has, at least, *happened.*

Contemporary, child-oriented literary studies are quite different; here we are talking about childhood, about *use*, about books being touched, eaten, rejected, banned, pulped—in short, about *live* issues. For example, that John Newbery produced trash of the worst commercial order is historically scarcely mentioned, because it is part of a historical process, because the books are rare, and because they show us the development of printing through the reuse of woodcuts, or of different printers and so on. In contrast, that the Ninja Turtles or the Power Rangers or Sonic the Hedgehog or "Point Horror" galvanize our children is not a matter of abstract curiosity; it is a matter that has to be understood and confronted.

Children's books do different things at different times, and it is at least questionable to assume that they can constitute, diachronically, a cohesive subject. All of this, of course, is gloriously arguable. What is not so arguable is one of the implications. Too often we do not acknowledge that "children's literature" is a big subject; we cannot be experts in "children's literature" any more than anyone would be an expert in the whole of "literature." If we do not acknowledge that theory and history and the application of texts may inform each other but are *not* the same, then we are dooming the whole subject.

Works Cited

Avery, Gillian. "Scamper Through the Ages." *Times Educational Supplement* 10 March 1995, Supplement IV.

Hunt, Peter. "Criticism and Children's Literature: What Can We Say, and Who Wants to Listen?" *International Review of Children's Literature and Librarianship* 9 (1994): 1-7.

——. *Criticism, Theory, and Children's Literature.* Oxford: Blackwell, 1991.

——. *An Introduction to Children's Literature.* Oxford: Oxford UP, 1994.

——. "Researching the Fragmented Subject." *Researching Children's Literature: A Coming of Age?* Ed. Neil Broadbent et al. Southampton: LSU, 1994. 6-12.

——. "Scholars, Critics, Standards." *Children's Literature History Newsletter* 52 (1995): 18-22.

Nodelman, Perry. "The Second Kind of Criticism." *Children's Literature Association Quarterly* 17 (1992): 37-39.

Postscript (2005)

This article, which I thought merely described the *status quo*, provoked a spirited response, notably in the *Children's Literature Association Quarterly*. Dieter Petzold saw it as "another version of the 'book-people vs. child-people' controversy ... or 'pluralists vs. educationalists' or ... 'elitists vs. populists.'" (146) He argued that the "tension between the two poles" of the old book people and the new book people "can be a powerful source of energy"—and I agree. However, he also argued that "it is the business of the academy to keep our literary heritage alive and to teach students [and, I imagine, ultimately, children] to *appreciate literary excellence*" (146). This seems to me to make my point: "literary excellence"—whatever that may be, does *not* reside in the past; the books of today and the readers of today make their own kind of excellence. It may be useful to know about other kinds of excellence, but they should not be privileged. If *Harry Potter* can never be as good as *Alice*, by definition, then what are we condemning our children to?

Richard Flynn, on the other hand, who thought the article "reductive and wrongheaded" (143), gave a spirited defence of what I would see as the tendency to remoteness and solipsism in criticism, and pointed to a very productive future model. "Childhood Studies" represents a "better, more visible, more inclusive network," and would, I hope, focus on the child, and the child-and-the-book.

Works Cited

Flynn, Richard. "The Intersection of Children's Literature and Childhood Studies." *Children's Literature Association Quarterly* 22.3 (Fall 1997): 143-45.
Petzold, Dieter. "Another 'Querelle des ancients et des modernes'? Some Commonplaces to Remember." *Children's Literature Association Quarterly* 22.3 (Fall 1997): 145-46.

Report from Limbo:
Reading Historical Children's Literature Today (1998)
Susan R. Gannon

In a recent issue of the *Horn Book* Brian Alderson confessed a prank he played on some academics running a conference on children's literature. Pretending to be one Dr. Quashi-Idun, an aspiring children's literature scholar, he'd sent them a jargon-filled and meaningless paper proposal. When the paper-call committee welcomed it warmly, the trap was sprung. Alderson's acid account of his hoax stresses the way the committee's taste for fashionable nonsense blinded them to the obvious deficiencies of the proposal, including a reference to a nonexistent nineteenth-century children's journal that should have been a clear signal that something was amiss. Alderson's impeccable credentials as researcher and scholar make his outrage at the committee's carelessness and sheer ignorance understandable. In a gentler but no less stern vein, Anne Wilson, writing in last September's *Signal,* observes that genius demands independence of thought, imagination, realism, the ability to predict what may happen next, a love of challenge and a desire to take scholarly work forward in a very practical way—qualities she finds in short supply among today's scholars. She commends researchers who meticulously gather and analyse the evidence needed to read texts properly, but Wilson thinks "the way of genius should be a model" for scholarship and notes with concern some current trends that impoverish thought: "narrower and narrower specialization," "the use of jargon and other special language," a detachment from "real problems and practical means." Though Wilson doesn't specifically mention a single scholar specializing in children's literature, the venue of her piece suggests that her comments are politely directed towards the children's literature community, and Wilson's words need to be taken very seriously—coming as they do from a critic whose brilliant practice embodies the "way of genius" she preaches.

It is hard not to sympathize with Wilson and Alderson in their impatience with the follies and impostures of the muddle-headed. But Peter Hunt's recent piece in the *Children's Literature Association Quarterly*, "Passing on the Past: The Problem of Books That Are for Children and That Were for Children," is another matter. He complains that there are two quite different disciplines operating within the field of children's literature—one "the study of books that *are* for children," the other "the study of books that *were* for children" (200). Earlier Hunt had distinguished between what he termed "live" and "dead" books, the latter comprising "books which no longer concern their primary audience" and which therefore "concern no-one else except historians." "Concepts of childhood," he contended then, "change so rapidly that there is a sense in which books no longer applicable to childhood must fall into a limbo in which they are the preserve of the bibliographer, since they are of no interest to the current librarian or child" (Hunt 1991, 61).

Hunt thinks that children's books of the past and present have been studied together as part of one intellectual enterprise for a purely political reason: because historical studies have always had more status in the academy, they have been used to lend a certain respectability to the less prestigious work on contemporary books for the young. But, he believes, the "primary, interdisciplinary, intercultural, intellectually challenging, innovative and unselfconscious centre of our study" should be the study of books currently read by children. The study of historical children's literature, he says, "far from being the root or the foundation of our work, is in fact a subdivision of historical and literary studies, and has little connection with our study of *today*" (Hunt 1996, 202).

Hunt's *Quarterly* piece was intended to raise hackles and to be, as he suggests, "gloriously arguable." But in it he draws a picture of historical children's literature study that I barely recognize—as something that is merely "the province of the academic and the collector interested in the sociology of childhood, or the development of printing techniques, or the development of literary trends," as opposed to "contemporary, child-oriented literary studies" that are "quite different; here we are talking about childhood, about *use*, about books being touched, eaten, rejected, banned, pulped—in short, about *live* issues."

Hunt asserts that "the study of past books requires and implies different skills from the study of books currently read by live children." He sees the philosophy and methodology of traditional historical children's literature study to be "more concerned with the book than the interaction" and "wedded to concepts of canon and to certain value systems (male, white, adult)" and "essentially adultist and universalist." Yet far from romanticizing or idealizing a set of "children's classics" to be studied as touchstones of excellence, many recent studies of historical children's literature focus on the experience of ordinary, sometimes quite obscure, readers of the past—their practices, their favourite texts, their interactions with the people and institutions that shaped them as readers. And these inquiries have been informed by an agenda concerned very much with issues of gender, class, and power relations.

I don't know that I can offer much consolation to Brian Alderson or Anne Wilson. Their concern for a field of study that has its share of politics and pretension, narrow specialization and intolerance is quite legitimate. But at least Peter Hunt may take heart: there is good evidence that many of his historically minded colleagues value, have profited from and are trying—in their own way—to contribute to the sort of work he cherishes. Currently scholars *are* asking fresh, realistic and practical questions of historical texts very much informed by hands-on work with present-day readers and their books.

For example, a treasure trove of handmade nursery library and artefacts produced by Jane Johnson (1706-59) and discovered in 1986 in the collection of Elizabeth Ball (now held at the Lilly Library of the University of Indiana) has opened a debate over the texts written and read to the very young, the way reading shapes children's consciousness, and the much-neglected subject of women's role in educating young children in the home. The intensity of critical interest in the teaching materials developed by this obscure English vicar's wife is demonstrated in the prominence given them at a conference at Princeton last October called "Playing with Knowledge: Text, Toys and Teaching Children" that focused on the rise of child-centred teaching methods in the late eighteenth century, bringing together scholars to talk about Johnson's home-made instructional materials for her children (Brian Alderson), the Edgeworths (Mitzi Myers), Barbauld's *Lessons* (William McCarthy), and the development of educational toys and games (Jill Shefrin). And in keeping with its lively interest in real children touching and using the precious ephemera of their nursery worlds, the conference, inaugurating the Cotsen Collection, included exhibitions of historical toys and games along with the discussions and celebrations.

A recent collection of essays called *Opening the Nursery Door*, edited by Mary Hilton, Morag Styles, and Victor Watson, also derives its impetus from study of the Johnson material—that loving creation of one of the many forgotten mothers who knew how to draw children into stories, engage them in dramatic play, making them "active, mindful, imaginative, and artistic conversationalists and performers" (Heath 29). The nursery culture of which Jane Johnson was mistress can only be reconstructed with careful scholarly effort, but such scholarship reflects great respect for the work of ordinary mothers with real children, and draws actively on contemporary work on children and their introduction to literacy. As Mary Hilton puts it, Johnson, in creating her tiny books, card sets, mobiles, was doing far more for her children than presenting them with "predictable, graded and utilitarian exercises"; she was

involving them in a vital project of mutual, loving and moral interpretation of the social and physical world around them. She was, possibly like many other women educators in the private sphere, engaging the young in a dialogic and imaginative construction of their social possibilities. (1)

Shirley Brice Heath's essay describes in loving detail the sets of pictures Johnson put together for her children's educational play. These seem designed to be cues for simple word and sound recognition and the generation of sentences and stories, but they also embody social critique and opportunities to discuss problem-solving in real-life situations. And Victor Watson's essay on Johnson's "A very pretty Story to tell Children when they are about five or six years of age" demonstrates the originality and cleverness with which Johnson put her own children into a story combining elements of domestic fable, French fairy tale and oral family performance. The discovery of such a charming and sophisticated home-made nursery story written in the 1740s suggests for Watson "the powerful need of a developing print-based culture to take its materials from oral practices." And it throws into question "the old orthodoxy that children's literature began because a philosopher had an idea and a printer put it into practice," in favour of the likelihood that what really happened in the eighteenth century was

> the emergence into public scrutiny ... of a traditional private and domestic nursery-culture—undervalued, orally transmitted from one generation to the next, responsive to changes in contemporary thinking, making a pragmatic use of available materials, and mostly sustained by mothers. (45)

There is a great deal yet to be learned about the ways women of all classes have, historically, nurtured their children's early intellectual growth. Johnson's practice may be illuminated further as scholars study her daughter's scrapbooks and her own other writing. Contemporary interest in observational study of parent interventions in children's cognitive development has set historical scholars to reading parent and child diaries of past generations with "live" questions in mind. J.A.V. Chapple and Anita Wilson have recently edited the parent diaries of novelist Elizabeth Gaskell and her cousin Sophia Holland, recording the early childhood years of Gaskell's daughter Marianne and Sophia's son Edward, who were later to marry. These diaries offer highly personal accounts of what it meant to be a Victorian mother and document daily interactions with young children in significant detail. Other scholars are mining memoirs and autobiography, journals and diaries to find more accurate information on children's introduction to literacy. The diaries of Marjory Fleming (1803-11) have been explored to show the way she was taught by her sister, Isabella, and to reveal her vivid reactions to literature—not only "Gray, Swift, Fielding, Addison" but also "Shakespeare and Mother Goose, Scott and Maria Edgeworth, Robert Morehead's sermons (ignored) and the *Newgate Calendar* (pored over)" (Johnson 87).

Hilary Minns writes in a piece in *Opening the Nursery Door* about the way Irish children in Derby between 1841 and 1861 were introduced to literacy, noting the effect of a gifted teacher like Mother Cornelia Connelly, whose method of teaching was meticulously followed by the nuns who taught in Derby's Roman Catholic schools. And Minns offers a fresh look at the surprisingly clever and effective Irish *Lesson Books* from which many Derby boys and girls learned to "reconstruct, remake, extend and understand their experience of living in a social context with each other" (Meek, qtd. in Minns 190). (It is interesting that when Minns goes to examine the likely effect of the reading of a little fable on a child audience she turns for inspiration to the work of Margaret Meek in a modern piece, observing that "her message is equally valid when applied to this nineteenth-century text.") And Minns, no victim of dreamy nostalgia for a romantic past, but a practical educator and specialist on children and reading, concludes by suggesting that the textual world presented to today's children by schoolbooks that give them "no opportunity to go out and look, smell, touch, and feel, and to take their own emotional and practical worlds of knowledge to the world of the book" is sadly impoverished. "There are surely," she suggests, "lessons in the Irish *Lesson Books* that we can learn from today" (196).

The new questions contemporary historical scholars of childhood and of children's literature are learning to ask are reshaping our picture of education history. Not only is it important to see education in the context of changes in philosophy, politics, religion, but changes in nursery culture as well. David Vincent suggests that studies of the history of childhood need "a more rigorous and theoretically informed treatment of issues such as cognitive development, social psychology, orality and literacy" and "the economics of supply and demand" including a sense of what might have been the relative roles played by parents and official providers in valuating and shaping education (175). And since the parent-child relationship is very much implicated in the structuring of literature for a child audience an understanding of the way real families functioned in the past has been a subject of vital interest to critics.

Mitzi Myers's work on the way the nurturing mother as tutor and guide figured in fictions of moral education in the eighteenth and early nineteenth centuries, for example, raises questions about "the relation between nurturance and autonomy, connectedness and individuation, child and parent, dependence and dominance, feeling and reason ... experience and the discursive practices that figure it" (Myers 1991, 98) that seem to me to be as relevant to contemporary children's books as they are to the Georgian texts that are her primary focus—though perhaps the historical scholar has the advantage of a distant perspective. Immediacy has its perils: the transparency of the contemporary context can be deceptive when the observer is too close to see clearly. And the present, after all, is every moment becoming the past, its full story never completely available as it unfolds. As Juliet Dusinberre has eloquently reminded us, sometimes the true nature of the vital interaction between a generation of young readers and their reading is not apparent until they have grown up and written books of their own.

For Peter Hunt "*children's children's books* are studied in education and *adults' children's books* are studied in literature departments" (Hunt 1996, 202). But things are rarely so simple. How are we to *know* which literature is for children and which for their elders? It is not so easy to assess those subtle alterations of tone and register that determine questions of address. Barbara Wall, believing that "the narrator-narratee relationship ... is the distinctive marker of a children's book" (9), has given considerable critical attention to analysing the various effects authors in different periods have been able to achieve in narrative address. Though Wall's warmest sympathies, like Hunt's, lie especially with modern writers and their very real and live audiences, she makes useful observations about the relationship between the speaking voice and its narrative audiences in the work of a great range of historical authors including Charlotte Yonge, Mary Louisa Molesworth, Juliana Ewing, Charles Dodgson, Thomas Hughes, J.M. Barrie and Kenneth Grahame. While I don't agree with Wall's view of children's literature as having progressed gradually from less effective forms of address to the "single address" that dominates recent writing, her clever and insightful close readings offer convincing evidence that anyone who cares about children's literature criticism must attend to narrative address and its implications.

As editors of a special issue of *Children's Literature* on cross-writing U.C. Knoepflmacher and Mitzi Myers have focused attention on the "dialogic mix of older and younger voices" to be found in "texts too often read as univocal. Authors who write for children inevitably create a colloquy between past and present selves" (vii). And of course many famous children's stories have had their genesis in real-life, face-to-face sessions between adults and the children they wanted to entertain, instruct, amuse. In "Kipling's 'Just-so' Partner: The Dead Child as Collaborator and Muse" Knoepflmacher explores the way Kipling transformed his favourite auditor, his daughter Effie, into the "Best Beloved" addressed in his stories. Kipling had a subtle understanding of the process of cross-writing with its delicate balance between child and adult perspectives and selves. Particularly in the stories written after Effie's unexpected death Kipling managed to dramatize "an alliance or collaboration designed to counter not only the separation between adult and child, but also gaps between the sexes and between the living and the dead" (25).

Questions of status have dogged children's literature in every era. Hunt is concerned about the downgrading of contemporary children's literature by those who prefer to study the literature of the past. But historical children's literature, its writers and their work, its critics and theirs, have suffered greatly from the same prejudices that trouble Hunt. Consider the case of Maria Edgeworth, whose literary status seemed, as Mitzi Myers has pointed out, secure. But "writing for, to, about, and as a child, however brilliantly successful in its day, hasn't proved good for Edgeworth's long-term canonical health" (Myers 1997, 122). Myers looks at Edgeworth's work from the perspective of post-colonialist criticism, seeing her as a daring border-crosser projecting "her political and cultural answers within child characters and within the childlike genre of the tale." "Ironically," says Myers, it is Edgeworth's bold transgression of "the usual demarcations between children's and adults' literature" in aid of her "revisionist political agenda" that "—misread and mis-valued—have done in the author's literary standing today" (126).

Hunt is right to want to see children's literature of the present taken seriously. But the sort of historical scholarship Myers practises offers a useful model to students of contemporary children's books as well. Myers, in taking Edgeworth's "child-centred texts seriously *politically*, as reformist spaces intertextual with grown-up works and lives and perhaps more radical than adultist conformities permit," adds an important dimension to current "theorizing about the role of the juvenile in both our cultural construction of ourselves and our historical reconstruction of the past" (126). As Margaret Meek pointed out, from study of children's books of the past can be derived

a theory of children's literature that includes children reading as authors taught them to. The advantage of so doing is that it helps us to do the same for our contemporary children's books. (169)

Meek noted with admiration the way J.S. Bratton's extensive work on popular formula fiction "demonstrates that we can judge the skill of a writer like Hesba Stretton in interpreting and manipulating the given formula" only when Stretton's work is set against the conventions of the genre in which she wrote. "Where once critics lumped these books together, she now exercises a more refined literary discrimination" (169).

Sally Mitchell's *The New Girl: Girls' Culture in England, 1880-1915* draws not only on formula fiction but memoirs and advice manuals to study the way reading shaped and expressed the experience of the "new" girl. She also offers a reading of Stretton's *Jessica's First Prayer* and the vast body of street Arab literature it spawned. Mitchell's study of reader interaction with texts is grounded in an interest in "what girl readers were taking and using from their stories" (6), and she chooses to study not the fiction adults might have prescribed for their improvement, but the (often now quite forgotten) books they loved. In taking seriously ephemeral books that were, for a moment, intensely satisfying to a young audience, Mitchell offers a useful model for the study of more recent readers and their tastes. Indeed, her book raises a troubling lesson from the past that students of contemporary children and their books might ponder as they contemplate the future of child culture in a new century: she finds girls' culture in the period immediately after 1920 to have been "less open, less fluid, less promising than the new culture of the nineteenth century's final decades" and lacking "the range and promise and daring agency of its first generation" (188).

One of the pleasures of telling stories is the fun of watching the children you know making meaning: taking in what the text says, struggling against it, extending and playing with it. (And—often enough—helping to shape the next story that comes along.) My own research interests have recently involved me in reading nineteenth-century children's periodicals, especially America's *St. Nicholas*, the pages of which offer ample evidence of the involvement of a young readership in shaping the magazine's contents. In a piece included in the Myers and Knoepflmacher volume I examined the way child readers responded to their reading of Burnett's *Little Lord Fauntleroy* in the magazine's "Letter-Box" feature, framing each serialized episode in a multidirectional, intergenerational conversation (Gannon 153-80). Many letters described readings aloud in the family circle, sharing reader's hopes, fears and expectations about the way the story would turn out. The immediacy of the children's response, and their eagerness to share their feelings with other readers still come across as you pore over the dusty volumes. The magazine's editor, Mary Mapes Dodge, put her own editorial spin on the cult of Cedric Errol, who seemed to her a wonderful role model for her readers, and she shamelessly puffed the play Burnett made from the novel when it appeared in London and then on Broadway. Anyone interested in the intricacies of a young audience's response to the culture-text (the sum of a popular text's many versions) of a novel as reshaped into drama will vastly enjoy the sometimes starry-eyed, sometimes brusque and cutting critiques offered by young readers who saw the stage production, as well as their letters praising the young actress who played Ceddie on Broadway (a protegée of Dodge and a sentimental child-friend of Mark Twain). Together with "The St. Nicholas League," the literary department that offered children the chance to write fiction and poetry of their own and see it published, the "Letter-Box" gives us a privileged view of the process of active reading as practised in the community of readers created by the magazine.

It is more than a dozen years now since Jacqueline Rose drew our attention to the "impossibility" of a children's literature that "sets up a world in which the adult comes first (author, maker, giver) and the child comes after (reader, product, receiver) but where neither of them enter the space in between" (1-2). Today, anyone interested in studying or writing about it must deal with the fact that "children's literature is not just literature written with children in mind, nor is it just literature that happens to be read by children. It is a genre, a special kind of literature with its own distinguishing characteristics" (Nodelman 81), among which are its peculiar kind of interactivity and the way it handles the balance of power between child and adult. Coping with the "impossibility" of the genre and identifying its defining characteristics are not easy, and a "rich but unstructured area" (Hunt 1990, 7) of study has arisen, providing a different and invaluable kind of "space in between" where intellectual border-crossers can meet to find ways to "understand its particularity; as well as its continuity with literature in general" (Meek, qtd in Hunt 1990, 11).

Of course, it is hard to theorize the interdisciplinary practice of children's literature studies. The field is neither stable nor unified, and there is no consensus on any *best* way to approach the literature. But why should we be surprised that a field of study might reflect the variety, the complexity, and perhaps even the "impossibility" of its subject? However much children's literature specialists may occasionally long for the simplicities of a more clearly defined, integrated and coherent discipline, there are distinct advantages to working within a scholarly subculture that sustains a lively—though sometimes contentious—conversation among colleagues with quite different critical agendas. What is important, I think, is that those of us engaged in this conversation listen to each other carefully and patiently, ready to discern potentially useful lines of inquiry even when they are cast in unfamiliar terms (or irritating jargon).

Most academics working with children's literature have encountered enough snubs and sneers from colleagues in more academically prestigious fields to make them sensitive to the particular kind of pain expressed in Hunt's irritable reaching after the certainties of disciplinary purity. There is an understandable edginess to his complaints that the academic institution of "Children's Literature" "with its conferences and its journals and papers and theory—has played the adult game, valuing history above the new challenges of literary interaction" (Hunt 1996, 202). But these objections are being voiced at a moment when the study of children's literature of the past is—as never before—informed by precisely the sort of hands-on contemporary work with real children and their books that Hunt most keenly appreciates. Such study recontextualizes historical texts without suggesting a false continuity between past and present or assuming a romantic attitude that overvalues texts celebrated for their nostalgic associations. And I think it extends our understanding of the variety of real transactions it is possible for child readers to have with their books, provides valuable evidence about the "interplay of gender and genre" and can "assist modern critics in their canonic and generic reconceptualizations" (Myers 1992, 132). Why anyone should want to marginalize such work beats me.

Works Cited

Alderson, Brian. "A View from the Island: How to Get Your Ph.D. in Children's Literature." *Horn Book* 73.4 (July/August 1997): 438-42.

Chapple, J.A.V. and Anita Wilson. *Private Voices: The Diaries of Elizabeth Cleghorn Gaskell and Sophia Isaac Holland.* New York: St. Martin's, 1996.

Dooley, Patricia, ed. *The First Steps: Articles and Column from ChLA Newsletter/Quarterly,* Volume I-IV. West Lafayette, IN: ChLA, 1984.

Dusinberre, Juliet. *Alice to the Lighthouse: Children's Books and Radical Experiments in Art.* New York: St. Martin's, 1987.

Gannon, Susan R. "'The Best Magazine for Children of All Ages': Cross-Editing *St. Nicholas Magazine* (1873-1905)." *Children's Literature* 25 (1997): 153-80.

Goodenough, Elizabeth, Mark A. Heberle, and Naomi Sokoloff. *Infant Tongues: The Voice of the Child in Literature.* Detroit: Wayne State UP, 1994.

Heath, Shirley Brice. "Child's Play or Finding the Ephemera of Home." Hilton, Styles & Watson 17-30.

Hilton, Mary. Introduction. Hilton, Styles & Watson 1-13.

Hilton, Mary, Morag Styles, and Victor Watson, eds., *Opening the Nursery Door: Reading, Writing and Childhood 1600-1900*. New York: Routledge, 1997.

Hunt, Peter. *Children's Literature: The Development of Criticism*. New York: Routledge, 1990.

——. *Criticism, Theory and Children's Literature*. Malden: Blackwell, 1991.

——. "Passing on the Past: The Problem of Books That Are for Children and That Were for Children." *Children's Literature Association Quarterly* 21.4 (Winter 1996-97): 200-02.

Johnson, Alexandra. "The Drama of Imagination: Marjory Fleming and her Diaries." Goodenough, Heberle and Sokoloff 80-109.

Knoepflmacher, U.C. "Kipling's 'Just-So' Partner: The Dead Child as Collaborator and Muse." *Children's Literature* 25 (1997): 24-49.

Knoepflmacher, U.C. and Mitzi Myers. "From the Editors: 'Cross-Writing' and the Recontextualization of Children's Literary Studies." *Children's Literature* 25 (1997): vii-xvii.

Meek, Margaret. "What Counts as Evidence in Theories of Children's Literature?" Hunt 1990 166-82.

Minns, Hilary. "'I Knew a Duck': Reading and Learning in Derby's Poor Schools." Hilton, Styles and Watson 180-98.

Mitchell, Sally. *The New Girl: Girls' Culture in England, 1880-1915*. New York: Columbia UP, 1995.

Myers, Mitzi. "Canonical 'Orphans' and Critical *Ennui*: Rereading Edgeworth's Cross-Writing." *Children's Literature* 25 (1997): 116-36.

——. "Little Girls Lost: Rewriting Romantic Childhood, Righting Gender and Genre." *Teaching Children's Literature: Issues, Pedagogy, Resources*. Ed. Glenn Sadler. New York: MLA, 1992. 131-42.

——. "Romancing the Moral Tale: Maria Edgeworth and the Problematics of Pedagogy." *Romanticism and Children's Literature in Nineteenth-Century England*. Ed. James Holt McGavran, Jr. Georgia: U of Georgia P, 1991. 96-128.

Nodelman, Perry. "Beyond Genre and Beyond." Dooley 81-83.

Rose, Jacqueline. *The Case of Peter Pan: Or the Impossibility of Children's Fiction*, Rev. Ed. Hampshire: Macmillan, 1994.

Vincent, David. "The Domestic and the Official Curriculum in Nineteenth-Century England." Hilton, Styles, and Watson 161-79.

Wall, Barbara. *The Narrator's Voice: The Dilemma of Children's Fiction*. Hampshire: Macmillan, 1991.

Watson, Victor. "Jane Johnson: A Very Pretty Story to Tell Children." Hilton, Styles and Watson 31-46.

Wilson, Anne. "A Don May Look at a Genius." *Signal* 84 (September 1997): 161-71.

The Picturebook[1]

Every experienced reader is confident with written material, but how pictorial art communicates is, for many, unfamiliar territory. While this does not affect our delight in picture books, it certainly limits our understanding of them. (7)
—Jane Doonan, *Looking at Pictures in Picture Books* (1993)

The simplicity of a picture book in terms of narrative structure, visual appeal and often fable-like brevity might seem to suggest that it is indeed ideally suited to a juvenile readership. It's about showing and telling, a window for learning to "read" in a broad sense, exploring relationships between words, pictures and the world we experience every day. But is this an activity that ends with childhood, when at some point we are sufficiently qualified to graduate from one medium to another? Simplicity certainly does not exclude sophistication or complexity; any serious reader, writer or artist would know that the truth is otherwise. "Art," as Einstein reminds us, "is the expression of the most profound thoughts in the simplest way." (1)
—Shaun Tan, "Picture Books: Who Are They For?" (2001)

Because the words and pictures in picture books both define and amplify each other, neither is as open-ended as either would be on its own. And while the same paradoxical amplification and limitation of different means of communication by each other also occur in filmed or staged narratives, picture books also differ significantly from these; instead of providing different modes of communication simultaneously, they alternate between their two modes, and we cannot both read the words and peruse the pictures at the same time....

As a result of these unusual features, picture books have unique rhythms, unique conventions of shape and structure, a unique body of narrative techniques. (vii)
—Perry Nodelman, *Words About Pictures: The Narrative Art of Children's Picture Books* (1988)

I consider it to be most important that we avoid presumptions in favour of any one type or kind of picturebook. If we begin by assuming that we already know what the essential characteristics of the picturebook are, then there will be less to investigate, our investigations revolving around a diminished set of characteristics. If, for example, we take the work of Quentin Blake or Anthony Browne to possess what the essential characteristics of a picturebook are, then the further away from the Blake or Browne model a picturebook appears to be, the less like

a picturebook it will seem. By examining a range of books, and withholding judgements as to which ones are more picturebook-like than others, we are able to construct a more generous description of the form. (27)
—David Lewis, *Reading Contemporary Picturebooks: Picturing Text* (2001)

Introduction

As the quotations above point out, picturebooks are an unusual art form. They reward sophisticated reading involving two kinds of literacy: visual and verbal. That is, with many picturebooks, readers can gain a great deal from knowing theories and strategies of both visual art and literature. Ironically, these are the books we tend to think of as most suitable for the least experienced readers, and we ignore them as we grow up. Children sometimes scorn picturebooks when they've finally learned to read on their own because society and schools tell them that reading books with pictures is what babies do; few children want to be babies.

Over the past 30 years, however, the art of the picturebook has been recognized and discussed in some detail, and picturebooks, along with their cousins, comics, now come in a range of artistic merits, from disposable, market tie-ins by Disney and Mattel to the technical and artistic virtuosity of books such as Maurice Sendak's *Where the Wild Things Are*, Anthony Browne's *Voices in the Park*, or Peggy Rathmann's *Gloria and Officer Buckle*, to name too few.

Learning to read picturebooks to their full potential is both fun and rewarding. The most important step is taking time to look and absorb details of both the visual and the verbal texts and then becoming conscious of the ways in which they communicate to us. In "Introduction to Picturebook Codes," William Moebius begins the work that has continued over the past 20 years. He identifies different codes or conventions that appear in the visual texts. Often we are influenced by those conventions without being aware of their presence. Other critics have continued that work, and so a basic list of important conventions can be a starting point for reading visually:

Style. Examine whether the pictures are realistic, cartoon-like, or stylized (based on stylized patterns rather than on nature). Consider if the style matches, adds to, or creates a tension with the words.

Border. A large border and small picture might suggest that the character is trapped or, alternatively, secure. A small border and a large picture can mean the character is free, or perhaps abandoned. Some borders are decorated or have pictures that connect to the story in some way. There may not be a formal border, just space around the picture, in which case, consider the effect of that space; sometimes unframed pictures involve readers in the story rather than setting them outside the story.

Character movement, direction, and placement. If characters face or move right, they are often moving into adventure or the unknown, while those facing or moving left are moving into safety or the known—although facing left sometimes means the journey is blocked in some way. Placement at the top of the page suggests a character is dominant, powerful, happy, while those at the bottom of the page may be dominated, powerless, sad. Placement in the middle of the page can indicate that a character is the centre of attention, though one should pay attention to whether the character is all alone and isolated, or surrounded by friends and happy.

Colour. Consider that cool colours, like blues and greys, tend to communicate calmness, while warm colours, like reds and yellows, tend to communicate activity and action. Light, happy colours or dark, sombre colours can support the action and events in the story.

Page layout. Sometimes, more than one picture will be on a page; there may be multiple views of a character or event. In some cases, the multiple pictures help show a series of connected actions or events. In other cases, they may help show a transformation taking place.

Looking at the pictures is, however, just a starting point. The book as a whole can contribute to meaning. The cover, the endpapers or endpages, the half-title page and the full-title page, the copyright page, the dedication page are all important. And, of course, the words—how they are arranged and what they say—contribute to meaning.

The articles presented here discuss different aspects of understanding and assessing picturebooks. Although originally written in 1949, many of Marcia Brown's points in "Distinction in Picture Books" continue to hold true, with the exceptions of some of the technical aspects of printing and the fact that retail sales have largely replaced trade sales due to increasing cutbacks in public and school libraries. In a letter, Marcia Brown explains that her piece "appeared in *The Horn Book*, September-October, 1949. It was a speech given at a meeting of the New York Library Association in Syracuse, New York, 1949. The original title was 'What is a Distinguished Picture Book?'" The version reprinted here "was later published in [her] book, *Lotus Seeds: Children, Pictures and Books*, published by Charles Scribner's Sons in 1986." Regrettably, we have had to omit the pictures that accompanied the original version of Brown's article in this chapter due to constraints of space.

Deborah Stevenson's exploration of the narrative considerations of picturebooks, "Narrative in Picture Books or, The Paper That Should Have Had Slides," provides many pointers on things to look for when reading picturebooks, while the excerpts from Scott McCloud's *Understanding Comics* introduce elements to consider when reading comics, graphic novels, and even Dav Pilkey's ever popular Captain Underpants series. The excerpts from Aidan Chambers's *Tell Me: Children's Reading and Talk* provide insights into productive means of exploring picturebooks with children and demonstrate children's critical acumen when they are given the chance to display it. Finally, Emer O'Sullivan's article "Translating Pictures" addresses the sometimes drastic changes that can result in the process of translation from one language to another because of variations in what adults in different countries think is acceptable for children.

Note

1 The current consensus, started in this century with David Lewis's *Reading Contemporary Picturebooks* (2001) and Maria Nikolajeva and Carole Scott's *How Picturebooks Work* (2001), is that the single word *picturebooks* refers to those particular books in which the pictures are an integral part of the overall text. The single word picturebook signals symbiosis or integration of pictures and words, whereas the space in "picture book" signals the division or separation between the visual and the verbal texts within the book.

Works Cited

Doonan, Jane. *Looking at Pictures in Picture Books.* Stroud, Glos.: Thimble, 1993. 7.

Lewis, David. *Reading Contemporary Picturebooks: Picturing Text.* London: Routledge Falmer, 2001. 27.

Moebius, William. "Introduction to Picturebook Codes." *Word and Image* 2.2 (1986): 141-58.

Nodelman, Perry. *Words About Pictures: The Narrative Art of Children's Picture Books.* Athens and London: U of Georgia P, 1988. vii.

Tan, Shaun. "Picture Books: Who Are They For?" A paper presented at the 2001 AATE/ALEA Joint National Conference. 4 Jan 2006. <http://www.education.tas.gov.au/english/tan1.htm>.

Distinction in Picture Books (1958)

Marcia Brown

What is a distinguished picture book? With the changes that have come about in publishing in the last few years, the fate of the picture book lies squarely in the hands of librarians. Today it takes real courage for a publisher to produce a picture book, especially one that is a little unusual. With the great competition from mass-produced, inexpensive books, the individually produced picture book can remain in print only through continued library sales.

A librarian hands along to others what she has found significant, interesting and beautiful in books. From the flood of picture books that pour off the presses each year it is increasingly difficult to select any that merit the designation "distinguished." In selecting and interpreting books for children, librarians can actively encourage the production of good picture books. The problem of choosing good illustration in the books we give our children has many ramifications in our contemporary life.

A child can and must be trained in visual awareness if he is to become an aware adult. For the city child, there is the staccato excitement of geometry, subway lights, neon signs, sharp contrasts of light and shade, mass groupings of buildings and humanity. Human warmth becomes even more precious in such an atmosphere. For the country child there are the subtle curves of landscape, a close-up of seasonal changes, the design of plant forms, a chance to observe the relationships of the parts of nature to the whole. Each child can be taught to enlarge his horizons.

Taste, the ability to discriminate, to cast off the false, the unworthy, and to retain the genuine; the capacity to see what is before us, to be alert; the pleasure in what is harmonious and at the same time various; the poise that is born of inner rhythm and balance—all these are best formed in early childhood.

In our mechanized environment, mass media such as the comic book, the greeting card, magazine advertising, television, the motion picture and the animated cartoon influence the visual perception of a child. The child's avidity for information, his need for excitement and adventure, his imagination, are exploited in this mass production of taste, with all its accompanying paraphernalia of saccharinity, sadism, and frenzied destruction. Now, added to this we have the mass-produced, inexpensive picture book that must cost as little as possible to produce and be easy to sell, since the motive for production is profit. Millions of copies of this style of book appear on the market each year. The public library, the school library and the home—if in these places adults select good books for children—become islands in the flood. None of us would quarrel with the cost of these books to the children. Would that all their books could cost so little! But we can question their quality.

A picture book evolves from the combined effort of author, illustrator, publisher, and printer. All, I believe, are interested in producing a good book, but they must also produce a salable book. From our discussion we shall have to exclude the book produced entirely as a business commodity by huge combines and those concerns whose large reserves of funds afford them vast machines for production and distribution. The average publisher cannot afford to publish and keep in print a book that will not sell. And just as any united group of people accomplishes its work through a certain amount of personal compromise and mutual understanding of each other's needs and problems, so the production of a picture book entails concessions from one member of the group to another.

When the artist is also author the chance for unity between text and pictures is usually greater, although it is conceivable that other artists could provide better illustrations than those of the author. Whether or not the author is artist, whether pictures and text form simultaneously in the author's mind or the writing of the text precedes the execution of the pictures, the problem of unity remains. For the pictures must be true to the spirit and feeling of the book as a whole, the spirit of the author's concept and the child's acceptance. Once the artist has grasped this concept, and this can happen in the short space of time needed to read the text because all his life has been a preparation for this moment, the plan of the book's appearance begins to take place in his mind. Perhaps he asks himself questions such as these:

What shape? How much space will I need for double spreads? Is the feeling of the book one of height, with tall buildings, trees that reach up, or is it horizontal, with long roads, the sea, a procession to stretch across a page? When Plato Chan had just finished the pictures for *Magic Monkey* he told us in the Children's Room of the New York Public Library that he made the book vertical because monkeys go up and down and *The Good-Luck Horse* horizontal because a horse is shaped that way.

What colours are appropriate to the story? Also, how many colours can the publisher afford to let me use? If I must use only two colours, what two will suggest the atmosphere of the story and provide one dark enough for a legible text? If the story has an exotic or historical background, how much of the style determined by the background shall I use in my pictures? What technique shall I use: fine line, reed pen, water colour, flat colour, wash and line, crayon, spatter, linoleum cut, pastel and line? What type face shall I keep in mind that will be harmonious with my drawings and also with the spirit of the book?

Each book presents a completely new set of problems. That is one reason why illustrating is such interesting work. Certain methods of reproduction are suitable to certain media, and the costs of these vary greatly. Just as the printmaker does not expect from an etching the same effect he can get in a wood block, so the illustrator cannot expect from line reproduction the nuances of a water colour. An illustrator today must acquaint himself with all these methods of reproduction to realize the best results from his work. His job does not end with the completion of his drawings, but only when the finished, bound book is in his hands. Many illustrators see their books through the entire ordeal of proving and printing.

To anyone who has taken the trouble to show fine paintings or reproductions to little children it should be apparent that there need be no condescension to their ages in the types of drawing and painting we offer them. They embrace all kinds and all subjects freely. Their own drawings may be realistic, near abstract or conceptual. The child of six does not become lost in a tangle of associations and rules as he looks at a drawing. If its message is clear, whether simple or complex, he will comprehend it. Perhaps not all at once. But most worthwhile things bear more than one examination.

As for deciding which medium of illustration is best for children, the great variety of media and the many fine examples of each type prove the foolishness of dogmatism. The important question is what medium is best for this book, tells its message clearly—and is economically practicable. The photographs of *Tobe*, the coloured woodblocks of Falls' *ABC*, the poster technique of LeWitt and Him in *Locomotive* and *The Little Red Engine Gets a Name*, Thomas Handforth's stylized pen line in *Tranquilina's Paradise* and his bold brush and crayon work in *Mei Li*, the black and white rhythmic line and mass of *Millions of Cats*, the beautiful abstract design of some of the Russian pictures books of the '30s, the water colours of *Little Tim and the Brave Sea Captain*, the coloured lithographs of *A Child's Good Night Book*: these are just some of the media available to the illustrator. Why do many illustrators utilize so few of them?

Nor can we make rules about colour in children's books, except that it be harmonious and appropriate to the subject. We have become so saturated with colour in our advertising, in our magazine illustration, and now in our motion pictures that we almost lose sight of the fact that children enjoy equally books with little or no colour and books in full colour. To refute the demand of those who want many colours, there are the richness of Wanda Gág's black and white drawings, the sepia of *Make Way for Ducklings*, the two colours of *Andy and the Lion*, *The Five Chinese Brothers*, and many others. Colour is not so important as the richness of the message told by the illustrations in these books so well liked by children.

At a time when production costs are more than double what they were before the war, the illustrator is obliged to become more skilled in the utilization of small amounts of colour. He must know how to get everything out of his colours through overlays in his colour separations. Some illustrators, like Nicolas Mordvinoff, Roger Duvoisin and Leo Politi, use two or three colours more effectively than others use five. The line drawings themselves must provide more colour.

After the artist makes a dummy and has completed some of his final drawings he may help select a type face with the book designer or person in charge of manufacturing details. This type must be legible to children and harmonious with the pictures; it must fit into the proper space on the page and usually be available in linotype, since the cost of hand-set type is often prohibitive [editors' note: this point no longer applies today].

Before I worked on picture books I never realized the great number of manipulations that drawings and text go through before the completion of a book. I wish it were possible for everyone using books with children to observe a large offset press in operation, to see how negatives are made, how they are stripped up for making the final printing plates, and then to witness the actual printing of the large sheets that form the body of the book.

But from all the picture books produced, how are we to pick those which are exceptional? I believe that they must be regarded as are other forms of visual art. There is no recipe for judging illustration any more than there is a recipe for producing it.

It is extremely difficult to be objective about a picture book because each of us brings something different to what he sees. What is beautiful to one of us might be merely dull to another—or worse. Recently I gave a coloured wood-block print to a friend of mine in the hospital. The print was an abstraction of a mask in which I attempted to show two aspects of ennui, the giddy gaiety that tries to forget and the withdrawal into oneself. When the nurse's aide saw the print the next morning she said to my friend, "Miss, if you did that you deserve to be in the hospital! Them that can draw should draw pretty."

All that the artist has seen and felt deeply, his subconscious feelings and reactions to life, contribute to his work and will often be discernible there, setting up similar reactions in us as we look at it. Some illustrations set up reactions that continue long after we have ceased to look at them. Others we grasp at a glance because of the very narrow range of the experience they offer. Some books for children can be returned to again and again, not only because the child enjoys repetition, but because he will always find in them the reward of enjoyment.

Such books are those of the artist whose name is given to the greatest honour conferred on an illustrator of children's books, Randolph Caldecott. From the insipid, oversweet atmosphere of many of our picture books today, it is like stepping out of doors into a fresh wind to enter his picture books. Here are vitality in every line, sweep, humour without acerbity that never had to worry about age-levels or suitability for children because it was born of rich observation of and enthusiasm for life itself. Here is such a thorough familiarity with the English countryside and its people that these scenes and characters could have sprung from no other soil. And all that is essential is clear to the youngest mind and yet stimulating to the adult who returns to it again and again. Much has happened in illustration and bookmaking since Caldecott's time, but the positive quality of his spirit remains in our best picture books.

In his *Last Lectures* Roger Fry suggests a method of examining works of art by confining attention to one or two qualities at a time and by comparing a number of different works to see to what extent they possess or lack these qualities. He chose sensibility and vitality. It might be profitable for us to study how these qualities can be reflected in the picture book.

The term sensibility includes two basic desires, the desire for order, harmony, and the desire for variety, chance, the unexpected. The first is expressed in the over-all design of a work, the coordination of the parts in the whole. The other is subject to the feeling and sensitivity of the artist in executing the design or plan.

Since the picture book is a unit composed of text and pictures, I am assuming that the text of the book is at least good, if not distinguished in itself. Without making set rules only to break them, let us subject the visual elements that compose a picture book to an examination for those qualities Fry suggests. We can learn something from asking ourselves questions such as these:

How appropriate are the illustrations to the spirit as well as the facts of the story? If the illustrations are merely decorations, is this treatment all the story demands? Is there extraneous gingerbread in the decoration that might better have been left out? Do treatments vary from page to page, or are many pages monotonously alike in design? Do the margins allow enough air for the pictures to move in? If the page is bled, is it best that way?

Is the type legible and harmonious with the pictures and feeling of the story? Is there a pleasant visual play between pictures and type? Is the type attractively placed in relation to the pictures?

Is the colour appropriate, interesting, or watered-down, sugary? If it is bright and harsh, is it appropriate so? We can expect bright colour from a fire engine or a circus. How has the illustrator seen the whole book—in masses of colour, in line, in rhythm? Why?

Is there a discernible build-up in the dramatic interest of the pictures as there is in the text? Is the characterization rich or meagre, the people merely stereotypes, or do they have the qualities of individual human beings observable in life? Is there a build-up in characterization if the story requires it? Does the illustrator impose on us a reaction toward the characters that he wants us to feel? Does he nudge us to say, "This child, or this puppy, isn't he charming? Do you see what I mean?" If pushed too far we are apt to be aware of nothing but a sense of falseness.

How honest is the portrayal or various races and peoples? Do all of them resemble tinted Anglo-Saxons? What is the illustrator's feeling toward races other than his own? What appreciation of differences are we going to give our children? False generalizations about the goodness or evil of a race do little to create understanding.

Is the humour genuinely funny, or is it the tongue-in-cheek humour of the over-sophisticated adult?

How do the varieties of treatment reflect the sensibilities of the individual artist?

As we consider vitality we see how even more difficult it is to formulate any rules concerning this quality. Is there rhythm of line, of movement, of shape and mass in the drawings, and are these rhythms suitable to that of the story? If the text has sweep, do the pictures move likewise? Are the drawings so finished, so slick and photographically perfect that they were dead before we had a chance to look at them? This question is related to that of sensitivity of drawing. Do the drawings continue in the mind, as do those of Edy-Legrand, or are they so complete there is nothing for our minds and imaginations to do? Sheer virtuosity is often more useful in a juggler than in an artist. Is the drawing alive by itself on the page, as Andy and his lion are so thoroughly alive, or does it seem to live only because of its accurate resemblance to life? In his *The Spirit of Man in Asian Art* Laurence Binyon wrote, "The full mind, the rich mind, makes itself felt in the tracing of a few vivid lines; the empty mind, the poor nature, is betrayed in the most elaborate composition."

As we look at picture books we can find answers to all of these questions that will heighten our powers of discrimination. Perhaps the question that includes much of the foregoing could be—how rich is the experience in living the child gets, that I get, from looking at this book?

In their first books children begin to form their taste for art and literature. Any of you who have struggled to introduce mature writing to high school students saturated with comic books can appreciate this. It leads us into the question of our responsibility to children in training them to discriminate, to discard the cheap and ugly.

Perhaps exposure to good picture books in childhood will not assure an adult taste capable of appreciating fine art, but I do believe that a child unconsciously forms an approach to his visual world of order, rhythm, and interesting arrangements of colour from the books he sees when young. The cleanness and simplicity of a well-designed page may start a chain of reactions that will continue into adulthood. If the child is accustomed to seeing varied and interesting shapes in his picture books, abstract art will not have the terrors for him that it seems to have for some adults. His discrimination, along with whatever of his individuality he can manage to preserve, will be his main defence against the bombardment of visual material on his eyes in most of his waking hours.

Librarians can play an important part in the future production of good books. They can select a few good picture books rather than many mediocre ones. We often forget that each year new groups of children are seeing for the first time books we have long known. Librarians can write to publishers about their reactions to books as they come out. They can award honours to books that are truly distinguished.

An author expects the librarian to bring some experience with literature to her judgement of a text. I feel that an illustrator or artist has a right to expect in those judging his work some art background. Just as an appreciation for great poetry is fed by great poetry and not by doggerel, so an appreciation of art must be fed by something more than book illustration. I know from experience how difficult it is to nourish an interest in painting if one lives in a small community, but through the state library, through art publications, it is possible at least to see reproductions of paintings of our own time, as well as earlier ones. Some of the paintings I remember best from my childhood are those reproduced on slides that my seventh-grade teacher obtained for us from the state library. Most of the names of the artists were forgotten until I met them again as an adult, but the images of the pictures remained.

If more adults were familiar with modern art movements and the problems artists today are trying to solve, we might hear fewer set conceptions and snap judgements of drawing and painting such as: "It's too modern! There's no perspective! I could draw as well myself and I can't draw a straight line! A child could do better!" Since art is a communication only in its own terms of line, colour and mass, we must learn to enjoy pictures with our senses instead of demanding logical explanations. It is senseless for us to be indifferent to art and to the training of children to see and select and then to deplore their lack of taste once they have become adults.

Let there be among librarians a wider examination of picture books of all types, past and present, American and foreign, so that their judgements will reflect a rich acquaintance with the whole field of illustration. Familiarity with some of the best picture books will show us how often we are content with the shoddy and the ordinary.

The effect of the popularity in America of Hollywood-inspired illustration is now coming back to us from Japan, France, Argentina, even from Switzerland—all countries that are also making beautiful books for children. Our responsibility to children does not stop with our own boundaries. We must show to other countries the best we have to offer.

In judging I believe we should leave our personal prejudices for the illustrator or subject out of consideration. If an award is to be given to a distinguished book, let it be given to just that, the book that will carry the seal of your recognition to the public. If a picture book does not wear well, can't we rightly ask ourselves was it ever really good, or merely timely? The book itself has not changed.

This awarding of honours has an effect on other librarians who do not have an opportunity to see much of a year's output of books, as they buy for school and public libraries, as they suggest purchases to parents. It has a great effect on bookstore sales and the production of similar books by publishers. A great part of the public is impressed by prizes, and slavishly follows the edicts of the critics and book reviewers, instead of judging for itself. Most people have neither time nor opportunity to examine large numbers of children's books, even if they were interested. They rely on the judgement of those they consider experts.

Awards have an effect on the artists themselves. It has always been the fate of some artists to be either misjudged or to feel that their best work is unrecognized. Often an artist receives recognition for work inferior to what he has done previously.

Librarians can demand high standards from their illustrators and publishers. Why is it that as we examine the output of many of our outstanding illustrators we find so few who have grown appreciably since their first books? A story about a child of 1800, one of 1949, one in Mexico, one in Alaska—all get the same illustrative treatment from them. Their growth has been in perfecting what they already could do rather than in experimenting and reaching out into new fields. Perhaps we have directly or indirectly asked these artists to repeat themselves. An illustrator must produce what sells in order to live. But to do his best work he must also be free to listen to his own inner voice and act upon it. Many illustrators are doing other art work as well as illustration in order to work in complete freedom. By buying only work that resembles an illustrator's earlier books we force him to stunt himself to our prescription. Let us encourage him to grow, to experiment, to try new techniques, by being at least receptive to the new.

Narrative in Picture Books or,
The Paper That Should Have Had Slides (1998)
Deborah Stevenson

I'm not sure my title is quite right—while the product is a unified one, I think there are narra*tives* in a picture book, not just one narrative. As Perry Nodelman says:

> [the picture book] is unique in its use of different forms of expression that convey different sorts of information to form a whole different from the component parts—but without those parts ever actually blending into one, as seems to happen in other mixed-media forms such as film and theatre, so that someone reading a picture book must always be conscious of the differences of the different sorts of information. (21)

The literary world is so verbally attuned that it's easy to consider narrative as words only, and therefore to consider a picture book as a narrative with pictures; the art world focuses on the pictures, considering the picture book as an art object with extended captions. These views both seem to me unfortunately limited—if narrative were merely the words on a page, people wouldn't attend conferences—and this side-taking also seems to me to overlook the nature of the picture book as synthesis of art and words. To read a picture book aloud, as most were intended, is to dramatize it. One might almost consider a picture book a variant of a play, one that carries its own set design with it.

In this sense picture books resemble other combinative art forms, such as opera or musical theatre, films, and ballet; older examples include the courtly masque and the emblem book. This resemblance is good for me, since I thrive on analogies (I was apparently permanently warped by that section of the SATs), and I therefore often find it useful to consider picture books along with those other media, without, of course, ignoring the fact that picture books also have their own individual charms and characteristics. I'd like to examine the aspects of the picture book—the text, the art and other physical factors—and then discuss how these narratives work together to affect each other and the final outcome.

Text: The Downtrodden Partner

Despite its primacy, the text is often the downtrodden partner in the picture book form. A picture book can, after all, be a picture book without a text; it can't be one without pictures. It's tempting to consider the relative responses to the term "textbook" and the term "picture book"; the former is dull, the term occasionally used pejoratively; the latter is pleasurable and imaginative. Because the text of a picture book is short (*Where the Wild Things Are* by Maurice Sendak contains 338 words in all), the writing of it can seem easy; because the text accompanies the pictures, it may seem insignificant. This apparent insignificance can lead to underestimation of the author's role. It's difficult, for instance, for the author of picture books to gain a reputation solely for that skill; many of the best known write for older readers or illustrate as well. The number of critical articles addressing picture book illustration far outweighs those dealing with picture book text, nor is it usual for the author of a picture book to win any writing award such as the Newbery (Nancy Willard's medal for *A Visit to William Blake's Inn* is an obvious exception, but one that was supported by well-received illustrations that made the title a Caldecott Honor book as well). The late Margaret Wise Brown was one of the first picture book authors to gain wide repute; two of the currently most prominent are Eric Kimmel and Robert San Souci, both of whom specialize in folktale adaptation, a type of text that frequently draws more attention, because of cultural interests, than does an original story (Tony Johnson is one of the writers of original texts whose reputation is growing). A likelier way to gain an authorial reputation is as part of an author-illustrator team, such as Arthur Yorinks and Richard Egielski or Jon Scieszka with Lane Smith (Scieszka's one book with a different illustrator was nowhere near as successful); better still, create both text and art and allow the illustrator's fame to be the same as the author's.

This deceptive simplicity of picture book texts may be one reason why it's so easy to find bad ones. It can become a vicious and self-fulfilling circle: since it seems so easy to write a picture book, it must mean that anyone can, and picture book texts are further cheapened. Picture book authors are also likelier than illustrators to think or be told to think in terms of education rather than art. The pressure on a picture book to be educational, whether pedagogically, politically, or socially, falls almost entirely on the text, so desirable subject matter or an important message can outrank good writing. I have no objection to narratives with lessons: most stories have a point, and didactic tales are alive and well and often absorbing and frequently well-received by children as well as adults, but a lesson in itself is not sufficient for a story. Some picture books seem quite content with the idea that pictures exist as sugarcoating for the textual pill, because that arrangement relieves the text of the burden of being interesting; the result is artistically inferior and unappealing to most children and adults.

Fortunately, however, many writers of picture books craft their work well, rising to the challenge of writing a text that will meet an illustrator at least halfway. The restraint involved in writing a picture book is a challenge; authors of other kinds of books generally employ narrative to tell the "whole" story, but picture book text must leave some meaning to the illustrations while still possessing its own spirit. It is the text through which adults hope to shape children and inspire them, and the text that an adult will reread a multiplicity of times to an importunate child.

The reading aloud is an important consideration, since most literary texts are designed with a different kind of reading experience in mind. It's odd that the otherwise perceptive Nodelman, in his *Words About Pictures*, a detailed examination of the operation and process of picture books, focuses almost entirely on silent reading of the written text; he finally suggests that the "ironies and rhythms" he analyzes may not be apparent if those texts are read aloud (263). In practice, this seems incorrect. Most picture book creators seem attuned to the auditory aspects, since with most picture books those ironies and rhythms are generally most apparent when the book is read aloud as intended. Many picture book texts read quite blandly on the page, but their patterns of rhythm and energy appear with force when one speaks them aloud.

There are a multiplicity of possibilities even in this compressed and focused genre that will change the narrative completely: the text prose or rhymed; present tense or past; first person, second person, or third person. From a formal point of view, a text can be visually end-stopped, to borrow a term from poetry, with sentences completed before every page turn, or there may be visual enjambment, with sentences continuing through page turns, as in *Where the Wild Things Are* when Max makes "mischief of one kind / and another." The text may be separated from the art (as in *Wild Things*), interspersed with it, or winding around it; or it may only appear in speech balloons (Raymond Briggs's *Father Christmas*). Every page may have text, or text and illustration pages may alternate; or illustration alone may carry many spreads (*Wild Things* again). Or it might be primarily a wordless book with only a small bit of text (Rathmann's *Good Night, Gorilla*). Even before you get to the myriad vagaries of individual style, there are narrative choices that will change a story completely.

As there are, of course, with the illustrations.

The Language of Illustrations

I've found it very challenging, at times, to write about picture books, because the critical vocabulary is geared to words. The term "text" in critical circles, meaning the thing that is contained within every edition of the book, that sense of a title that exists without regard to the physical objects, linguistically excludes illustration. In a larger sense, however, picture book illustration is inarguably part of (and in wordless books, completely) a picture book's text; it is read, it conveys intentional and unintentional meanings, it imparts the story.

As someone whose skills lie entirely in the writing area of the equation, I find myself overwhelmed with the technical side of illustration, with gouache versus watercolour, with colour separations each painted in black and then photographed in a different colour, with selecting two different kinds of black inks to approximate the brown tones on an original (as happened for Tom Feelings's *The Middle Passage*). I find it hard to imagine making it beyond these technicalities to the creative sweep of artwork, but I suppose it's not that dissimilar to fierce preferences for certain wordprocessing software, an understanding of the different effects between the passive and active voice, or the authenticity conferred by specificity.

Yet every technical aspect of illustration is an aspect of the visual narrative. Oils tell a story differently from watercolour, photo collage from pastels. Black and white (Isadora's *Ben's Trumpet*) obviously differs from colour (Ehlert's *Circus*), or even from sepia tones or other monochromatic palettes (Van Allsburg's *The Sweetest Fig*) and even other black and white (Van Allsburg's *Jumanji*); illustrators, like filmmakers, know that the pictorial narrative changes if the colours are different. Look, for instance, at the stylistic and colour differences between wordless books, which remove the additional possibility of textual difference (*Anno's Journey* and Raymond Briggs's *The Snowman*).

Differences in the visual treatment make for a completely different narrative. Sometimes it's a matter of interpretation. We're all familiar with songs that have been covered by two different artists. The difference can be substantial (I'm particularly remembering the anecdote about music-hall legend Marie Lloyd performing a rendition of the innocent drawing-room song "Come into the Garden, Maud" that had critics of her morality blushing on account of what they allowed into their own homes). That additional effect can be entirely the province of illustration. It's impossible that a story would be the same when illustrated by David Wisniewski as by Chris Van Allsburg, or by Ed Young and by Arthur Geisert.

Even very small differences alter the construction of the visual narrative. Betsy Hearne has a nifty set of slides that she uses in teaching—the artist Adrienne Adams redid her pictures for Priscilla and Otto Friedrich's *The Easter Bunny That Overslept* 20 years later, and the two sets of illustrations make a provocative contrast. The artist has clearly gained in skill and expertise over the years, and the changes are in keeping with the enhanced sophistication and subtlety of the genre and printing technology; the later illustrations have subtler hues compared to the primary colours of the earlier versions, and the compositions have gotten more diverse and less uninflected, and there's much more sensitivity to the sweep and drama of line. The text remains the same and the pictures are really only slightly altered. Yet, the result is not the same story.

There is always the question of the necessity of such artistic achievement when the young audience may well not notice. I go now for my analogy to the world of musicals for Oscar Hammerstein's metaphor—he pointed out that when the Statue of Liberty was carved, Bartholdi took pains with the top of her head even though he had no reason to believe anyone was going to see it. Merit lies in careful craftsmanship of areas that few will notice as well as those that all will notice; Hammerstein was discussing underlying musical themes and verbal plays that may not be noticed as they go by quickly in live theatre, but are nonetheless there.

And, of course, people do now see the top of the Statue of Liberty's head. Changing times mean different viewpoints and different sets of knowledge, and contemporary children are much more visually schooled than previous generations. Take, for example, the Cottingley fairy incident, which is depicted in a movie called *Fairy Tale* in the US. For those who don't know the incident, a pair of young sisters, at the beginning of the century, claimed that fairies were visiting their garden and that those visitors had been captured on film—and indeed, they had pictures of themselves with fairies so convincing that Arthur Conan Doyle, for instance, believed them. Yet these photographs very obviously, to modern eyes, feature living girls and cardboard cutout fairies. Even without tackling the issue of our greater scepticism about such visitation, our visual sophistication makes differentiating between cardboard cutouts and real figures elementary ... my dear Watson.

Visuals, after all, have their own language; some of it is literal, but some of it, particularly in narrative, is not. Apparently, for instance, many small children have difficulty understanding the convention that sequential pictures of the same object indicate passage of time rather than just several similar objects at the same time. It's also possible that a child who has recently learned that the shimmers of green and yellow outside do constitute a tree will not be overjoyed at an Impressionist's careful return to the predistinguished vision. Nor is it fair to judge children's visual sophistication by their capability in production. Adults, after all, do not necessarily appreciate a mediocre violinist just because they are themselves execrable musicians. Evelyn Goldsmith notes the difficulty children have in recognizing some theoretically "childlike" abstractions (150). What we have here is a literary and artistic equivalent of what psychology terms the "fis phenomenon," wherein a child whose developing motor skills aren't yet up to the consonantal cluster pronounces "fish" "fis," but whose linguistic knowledge makes him insist that an adult's use of "fis" was incorrect; his ability to produce lags behind his ability to understand.

Children also react to pictures at a startlingly early age: Dorothy Butler's granddaughter Cushla, for instance, in one of the great longitudinal examinations of reading, responded to pictures and abstract symbols with fascination at nine months of age. Leonard Marcus argues that it can be appropriate to speak of "readers" of the picture, since a child's response to them is centered on words and names (35). In many books, especially alphabet books, art is simultaneously picture and language, as in *Anno's Alphabet,* Stephen Johnson's *Alphabet City,* and David Pelletier's *The Graphic Alphabet.* In a different vein, if you'll pardon the circulatory system pun, Ed Young's *Voices of the Heart* refigures the meaning of Chinese characters in new metaphoric images—in these books, the pictures are *about* language. From the child's point of view, the experience is no less reading for involving pictures. A toddler on a parent's lap experiencing *Wild Things* may not be literate in the technical sense of the term, but she is reading in the broad sense; she is decoding messages and meanings from the volume in front of her in order to recreate a story. Whether young children are poring over a wordless book, sharing a picture book read aloud, or privately experiencing both text and pictures, they are increasing their visual literacy and their understanding of the breadth and diversity of narrative.

Format and More

We often break up our discussion of picture books into two components of words and pictures, but a recent spate of variations in form and physical effects reminds me that those aspects of a book, which don't fit neatly into the categories of words or pictures, also affect a narrative. Even before children can read books, the sheer physicality of a volume is very important to them; they are little inclined to abstract "text" or "pictures" from the construct of the book. Various studies have made it clear that physical makeup of a book greatly affects a child's response to it, and that children, who don't worry about shelving constraints, can warm to books both oversized and undersized. Children pet books and wear them, taste them and listen to them, creating a material connection with books that adults rarely envision. In reviewing Nodelman's *Words about Pictures*, Juliet Dusinberre reasonably criticizes him for failing to consider as a factor a book's smell (397); olfactory appeal rarely enters into a critical discourse, but it can play a large part in a child's reaction. Maurice Sendak describes his reaction to a book received as a child:

> The first thing I did was to set it up on the table and stare at it for a long time. Not because I was impressed with Mark Twain; it was just a beautiful object. Then came the smelling of it. I think the smelling of books began with *The Prince and the Pauper*, because it was printed on particularly fine paper, unlike the Disney Big Little Books I had gotten previously, which were printed on very poor paper and smelled poor. *The Prince and the Pauper* smelled good, and it also had a shiny cover, a laminated cover. I flipped over that. And it was solid. I mean, it was bound very tightly. I remember trying to bite it, which I don't imagine was what my sister had in mind when she bought the book for me. The last thing I did was to read it. It was all right. ("Notes" 173)

Sometimes these forms are variations of books originally published in a more traditional arrangement. Picture books get reissued as big books, for instance, and more and more of late turn up again in board book form. Pop-up versions have been around for awhile, but a new (or perhaps resurrected) form, so far used for original books only, has been the foldout frieze (or pull-out panorama, as I note a new one calls itself), which accordion-folds neatly between the book covers but opens up into a single lengthy, connected page. Then, of course, there are the newer versions, the downloadable electronic text, or the book on CD-ROM. (There are also movies and television, but I'm speaking of forms in which the illustration and the verbal text are the same as the original.)

I don't mean to suggest some sort of purist hierarchy, whereby the sewn binding and paper pages are some holy literary grail. I like board books, and popups, and CD-ROMs. Nor do I think the conversion of any book into a different format is a recipe for disaster. But the medium is at least part of the message, and the book's narrative alters with its format and appearance. The very way readers interact with the book is changed, which Beatrix Potter so wisely noted in specifying the tiny trim size of her volumes. A book you can make a clubhouse out of is obviously going to demand different treatment than a book you can tuck under your pillow, or one which can only be handled occasionally and gently. In her excellent *Horn Book* article, Sarah Ellis discusses some of the advantages and disadvantages of the electronic format of Bjarne Reuter's *The End of the Rainbow*, noting such important and over-lookable details as the physical warmth of the laptop and its comparative unportability. [original *Editor's note: The electronic format cited no longer was avail-*

able at the time this publication went to press.] A CD-ROM has its own momentum which can remove the onus from the reader. Scrolling is not the same as "the drama of the turning of the page," as Barbara Bader so eloquently puts it (1). This drama, too, is lost in the frieze, which offers a chance at a more sustained, less discretely episodic narrative, and indeed a more literally circular one. The story of snakes in *The Snake Book* would be a muted and lost one in a tiny format (though it might make a terrific frieze, with snakes all around). The focused and hemmed intensity of *Grandmother Bryant's Pocket* would lose its impact in a large trim size.

Working Together: Synthesis of Art Forms

But it's all got to come together somehow. Maurice Sendak, when discussing illustrating his own text, suggests that in order to attain this synthesis of art forms, a picture book creator not only deliberately balances the text and illustrations but "must not ever be doing the same thing, must not ever be illustrating exactly what you've written. You must leave a space in the text so the picture can do the work. Then you must come back to the word, and now the word does it best and the picture beats time. It's a funny kind of juggling act. It takes a lot of technique, a lot of experience, to really keep the rhythm going between word and picture" ("Notes" 185-86).

There's a story, for instance, about Katharine Hepburn and friends watching Charlie Chaplin's *A Countess from Hong Kong*, his big flop, and finding it awful. Then someone suggested turning the sound off, and they suddenly found it effective. Chaplin had written successful visual narrative, as he had done so many times before, and then added superfluous words, creating an unsuccessful combination and an ultimately unsuccessful narrative. He had not performed what Sendak terms the balancing act.

Linda Ellerbee, discussing television news, suggests that if the news report makes equal sense without looking at the visuals, the program's doing it wrong, and that pictures that are merely redundant are superfluous. Dramatically speaking, there are a multitude of differences between television and picture books, particularly television news. But as Nodelman notes, television—like the picture book—is "a medium dependent upon the interrelation of words and pictures." In his attack on wordless books, Patrick Groff suggests that, given the predominance of television in their lives, children are "prewired" to see plots in pictures, but not in writing. "Given the predominance of television, I suspect that children are actually 'prewired' to see plots in pictures accompanied by words" (Nodelman 186). And the principle of pointless redundancy applies as well to both media, pictures may reinforce the text, but if they do only that, they are not using the medium to its fullest.

Text and pictures, in fact, can achieve remarkable effects in contradicting one another, expanding one another, or even limiting one another. Joseph Schwarcz speaks of Tomi Ungerer's pictures as "*spiting* the text" (16), and Perry Nodelman mentions that they are both narratives of dramatic irony (221), each speaking about matters on which the other is silent. He also notes the effect of illustrations not only in expanding the text but in opposing expansion, in buffering imagination and allowing it to explore dangerous areas in safety:

> When I have read the text of Sendak's *Where the Wild Things Are* to adults who have not previously heard of it, without showing them the pictures, many feel it to be a terrifying story, too frightening for young children. Without Sendak's particular Wild Things to look at, they conjure up wild things out of their own nightmares, and those they find scary indeed. When I then tell them the story accompanied by the pictures, they always change their minds. (197)

Nor are the authorities of text and illustration identical. (We believe what we see, not what characters say—I just watched a show where we saw what the character did and then heard him deny it, which "means" that he's lying. How does that work? When did I learn this?) If, for instance, you see a television character saying one thing and the pictures demonstrating another, the picture is generally "the truth." This can also be true in picture books, as in Stoeke's Minerva Louise series or Hutchins's *Rosie's Walk*—the pictures tell what really happened, and the text is just the concept the joke needs to contrast against. In Swiftian terms, the text is that which is not.

Yet there is room also for the illustrations to be their own kind of non-literal truth, the truth, often, of the child protagonist. Whether you're talking about John Burningham's *Come Away from the Water, Shirley*, or Maggie Smith's *There's a Witch Under the Stairs*, the fact that the child's visions are pictured lends them credence. If *Where the Wild Things Are* pictured Max staring at the walls of his room or looking at a book of mythical beasts, it would be a book about the quaint imaginings of a thwarted child. In a genre, the picture book, where depiction of the legendary is commonplace and integral to the logic of many books, illustrations walk that narrow border between literal reality and imaginative reality, in a sense offering an authenticity that may not match objective experience.

It is partly out of the need for this balance that the best texts don't necessarily make the best picture book texts, and the best art doesn't necessarily make the best picture book illustration, just as the best poetry doesn't often make the best songs, and the Mona Lisa would have a hard time being an illustration of anything other than the Mona Lisa. When Christine Jenkins was describing the Graduate School of Library and Information Science's online classes, I was particularly intrigued by her ability to present picture books on the on-line environment with the text scrubbed out. And then I thought, with all the lovely neo-PhotoShop software available, that she could probably even fill in the text spaces or crop the pictures to present them as art that hadn't anything to do with words, and then I thought—maybe that's not quite fair? I'm reminded of Trina Schart Hyman, who responded to a gallery owner who lamented the empty blocks in the middle of her pictures, by stiffly pointing out that that those empty blocks were the reason for the art. It's surprising, for instance, even in our small manipulation of images at the *Bulletin* (either selecting for the Web page or choosing art to include on our cover) how often impressive illustrations lose their thrill as mere art. I'm not suggesting that these separate elements must be deliberately bad in some way, but rather that works of art, whether literary or painterly, that are successful independently rarely have the skills, as it were, to be good partners.

Those partnerships can take a variety of forms. When Stephen Sondheim first started learning about the writing of musicals under the tutelage of Oscar Hammerstein, the master set his pupil certain tasks for his education. "For the first one," says Sondheim, "he told me to take a play I admired and turn it into a musical ... Next, he told me to take a play I didn't think was very good and could be improved and make a musical out of it ... For the third effort, Oscar told me to take something nondramatic, like a novel or a short story ... For the fourth and last in his series, he told me to write an original ..." (Zadan 5). There are equivalents of those categories for picture books, too, and it's interesting to examine them when considering the relationship between the narratives. There are classic texts, such as Grimm and Perrault, that have been turned into picture books; there are not-so-classic texts that have been improved by their illustrations. Books such as James Michener's *South Pacific* are adaptations from another medium, and, of course, there is no lack of original books. Like musicals, picture books have components that are displayed independently and that sometimes are more successful separately than in their original setting. Yet together, the two aspects of those art forms are supposed to make something more than just the addition of the two, something greater than the sum of the parts and where the parts are no longer truly extricable from the whole. And surprisingly enough, they often do.

Like musicals, picture books almost always start with the text. This chronology is sufficiently established in the genre that books where the pictures have come first are rare indeed (thought one cannot entirely be sure of the procedures of author-illustrators, whose prerogative it is to switch back and forth between the two). Often these art-first arrangements use pictures not to illustrate but to inspire, to take off from them as a starting point, such as Barbara Porte's riffs on Bill Traylor's art or Joan Aiken's stories from Jan Pienkowski's images. Sometimes, as in Walter Dean Myers' words for Jacob Lawrence's narrative paintings of the life of Toussaint L'Overture, the words undercut the carefully architected silent drama of the art when they are added to pictures made to be self-contained. Some of the most successful, such as Gwen Everett's *Li'l Sis and Uncle Willie* or Toyomi Igus's *Going Back Home* use the art not as expansion and illumination but as portraiture of people and situations within the story. Then there is the additional complication that, with some of these works, the art was originally designed to be substantially larger and hung on a wall; the collectiveness, intense focus, and smaller size of book art makes for an entirely different display situation, so even without the words, the art has become a different thing. These books demonstrate that even the chronology of words and pictures changes a narrative.

Whether or not they employ the traditional hierarchy of words and pictures, many picture books manage an extraordinary fusion of narratives into a read-aloud drama that is, as critic Peter Hunt notes, the only literary genre that children's literature contributes rather than borrows (175). Nodelman states:

> Hearing someone else read a book, we are able to look at each picture during the whole time that the words printed with it are spoken.... Furthermore, hearing the words read aloud causes us to focus on them as a whole sentence—to want to know what happens next rather than to be content to pause and look at a picture when, for instance, a sentence has not been completed on a page. Children, then, encounter picture books when that literature is closest to its traditional ideal, but in a way far removed from most adults' reading experience. (236)

This is a unique effect. And to illustrate why it is worth taking pains to achieve, I go to one final borrowing mission, this time to Tom Stoppard's play *The Real Thing*. In the play, the character Henry, who is a writer, discusses the power of writing by using the metaphor of a cricket bat:

> This thing here, which looks like a wooden club, is actually several pieces of particular wood cunningly put together in a certain way so that the whole thing is sprung, like a dance floor. It's for hitting cricket balls with. If you get it right, the cricket ball will travel two hundred yards in four seconds, and all you've done is give it a knock like knocking the top off a bottle of stout, and it makes a noise like a trout taking fly.... What we're trying to do is to write cricket bats, so that when we throw up an idea and give it a little knock, it might ... *travel*. (53)

While literary physics may be a highly inexact science, we all know that it exists, and that properly formed picture books comprise several pieces of cunningly combined narrative to send those with which they connect a great distance. This is craftsmanship, and that is its goal. When all those pieces are put in place and they hit children at the right speed ... they travel.

Works Cited

Anno, Mitsumasa. *Anno's Alphabet: An Adventure in Imagination*. New York: Harper-Collins, 1975.
——. *Anno's Journey*. New York: Philomel, 1978.
Bader, Barbara. *American Picturebooks: Noah's Ark to the Beast Within*. New York: MacMillan, 1976.
Briggs, Raymond. *Father Christmas*. London: Puffin, 1973.
——. *The Snowman*. London: H. Hamilton, 1978.
Burningham, John. *Come Away from the Water, Shirley*. New York: Crowell, 1977.
Butler, Dorothy. *Cushla and her Books*. Boston: Horn Book, 1980.
A Countess from Hong Kong. Videocassette. Dir. Charlie Chaplin. MCA Universal Home Video, 1967. 108 min.
Dusinberre, Juliet. "Review of Perry Nodelman's *Words about Pictures*." *Word and Image* 6.4 (1990): 396-97.
Elhert, Lois. *Circus*. New York: HarperCollins, 1992.
Ellerbee, Linda. *"And So It Goes": Adventures in Television*. New York: Putnam's, 1986.
Ellis, Sarah. "Buster on the Screen." *The Horn Book Magazine* 73 (1997): 289-93.
Everett, Gwen. *Li'l Sis and Uncle Willie: A Story Based on the Life and Paintings of William H Johnson*. Washington: National Museum of American Arts, 1991.
Fairy Tale: A True Story. Dir. Charles Sturbridge. Paramount, 1997.
Feelings, Tom. *The Middle Passage: White Ships/Black Cargo*. New York: Dial, 1995.
Friedrich, Priscilla. *The Easter Bunny that Overslept*. New York: Lothrop, Lee and Shepard, 1957.
Goldsmith, Evelyn. *Research into Illustration: An Approach and a Review*. Cambridge: Cambridge UP, 1984.
Groff, Patrick. "Children's Literature vs. Wordless 'Books.'" *Top of the News* (April 1974): 294-303.
Hunt, Peter. *Criticism, Theory, & Children's Literature*. Oxford: Blackwell, 1991.
Hutchins, Pat. *Rosie's Walk*. New York: Scholastic, 1968.
Hyman, Trina Schart. "Zen and the Art of Children's Book Illustration." *The Zena Sutherland Lectures, 1983-1992*. Ed. Betsy Hearne. New York: Clarion, 1993. 186-205.
Igus, Toyomi. *Going Back Home: An Artist Returns to the South*. San Francisco: Children's Book Press, 1996.
Isadora, Rachel. *Ben's Trumpet*. New York: Greenwillow, 1979.
Jenkins, Christine. Personal conversation. Undated.
Johnson, Stephen. *Alphabet City*. New York: Viking, 1995.
Ling, Mary, Mary Atkinson, Frank Greenaway, and Dave King. *The Snake Book*. New

York: DK, 1997.

Marcus, Leonard S. "The Artist's Other Eye: The Picture Books of Mitsumasa Anno."
The Lion and the Unicorn 7-8 (1983-84): 34-46.

Martin, Jacqueline Briggs. *Grandmother Bryant's Pocket.* Boston: Houghton, 1996.

Michener, James. *South Pacific.* San Diego: Harcourt, 1992.

Nodelman, Perry. *Words about Pictures: The Narrative Art of Children's Picture Books.*
Athens, GA: U of Georgia P, 1988.

Pelletier, David. *The Graphic Alphabet.* New York: Orchard, 1996.

Rathmann, Peggy. *Good Night, Gorilla.* New York: Scholastic, 1994.

Reuter, Bjarne. *The End of the Rainbow.* Trans. Althea Bell. New York: Dutton, 1999.

Schwarcz, Joseph H. *Ways of the Illustrator: Visual Communication in Children's
Literature.* Chicago: ALA, 1982.

Sendak, Maurice. *Caldecott & Co: Notes on Books and Pictures.* New York: Noonday/Far-
rar, Straus, Giroux, 1988.

——. *Where the Wild Things Are.* New York: Harper & Row, 1963.

Smith, Maggie. *There's a Witch Under the Stairs.* New York: Lothrop, Lee & Shepard,
1991.

Stoppard, Tom. *The Real Thing.* London: Faber and Faber, 1982.

Van Allsburg, Chris. *Jumanji.* Boston: Houghton, 1981.

——. *The Sweetest Fig.* Boston: Houghton, 1993.

Willard, Nancy. *A Visit to William Blake's Inn: Poems for Innocent and Experienced Travelers.* New York: Harcourt, 1981.

Young, Ed. *Voices of the Heart.* New York: Scholastic, 1997.

Zadan, Craig. *Sondheim & Co.* Rev. ed. New York: Da Capo, 1994.

Why "Tell Me"? (1993)

Aidan Chambers

On the whole it is easier to put children off talking than it is to get them started. And one of the most offputting words is the interrogative "why?"

Early in our "Tell me" work we learned to ban "why?" from our teacherly
vocabulary. "I liked this book a lot," a child would say, the teacher would reply,
"Did you? Why?" and the answer would very often be a sigh or a look of pain
or shrugged shoulders or a puzzled frown: certainly a visible loss of enthusiasm.

What's the trouble with "why"?

Most obviously, it too often sounds aggressive, threatening, oppositional,
examinational.

But there are equally valid objections. First, it is a catch-all question, too big to answer all at once. No one can explain in a couple of sentences why s/he's liked or disliked a book. That's the reason children use shorthand catch-all words in reply: it was exciting, it was fun; it was boring, it was dull.

Second, the question "why?" gives you no help. To talk well about a book you have to start somewhere, you have to highlight a detail you can explain easily. In trying to help people talk well, the teacher's opening questions need to give them a starting point. As we've seen, the most obvious place to begin is by asking readers to talk about details they particularly liked or disliked.

Tell me ...

How to avoid asking "why"? The solution, when at last we hit upon it, was not only simple but proved a turning point, for it gave us a new style. We arrived at it by searching for what we thought of as "a conventional glottal stop." We meant an opening word or phrase that would prevent us asking "why?" straight out, would give us time for thought, and would provide a broadly useful start to more subtle questions.

The phrase we found was "Tell me ...".

It seems obvious now, since it has become the name for our approach, but it wasn't at the time. The qualities we liked about "Tell me ..." are that it suggests a desire for collaboration, indicating that the teacher really does want to know what the reader thinks, and that it anticipates conversational dialogue rather than an interrogation.

From "Scenes from 'Tell Me' in Action" (1993)
Aidan Chambers

Note: this scene is an account of Eileen Langley's work with a reception class aged five years to five years and eight months; one third of the class has been there for a month and the others for four.

One Monday morning I showed my class *Where the Wild Things Are* by Maurice Sendak. They were sitting happily on the carpet expecting a nursery rhyme session. When I showed the book several children got up on their knees in their eagerness to have a closer look. Several unprompted comments followed: "A monster book," "Look how big the monster is," "He's too big to go in that boat." One little boy grasped my ankle and said, "That monster has feet just like our feet." Someone else wondered why there was a ladder on the boat. I found it interesting that apart from Ryan, who kept a firm hold on my ankle, their attention was moving to the boat. "Is it a story about a boat?"

I opened the book so that they could see the complete [wrap-around] cover and Emma decided that it was night in the book and the monster was asleep. As I showed them the inside title page, Philip pointed out that there was a mummy and a daddy monster. These children, having just started school, were bringing their own experiences to the book [*world-to-text*], and the picture that they see as mummy and daddy monster is a very reassuring one, irrespective of the fact that it is a monster family. Another child informed me that the mummy monster was the one without the horns. The fact that the children were not frightened confirms Sendak's insight into children's minds.

The children had become quite excited but silence fell once I started reading, and they studied the pictures with avid interest. When I had finished the story several children asked to see the pictures again and I showed them, wishing that we had several copies of the book. The rumpus pages were top favourites. Lisa said that the monsters were having a disco. James said that his big brother had been to a disco and that these pictures looked like very noisy pictures.

I asked what they liked best. "The rumpus" was constantly repeated. Kate said that she liked these words best: "... they roared their terrible roars and gnashed their terrible teeth and rolled their terrible eyes and showed their terrible claws." These words have featured a lot in their language since then. When normally a very placid group were making too much noise in the Wendy house recently, I was assured that they were only having a rumpus! Neil, who is a very quiet child with a slight speech problem, volunteered that he liked Max in his private boat best.

Michelle said that she was puzzled by the forest growing in Max's bedroom. We had to sidetrack here as some children obviously did not understand what Michelle meant by being puzzled. After a short discussion they appeared to have grasped the meaning. Several children decided that they were puzzled when Max went sailing in such a little boat across the ocean. Others couldn't understand why he didn't remain and continue to be king of the wild things. Alan was puzzled by the wild things because of their strange hair. James interrupted: "They might not be true." I asked if he thought they were true. "No," he replied very firmly.

Teacher: Do you think Max is true?
James: Yes, but the wild things are not.
Teacher: How can that be?
James: Max just made up the wild things.

Lisa interrupted to say that the wild things must be real as they had skin on their feet.

I decided to move on and leave these ideas to float for a while. We discussed patterns in the story. Daniel, who has a rather forceful personality and who had remarked more than once that he would like to be Max, said "Max's mother put Max to bed without any supper and Max put the wild things to bed without their supper." Philip, who had been very quiet, astounded most of the children by saying, "I don't think Max really went to where the wild things are."

Teacher: Where do you think he went?
Philip: I think Max had a dream.
James (immediately): That's true, Philip. That's what I think.

A few of the children were still unsure but Philip had certainly enabled the majority to think as he did. A discussion on dreams followed, which I allowed to continue to let the children deliberate on the idea and on their own dreams. Friendly monsters appeared to feature in most dreams!

The children have requested this story on numerous occasions. I have read other Sendak stories to them but this remains their favourite. Parents have come in to check the title in order to buy the book as their child has talked about it so much at home. Other parents have come to tell me that when in the local library their child has picked this book and can read it ...

When I read a story with my class I always tell them who wrote and illustrated the book. The word illustrator fascinates these young children and they love using it. Emma asked if Maurice Sendak had written and illustrated other books. I showed her *In the Night Kitchen* and *Outside Over There*. Obviously she spread the news as after playtime I was asked to read *In the Night Kitchen*.

They listened and watched very attentively. Their faces reflected the immense pleasure they were getting from the story. They were very eager to tell me what they liked best. Alan was adamant that Mickey in the helicopter was what he liked best. Another child said, "I also like the little helicopter which is hanging over his bed at the beginning of the story." Others chorused that they liked when Mickey dived to the bottom of the milk. James interrupted to say he didn't like Mickey when he is out of his clothes. James is very reluctant to change his clothes for games so I was not surprised when he said this. Lisa commented that she liked lots of the words: "Thump, dump, blump, hump, bump. I like the sounds of these words," she said and kept repeating them.

Andrew commented that Mickey was in bed at the beginning of the story and at the end of the story.

Teacher: Where do you think the story happened?

Andrew: In Mickey's bedroom.

Teacher: Does the story remind you of any other story?

Lisa: *Where the Wild Things Are.*

Teacher: Why? [!]

Lisa: Max is in his bedroom before his journey and at the end of the story he is in bed.

Teacher: Do you think all of this really happened to Mickey?

Lisa: No.

Teacher: How do you know?

Lisa: Because when I watched television the ducks talked and ducks can't really talk.

Teacher: So what do you think Mickey was doing?

Lisa: He was dreaming in bed.

Chorus: Yes, because he was in bed at the beginning of the story and at the end of the story ...

The children were now capable, I felt, of having a longer story. I decided to read *The Elephant and the Bad Baby* by Elfrida Vipont, illustrated by Raymond Briggs ...

From "The Vocabulary of Comics" and "Blood in the Gutters" in *Understanding Comics* (1993)

Scott McCloud

27

LATER IN LIFE, I FOUND OTHERS WHO HAD SIMILAR DAYDREAMS AS CHILDREN. NONE OF US EVER REALLY BELIEVED THESE THEORIES, BUT WE HAD ALL BEEN FASCINATED BY THE FACT THAT THEY COULD NOT BE DISPROVED!

EVEN TODAY, AS I WRITE AND DRAW THIS PANEL, I HAVE NO GUARANTEE THAT ANYTHING EXISTS OUTSIDE OF WHAT MY FIVE SENSES REPORT TO ME.*

I'VE NEVER BEEN TO MOROCCO, BUT I TAKE IT ON FAITH THAT THERE IS A MOROCCO!

I'VE NEVER SEEN THE EARTH FROM SPACE FIRSTHAND, YET I TRUST THAT THE EARTH IS ROUND.

I'VE NEVER BEEN IN THE HOUSE ACROSS THE STREET, YET I ASSUME IT HAS AN INTERIOR, THAT IT ISN'T JUST SOME BIG MOVIE SET!

IN THIS PANEL YOU CAN'T EVEN SEE MY LEGS, YET YOU ASSUME THAT THEY'RE THERE.

EVEN THOUGH THEY'RE NOT!

*NOT TO SAY OUR SENSES ARE ANY KIND OF GUARANTEE!

62

THIS PHENOMENON OF OBSERVING THE PARTS BUT PERCEIVING THE WHOLE HAS A NAME.
IT'S CALLED CLOSURE.
IN OUR DAILY LIVES, WE OFTEN COMMIT CLOSURE, MENTALLY COMPLETING THAT WHICH IS INCOMPLETE BASED ON PAST EXPERIENCE.
SALE
SALE
SOME FORMS OF CLOSURE ARE DELIBERATE INVENTIONS OF STORYTELLERS TO PRODUCE SUSPENSE OR TO CHALLENGE AUDIENCES.
OTHERS HAPPEN AUTOMATICALLY, WITHOUT MUCH EFFORT... PART OF BUSINESS AS USUAL.
IN RECOGNIZING AND RELATING TO OTHER PEOPLE, WE ALL DEPEND HEAVILY ON OUR LEARNED ABILITY OF CLOSURE.
IN AN INCOMPLETE WORLD, WE MUST DEPEND ON CLOSURE FOR OUR VERY SURVIVAL.
63

Translating Pictures (1999)
Emer O'Sullivan

The "language" of pictures is generally regarded as international, capable of transcending linguistic and cultural boundaries. How, then, can we speak of translating pictures in picture books when, in most cases, these remain materially unaltered? It seems to me that in the translation of picture books, neither element—words or pictures—can be isolated, nor are they isolated when the translator translates. I think that, in a genre combining words and pictures, an ideal translation reflects awareness not only of the significance of the original text but also of the interaction between the visual and the verbal, what the pictures do in relation to the words; it does not verbalize the interaction but leaves gaps that make the interplay possible and exciting. The reader of the ideal translation is left to do the same work as the reader of the original. This paper looks at how translation changed this interaction in two picture books: Michel Gay's *Papa Vroum* (French into English) and John Burningham's *Granpa* (English into German).

First, a general point. The communication in children's books and around children's literature is asymmetrical; indeed asymmetry is one of the defining characteristics of this branch of literature. As is frequently observed, adults write, publish, and sell books for children, adult critics write about them, librarians recommend them, and teachers bring children's books into school. Adults act on behalf of children at every stage in this literary communication. In itself this is not a bad thing but it is not always easy to distinguish between adults enabling children and controlling them.

The asymmetrical communication is mirrored when children's literature is translated: the various steps from the selection of texts to the details of how individual lexical items are to be translated are subject to the assumptions of publishers and translators as to what children can understand, what they enjoy, what is suitable and acceptable. These norms and suppositions function on educational, sociocultural, ideological, and aesthetic levels. An example of a text being altered in translation to conform to views on suitability can be found in the German translation of Astrid Lindgren's *Pippi Långstrump*. In the original Swedish Pippi and her friends play in the attic with pistols (172ff); in the German edition Pippi declares that children shouldn't play with guns and that she will put them back in the chest (205).

Picture books present a special challenge to the translator, as the presence and interaction of two media make the process more complex. The more intricate the interplay between words and pictures the more complex the task of translating. Difficulties arise when pictures and words tell different stories or when the text consistently does not refer to what can be seen in the pictures.

A translator's reading of the original text is bound to be influenced by the pictures, though it is not always easy for her to disentangle the elements that contribute to the complexity.[1] The result can be problematic: the pictures stimulate the creative linguistic powers of the translator, who may in turn make elements explicit in the narrative where originally these were only seen in the pictures. In other words: gaps in the source text may be filled by translators in the target text.

Papa Vroum

The American edition of Michel Gay's *Papa Vroum* (*Night Ride*) reveals how the character of a picture book can be substantially altered in translation. In this night-time adventure Gabriel and his father, stuck in traffic, decide to spend the night in their van. While the father is asleep in the back, the van is towed away and Gabriel, who is joined by various animals as the night proceeds, is left "driving" the car. The present-tense narrative consists of direct speech for the most part and, though in the third person, is focused on Gabriel's point of view for the most part and thus relates directly what Gabriel is seeing, thinking and feeling. He thinks he is driving the van, and the reader is not told anything to the contrary. The pictures reveal that Gabriel is not the agent of the action, however, and the point of the story is that this is not made explicit so the reader shares Gabriel's trepidation and surprise.

A lorry, which Gabriel hasn't noticed, reverses close to the van and hits the front bumper. Gabriel thinks the noise is someone knocking at the door. In Figure [3.1] Gabriel tells the kittens not to wake his sleeping father, which implies that he believes they have made the noise. The kittens smell sausage in the van and ask to come inside. In the picture we see a monkey, again unnoticed by Gabriel, jumping onto the van. The text is narrated in the present tense with liberal use of direct speech, making action and words immediate for the reader/viewer.

The American text accompanying the same pictures describes what can be seen and interprets it, thus causing a shift in the relationship between picture and text. Whereas in the original the narrative is frequently constructed as a dialogue, in the translation Gabriel is made into the main actor, the narrative is now about him. What he perceives and how he reacts are now described rather than indicated in his own words. Immediacy is reduced by the elimination of direct speech and the substitution of past tense for present tense. Explaining that the kittens couldn't have made the noise because they are too small and that Gabriel didn't notice the monkey violates a central device of Gay's picture book: the variance between what is shown and what is said.

Il ouvre la portière et regarde.
«Moins de bruit, les petits chats,
Papa dort!»

«C'est ta voiture? On peut monter?»
demandent les petits chats. «Miam!
la bonne odeur de saucisson!»

Figure 3.1: From *Papa Vroum* by Michel Gay © L'école des loisirs, 1986. *American translation, left-hand page:* He opened the door and looked out. There were three kittens all by themselves in the parking lot. They were too little to have made that sound.
Right-hand page: Gabriel decided to let the kittens into the van.
He did not see the monkey that quickly, silently, climbed down to see what was going on.

When the van begins to move—the monkey has just been shown playing with the steering wheel—the French text exclaims *"Oh là là! Ça démarre!"* but the American text spells it out: "Suddenly the van jerked forward. They were moving! It wasn't the monkey's fault. The trailer was pulling out of the parking lot—and dragging the van behind," thus ruining the surprise of the later picture showing the van being towed by the lorry.

The narrative of the American translation also differs from the original in the stated reassurance that Gabriel is in control and that he is not afraid. Constant verbal reminders of the father's presence in the van—in the pictures he is visible only as a sleeping shape, until the final pages—further reassure the reader that there is no cause for alarm.

In the original the pictures tell a different story from the words, the text doesn't divulge more than Gabriel knows, but readers can experience the thrill of noticing more in the pictures than the words have told and draw their own conclusions. They can savour Gabriel's fear, excitement and surprise from a perspective of knowledge. The American translation eliminates the tension and, instead of playful irony, we have a nanny text which removes challenge and unexpectedness. Even the cover blurb tells all: "And when the van jerks forward—hooked by accident to the huge trailer parked in front of them—Gabriel bravely stays at the wheel as they roll faster and faster through the night." Much is lost in translation by everything being explained.

Granpa

John Burningham's *Granpa* is a collection of episodes about a girl and her grandfather, presented as scenes in a greenhouse, on a beach, sitting at home. In most of the doublespreads a full-colour picture in a distinctly naïve and childlike style, showing a situation experienced by the pair, faces a faint sepia picture depicting the old man's memories, the child's imaginings, or some form of association that illuminates or elaborates what is shown in its partner.

The links between the pictures are generally as open as those between pictures and fragmentary text,[2] which consists of snippets of dialogue between the old man and the girl. Different typefaces indicate the two speakers; they are shown in word and picture to have two distinct but equal subject positions. The same attention is given to their differing modes of perception, levels of experience, types of fantasies, their means of thinking and communicating. There is no narrator, no explicit commentary and, other than roughly following the pattern of the seasons, no apparent sequence of events until the final pictures portraying the grandfather's illness and death. The text is distinctly undercoded, and there are substantial gaps between the text and the pictures. What does a translator make of it all?

Two things are striking about the title page of the German translation. The first is that equal billing is given to John Burningham and Irina Korschunow. The translator—a figure traditionally ignored in children's literature—is elevated to the status of author. Irina Korschunow is a children's book author in her own right (it is quite common for German authors to translate children's literature) and has written extensively for all age groups from beginner readers to young adults. The double billing can, therefore, be seen as effective marketing of a name familiar to German readers and especially to those who buy the books. It also indicates that the German product is no longer a visual and verbal composition by Burningham but an amalgam of pictures by Burningham and text by Korschunow.

The second striking element is the title, "My grandfather and me." The girl is now clearly the focus of the story, which has become one about her relationship to her grandfather. The dialogue of the original is replaced by a text narrated in the past: the soundtrack is no longer immediate; what is being told happened a while ago. Where the first picture in the original shows the girl running into the arms of her grandfather, accompanied by the direct speech of the man, "And how's my little girl?", the German text, translated, runs: "Me and my grandpa, that was nice. 'Do you still love your old grandpa, my little girl?' 'You aren't old at all, grandpa.'" The past tense ("that was nice") tells us that their relationship is a thing of the past. The old man's death in the final pages is pre-empted by the tense used in the translation. The mode is sentimental: the grandfather wants to be assured of his granddaughter's love while she is at pains to tell him that he isn't old. As being old is not regarded by children as negative but simply a fact, we find here placed in the mouth of the young girl an adult sentiment which seeks to evade the inevitable end associated with old age. The pattern of communication—the simultaneity of the two discourses—has changed. Granpa has become the object of the girl's concern and no longer features as an autonomous subject in the text. Korschunow also verbalizes obvious details in the pictures. The first sentence accompanying the fishing scene reads "We also went fishing." By supplying this superfluous information, Korschunow degrades the picture to an illustration of her text.

The translator's reading of the text has begun with its ending, the grandfather's death. A popular topic in German children's literature in the 1980s, death is elevated to being the central theme around which the translator builds a continuous narrative. This has consequences for the characterization of the girl. Gone is the unburdened child perspective. Korschunow's girl is defined solely by what she thinks about and feels for her grandfather, she is fixated on him in an overprotective, anxious way.

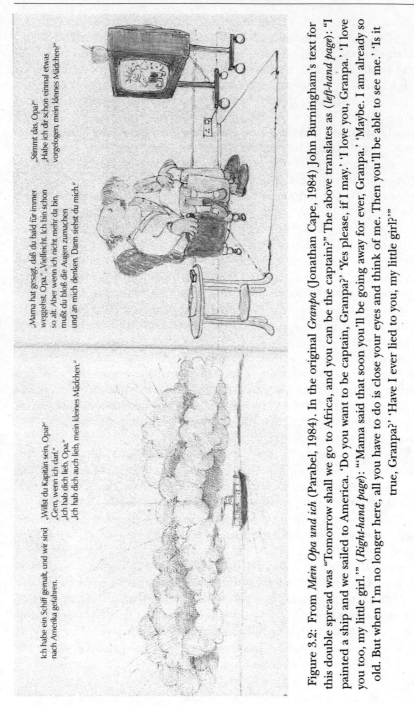

Figure 3.2: From *Mein Opa und ich* (Parabel, 1984). In the original *Granpa* (Jonathan Cape, 1984) John Burningham's text for this double spread was "Tomorrow shall we go to Africa, and you can be the captain?" The above translates as (*left-hand page*): "I painted a ship and we sailed to America. 'Do you want to be captain, Granpa?' 'Yes please, if I may.' 'I love you, Granpa.' 'I love you too, my little girl.'" (*Right-hand page*): "'Mama said that soon you'll be going away for ever, Granpa.' 'Maybe. I am already so old. But when I'm no longer here, all you have to do is close your eyes and think of me. Then you'll be able to see me.' 'Is it true, Granpa?' 'Have I ever lied to you, my little girl?'"

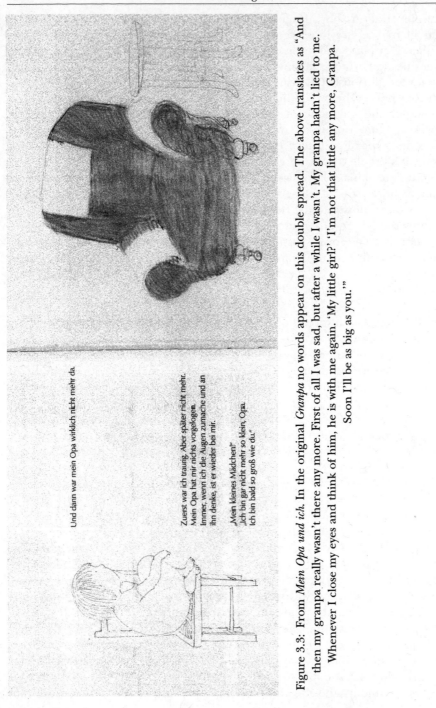

Und dann war mein Opa wirklich nicht mehr da.

Zuerst war ich traurig. Aber später nicht mehr. Mein Opa hat mir nichts vorgelogen. Immer, wenn ich die Augen zumache und an ihn denke, ist er wieder bei mir.

„Mein kleines Mädchen!"
Ich bin gar nicht mehr so klein, Opa. Ich bin bald so groß wie du."

Figure 3.3: From *Mein Opa und ich*. In the original *Granpa* no words appear on this double spread. The above translates as "And then my granpa really wasn't there any more. First of all I was sad, but after a while I wasn't. My granpa hadn't lied to me. Whenever I close my eyes and think of him, he is with me again. 'My little girl?' 'I'm not that little any more, Granpa. Soon I'll be as big as you.'"

The illustration above [Figure 3.2] shows the grandfather, who has been taken ill in the previous scene, and the girl indoors watching television together. Her plans and hopes for their continuing adventures are expressed in her question, which remains unanswered by the grandfather. A ship sailing away under gloriously billowing clouds can be seen in the sepia picture. We can't see whether the two of them are on board, as the girl probably imagines, or whether the old man, in what is more likely to be his association, is embarking alone on his last trip. The openness of picture and text allows a multitude of possible interpretations. The text of the German translation crowds this simple scene and closes most of the gaps.

The indeterminate ship has become one which the girl in the translation claims to have painted herself. In addition to reducing Burningham's pictures to mere illustrations, Korschunow makes one of them be explicitly drawn by the girl and then used as an illustration. The scene is taken by the translator as a cue for discussion about the impending death of the grandfather and about how the granddaughter will cope. Exclamations of mutual affection verbalize in an almost unbearably sentimental manner the closeness so eloquently expressed by the body language of the two people in the pictures.

In the final doublespread of the original the symbolic force of the empty chair is strengthened by the visual expression of silence on the textless page. The grandfather's chair is empty, the girl is left alone staring at it. There can be no words because words, in this book, have only ever been part of a dialogue, part of the pattern that characterized the communication. Once the grandfather is gone, dialogue is no longer possible. The almost deafening, and certainly moving, silence on this page is a fitting expression of loss. It also leaves room for the reader to grasp and respond to the death of the grandfather. There is room for sorrow. Not so in the German translation.

The translator obviously believes that the antidote to the final silence of death is garrulousness. On this page she tries to undo the grandfather's death or, at the very least, not to leave the reader alone to digest what has happened. The translator fills the vacuum with words and succeeds in bringing him back to life by having him talk in the familiar manner with the girl. The tone is one of hope for the future, the girl has coped quickly with bereavement. The picture is no longer an autonomous expression of loss but an incidental illustration to go with what the narrator of the German translation wants to tell us about death and how to deal with it.

Rather than translating the words of *Granpa*, Korschunow uses Burningham's pictures to tell a different story—a story about old age, death and mourning—in a different way. She clearly thought the original text far too open and thus not suitable for young readers who couldn't or shouldn't be expected to understand the complex narrative interaction between the pictures and fragmentary text. Her translation fills all possible gaps with elements of continuity, with a narrative focus and with numerous explanations, thus delivering an infinitely less interesting and less skilfully told story than Burningham's.

Korschunow's translation has had unusual repercussions. It is one of the rare instances where a licence has been withdrawn by the originating publisher. A second, "authorized," translation under the simple title *Großpapa*, true to the spirit of Burningham's text, was undertaken by Rolf Inhauser, who has served not only Burningham but many other celebrated picture-book artists well with his translations into German. It was published by Sauerländer Verlag in 1988, four years after the first translation.

The American edition of *Papa Vroum* and the first German edition of *Granpa* reveal how, even while remaining materially unchanged, pictures are indeed translated when their contribution to the dialogic whole of the original is usurped by translators and fed into the text. The implied readers of these translations are not identical to the readers of the originals, that much is made clear by the analysis. The translators obviously felt that they could not or did not want to reproduce a text in their language which trusts children to be able to read between the lines and the pictures, to be able to resolve the sophisticated connections between the verbal and visual elements of the books. Their solution was to resolve these connections themselves in the renarration of the stories.

Criticism of literature in translation—both for children and for adults—tends to speak of "changes," of "omissions" or "additions" in translations without identifying an agent in the text responsible for the changes. A translator is never invisible—despite the ideology of translation which insists that she is. Each translation has its own implied reader, and its own narrator, one who was not present in the original: the narrator of the translation. Two examples of clearly identifiable narrators of translation have been discussed here. The variations are infinite, but that is a different story, one that has been told in more detail elsewhere by the narrator of this paper.

Acknowledgements

I am grateful to Reinbert Tabbert for having drawn my attention to the American translation of *Papa Vroum* by some remarks made in his article "Bilderbücher swischen swei Kulturen." This piece was originally presented as a conference paper at the European Children's Literature Symposium in Stadtschlaining, Austria, in May 1998. It was subsequently published as "Translating Pictures: The Interaction of Pictures and Words in the Translation of Picture Books" in *European Children's Literature II*.

Notes

1 The Finnish translation scholar Riitta Oittenen was one of the first to point out the function of illustrations in the translation of children's literature.
2 Peter Hunt writes of *Granpa* that "the relationships between the fragmentary text and between the full-colour pictures and the sepia pictures ... are as important as whether the book is read in a conventional sequence or not" (183).

Works Cited

Burningham, John. *Granpa.* London: Jonathan Cape, 1984.

———. *Großpapa.* Aus dem Englischen von Rolf Inhauser. Von John Burningham autorisierte Ausgabe. Aarau, Frankfurt/M, Salzburg: Sauerländer, 1988.

Burningham, John/Irina Korschunow. *Mein Opa und ich.* Zürich, Schwäbisch Hall: Parabel, 1984.

Gay, Michael. *Night Ride,* story adapted from the French by Margo Lundell. New York: Morrow, 1987.

———. *Papa Vroum.* Paris: L'école des loisirs, 1986.

Hunt, Peter. *Criticism, Theory and Children's Literature.* Oxford: Blackwell, 1991.

Lindgren, Astrid. *Pippi Långstrump.* Stockholm: Raben and Sjögren, 1945.

———. *Pippi Langstrumpf.* Trans. Cäcilie Heinig. Hamburg: Oetinger, 1965.

Oittenen, Riitta. "The Dialogic Relation between Text and Illustration: A Translatogical View." TEXTconText 5 (1990): 40-53.

O'Sullivan, Emer. "Translating Pictures: The Interaction of Pictures and Words in the Translation of Picture Books." *European Children's Literature II.* Ed. Penni Cotton. Kingston: Kingston UP, 1998. 109-20.

Tabbert, Reinbert. "Bilderbücher swischen swei Kultern." in *Kinderbuchanalysen II. Wirkung—Kultureller Kontext—Unterricht.* Ed. Reinbert Tabbert. Frankfurt: dipa 1991. 130-48.

IV

POETRY AND NURSERY RHYMES

What should we expect from poetry written for children? First and foremost, reject the patronizing view that poetry for children is a sub-genre of literature, like SF or crime fiction, and that it won't matter too much if standards are lowered in the interests of "accessibility." (3)
—Brian Morse, *Poetry Books for Children* (1992)

Children also need to hear how poems sound. How distressing it is to meet a child with an obvious enthusiasm for poetry who then proceeds to read a poem aloud as if the line endings didn't exist, as if the poem wasn't organized as a structure of sounds and meanings. Some poetry may not be meant for reading aloud—or rather it's meant to be read in the privacy of your own head—but much of it, whether performance verse or not, gains from being spoken: rhythms, rhymes, sound values, the whole movement of the poem is enhanced. So children will benefit greatly if we show them how a reading can be made. (2)
—Brian Morse, *Poetry Books for Children* (1992)

Recognizing the communal characteristics of orality, of a literature "meant to be spoken out loud," Sheree [Fitch] formulated the term "utterature": "all literature that is dependent on the human voice and a community of listeners to have its life." This concept feeds readily into the genre of children's poetry, one which, Sheree asserts, "is dependent on rhythm and the human voice ... a thing that's meant to be shared." "The early 'readers' are not readers at all," she says. "What they really are are listeners of the literature, which means it's utterature." "Uttering" strikes Fitch as an appropriate term for reaching out, for moving toward a community of listeners. "I love the origins of the word 'utter,'" she says, "which means to 'outer,' to take what's inside and to make it out loud." (29-30)
—Jeanette Lynes, "Profile: 'A Purple Sort of Girl':
Sheree Fitch's Tales of Emergence" (1998)

[I]f poetry were visibly part of the required curriculum, more teachers might make an effort to read, to understand, and even enjoy it, and help children enjoy it, too. Last April, I visited a friend's fifth-grade classroom as a guest poet during National Poetry Month. The children there were (I found out afterwards) the "at risk" group—those having difficulty with reading. And yet they responded to poetry with great interest. Because they seemed to take to poetry, I gently chided my friend for relegating poetry to "National Poetry Month." She informed me that she was the only teacher in the entire elementary school that ever did *any-thing* with poetry in the classroom. (81)

—Richard Flynn, "Consolation Prize" (2003)

Introduction

Mentioning the word *poetry* can often elicit a response of dread, if not out-right terror. Too often, reading and discussing poetry is an exercise in humil-iation, as students offer their responses to a poem and then are told that they've completely misunderstood it. Ironically, however, poetry is often the first form of literature many of us encounter and enjoy, and it tends to be the form we remember the longest. Sit any group of people down and ask them to remember nursery rhymes, silly parody songs ("Jingle bells, Batman smells, Robin laid an egg"), or skipping rope songs, and with a bit of warm up, a live-ly discussion generally ensues. We learned many of those rhymes and ditties outside the pages of a book, picking them up from friends or family. Thus, some poetic forms of today are closer to the older, oral traditions than most prose narratives. And, as Perry Nodelman's introduction to nursery rhymes, "The Nursery Rhymes of Mother Goose," shows, there are also plenty of tra-ditional tales *about* nursery rhymes that are as entertaining as the rhymes themselves.

Moving from nursery rhymes to more formal poetry introduces the com-plexity of defining poetry for children, a process as difficult as doing so for children's literature itself. In the Introduction to *The Garden to the Street: 300 Years of Poetry*, Morag Styles writes,

Can we identify such a thing as a child's poem? The answer is "not easily," except for the negation; that is to say, I can show you poems that are not for children because they are about things children do not understand or are written in language too complex for young readers to take in. Even a statement like that must be qualified since children with a good start in poetry can manage quite sophisticated texts from writers such as Shake-speare, Gerard Manley Hopkins, or Emily Dickinson, especially if the verse is musical, lyrical, or tells a good tale. (xv)

As the chapter "'From the Best Poets'?" from *The Garden to the Street* includ-ed here indicates, poetry for children suffers from the same disregard or ignorance that much of children's literature does; poetry anthologies fre-quently reject poetry written for children in favour of poetry created for adults and thought to be accessible to children. As a result, Styles argues, a great deal of fine poetry written for children does not receive the attention it deserves.

Listening to children on the topic of poetry, as with other areas of children's literature, can be enlightening. Kaye Webb's *I Like This Poem*, a collection published for the Year of the Child (1979), was compiled by asking children to send in their favourite poems. Although an adult made the final decisions for the poetry included, the mix of poems from collections aimed at children and those aimed at adults, coupled with the often insightful comments about those poems from the children, suggests that, as in the dress-up box and in other areas of their lives, children are happy to mix those things meant for them with those they borrow from the adults around them. Trying to draw hard and fast lines by looking to intended audience is ultimately less useful than looking at what *does* attract an audience and thinking about the implications therein.

Works Cited

Flynn, Richard. "Consolation Prize." *Signal* 100 (2003): 66-83.
Lynes, Jeanette. "Profile: 'A Purple Sort of Girl': Sheree Fitch's Tales of Emergence." *Canadian Children's Literature* 90 24.2 (1998): 28-37.
Morse, Brian. *Poetry Books for Children*. Stroud, Glos.: Thimble Press, 1992. 2-3.

The Nursery Rhymes of Mother Goose:
A World without Glasses (1987)
Perry Nodelman

Of all the great works of children's literature, the oddest is the body of poetry surrounding the name of Mother Goose. It is amorphous. It is various. Above all, it is absurd.

The canon of Mother Goose is so amorphous that trying to pin it down might be something like doing a bibliography of the complete works of Anonymous. In Iona and Peter Opie's *Oxford Dictionary of Nursery Rhymes*, there are 550 different rhymes (not including variants); in William and Ceil Baring-Gould's *The Annotated Mother Goose* there are 884. The reason for this uncertainty about how much Mother Goose wrote is obvious—there is not now and there never was a Mother Goose, at least not one who wrote poetry.

That has not prevented scholars from trying to invent one. Their candidates have ranged from Charlemagne's Mother Bertha (who went by the nickname "La Reine Pedauque," or Queen Goosefoot, and who has become confused with another Queen Bertha, blood relative and wife of Robert II of

France, who is said to have given birth to a goose-headed child) to one Eliza-beth Foster Goose (or maybe Vergoose or Vertigoose) of Boston, Massachu-setts, who may or may not have recited rhymes to her grandchildren in a man-ner that suggested the cackling of geese. Somehow, somewhere in history, the idea of literature for the young became connected with the name Goose; it seems to have already been an old idea when Perrault subtitled his collection of fairy tales "CONTES DE MA MERE LOYE"—stories of Mother Goose—in 1697. But where or how the connection was first made nobody knows.

What we do know is what goes under the name of Mother Goose—a body of verse that has become separated from its original contexts, and therefore, its original authors. In some instances, we either know or can guess some of those authors: we know that "Twinkle, Twinkle, Little Star" first appeared in Jane and Ann Taylor's *Rhymes for the Nursery* in 1806, and that Sarah Catharine Martin had something to do with *The Comic Adventures of Old Mother Hubbard and Her Dog* published in 1805; if she didn't make it up, at least her version of it was what first made it popular. And we know that no less a literary figure than the great Samuel Johnson was responsible, not just for compiling the dictionary and providing James Boswell with an object of worship, but for

> If a man who turnips cries,
> Cries not when his father dies,
> It is proof that he would rather
> Have a turnip than his father. (Opie 284)

That the sententious Dr. Johnson improvised this as an example of bad writ-ing may say less about the quality of the verse ascribed to Mother Goose than it does about Johnson's taste; a similar lack of appreciation backfired on Samuel Griswold Goodrich, better known as "Peter Parley," when the rhyme he made up in the eighteen-forties as a parody of the irrationality of Mother Goose rhymes also entered the canon:

> Higglety, pigglety, pop!
> The dog has eaten the mop;
> The pig's in a hurry,
> The cat's in a flurry,
> Higglety, pigglety, pop! (207)

The Opies suggest that many of the rhymes ascribed to Mother Goose may have been written by professionals: "we believe that if all the authors were known, many more of these 'unconsidered trifles' would be found to be of distinguished birth, a birth commensurate with their long and influential lives" (3).

But scholars have not often been able to identify authors, for a simple but important reason. Whoever wrote these verses in the first place, and whatever the occasions of their having been written, they are the kinds of words that get stuck in human minds, so that people can pull them out on those occasions when they need to say or sing something that sounds pleasant or just plain interesting. Whatever their sources, then, people who found these verses easy to remember remembered them, and passed them on to others by word of mouth; and so, the poems became part of an oral tradition that cares much less for authorship than it does for memorability.

As a result, we can't figure out exactly what Mother Goose wrote; and because memory tends to be eclectic in its tastes, we can't any more easily determine the characteristics of her work. This body of verse includes everything from gentle prayers like "Now I lay me down to sleep" to counting out rhymes like "Eena meena mina mo," from parts of old ballads like "Lavender's blue, diddle diddle" to tongue twisters like "Peter Piper picked a peck of pickled peppers." Obviously, this variety of rhymes had a variety of difference sources, mostly in forms of jollity of the sort that people used to enjoy in their free time, in the days before soap operas and singles bars. Some rhymes were intended as riddles or jokes, some were parts of mummer's plays, some were drinking songs or just pleasant songs to sing at parties; and some were words that allowed reluctant performers to get out of singing at parties:

> There was an old crow
> Sat upon a clod;
> That's the end of my song.
> That's odd. (138)

"Oh where oh where has my little dog gone?" was originally a comic ballad, "Der Deitcher's Dog," published by Septimus Winner in 1864; luckily, its transition to the oral transition divested it of its tasteless mock-German accent and its cheap jokes about "very goot beer" and sausage made "mit dog" and "mit horse."

Some of the rhymes had less playful origins. Some, like "Hot cross buns" and

> Young lambs to sell! Young lambs to sell!
> I never would cry young lambs to sell
> If I'd as much money as I could tell,
> I never would cry young lambs to sell (264)

were once street cries; and the stern advice to

> Come when you're called,
> Do as you're bid,

Shut the door after you,
    Never be chid (136)

seems to have been directed at servants before it was inherited by children.

Not surprisingly, this grab-bag of various types of verse ranges widely in tone and effect. There is somewhat imbecilic absurdity of

Goosey, goosey gander
    Whither shall I wander?
Upstairs and downstairs
    And in my lady's chamber. (191)

But there is also the mysterious beauty of

Gray goose and gander,
    Waft your wings together,
And carry the good king's daughter
    Over the one-strand river. (190)

There is the smarmily gentle

I love little pussy,
Her coat is warm, and if I don't hurt her
    She'll do me no harm. (356)

But there is also the bloodyminded nastiness of the boy who drowns another pussy in a well, the farmer's wife who amputates the tails of defenceless handicapped mice, and numerous other tales of sometimes breathtakingly brutal violence:

When I went up sandy-hill,
I met a sandy-boy;
I cut his throat, I sucked his blood,
And left his skin a-hanging-o. (377)

(Somehow, it doesn't help to know that this is a riddle, and that the sandy-boy is merely an orange.) There is the wistful sadness of

The north wind doth blow
And we shall have snow
And what will poor robin do then?
    Poor thing. (426)

But then there is the raucous vulgarity of another verse about a robin as it appeared in the first known collection of nursery rhymes, *Tom Thumb's Pretty Song Book*, in 1744:

Little Robin Redbreast
Sat upon a rail
Niddle noddle went his head
and Poop went his hole.

In modern versions designed more for the adult sense of decorum than the juvenile sense of humour, the last line is "Wiggle waggle went his tail." But even when the vulgar bits have expurgated, a free spirited breeziness survives everywhere in Mother Goose, in references to "dirty sluts" (297) and "Greedy-guts" (390) and to a disrespectfully described "gaping wide-mouthed waddling frog" (181).

But more often than not, the most widely known verses of Mother Goose are merely absurd—absolutely and unreservedly absurd. What are we to make of poems that express no surprise or alarm about weird events like cows that jump over the moon or people that jump over candles, or weird characters like groups of tradesmen who climb into small containers intended for bathing and husbands who incarcerate their wives in large vegetables? What are we to make of a logic which assumes that a refusal to submit oneself to the divine will is grounds for having one's lower extremities grabbed by a large domesticated fowl and being tossed down the stairs, or that the thought of having one's cradle blown out of a tree by the wind should comfort an infant and assist somnolence? (Nor does "Rockabye Baby" express an attitude unusual in Mother Goose; there is also

Baby, baby, naughty baby,
Hush, you squalling thing, I say.
Peace this moment, peace, or maybe
Bonaparte will pass this way

And he'll beat you, beat you, beat you,
And he'll beat you all to pap,
And he'll eat you, eat you, eat you,
Every morsel, snap, snap, snap. (59)

Pleasant dreams?)
Furthermore, what are we to make of poems that do the opposite, and instead of taking oddities for granted, imply that there is great significance in

quite obviously insignificant events, such as a child falling asleep half-shod, or another child pulling a plum out of a plum pie, or a couple who

> walked on their feet
> And t'was thought what they eat
> Helped, with drinking, to keep them alive! (171)

Given their history, of course, these verses may once have made sense. Before the vagaries of memory distorted them, they may have been associated with events that explained them, or had further verses that eventually offered rational explanations for some of the bizarre behaviour they describe. But once these verses have been divorced from those contexts, there is no question about it: they are unquestionably loony.

That lunacy interests, and bothers, a lot of adults. Here are words that we have in our heads, words as familiar to us as our own names and telephone numbers, words we seem to have always known, for we probably can't remember when we first heard them; but if we stop to think about it, these ever-so-familiar words make no sense at all. A lamb going to school? A garden with pretty maids growing in it? A blackbird that bites off noses? How could something so familiar—something we all know and take for granted—be so strange? So irrational? So just plain loony?

That strangeness bothers some people so much that they invent all sorts of theoretically rational explanations for it—ways of accounting for the lunacy by denying it. Sure, they say, Mother Goose rhymes *sound* strange—but they actually have hidden meanings, and once you know what those meanings are, then they aren't strange at all anymore. About once a year or so, I get a phone call, usually late in the evening, from someone who asks, in a slightly slurred voice over a background of tinkling glasses and loud music, for the guy who knows all about children's literature. When I admit to being that guy, the slurred voice says, "You don't know who I am, but we're having an argument here and somebody said you could settle it. Isn't that there rhyme 'Georgie Porgie, pudding and pie' all about one of them kings of England back in the olden days, and, like, he had all these mistresses and he killed them all, like Henry the Eighth?" When I say that, no, it isn't, that in fact old versions don't even have the name George in them (the Opies report that the first printed version, in Halliwell's *The Nursery Rhymes of England* of 1844, is about "Rowley Powley") and that in any case these rhymes rarely have that kind of secret allegorical meaning, the slurred voice gets a little angry, and says, "But I heard it from a guy who says he read it in a magazine somewhere—so it must be true. I thought you professors were supposed to know everything."

In asking about the hidden meaning of nursery rhymes, my callers are partaking in another significant aspect of oral culture, the transmission of pseudo-scholarship by rumour and word of mouth. Some of the demystifying explanations of nursery rhymes they ask me about have a long history of their own, going back at least as far as 1708, when William King included speculations about who the original King Cole might have been in his *Useful Transactions in Philosophy* (Opie 134). In 1834, John Bellenden Ker published *An Essay on the Archaeology of Popular English Phrases and Nursery Rhymes*; almost a hundred years later in 1930, Katherine Elwes Thomas published *The Real Personages of Mother Goose*, which, the Opies say, expressed "a cheerful determination to prove that the nursery characters were real persons regardless of what the sources quoted say" (29). This book formed the basis of an MGM documentary which probably put these silly theories into popular circulation, where, as my phone calls reveal, they still survive.

One of the main delights of the *Oxford Dictionary of Nursery Rhymes* is the Opies' levelheaded discussions of these theories, which are often more absurd than the rhymes themselves—and just as entertaining. The Opies say, "Much ingenuity has been exercised to show that certain nursery rhymes have had greater significance than is now apparent.... it should be said straightway that the bulk of these speculations are worthless" (27). Thus, Ker himself invented the early form of Dutch which he claimed that the rhymes were actually Anglicized versions of, so that "Ding Dong Bell" was originally

> Ding d'honig-beld,
> Die kaetst in de weld
> Hwa put heer in?
> Lyt'el Je haen, Je Grjn (Opie 28)

which supposedly meant, "It is the honey-bearing image that brings this revenue, it is this that affords all this wealth. Who is it takes it out? That curse to us all, the sneering bully (the monk)"—an attack on the Catholic Church by early Dutch Protestants, it seems. In 1866, the Rev. Sabine Baring-Gould proposed that Jack and Jill were originally Hjuki and Bil of the Norse Edda; he could only explain how Bil became Jill by suggesting that one of the children ought to have a female name, and he conveniently forgot the much simpler explanation that Jack and Jill have often been used as generic names for boys and girls, as in Shakespeare's "Jack shall have Jill; nought shall go ill" (*Midsummer Night's Dream* 3.2.461-62). A particularly rich example of the wild extremes to which pseudo-explanation has gone is the Opies' list of sources proposed for "Hey diddle diddle," which begin with James Halliwell taking seriously the practical joke of someone who presented him with a parallel to the verse in supposedly ancient Greek:

> some other of the 'origin' theories that may safely be discounted are (i) that it is connected with Hathor worship [whatever that is]; (ii) that it refers to various constellations (Taurus, Canis Minor, &c.); (iii) that it

describes the flight from the rising of the waters in Egypt (little dog, the Dog Star, or 'Sohet'; fiddler, beetle, hence scarab; cow jumping over moon, symbol of sky, &c.); (iv) that it portrays Elizabeth, Lady Katherine Grey, and the Earls of Hertford and Liecester; (v) that it tells of Papist priests urging the labouring class to work harder; (vi) that the expression 'Cat and the fiddle' comes (a) from Katherine of Aragon (Katherine la fidèle), (b), from Catherine, wife of Peter the Great, and (c) from Caton, a supposed governor of Calais (Caton le fidèle). (203-05)

Alternately, the Opies suggest that "The sanest observation on this rhyme seems to have been made by Sir Henry Reid, 'I prefer to think,' he says, 'that it commemorates the athletic lunacy to which the strange conspiracy of the cat and the fiddle incited the cow.'"

This perfectly logical explanation for one particular rhyme points to an important generalization about all the works of Mother Goose. Since most of us remember these rhymes without knowing or caring about their original reasons for existence, any satisfactory explanation of their significance will not depend on their origins. Because we know them and treasure them in apparently meaningless forms, we must account for their lack of meaning instead of attempting to find meaning in them.

A good way of doing so may be found in the circumstances in which they have been remembered. The British call these verses nursery rhymes because they have a history of having been often said or sung to young children by people with no books handy. Somewhere in the history of each of the rhymes of Mother Goose there is probably a nanny or a mother trying to calm down a child, and plucking some words out of her brain in order to do so. In these circumstances, the original purpose of the words is quite beside the point; as the Opies say, "the mother or nurse does not employ a jingle because it is a nursery rhyme *per se*, but because in the pleasantness (or desperation) of the moment it is the first thing which comes to her mind" (6). I can recall my own mother singing to my younger brother about how he'd wonder where the yellow went when he brushed his teeth with Pepsodent; if other mothers also sang it, and if their children remember it and later pass it on to their children, then someday that verse may turn out to be a nursery rhyme, for people who haven't the vaguest idea about who or what Pepsodent might once have been.

In fact, the *real* explanation for the often absurd nature of nursery rhymes is less often a forgotten historical significance than it is merely the vagueness of memory. Again and again, the Opies report that familiar rhymes are actually parts of simpler versions of older songs—most often their openings or their choruses; and the rest of the song often grounds the apparent nonsense in quite logical circumstances. For instance, Mother Goose tells us merely that

Elsie Marley is grown so fine,
She won't get up to feed the swine,
But lies in bed till eight or nine
   Lazy Elsie Marley. (159)

But a later verse of the original verse of the original song Mother Goose borrowed these lines from provides the reason for this indolence: Elsie can afford to be so lazy because she's become rich on the proceeds of booze, and maybe even prostitution:

Elsie keeps wine, gin and ale,
In her house below the dale,
Where every tradesman up and down,
Does call to spend his half-a-crown.

The memories of those who brought rhymes to the nursery were not just selective; they were often inaccurate. "Goosey Goosey Gander" is as illogical as it is because the last four lines about throwing an old man down the stairs actually have a separate source:

They are much the same as the lines which school-children address to the cranefly ("Daddy-long-legs"), sometimes pulling off its legs as they repeat,
   Old father long-legs
      Can't say his prayers;
   Take him by the left leg,
      And throw him downstairs. (191)

An even vaguer memory than the one that joined these two separate bits of memorable verse into one strange poem is the one responsible for "Rub a dub dub" as we now know it. This story of three men in a tub is based on

Hey! rub-a-dub, ho! rub-a-dub, three maids in a tub,
And who do you think were there?
The butcher, the baker, the candlestick-maker
And all of them gone to the fair. (376)

Replacing "were there" with "they were" makes for a whole different story: the sordid and less memorable truth behind the memorable nonsense is that the three tradesmen weren't taking the bath themselves; it was their minds that were dirty, for they were just spectators of the tub scene, apparently at a sideshow involving three, count 'em, three beautiful wenches.

The fact that easy (if sometimes confused) memorability is what made a rhyme part of the nursery canon is an important clue to the significance of

Mother Goose rhymes as touchstones for children's literature—especially children's poetry. These rhymes have that insidious insistence that writers of popular songs aspire to—we find them running through our thoughts even when we'd rather forget them altogether. The important question is, why are they so insistent? What makes them so memorable? Knowing that should tell us much about how poetry in general affects and delights us.

The first thing to be said is that the memorability of these rhymes has little or nothing to do with their content; the mere fact that so many of them make so little sense should tell us that. In some cases, in fact, the content is quite literally something we would otherwise find hard to remember, so that the rhymes have the express purpose of assisting memory, of helping us to recall the days of the month in "Thirty days hath September" or the letters of the alphabet in

> A was an archer, who shot at a frog,
> B was a butcher, and had a great dog. (48)

Rhymes like these allow us to remember otherwise unmemorable information because they use patterns of language, rhymes and rhythms, that place the useful information into predictable slots; all we have to do is remember the frog in the first line, and we're well on the way to remembering the rhyming "dog" in line two, and thus, the butcher who owned him and the letter B that begins the word "butcher." The information survives because it is carried within an easily recognizable and highly repetitive structure. It is accompanied by a great deal of what theorists of information call "redundancy": that part of our communications with each other that we already know, for paradoxically, we cannot communicate anything new without reminding ourselves of a great deal that we know already:

> A written message is never completely unpredictable. If it were it would be nonsense. Indeed, it would be noise. To be understandable, to convey meaning, it must conform to rules of spelling, structure and sense, and these rules, known in advance as information shared between the writer and the reader, reduce uncertainty. They make the message partly predictable, compelling it to carry extra luggage in the form of superfluous symbols. Rules are a form of redundancy.... (Campbell 68-69)

Because nursery rhymes often don't conform to rules of sense, they might seem to lack this sort of redundancy; but in fact, their obvious patterns of rhyme and rhythm and repetition quickly become redundant, and thus, help us to remember the nonsense they contain. According to Jeremy Campbell, psychologists have discovered that people "are poor at remembering sequences which contain little or no redundancy ... most people can sense a distinct change that occurs when unorganized strings of words acquire structure. Some sort of barrier is crossed, with powerful effects on the effectiveness of memory" (218).

Nursery rhymes often have very short lines, so that the rhymes come frequently and thus, are hard not to notice:

> Jack be nimble,
> Jack be quick,
> Jack jump over
> The candlestick. (226-27)

They also tend to have strong, assertive rhythms, as in

> American jump, American jump,
> One—two—three (55)

and strongly repetitive patterns of language, so that nouns and verbs appear at the same place in series of lines:

> He *put* in his thumb,
> And *pulled* out a plum,
> And *said*, What a good boy am I! (234)

Here the second word in each line is a verb, "put in" is balanced by "pulled out," and "out a" is echoed by "what a." Sometimes, the patterns are all reversals:

> As I went over the water,
> The water went over me. (220)

There are also often repeated words or phrases, repeated refrains or choruses as in "There was a man lived in the moon, lived in the moon, lived in the moon" (52) or "Curly locks, curly locks" (140) or "Pussy cat, pussy cat, where have you been?" (357). When all of these rhymes and patterns and reversals and repetitions combine in one short verse, the result is hard to forget:

> Hickory, dickory, dock,
> The mouse ran up the clock.
>> The clock struck one,
>> The mouse ran down,
> Hickory, dickory, dock. (206)

But redundancy makes, not just for memorability, but also, and more significantly, for enjoyment: as their long history of service in the nursery shows, we recall these rhymes in circumstances in which we wish to give pleasure, to both ourselves and to children. They are a pleasure to hear, and they are a pleasure to say.

That they are a pleasure to hear accounts for the rhymes that the Opies call "infant amusements": words meant to accompany games that adults play with babies, such as "This little piggie went to market," designed as an accompaniment to tickling, or this rhyme meant to be said while hiding an object in one of two closed fists:

Handy dandy, riddledy ro,
Which hand will you have, high or low? (197)

The pleasure is not just the physical activity, but the silly sounds that go with it: the mere fact that the words make no sense focuses attention on their patterns, and it is these satisfying structured patterns that give listeners pleasure. When my own children were younger, they were particularly fond of our own variation of one such game:

This is the way the lady rides—
    Easy, easy;
And this is the way the gentleman rides—
    A gallop a trot, a gallop a trot;
And this is the way the farmer rides—
    Hobbledy hoy, hobbledy hoy;
And this is the way the maniac rides—
    Eeeeee-AW!

The traditional game consists of holding the child's hands and of jumping it up and down ever more quickly on one's knees; at the end of the last verse which I made up myself, I'd toss the child up into the air—and that toss, accompanied by a high pitched scream, always got more laughs than a toss without a scream, and without a redundant pattern of every quickening nonsense syllables preceding it.

That the rhymes are a pleasure to say is also apparent in games like these; "A gallop a trot" is a wonderful workout for the tongue, and it's hard not to want to say it, and then say it again. And it's easy to understand why children like to choose sides with counting out rhymes that are as much fun and as challenging to say as

Inter, mitzy, titzy, tool,
Ira, dira, dominu,
Oker, poker, dominoker,
Out goes you. (223)

Some of the rhymes are even more obviously intended to be fun to say— among them tongue twisters like "Peter Piper picked a peck of pickled peppers" or

I need not your needles, they're needless to me,
For kneading of needles is needless, you see.
But did my neat trousers but need to be kneed, I then should
have need of your needles indeed. (326)

In all these rhymes, basic characteristics of language—for instance, the fact that words or sounds that are similar to each other create rhythmic patterns— have been exaggerated, so that they become much more obvious than they usually are in speech or in written prose. Having been exaggerated, they become the centre of attention: these tongue twisters are less about their apparent subjects than about the pleasure of the patterns formed by words used to describe those subjects. And to some extent, that is true of just about every rhyme in the Mother Goose canon.

But the qualities of words in themselves can be foregrounded in this way exactly because the meanings of the words in these rhymes are so relatively unimportant. Like conversations in languages we don't understand, we can hear the music better when we aren't conscious of the significance of the words. Not knowing Italian, I used to think that Puccini's aria "Mi chiamano Mimi" sounded extravagantly romantic—until I read a translation of the libretto for *La Bohème,* and discovered that all it meant was, "People call me Mimi, and I live by myself in a chilly room making artificial flowers."

That part of the effect of Mother Goose rhymes depends on their lack of meaning becomes particularly obvious when we consider the works of poets who try to imitate Mother Goose, like the Canadian poet Dennis Lee. When he writes absurd nonsense, the rhymes and patterns become as significant as they are in the originals, and Lee creates some magnificently persuasive rhymes:

Mississauga rattlesnakes
Eat brown bread.
Mississauga rattlesnakes
Fall down dead.
If you catch a caterpillar
Feed him apple juice;
But if you catch a rattlesnake
Turn him loose! (16)

But when he uses almost the same rhythms for poems that try to convey realistic emotions, they only seem shoddily sentimental, more Eugene Field than Mother Goose:

I've got a Special Person
    At my day-care, where I'm in.
Her name is Mrs. something
    But we mostly call her Lynn.

Cause Lynn's the one that shows you
    How to Squish a paper cup.
And Lynn's the one that smells good
    When you make her pick you up.
    She smells good when she picks you up. (24)

What is interesting however, is not just that the nonsense of the first example allows sound patterns to become apparent—it is that it is, unlike the second example, satisfyingly mysterious—a strange set of events delightful both because they are strange and because the patterns of their saying make them seem so inevitable, so to be taken for granted.

The same is true of all the important works of Mother Goose. They are memorable not just because they are highly patterned, but also because they are so successfully strange. Their main strangeness is that they use quite sensible language in the service of quite nonsensical situations, as in the story of a man who lived in the moon.

And his hat was made of good cream cheese, good cream cheese, good
   cream cheese,
And his hat was made of good cream cheese,
And his name was Aiken Drum.

His breeches were made of haggis bags, haggis bags, haggis bags,
His breeches were made of haggis bags,
And his name was Aiken Drum.

This is redundancy without any comprehensible information to convey—the use of the very means which make communication possible to communicate nothing sensible. It becomes interesting and pleasurable exactly because the meaning it conveys is so unrecognizable. Short-sighted people will understand when I say that the work of Mother Goose is something like taking your glasses off and enjoying what you see, or rather, don't see—wrongheadedly using your eyes, your tools of vision, to see unclearly, and enjoying the mysterious and meaningless world you see.

There is, of course, some pleasure in putting your glasses back on again, and realizing that that wonderful reddish cloud with green and yellow bits was just an ordinary phone booth after all. It's something like solving a riddle: that which seemed so peculiar, so absurd, so entirely inexplicable, had a quite commonplace explanation after all. That may explain why so many people try so hard to find explanations for these rhymes: they are so strange that we assume they must be riddles—that they must have quite rational explanations after all, if only we could apply our ingenuity and figure out what they are.

And of course, many of the rhymes are actually riddles—very weird descriptions with very ordinary explanations:

> Four stiff standers
> Four dilly-danders.
> Two lookers, two crookers,
> And a wig-wag. (397)

To a nasty mind like mine that sounds exceeding sexual; but in fact it's just a cow. Or how about

> Little Nancy Etticoat
> With a white petticoat,
> And a red nose;
> She has no feet or hands,
> The longer she stands
> The shorter she grows. (326)

This apparently deformed Elephant Girl is actually just a candle.

But so what? What is most revealing about the riddles of Mother Goose is that their answers are not very memorable. It's the riddling descriptions themselves that capture our attention, so much so that in a few cases we have even forgotten that the verses we take such pleasure in reciting started life as riddles. One example is

> Little Dicky Dilver
> Had a wife of silver; He took a stick and broke her back
> And sold her to the miller;
> The miller wouldn't have her
> So he threw her in the river. (148)

This apparently gruesome tale of horror is part of a longer ballad which makes it clear that Little Dicky Dilver's wife is actually a grain of wheat, whose travels after the miller breaks her back are chronicled in a series of verses. An even more telling example of a riddle now divorced from its answer is one of the most famous of the rhymes: few people who recite the story of "Humpty Dumpty" realize they are giving a riddling description of an egg.

Like most of Mother Goose's riddles, "Humpty Dumpty" really needs no answer. It's the peculiar description, the strange world evoked by language used in an unusual way that gives it its power. When we do find out the answer of a Mother Goose riddle we've not heard before, we tend to immediately go back and consider the riddle again, and only partially to see how the answer explains what seemed so weird; the other reason we return is to enjoy the pleasure or familiar things turned so strange, so magical—the world of the commonplace made wonderful by magic. Knowing that it's a phone booth, we take our glasses off again to enjoy how it becomes a strange red cloud. Knowing that it is a description of an egg only heightens the mysterious intensity of this extravagantly beautiful description:

> In marble halls as white as milk,
> Lined with a skin as soft as silk,
> Within a fountain crystal-clear,
> A golden apple doth appear.
> No doors there are to this stronghold,
> Yet thieves break in and steal the gold. (196)

And the fact that it represents something so mundane as teeth and gums does nothing to dispel the magically mysterious behaviour of

> Thirty white horses
> Upon a red hill,
> Now they tramp,
> Now they champ,
> Now they stand still. (212)

The irony in the history of attempts to explain away, conventionalize, normalize nursery rhymes is that the absurdity that so disturbs a certain kind of adult mind may be exactly what most delights those children and adults who most enjoy these rhymes. It is an anarchic absurdity, a defiance of convention and normalcy; it's no accident that Mother Goose's version of the old proverb

> A man of words and not of deeds
> Is like a garden full of weeds (286)

should continue with a series of absurd statements that send up the seriousness of the proverb:

> When the weeds begin to grow,
> It's like a garden full of snow;
> when the snow begins to melt,
> It's like a ship without a belt;

When the ship begins to sail,
It's like a bird without a tail.

(I've changed the tense here to fit the first verse, which, not surprisingly, has been discarded in many modern versions.) To explain away this sort of deliberate absurdity is merely to restore the pomposity of the proverb, merely to replace the wonderful image of stamping horses with a picture that could delight only a dental hygienist.

Like the story about the garden or the riddle about the horses, Mother Goose's best work contains nothing much that we aren't familiar with— although its daily acquaintance with cows and candles makes it even more magically foreign for us than it once was for our ancestors. But it combines common words for common objects in such a way that they become strange; due to accidents of history, furthermore, or sometimes due only to our lack of knowledge about their origins, even those rhymes that once did make sense have come to be mysterious. Making the ordinary seem weird is a way of shooting holes in our usual vision of the world—focusing our attention on things we are otherwise so familiar with that we no longer even notice them. Above all, in making the ordinary noticeable and strange, the language of Mother Goose draws attention to its own power, its own mystery. In these ways, in revealing the power of language to make the ordinary wonderful and to be wonderful in and for itself, the rhymes of Mother Goose offer their young hearers an introduction to the main pleasure of poetry—indeed, of all literature.

The rhymes of Mother Goose have given rise to a vast body of pictures, including many by great children's illustrators from Caldecott and Greenaway and Crane in the last century to Maurice Sendak and Nicola Bayley in more recent years. While many of these illustrators have produced fine books based on Mother Goose, new creations that result from combinations of these old words with new pictures, their work never adequately represents the rhymes themselves. This is not just a question of our being better able to imagine our own pictures without the interference of Caldecott or Sendak; the fact is that *any* specific picture at all, even one we invent for ourselves, is bound to destroy some of the special impossibility, perhaps even unimaginability, of the images evoked by the rhymes themselves.

Consider the thirty white horses: while a picture of a set of dentures would obviously deflate the grand mystery of the image, a picture of thirty horses doesn't serve much better, for looking at a bunch of horses is not the same as having words evoke them for us; and in any case, the illustrator would have to resort to a hill covered with red posies or something equally literalizing. The fact is, the best picture is an impossible one that could be both teeth and horses at the same time—and not as silly as that sounds, but grandly strange. The pictures evoked by most Mother Goose rhymes are equally impossible.

Breeches made of haggis bags? Somebody sitting on a tuffet (especially when there is no such word or thing as a "tuffet")? Boys made of frogs and snails and puppy-dog's tails? All are equally unimaginable to the eye but easily understandable to the mind.

But most illustrations for nursery rhymes are anything but impossible; illustrators tend to explain the rhymes away in the same doggedly single-minded way that scholars have tried to allegorize them. Sometimes this makes for good jokes, as when Randolph Caldecott or Maurice Sendak turn simple rhymes like "This is the house that Jack built" or "Hector Protector" into long, complicated narratives in an extended sequence of pictures; the effect of these is something like the relationship between complex riddles and their commonplace answers, except in reverse: the riddling words are relatively simple, the pictures that provide the answers complex. But more often than not, literalizing illustrations merely make the rhymes seem point-lessly commonplace rather than magically absurd. The actual silver bells growing on the plants in both Blanche Fisher Wright's and Nicola Bayley's gardens look manufactured, like chintzy Christmas ornaments; and the ath-letic lunacy of the cow in "Hey diddle diddle" seems hardly even worth not-ing when illustrators again and again depict it as an optical illusion—a mat-ter of a cow in the foreground seeming to jump over a moon low in the sky in the background. Either taking these rhymes literally or attempting to lit-eralize them, as Wallace Tripp does when he makes the fox who "gives warn-ing/It's a cold frosty morning" into a TV weatherman, results in a flattening of their mystery.

Consequently, while children should certainly have access to the many ingeniously humorous stories that good illustrators have made out of Mother Goose, we shouldn't allow the existence of those stories to deprive children of the quite different pleasure of the rhymes on their own—the pleasure of hearing or of saying these enjoyable and evocative words without the inter-ference of accompanying illustrations. For this purpose, any large collection of the rhymes will do; but since the main audience for Mother Goose is like-ly to be those too young to be able to read the rhymes for themselves, the best collection will be one that offers the most to the adult readers who will actu-ally speak the rhymes.

Like many other editions, the Opies' *Oxford Dictionary of Nursery Rhymes* gives adults access to a lot of fine rhymes to read aloud to their children; unlike most other editions, it has the added virtue of explaining the rhymes in a sensible and useful way—offering answers to the riddles, and easily fol-lowed directions for the infant amusements. As an added bonus, the *Dictio-nary* offers careful scholarship that doggedly traces rhymes back to often fas-cinating origins, happily debunks silly ideas—and meanwhile, offers a rich ragbag of delightfully useless information about subjects as diverse as Ameri-can slang and Old Norse deities. Reading the *Dictionary* is like exploring the attic of an old house—there is lots of stuff to rummage through, and most of it is just useless and dusty, and some of it is useless and fascinating, and some of it is not just fascinating but useful indeed. The *Dictionary* is much like the rhymes it contains—it has a lot to offer because it's more than a little crazy.

Works Cited

Baring-Gould, William S. and Cecil Baring-Gould. *The Annotated Mother Goose Rhymes, Nursery Rhymes Old and New.* New York: Bramhall House, 1962.

Bayley, Nicola. *Book of Nursery Rhymes.* Harmondsworth, Middlesex: Penguin Puffin, 1981.

Caldecott, Randolph. *The Randolph Caldecott Picture Book.* London and New York: Frederick Warne, 1976.

Campbell, Jeremy. *Grammatical Man: Information, Entropy, Language, and Life.* New York: Simon and Schuster, 1982.

Lee, Dennis. *Alligator Pie.* Toronto: Macmillan, 1974.

Opie, Iona and Peter Opie. *The Oxford Dictionary of Nursery Rhymes.* 1951. Oxford: Oxford UP, 1984.

Sendak, Maurice. *Hector Protector and As I Went Over the Water.* New York: Harper and Row, 1965.

Tripp, Wallace. *Granfa' Grigg Had a Pig and Other Rhymes Without Reason from Mother Goose.* Boston: Little, Brown, 1976.

Wright, Blanche Fisher. *The Real Mother Goose.* 1916. Chicago: Rand McNally, 1974.

"From the Best Poets"?:
How the Canon of Poetry for Children is Constructed (1998)
Morag Styles

"From the best poets" is the sub-title to Coventry Patmore's highly regarded anthology of poetry, *The Children's Garland*, which was published in 1862. Patmore, like many anthologists of the past and present, was a poet himself and he explains the reasons for his selection of poetry in his preface—a convention many anthologists feel the need to do. He writes:

I have excluded nearly all verse written expressly for children and most of the poetry written about children for grown people ... this volume will, I hope, be found to contain nearly all the genuine poetry in our language fitted to please children.

Thus Patmore introduces several of the ideas I want to deal with in this chapter on anthologizing poetry for children: the extraordinary exclusion from anthologies of nearly all *verse written expressly for children*; the notion of "genuine" poetry which ought to be included in a good anthology; the concern to "please children."

Now pleasing children is a difficult idea to grapple with, particularly when the time-scale I deal with in this book covers three centuries, during which the notion of children or "childhood" has been constructed in many different ways and is constantly evolving. Untangling what might be meant by "pleasing" one young person, let alone children in their infinite variety, is also tricky. Sales figures and regularity of new editions are helpful indicators, but we must not forget that it is adults, by and large, who buy children's poetry— and write, sell, publish and teach it. And adults are often dismissive of children's taste. Indeed, one of my guiding principles in writing this book has been to take as much account as I can of what evidence there is about what children choose to read with pleasure. More importantly, there is Patmore's extraordinary determination to avoid poetry written specifically for children. This exclusion is even more perplexing when one learns that it was commonplace: Patmore, as we shall see, was by no means alone in taking such a stance.

To help us grapple with this issue, it might be instructive to ask some questions. What did Patmore actually select for children? What did he mean by "genuine" poetry? Did all the poetry written for children at that time somehow fail to be "genuine"? What did he think would please children? Why was he so firm about excluding poetry written with children in mind?

I want to bring E.V. Lucas (1868-1938), writing 30 years later, into this discussion. Lucas was another distinguished anthologist with a wide knowledge of and interest in children's poetry. In one of the earliest essays dealing seriously with poetry for children (1896), he takes Patmore's *The Children's Garland* to task:

> As a collection of poems about childhood each in its own way is delightful, although even then not satisfactory. It is as vehicles for the entertainment of young readers that they are so sadly to seek.... (391)

Lucas's view of childhood was as a time of "fun and irresponsibility" where literature "should amuse and delight from first page to last." Do we seem to have a champion for children's poets? Not quite; in the Introduction to Lucas's own anthology, *A Book of Verses for Children*, he writes:

> When you feel ... that these pages no longer satisfy, then you must turn to the better thing. You must understand that there is a kind of poetry that is finer than anything here, poetry to which this book is only a stepping stone.

In the end, Lucas wants children to read the same sort of poetry as that anthologized by Patmore, but not until they are older. This is the classic example of the golden staircase metaphor: start with easy accessible things on the lower rungs and gradually progress to the higher steps where you will encounter "real" poetry. Could this be poetry for adults written in language children can understand on topics they might be interested in? Nature, perhaps, some narrative verse, simple forms, universal sentiments? And does that not lead to poetry predominantly written, as the cliché goes, by dead, white, university educated, middle-class men? One of the motivations for writing this book is to challenge these assumptions, take children's poetry out of its ghetto, and to declare loudly that *this is good poetry for everyone.* Not only do I take issue with Lucas and Patmore who held, after all, the conventional views of their day, but I want to open the debate with many contemporary anthologists and critics who still seek to marginalize poetry written expressly for children.

My argument is that Patmore and Lucas, despite their disagreements, held views about poetry and children in common which also had currency with most anthologists of influence who preceded them and with many who have succeeded them. They believe in a canon of great or 'genuine' poetry which children must read, sooner or later. They believe that what is written with children in mind is inferior to what is written by "great" poets for adults. They want to please young readers, but that does not necessitate being interested in what they actually choose to read. Despite the protestations of many anthologists that they are guided by their own personal preferences, clear patterns and continuities of editing poetry for children have developed over time.

Here is John Rowe Townsend:

If an editor doesn't please himself he doesn't intend to please anyone ... an anthology is a personal thing: that is what gives it its flavour. This may be true, but the established canon of poetry for children which has emerged over time marginalizes the very poetry actually written for young readers. The main reason for this has been the role played by editors of anthologies for children, many of whom, while believing they were making unique and fresh collections, have actually been strongly influenced by a tradition of anthologizing from the so-called "best poets". (212)

Let me tell you the story and show my evidence.

Early Anthologizing

We have already encountered (in Chapter 4) one of the earliest, if not the first, poetry anthology for children, *Mother Goose's Melody,* 1760, a delightful chapbook compilation of nursery rhymes, plus a selection of Shakespeare's songs. The contemporary reader immediately recognizes at least two familiar features of poetry anthology—nursery rhymes and poems by Shakespeare. It does not seem surprising that as soon as anthologies started to be published for children, nursery rhymes were considered suitable material with their lively rhymes, humour, melody, enjoyable repetitions and simple forms, though they were not actually widely considered respectable until the middle of the nineteenth century. However, the successful children's publishers of the eighteenth century believed, like Patmore and Lucas 100 years later, that giving pleasure to children in their reading (as well as instruction) was desirable and commercially advantageous. So a trend began in the mid-eighteenth century for attractive compilations of nursery rhymes which is still in evidence as Mother Goose collections are a mainstay of children's bookshops today.

As for Shakespeare, "that sweet songster," the same extracts were chosen in *Mother Goose's Melody* that anthologists have drawn on ever since. "Where the bee sucks," "When icicles hang by the wall," "Under the greenwood tree," "Ye spotted snakes....". Lucy Aikin did not select any nursery rhymes in *Poetry for Children*, 1801, but she did include two Shakespeare poems. Since then Shakespeare has had a consistent place in anthologies for children, including many new books coming on the market in the twentieth century. As I write, a new, handsomely illustrated book of Shakespeare's poetry, *Something Rich and Strange*, is doing good trade in the shops. So drawing on the work of William Shakespeare in poetry books for children has been well-established practice for nearly 250 years.

That set me wondering about other poets writing for adults. Who gets anthologized for the young, and why? Which poets pass that test of time? In order to make the investigation manageable, I decided to concentrate on a handful of poets who filled the criteria described in the list below.

1. They were included in the Opies' *Oxford Book of Children's Verse*, a historical landmark of poetry for children, and/or Lucy Aiken's *Poetry for Children*, 1801, because it was one of earliest selections for children and because she included a wide cross-section of the poets of her time.
2. They were widely anthologized for children for some time after their deaths.
3. They were considered by many to be fine poets, either in their day or by posterity.
4. Their main poetic output was for adults rather than children.

In my choice of poets I tried to span the most popular genres and to be representative of the overall output of published poetry. I also tried to select equal numbers of men and women, but there were not enough published women poets to fulfil my stated criteria. In the end I chose Robert Burns,

Table 4.1   **Anthologies for children from 1801 to 1995**

Title	Editor
Poetry for Children, 1801	Lucy Aikin
First Book of Poetry, 1820	W.F. Mylius
Poetry for Children, 1825	Lucy Aikin
The Children's Harp, 1850	Unknown
The Golden Treasury of Songs and Lyrics, 1861	Francis T. Palgrave
The Children's Garland, 1862	Coventry Patmore
Easy Rhymes and Simple Poems, 1864	Unknown
Child Life, 1874	John Greenleaf Whittier
Poetry for the Young, 1883	Unknown
Blue Poetry Book, 1892	Andrew Lang
A Book of Verses for Children, 1897	Edward Lucas
Poems Every Child Should Know, 1904	Mary Burt
Another Book of Verses for Children, 1907	E.V. Lucas
The Golden Staircase, 1910	Louey Chisholm
Come Hither, 1923	Walter de la Mare
Tom Tiddler's Ground, 1931	Walter de la Mare
A Poetry Book for Boys and Girls, 1933	Guy Pocock
A Puffin Book of Verse, 1953	Eleanor Graham
The Faber Book of Children's Verse, 1953	Janet Adam Smith
This Way Delight, 1957	Herbert Read
The Cherry Tree, 1959	Geoffrey Grigson
The Dragon Book of Verse, 1977	Harrison & Stuart-Clark
A New Treasury of Poetry, 1990	Neil Philip
Classic Poems to Read Aloud, 1995	James Berry

John Clare, William Cowper, Oliver Goldsmith, Felicia Hemans, Thomas Hood, Alexander Pope, Alfred Tennyson, and William Wordsworth who straddle between them the eighteenth and nineteenth centuries. Felicia Hemans did write for children occasionally, but her main output was for adults.

I then set about choosing some key anthologies, from the nineteenth century to the present day, in order to trace the representation of my chosen poets. I added a number of large, mainstream anthologies of poetry for children by well-qualified editors published more recently. My rough rule of thumb has been (a) poetry for children aged roughly between 6 and 12 and (b) one or two anthologies per decade. I believe my sample contains most of what would be widely regarded as the influential anthologies of my chosen period. I included poetry books intended for school use and those for sale to the general reader, though the latter predominate.

It is as well to underline certain principles regarding the anthologizing of poetry. Most editors compiling large, general anthologies select a personal collection of poems which they believe to be good for their chosen age group,

Table 4.2   British poets writing for adults represented in key anthologies for young readers from 1801 to 1995

(Note: The date given below each poet's name is the date of first publication of a book of poetry likely to be used by anthologists for children. The dates in the left-hand column represent the poetry anthologies.)

	Burns 1780	Clare 1820	Cowper 1782	Golds 1760	Hemans 1834	Hood 1825	Pope 1730	Tennyson 1842	W'worth 1798
Aikin 1801		x	*	*	x	x	*	x	
Aikin 1825			*	*	x	x	*	x	
Mylius 1820	*	x	*	*	x	x	*	x	
Harp 1850	*		*		*				*
Palgrave 1861	*	*	*	*		*	*	*	*
Patmore 1862		*	*	*				*	*
Easy 1864				*		*		*	*
Whittier 1874		*		*		*		*	*
Young 1883	*	*		*		*			*
Lang 1892	*	*	*			*			*
Lucas 1897	*	*	*			*			
Lucas 1907						*		*	*
Burt 1904	*			*		*		*	*
de la Mare 1923	*	*	*	*	*	*	*	*	*
de la Mare 1931	*	*				*		*	*
Pocock 1933		*							*
Graham 1953		*	*						*
Smith 1953	*	*	*	*				*	*
Read 1957		*						*	*
Grigson 1959	*	*	*			*			*
Dragon 1977	*	*		*		*	*		*
Philip 1990	*	*		*		*	*		*
Berry 1995	*		*	*		*	*	*	*

* = at least one poem included in anthology

x = couldn't be included in anthology because writing at a later date.

sometimes by theme, sometimes by other criteria. In almost every case, editors try to include the poets and poems they most admire. If a poet is neglected, it is either because the editor does not know of her/his existence, lack of space, or because the exclusion is intentional. There will, no doubt, be some chance omissions, but if general trends are indicated, then there are probably reasons for them.

What can we make of the pattern that emerges? The most obvious point is that poets who write for adults are very popular in anthologies for the young. Some poets quickly get incorporated into the children's canon and maintain their popularity right up to the present day: Wordsworth, Tennyson, and Burns share that distinction. Some poets are popular for a while, then disap-

Table 4.3 British poets writing for children represented in key anthologies for young readers from 1801 to 1995
(Note: The date given below each poet's name is the date of first publication of a book of poetry likely to be used by anthologists for children.)

	Howitt 1834	Lear 1846	Milne 1923	Roscoe 1809	Stevenson 1885	Taylor 1804	Watts 1715
Aikin 1801	x	x	x	x	x	x	x
Aikin 1825	x	x	x		x		x
Mylius 1820	x	x	x		x		
Harp 1850	*		x		x		
Palgrave 1861			x		x		
Patmore 1862			x		x		
Easy 1864			x		x	*	*
Whittier 1874	*	*	x		x	*	
Young 1883	*		x		x	*	*
Lang 1892			x				
Lucas 1897	*	*	x	*	*	*	
Lucas 1907			x		*	*	
Burt 1904	*		x		*	*	*
de la Mare 1923	*		x		*		*
de la Mare 1931	*				*	*	
Pocock 1933					*		
Graham 1953		*			*	*	*
Smith 1953		*			*	*	*
Read 1957							
Grigson 1959		*					
Dragon 1977					*		
Philip 1990		*			*		
Berry 1995		*	*		*		

pear from view. Whereas Cowper has fallen out of favour since the 1960s, Goldsmith and Pope seem to go in and out of fashion. But in my final anthology representative of 1995, all but two of the poets (Clare and Hood) are included; and they feature in Philip's *New Treasury* of 1990. One might wonder if Pope's poetry would seem dated for the young, yet he is included in nine out of 24 anthologies.

Lucy Aikin drew extensively on Cowper, Shakespeare, and Pope in the first edition of *Poetry for Children*, but in the 1825 edition she cut down on Pope and brought in Wordsworth. She did *not* choose to include popular children's poets like Ann and Jane Taylor, William Roscoe, or Elizabeth Turner and she drops Isaac Watts after the first edition. She does not offer any clues as to the reasoning behind the selection in her Introduction, which is liberal and enlightened about both children and poetry. Whatever her reasons, Lucy Aikin preferred to draw from what she presumably considered to be the best poetry of her day that was accessible to children. *And that is what anthologists have done ever since.*

How then do the poets fare who *are* well known for writing for children in the same anthologies? Was I right in believing that this poetry was under-represented? This time I chose children's poets who were popular in their day and who fulfilled the criteria outlined above: Mary Howitt, Edward Lear, A.A. Milne, William Roscoe, R.L. Stevenson, Jane Taylor and Isaac Watts. I added four more poets whose work was or is equally well known for children and adults—Anna Barbauld, Charlotte Smith, Christina Rossetti, and William Blake.

What conclusions can we draw? Poets writing for children are half as likely to be included in anthologies as those writing for adults. The poor representation of some poets is remarkable. Milne remains popular in early-years classrooms today, yet only one out of ten possible editors chose to include him. Although Lear and Stevenson are well represented, Lear is ignored in 14 out of 21 and Stevenson in four out of 15 poetry books. Compare that with the representation of Wordsworth or Tennyson in Table 2. Of course, many will argue that Wordsworth and Tennyson are anthologized for children simply because they wrote some of the best poetry ever written. Best poetry *for whom?*

None of our children's poets was included in Andrew Lang's influential *Blue Poetry Book.* Sixteen editors chose to include only two or fewer of our representative children's poets in their anthologies. Women poets writing for children do better in this table than the last. Mary Howitt and Jane Taylor fare pretty well until this century; William Roscoe hardly survives his lifetime, though Isaac Watts lasted right up to 1953 and is still occasionally anthologized today.

Once Blake's poetry was well known and widely circulated, he solidly maintained his place in children's anthologies. Not so Rossetti, who is excluded (10 omissions) more often than she is included (she is selected in eight texts). There is neither rhyme nor reason for this neglect and it certainly cannot be justified on any grounds to do with the quality of the poetry. Barbauld and Smith are even more poorly represented. As relatively few women were able to get published at all, it would appear that because of the marginalized status of poetry written for children, they suffer a double disadvantage. The neglect of women poets from anthologies is a sad part of this tale.

This evidence seems to confirm my suspicions that children's poets are less likely to gain a place in anthologies for the young than poets writing for adults. The editor of *The Children's Harp* (1850) brings us up full square with the main thesis of this chapter:

Table 4.4   British poets writing for children and adults represented in key anthologies from 1801 to 1995

	Barbauld 1782	Blake 1789	Smith 1804	Rossetti 1872
Aikin 1801	*		x	x
Aikin 1825	*		*	x
Mylius 1820	*		*	x
Harp 1850				x
Palgrave 1861	*	*		x
Patmore 1862	*	*	*	x
Easy 1964	*			x
Whittier 1874		*		
Young 1883		*	*	
Lang 1892		*		
Lucas 1897		*		*
Lucas 1907	*	*	*	
Burt 1904	*			
de la Mare 1923		*		*
de la Mare 1931		*		*
Pocock 1933		*		
Graham 1953		*		*
Smith 1953		*		
Read 1957		*		*
Grigson 1959		*		
Dragon 1977		*		*
Philip 1990		*		*
Berry 1995		*		*

So far as possible, we have taken our specimens from standard writers, who, with the true sublimity of genius, have often, amid their loftiest flights, poured forth simpler melodies than *meaner bards can command* when handling the lute with a purposed *view to meet the infantile capacity.* [my emphasis]

Meaner bards seems to imply those who write for children. It is amusing with hindsight to read editors' introductions to poetry anthologies, as so many seem to believe that others have got it wrong while they hold the key to selecting just the right poetry for children. In fact, most of them share the same prejudices and, indeed, feed off one another's choices. John Greenleaf Whittier was a fine selector of poetry for the young, but his preface is revealing when he describes the limitations of poetry anthologies: "... noticing in nearly all of them much that seemed lacking in literary merit." He sought to combine "simplicity with a certain degree of literary excellence, without on the one hand descending to silliness, or, on the other, rising above the average comprehension of childhood" (vii).

Thus poetry written specifically for a young audience gets marginalized by influential editors and a tradition becomes established where adult poetry by the so-called "great" poets is considered preferable to writing directed at children. And it is still happening today. Here is Angela Huth, author of *Island of the Children*, writing her introduction in 1987:

> The discovery that there was a certain scarcity of modern poetry for children ... came to me when searching for new poems to entertain my daughter, Eugenie. I had been reading her poetry from a very young age, and found with surprising swiftness we were running out of material. What was plainly missing was a rich anthology of contemporary poetry written ... by disparate modern poets ... I hope their efforts (i.e., the poets included in her anthology) will delight many a poetry-starved child in the future. ([ix])

Such comments are insulting to the many talented poets writing today and show ignorance on the part of the editor. Huth subscribes to a form of elitism quite in keeping with the well-established tradition of editing poetry for children. Here is Robert Hull being slightly condescending about Brian Patten's *Puffin Book of 20th Century Verse*: "Brian Patten's volume is a book of good poems for children written in the twentieth century, and that's about it" (21). What else should it be? Or Anthea Bell discussing Prelutsky's *The Walker Book of Poetry for Children*: "If I am lukewarm ... it is because I feel that Prelutsky has been compiling down.... He draws largely on specifically children's poets...." (Philip and Bell 82). Or Neil Philip in his introduction to *A New Treasury of Poetry* 1990:

> I have also been cautious with poems written specially for children, preferring on the whole work which makes itself available to a young reader without any sense of talking or writing down. Of course, some poets have written marvellously for children ... (15)

Or consider Gillian Avery's comments in her *Everyman Anthology of Poetry for Children*, 1994, where she talks of avoiding: "poems deliberately aimed at youth which—with the exception of nonsense—tend to be worthy and dull, if not arch and fey." But does it follow that poetry written for children will talk down or be dull and fey?

How does this prejudice on the part of editors affect the representation of women? Coventry Patmore declares that *A Children's Garland* is only from "the best poets" and *Poems Every Child Should Know* is a selection from "the best poems of all time." Both excluded most women. Although the latter purports to deal with poems *every child* should know, the introduction is addressed exclusively to boys. Other editors do likewise. I could only identify for certain three women in Lang's *Blue Poetry Book* which contains about 100 poems, and only six out of 170 entries in Geoffrey Grigson's otherwise magnificent *The Cherry Tree* (1959) are not by men. Yet this is not inevitable. The editors, of whom I am one, of *Mother Gave A Shout*, an anthology of women poets writing for children, declared that their only problem in selection lay in deciding what to leave out. Nor have editors of the calibre of Carol Ann Duffy or Wendy Cope had any difficulty in finding excellent poetry by women in similarly focused anthologies. There is no scarcity of good poetry written by women, now or in the past.

It is *not* natural for anthologists to select poems written mainly by men for other adults in poetry books for children. A tradition has developed in anthologizing for children which needs to be challenged. Traditional often means conservative, sticking with the "tried and tested" rather than appreciating what is new, unusual, different, or risky. When you combine this conservatism with nostalgia for some idealized past, often associated with adults' interest in children's poetry, then it is easy to see why anthologies for young readers fall into this pattern. There are unrecognized and unexamined historical continuities in anthologizing for children that most editors seem unaware of, and too little understanding about the poetry children actually like and choose to read. It is not surprising that black British poetry, which was developing in innovative and exciting ways in the early 1980s, took a long time to get any place in the canon and is still under-represented. It surely is time to open up the canon particularly to show what women and poets from other parts of the world can write for children. This does not mean discarding the poetry from the past, but appreciating its value alongside new and changing voices. There is a great heritage of children's poetry in Britain and some of it is by women and working-class people and black writers, and of course, those who choose to concentrate on writing for the young.

Works Cited

Aikin, Lucy. *Poetry for Children*. London: R. Phillips, 1801.

Avery, Gillian. *Everyman Anthology of Poetry for Children*. London: David Campbell, 1994.

Burt, Mary, ed. *Poems Every Child Should Know*. London: Doubleday, 1904.

The Children's Harp. London, 1850.

Cope, Wendy, ed. *Is That the New Moon?* London: Collins, 1989.

Duffy, Carol Ann, ed. *I Wouldn't Thank you for a Valentine*. London: Viking, 1992.

Grigson, Geoffrey, ed. *The Cherry Tree*. London: Phoenix House, 1959.

Hull, Robert. "A Jostle of Poetries." *Books for Keeps* 72 (January 1992).

Huth, Angela, ed. *Island of the Children*. London: Orchard Books, 1987.

Lang, Andrew, ed. *The Blue Poetry Book*. London: Longmans, Green & Co., 1891.

Lucas, E.V. *A Book of Verses for Children*. 1897. London: Grant Richards, 1904.

———. "Some Notes on Poetry for Children." *Fortnightly Review* LX [old series LXVI] (1896): 391-407.

Mother Goose's Melody. London: Marshall, 1760.

Opie, Iona and Peter Opie, eds. *The Oxford Book of Children's Verse*. Oxford: Oxford UP, 1973.

Patmore, Coventry, ed. *The Children's Garland*. London: Macmillan, 1862.

Patten, Brian, ed. *The Puffin Book of Twentieth Century Verse*. London: Penguin, 1991.

Philip, Neil, ed. *A New Treasury of Poetry*. London: Blackie, 1990.

Philip, Neil and Anthea Bell. "The Signal Poetry Award [*What is the Truth?* by Ted Hughes]." *Signal* 47 (May 1985): 71-85.

Pollinger, Gina, ed. *Something Rich and Strange*. London: Kingfisher, 1995.

Prelutsky, Jack, ed. *The Walker Book of Poetry for Children*. London: Walker, 1984.

Steele, Susanna and Morag Styles. *Mother Gave a Shout: Poems by Women and Girls*. London: A&C Black, 1988.

Townsend, John Rowe. *Modern Poetry*. London: Oxford UP, 1973.

Whittier, John Greenleaf, ed. *Child Life: A Collection of Poems*. London: Nisbet & Co., 1874.

V

FAIRY TALES AND FANTASY

Although adults have discarded fairy tales in their own reading, judging them childishly fanciful, unreal, and unrelated to the world as they know it—a world in which the workings of natural law are familiar and accepted—it is remarkable how many references to fairy tales are found in adult speech and writing. We all understand the implication of such phrases as it's a Cinderella tale; he's an Ugly Duckling; he killed the goose that laid the golden egg; it's a case of Beauty and the Beast; a veritable Bluebeard; Sister Ann, Sister Ann do you see anyone coming; Open Sesame; an old man of the sea; and many others. These allusions in common speech testify to the memorable quality of fairy tales. But do they not also in some sort refute the judgment of grownups that theses stories are unrelated to everyday life? (46)

— Lillian Smith, "The Art of the Fairy Tale" (1953)

[A] scientific theory is a kind of fantasy which is required to match the world in a particularly strict sort of way. We have ample testimony from great scientists of the importance of fantasy to creative scientific thought. Einstein said: "When I examine myself and my methods of thought, I come to the conclusion that the gift of fantasy has meant more to me than any talent for abstract, positive thinking." (566-67)

— Chet Raymo, "Dr. Seuss and Dr. Einstein:
Children's Books and Scientific Imagination" (1992)

Fantasy is the poetry of ideas. We tend to be told that the prime aim of fantasy is to arouse a sense of wonder. It is an ambiguous phrase. If you take wonder to mean awe, and the marvelous, then I think it isn't true, and even if it were it wouldn't get us very far. It might have been true once, when our ancestors listened open-mouthed to the travelers' tales. But if we take wonder to mean speculation, then I think we are on to something. That's the beginning. Speculation begins with "If." It goes on from there and discovers new worlds. (48)

— Peter Dickinson, "Fantasy: The Need for Realism" (1986)

Introduction

Fairy tales and fantasy are connected to the oldest narratives from the oral tradition, and, according to many, embody humanity's deepest thoughts and desires. Despite attacks on their suitability for children throughout the ages, fairy tales have firmly held their place in many cultures, and fantasy, as a literary form, has been steadily popular for children since the nineteenth century.

The articles in this section are only the tip of the iceberg that is fairy tale and fantasy criticism, but each one introduces useful background and terminology. Hugh Crago's "What Is a Fairy Tale?" gives some sense of the history of fairy tales in Europe, examines terms commonly used in discussions of them, and provides an introduction to some approaches used in studying them. Anna Altmann's "Parody and Poesis in Feminist Fairy Tales" narrows the focus, looking particularly at the trends of folk tale parodies and of fairy tale and fantasy creation in the twentieth century. Finally, C.W. Sullivan's "Fantasy" discusses the development of fantasy, and then focuses on a particular branch of the form: high fantasy.

As the beginning paragraphs of Crago's article suggest, terminology used in the study of fairy tales is not consistent; scholars employ a variety of terms in differing ways. Generally speaking, it is agreed that there was an oral narrative tradition in which stories were passed around verbally, either by professional storytellers or by family or friends in informal settings. The stories familiar to many of us today, such as the Red Riding Hood, Sleeping Beauty, or Jack tales were at some point, generally after the sixteenth century, recorded in writing. The process of writing down the tales started a new tradition of recorded folk tales and fairy tales. Collections of tales by Basile in Italy (1634-36), Charles Perrault in France (1697), the Grimm brothers in Germany (1812), and Abjørnsen and Moe in Norway (1837) are examples of recorded folk tales.

This is not to say that the oral tradition has disappeared; however, the print culture is dominant today, and we are familiar with the oral transmission of tales mostly from what are now known as urban myths or legends, such as the persistent story of the ethnic restaurant that is reputed to serve cat, dog, or rat. In recent years, the Internet, an odd mixture of oral and print transmission, has become a thriving source of such tales.

The terms *fairy tale* and *folk tale* are often used interchangeably. Since many of the older, traditional tales don't actually have fairies in them, many scholars prefer the term folk tale. Some scholars use the term fairy tale for tales that began to appear during the nineteenth century, also known as literary tales or *kunstmärchen* (art fairy tales). Such tales resembled those of the oral tradition in form but had no particular antecedents, each being chiefly the invention of one specific writer. We must be careful, however, about making too firm a delineation between the oral tale, the recorded folk tale, and the literary tale, all of which can be considered under the broad term fairy tale. They do have their distinctions: oral tales and folk tales tend to have very spare characterization and setting, with minimal description, while literary tales are usually longer with more detail and development. They also have many similarities, and the line between them is so often blurred that being too rigorous in trying to classify them can distract from the more important process of reading and understanding them.

Crago and Altmann both indicate ways of thinking about fairy tales, which is a large part of folk and fairy tale studies. Certainly, with their odd short-hand manner of communicating human fears, emotions, foibles, and actions, these stories practically beg for interpretation beyond the surface plot. As Crago notes in his article, there are many different approaches to understanding the tales. Altmann's article points to a trend toward reimagining in fairy tale writing that has been around for a while, but has gained a great deal of popularity since the women's movement of the 1970s. Revisions and rethinkings of fairy tales have become very popular, both in adult and children's literature.

Although she uses fairy tales as her main example, Altmann's article also has applications for the study of fantasy, a form generally agreed to have evolved from all the forms of fairy tales, and particularly from the popularity of literary tales. Over the past 150 years, the form has developed many branches, including science fiction, the extrapolation of scientific ideas or practices; high fantasy (on which Sullivan focuses) set in other worlds and usually written in a high style and tone; magical realism, with a mix of the real world and the supernatural; and animal fantasy, in which animals possess human characteristics. Although we have not covered all those various forms in these readings, Sullivan's and Altmann's Works Cited give suggestions for further reading about fantasy, as does Crago's for fairy tale criticism.

Works Cited

Dickinson, Peter. "Fantasy: The Need for Realism." *Children's Literature in Education* 17.1 (1986): 39-51.

Raymo, Chet. "Dr. Seuss and Dr. Einstein: Children's Books and Scientific Imagination." *Horn Book* 68.5 (Sept. 1992): 560-67.

Smith, Lillian. "The Art of the Fairy Tale" *The Unreluctant Years: A Critical Approach to Children's Literature.* New York: Viking P, 1953: 44-63.

What Is a Fairy Tale? (2003)
Hugh Crago

"Once there was—and twice there wasn't"

Almost everyone can name a few fairy tales—probably "Cinderella," "Snow White and the Seven Dwarfs," "Red Riding Hood," "Sleeping Beauty," and "The Three Bears." Pushed a bit harder, our hypothetical person-in-the-street might add "Hansel and Gretel," "Puss in Boots," "Jack and the Beanstalk," or "The Three Billy Goats Gruff."

Almost everyone can tell you what the adjective "fairy-tale" means: a fairy-tale wedding is one like the late Princess Diana's. A fairy-tale ending is *not* one like the late Princess Diana's. "It's just a fairy tale" refers to a gratifying illusion. A fairy godmother is someone you don't expect to meet in your life. Almost everyone will associate fairy tales with children and childhood. However, the reasons most people give for this link will be vague and circular: "You like fairy tales when you're a kid, because they're all about fairies and that sort of thing," or, "Well, fairy tales are *for* kids, aren't they?" Overwhelmingly, the assumption is that fairy tales have to do with a wish-fulfilling, basically irrational view of life, which we outgrow when we put aside childish things.

Educated adults will possess a little more learning—which, as Pope reminds us, can be dangerous. They may know, for instance, that fairy tales are part of a larger category called folk tales, and originated as stories told aloud in peasant communities to both adults and children. They will know that many folk tales involve events and characters that are potentially frightening and cruel rather than simply gratifying. They may know that in the "original" version of "Cinderella," the ugly sisters actually cut off parts of their large feet in order to force them to fit the Prince's slipper, or that the "original" Red Riding Hood was eaten by the wolf, not saved by the woodcutter. They will probably know that some of the stories normally categorized as fairy tales (such as "The Little Mermaid" or "The Three Bears") are not orally transmitted stories but were composed by individual, known authors. They will distinguish these from "true folk tales"—probably thinking of the Grimm brothers' tales when they speak of the latter.

Adults who have majored in women's studies or cultural studies may have qualms about the supposed affinity between children and fairy tales, arguing that fairy tales are violent, sexist, classist, and may in fact be covert agents of a cultural hegemony which seeks to keep the poor and the female in their place. By contrast, another group of adults, influenced by the well-publicized views of psychotherapists like Bruno Bettelheim, asserts that fairy tales are uniquely good for children because they preserve deep truths about life, expressed in patterns and images that speak to the minds of the young.

Unfortunately, where fairy tales are concerned, the smugly educated and the politically correct often prove to be almost as wrong as the cheerfully ignorant. Once we start examining the facts, all certainties dissolve as spectacularly as the Wicked Witch of the West. Over the past century or more, fairy tales have been the subject of an enormous scholarly literature, studied and debated by folklorists and anthropologists, critics of literature and illustration, social historians, psychoanalysts both Freudian and Jungian, feminists, structuralists and post-structuralists. The mere existence of this continuing fascination is highly significant. Why can't rational, highly educated adults agree about what fairy tales are, or what they mean, let alone on whether they are "harmless," "dangerous" or "therapeutic"?

The "Truth" about Fairy Tales

The fairy tales that everyone can name are in fact a tiny selection from a far wider range of stories, which only a small minority of children today ever hear, read, or see. "Snow White," "Cinderella" and their ilk are well known because publishers keep them in front of parents (and hence children) in the form of endless cheap reprints and "new" version, often with recycled illustrations. The place of this selected group has also been assured by the fact that the Disney studios have produced animated movie versions of them, all readily available on video.

Today's child, and tomorrow's adult, know these tales in quite different forms from the ones in which they first appeared in print, in the seventeenth, eighteenth and early nineteenth centuries. Snow White's stepmother is now almost universally depicted as a stereotyped witch because the 1937 Disney movie showed her in this guise. Far from being comfortingly fixed points of cultural reference, fairy tales are in fact shifting, evanescent, subject to almost as many reversals of emphasis and periodic recyclings as the fashion industry.

That same shifting quality seriously undermines attempts to attach moral value (positive or negative) to fairy tales. Bettelheim, like other therapeutic commentators before him, wrote as if the tales had a single, definitive form. Yet, as social historian Robert Darnton points out, Red Riding Hood's red cap features in only a few of the many oral variants of the tale collected (albeit a century and a half later) in France. Psychoanalyst Erich Fromm's insistence that the red cap represents menstrual blood, and that the story must deal symbolically with puberty, becomes questionable as a result. Similarly, how does it alter the argument that "Cinderella" is a sexist tale encouraging oppressed women to dream passively of rescue by a handsome prince, when we know that in a far earlier Chinese version of the tale, there was no hand-some prince at all? So: are fairy tales dangerous or therapeutic? We cannot say, unless we specify which version of a tale we are talking about.

Although the average informant will tell you that fairy tales are "about magic," or "things which can't really happen," in fact many fairy tales (apart from the most commonly cited ones) contain no fairies and little or no actual magic, though they do contain talking animals and other supernatural and grotesque elements. *Contes des fées* ("Fairy Tales") was in fact a name popularized by the courtly French writers of the late seventeenth and early eighteenth centuries, who saw that traditional tales had potential for educating young noblemen and women in socially approved ways of behaving. They rewrote "folk" tales accordingly, censoring and "improving" them as ruthlessly as ever Disney did two hundred years later (Zipes, *Fairy Tales and the Art of Subversion*), even inventing completely new ones. For Mme L'Héritier, M. Perrault, Mme d'Aulnoy and Mme LePrince de Beaumont, the fairies and the magic were a way of gaining the fascinated attention of the young, while subtly inculcating the "right" values. What counted was the *effect* of the tale, not any notion of literary purity. So, were fairy tales originally about magic? No—and yet they became more and more so, for *didactic* reasons. And for all their supernatural content, fairy tales are curiously hard-headed and pragmatic, something that gives the lie to the equation of fairy tale with myth or illusion.

Our educated respondent may recognize that folk literature consisted of stories not originally addressed to children—but then, very little literature was addressed to children until childhood itself began to be seen as a distinct stage of life with its own special characteristics and requirements (Ariès; de Mause). And it remains true that when children's literature began, it was to the body of folk tales that the *littérateurs* of the French court turned as a source of appropriate material for instructing and entertaining the young.

To what extent was the folk-tale material on which Perrault (and, later, the Grimm brothers) drew even "oral"? That folk tales were transmitted orally within illiterate peasant households there can be no doubt, but beyond this the certainties fail again. As Ellis shows in *One Fairy Story Too Many*, Jakob and Wilhelm Grimm's main informant was a *literate* woman within their own household, some of whose tales, at least, came from purely literary sources. One of Perrault's main informants, by contrast, appears to have been his children's wet nurse, who *was* of peasant stock. Marina Warner's sophisticated exploration of the tales and their early tellers in *From the Beast to the Blonde* goes so far as to claim that there is little point in trying to distinguish between "oral" and "literary" material at all. As she sees it, a male Perrault concealed his gender behind a stock Mother Goose figure, who in turn stood for, and yet subtly mocked, generations of real "feisty old women" who had told such tales to generations of children (including perhaps a young Perrault himself).

So the apparently clear distinction between the oral tales collected by the

Grimms and Hans Andersen's literary tales (for which the scholarly term is *kunstmärchen*, "art fairy tales") dissolves like all the other certainties. *Kunstmärchen* certainly contain elaborations that are the inventions of their individual, literate authors, but they are highly likely to borrow folk-tale plots (as Andersen's "Tinder Box" drew on the folk tale that the Grimms titled "The Blue Light"), and conversely folk narratives passed down in oral tradition sometimes owe key details to literary narratives (Boccaccio's *Decameron*, for example). And the Grimm brothers rewrote the tales dictated to them in accordance with their own (literate) ideas on what folk literature *ought* to sound like! It is significant that *The Oxford Companion to Fairy Tales*, edited by Jack Zipes, makes no attempt to distinguish between "art" and "folk" tales, or even between *kunstmärchen* and modern novel-length fantasies.

So, if fairy tales are not what we think they are, at least, not most of the time, what are they? Rather than try to summarize the body of scholarly work on fairy tales, a lifetime task at least as difficult as spinning straw into gold, I propose to concentrate on a few authors whose contributions—most of them published in the last thirty years—I have personally found most revelatory. With their help, we may be able to find our way through the mysterious twilight of the fairy-tale forest, and begin to understand what a fairy tale actually is.

Fairy-tale Plots: The Same Actions in the Same Order

We often forget, now, that the early years of the Soviet Union were not only a time of fear and misery for many but also a time of idealism and intellectual ferment, especially for those interested in folk culture, education and childhood—for most revolutions pay great attention to the New Order's future citizens. Vladimir Propp worked at the same time as illustrator Ivan Bilibin and educator Kornei Chukovsky, although his work did not achieve influence outside the USSR until fifty years later.

Studying Afanasyef's great collection of Russian folk tales, Propp became fascinated by the enduring patterns he could discern beneath the ever-changing surface details. A prince goes hunting and meets a magic fox; a girl wanders into the forest and encounters the hut of Baba Yaga; a fisherman plies his trade near the Black Sea, and finds in his nets a great golden flounder: what do all of these have in common? A sequence of events in which a protagonist moves away from home and encounters a person or creature with supernatural powers, whom Propp termed a donor, that is, one who offers something the protagonist comes to value. Moreover, the initial leaving of home is often accompanied by some lack or problem, which the protagonist must seek to correct; and the donor, whether benevolently inclined or not, is likely to be instrumental in the discovery of this solution or resolution. The protagonist can only interact with the donor in a limited number of ways, just as the initial leaving of home can only be under a strictly limited number of circumstances.

More important still, Propp found, the *sequence* of such incidents (which Propp termed "functions") is *invariable*. A donor never appears at the very beginning of a tale but can only be encountered after the protagonist has left home and travelled; a villain does not show up until after the encounter with the donor, and so on. While individual functions may be omitted from the narrative sequence in any given tale, the remaining functions still occur in the same order. Perhaps it is self-evident that a donor cannot figure in a tale until there is first a hero with whom the donor can interact, and a problem which the donor's appearance may help to rectify. But what Propp had uncovered through his close analysis of the Slav folk-tale corpus was in fact a glimpse of the "deep structure" (Chomsky) of narrative itself, a perspective which later narratologists would greatly expand. Very similar structural sequences occur, for example, in that enormous, multifarious collection of tales known in English as the *Arabian Nights* (even though it was not Arabian in origin at all).

In Propp's basic structure, a set of functions arranged in invariant order makes up a "move," that is, a sequence of events complete in itself, coming to a natural end in which the original lack or calamity is rectified and harmony restored. Propp recognized that in some tales a second move grew organically out of the first, leading to renewed departure, struggle, and return. Thus the second move of the tale of Aladdin begins with the evil Magician's tricking the Princess into giving up the magic lamp, and the consequent need for Aladdin to invoke the Djinn of the Ring. Propp's theory does not really explain such second moves; nor does it account for the thrice-repeated sequences of actions that are such a hallmark of fairy tales (the king has three sons, and each in turn attempts to complete a quest; only the third prince is successful, whereas the other two fail; or a fairy-tale hero makes three attempts to win a princess, or treasure, and only succeeds on the third attempt). For an understanding of these sequences, we need to turn to Anne Wilson (see below).

Propp also perceived that a folk tale consists almost wholly of a series of *actions*. There is no description to speak of (a prince is handsome, a witch is ugly, a kingdom is rich), and there is no introspection or reflection on events. When the protagonist tries a course of action and fails, he simply embarks on a different action. There is no *thinking about* anything. There is no attempt to portray the *passing of time* as there would be in modern realistic fiction. Character is not explored, and folk-tale characters are not individuals as we know them. Indeed, a key dictum of Propp's is that while functions are invariant, characters performing those functions may vary without any change to the underlying structure. Whether Jack finds a giant or an ogre in the castle at the top of the beanstalk is immaterial.

Propp's analysis helps us to see that a fairy tale presents a curiously fore-shortened view of the world (conveyed with great power in Maurice Sendak's illustrations for *The Juniper Tree*), a view in which the witch's forest tower seems close in space (because close in narrative time) to the town house where Rapunzel's mother craves rampion, a world where Snow White's seven-year sojourn with the dwarfs passes in a few sentences. It is a world in which security and danger are close together, where wolves and bears beset forest travellers as soon as they venture away from their homes. In part, these features can be explained when we examine the real world of three hundred years ago, the period when many of our best-known tales were first written down (see "Fairy-tale Content" below). But only in part.

The distinctive features of folk-tale narrative emerge even more clearly when we examine modern stories which for various reasons choose to flesh out their structure with descriptive detail, incorporate modern consciousness of the passage of time, and develop naturalistic character. Perhaps the most illuminating recent example of such stories is A.S. Byatt's collection *The Djinn in the Nightingale's Eye*, where "The Story of the Eldest Princess" deliberately reverses the conventions of traditional tales in a witty narrative that also functions as a sharper, more illuminating commentary on "proper" fairy tales than any dozen critical articles and books.

What Propp lighted upon was what we might call the *parsimony* of the folk tale. Folk tales ring a limited set of changes, oil a tiny set of underlying structural possibilities. What kind of *consciousness* might this repetitive, predictable, yet "unrealistic" kind of narrative represent? And why might there be a match between fairy-tale consciousness and young children?

Fairy-tale Consciousness: Magical Thought Dictates the Actions

Twenty years ago, British medievalist and narratologist Anne Wilson proposed a theory of "magical thought" in story (Wilson 1981; 1983; 1988) which illuminated many puzzling aspects of fairy-tale structure as well as offering important clues to the understanding of more complex forms of literature such as romance. Appropriately for readers of this final issue, Wilson's early essays on fairy tales were all published in *Signal*, and her second book by the Thimble Press.

Wilson's background included experience in Nigeria (where magical practices were still part of the culture) as well as the scholarly study of medieval literature, and personal experience of psychoanalysis. Her application of Freud to fairy tales attempts to describe the kind of *thinking* the tales represent, and although lucid enough in its exposition, requires an awareness of the workings of the unconscious that can best be attained as a participant in psychotherapy rather than from books. Consequently, her work seems mostly to have been ignored by critics; for example, she does not appear in the entry on psychological approaches to fairy tales in Jack Zipes's *Oxford Companion* and is not referred to in the index to Maria Tatar's *The Annotated Classic Fairy Tales* (2002). She has courageously pursued her larger-scale investigations into medieval narrative texts (Wilson 2001) without much support or comprehension from her academic peers. For Wilson, what distinguishes fairy tales is not whether or not they contain "magic" at the level of *content* (talking beasts or magic wands) but the fact that their *entire way of representing the world* is "magical," by which she means, as Freud did, pre-logical—the level of consciousness at which a child of two or three operates.

Wilson's point of departure is the fact that in most fairy stories characters act in a way contrary to common sense or rational thought. She permits herself to ask the "naïve question" (which is in fact the profound question): "How could Jack, of beanstalk fame, be allowed to rob the giant and giantess so easily three times running? Wouldn't they be increasingly on their guard as each serious loss occurred?" ("Magical Thought" 138).

Her answer to this question is that fairy-tale plots are "creations of their own protagonists." That is, they represent the protagonist thinking about ("contemplating") his or her internal conflicts. However, this thinking is not conscious, reflective thought as we know it, with a "self" or an "I" who *observes* his/her own feelings and actions. This helps to explain why there is no description of feelings and thoughts in fairy tales. *Those feelings and thoughts are represented by actions in the real world.* Donors, villains and the other separate figures described by Propp simply represent contradictory aspects of the protagonist him- or herself, or different versions of people significant to him/her. Similarly, the repetitive action-sequences typical of fairy-tale structure, which Propp's analysis fails to explain, are simply different *possibilities* in the protagonist's mind. When one set of actions fails to deal satisfactorily or fully with a conflict or dilemma, a rethink becomes necessary and takes shape as a sequence that replays the elements of the first in a somewhat different way.

In "Jack and the Beanstalk" the sequence of events that occurs when Jack climbs the magic beanstalk to the Giant's castle is a rethink of the earlier sequence in which Jack stupidly sells his mother's cow for a handful of beans. In the second version (a version more satisfactory to Jack) his *receiving* an apparently *worthless* object from one supernatural being is replaced by his *taking* several *valuable* objects from other supernatural beings. So much more satisfactory is this rethink that it is followed by two more, similar sequences, in which Jack steals again from the Giant. The tales play out for us the way *our thoughts and fantasies represent* the world, not the way it actually is. Although Wilson herself does not see her approach as psychoanalytic, it is certainly in the spirit of psychoanalysis, and this is evident in her notion of "disguise."

Disguise (see Freud's *Interpretation of Dreams*) operates throughout fairy-tale discourse in a variety of forms. Most basic is the "Once upon a time" formula, which asserts that the story is about "there and then," not "here and now." Internal conflicts may also be disguised. Thus "Jack and the Beanstalk" may be understood as dealing in disguised form with Jack's conflicts about growing up and becoming a sexually mature man, and the giant at the top of the beanstalk may be a disguised version of Jack's father (not mentioned in the tale).

In fact, "disguise" is probably a misleading term: it implies a conscious decision on someone's part to conceal something, and no such conscious intention is involved in magical thought. Rather, at the level of consciousness of early childhood, internal events and figures simply take symbolic shape as things external to the self. We can readily see this if we watch very young children at play. They cannot tell us in words what their inmost wishes and fears are, because they themselves do not "know" these wishes and fears in a conscious way. However, they can, and do, *show* us their inner preoccupations by repeating actions that represent those preoccupations. For example, a six-year-old girl repeatedly plays risky games with fire—perhaps indicating an awareness of something big and dangerous within herself, which she wants to be able to control.

Both Freud and Piaget agree that children below the age of five often believe their wishes to have real-world consequences, but by the age of seven or so, have come to recognize that their thoughts alone cannot bring about real outcomes—which might not be desirable in any case. However, all of us to some degree preserve vestiges of this kind of thinking into adulthood, and revert to it under stress. This is the kind of thinking that "magic"—including serious tribal magic and "black magic"—represents.

So, in fairy tales a protagonist's *wish* for help has real-world consequences: a "real" helper appears. Whether the donors actually perform a magical action or not is irrelevant; it is *their appearance at the right time* that is magical. The wolf is killed by the woodcutter *because Red Riding Hood needs him to be killed*, not for any real-world reason. Why did Red Riding Hood not 'arrange' for the wolf to be killed earlier? Because the scene where the wolf invites Red Riding Hood into bed with him represents the heroine's contemplation of the possibilities of sex with an adult man, and this contemplation needs to be allowed to take shape, until it becomes too frightening and overwhelming, upon which the wolf may be dispensed with, terminating that particular set of thoughts.

In Wilson's view, the repetitive quests of the three sons or the three daughters in fairy tales are best understood as occupying *mental* space rather than taking place in real-world time and space. That is, in "The Golden Bird" the quest of the three sons is a representation of a single protagonist splitting himself (but again, the active verb misleadingly suggests that this is the result of a conscious decision) into several possible attitudes. The two "elder sons," who refuse to help the fox, thus stand for the protagonist's selfish fixation on his own goals; the "youngest son," who delays his own quest to help the fox, represents the more mature thought that it is better to be helpful to others because "what goes around comes around." Why do the two elder sons react so similarly? Because the thought of ignoring the fox and getting on with the quest is so compelling that it must be tried twice before it can be given up.

Fairy-tale events lack any quality of elaborated emotion because such emotion is normally the product of a distinct "self" that can contemplate its own feelings and reflect on what others might be feeling. By contrast, the princess in "The Frog Prince" can casually hurl the frog against the wall, without feeling any remorse, because the frog represents a part of herself with which she is temporarily disgusted. The actions of the fairy-tale hero or heroine are entirely dictated by his or her own needs: its universe is, to use Piaget's term, egocentric in the extreme. (A historical analysis would offer a completely different explanation of the cruelty and egocentricity of the tales, as we shall see later.)

Nor is there any "narrator," separate from the hero or heroine, as there would be in the more sophisticated narratives that emerge from rational, conscious thought (Wilson refers to this latter sort of thought as "imaginative" rather than "magical"). Instead, the story *is* a bodying-forth of its protagonist. Who, then, tells the story? Although Wilson does not really answer this question, my own response would be as follows: the actions of the fairy-tale hero embody the *collective* magical thought processes of the community that told and received the tale. These thoughts focus upon some common dilemma or problem (for instance, the problem of how a boy gets to feel like a man, or how a girl should negotiate sexual encounters with males). The tales are not conscious attempts to teach things, couched in symbolic form—which would make them allegories. They are like dreams: *unconscious* narratives which nevertheless have shape and meaning for their dreamers. In the case of fairy tales, this unconscious is collective, not individual, which helps to explain the strong interest taken in the tales by Jung and his successors (e.g., Von Franz, 1956).

According to Wilson, fairy tale "must have an immediate, practical, popular meaning" in order to have survived the vagaries of oral transmission, in which almost every detail might be altered, while the basic core of the story stays the same and can be recognized across cultures and across centuries. Yet the alteration of detail as tales change over time does have important implications, at a different level of meaning from the one that Anne Wilson is concerned with, and it is to these alterations that we now turn.

Fairy-tale Content: Each Age Selects its Own Tales

Over the past two to three centuries, as print and electronic technology have taken over from oral storytelling, a large, diverse body of folk tales has been trimmed down to a smaller and more homogenous group, and the individual tales within that group have been systematically adapted, sanitized, elaborated and rationalized to produce, eventually, the body of tales we now think of as typical fairy tales, those narratives that have given rise to the expectations of magical intervention, happy-ever-after endings, wish-fulfilling details, and the presence of a generally moral tone. That process has been charted in detail by Jack Zipes (1979, and a long series of subsequent publications) and Marina Warner (1995).

As indicated earlier, the fairy-tale corpus known to an average contemporary child of say, six or seven, is now quite small. Of the eight tales in Perrault's *Contes de ma Mère L'Oye*, only "Cinderella," "Sleeping Beauty," and "Red Riding Hood" have survived with undiminished popularity, while "Bluebeard" and "Tom Thumb" have fallen away, and "Ricky of the Tuft" is now virtually unknown. Even "Puss in Boots" seems to be on the way out (*pace* a recent comics-style version by Philip Pullman). What immediately strikes us is that the three surviving Perrault tales all have female protagonists, whereas the genders were more evenly represented in the original collection.

In the case of the Grimm brothers, the modern corpus has retained "Little Snow White," "Rapunzel," "Briar Rose," "The Frog Prince," "The Twelve Dancing Princesses," "Hansel and Gretel," and "Rumpelstiltskin." "The Fisherman and His Wife," "The Bremen Town Musicians," "The Wolf and the Seven Little Kids," and "Big Klaus and Little Klaus" are beginning to appear less frequently. Once again, the shift has been towards stories featuring heroines (six of the above list) and princesses (four), and the stories that have fallen out of the most-reprinted and most-anthologized category tend to be those that feature males or animal protagonists, and low life rather than high. The trend towards idealization and gratification is clear, and confirmed by the fact that, of the large number of eighteenth-century French *kunstmärchen*, our modern reader will likely know only "Beauty and the Beast" (helped along by Disney) and Mme d'Aulnoy's "The White Cat": more images of luxurious palaces, magic and true love.

From the *Arabian Nights*, such a potent influence on a whole century of writers from Beckford and Coleridge to Dickens, the modern child will likely know only the ubiquitous "Aladdin" (recently Disneyfied), "Sindbad the Sailor," and "Ali Baba and the Forty Thieves." Hans Andersen's many humorous and cynical tales have largely been ignored in today's canon, except for "The Emperor's New Clothes." "The Little Mermaid" has been given a new lease of life by Disney, and the sentimentality of "The Little Match-Girl" and "The Steadfast Tin Soldier" still command a place in anthologies. Overwhelmingly, however, the Andersen stories that most people know remain "The Tinder Box," "The Ugly Duckling," and "The Snow Queen," the latter currently available in multiple picture-book versions. The addition of these tales to Perrault's and the Grimms' restores some male protagonists to the contemporary corpus, but continues the emphasis on idealized imagery and gratifying plots.

Today's fairy-tale canon is thus very much in the spirit of the aristocratic purveyors of the *contes des fées* in the seventeenth and eighteenth centuries. The emphasis is on youth, beauty (largely female), magic that is pretty rather than ugly, and the dream of True Love. Much (though not all) of the cruelty, aggression and overt sexuality of the earlier versions of the tales has been edited out. (I well remember telling "Rapunzel" to a group of seven-year-olds at my younger daughter's school; when I reached the point where the Witch puts out the Prince's eyes, one girl exclaimed loudly and censoriously, "That's *sick!*".)

Fairy-tale Content: Yesterday's Grim Reality is Today's Exotic Fantasy

Robert Darnton's wide-ranging, provocative essay "Peasants Tell Tales" has received little attention among fairy-tale scholars, perhaps because it appeared in a volume of social history called *The Great Cat Massacre*. For Darnton, the peasant narratives of the *ancien régime* reflect a world in which life was "nasty, brutish and short," a world in which inequalities between the great and the humble could only be overcome by precisely the qualities exemplified in "Jack and the Beanstalk": cunning, enterprise, and willingness to take huge risks. Not surprising, then, that some of the very tales which have fallen out of the corpus in our own time are those which feature tricksters (like Puss in Boots and little Klaus), and that Jack and his Beanstalk are no longer as popular. Tricksters we still have in our time, but they are more likely to be corporate whizzes and entrepreneurs than humble people who make good with the help of ever-filled purses or magic beans.

Darnton's peasants lived in a world of real kings and queens, a world where towns and castles were separated by genuinely intractable forests and long, gruelling hours of travel at a pace no faster than a horse's gallop. Those guilty of crimes were literally subject to having their heads chopped off, or their eyes put out. Stepmothers were far more common than stepfathers, because men were twice as likely to remarry as women. And young men (and sometimes women) did really "set off to seek their fortunes," a euphemistic phrase which actually meant leaving home to undertake a shiftless, vagrant existence because their parents could not afford to feed them any longer. Younger sons were particularly likely to leave home in this way, in nations like England where primogeniture meant that the family acres went automatically to the eldest.

Darnton's analysis of the folk originals which Perrault rewrote for a courtly audience shows that their protagonists' greed for simple food (magically granted wishes nearly always take the form of "a square meal") reflects quite literally a peasant society in which the lowest in the social order could imagine little more gratifying and escapist than having enough to eat. His survey, like Propp's, supports the proposition that details of tales changed constantly to fit local realities, and strongly suggests that the ogres, giants and bluebeards of many tales were actually hyperbolic representations of the local *seigneurs* (who appeared undisguised in other versions of the same tales). In the same way, images of spinning straw into gold, emptying lakes with sieves, and other "impossible tasks" may well have been hyperbolic images for the literal reality of a peasant life of ceaseless, grinding labour, in which no sooner was one sequence of tasks accomplished than the entire cycle had to begin all over again.

All these details, then, were both meaningful and credible two or three hundred years ago. But for today's listeners, they no longer correspond to observed daily life. They have become exotic, fantastic, and hence meaningful at a psychological rather than a literal level. In a way, then, the disappearance of the tales' original social context highlights their deep structure and invites us more insistently to identify with them at the level of magical thought.

The vanishing of the original significance of some fairy-tale details also leads to the need for retellers to rationalize what originally was self-explanatory. If peasants exposed unwanted babies because there was nothing to feed them with, this was a practice which, though cruel, was pragmatic and, in the circumstances, explicable. Moreover, it would be assumed that both the child's parents would be in agreement about the necessity of the action. Once the tale is retold for an audience who have never known starvation and infanticide, it is necessary to demonize the caregiver who puts her children at risk. So what would once have been an undisguised mother becomes a stepmother, and then a "wicked" stepmother, contrasted with a weak but kinder-hearted father. The misogyny of "Hansel and Gretel" and "Babes in the Wood" was not built into the tales from the beginning, although it is certainly there now.

The Fairy-tale Worldview: Why the Tales Speak to Children

For all the changes to fairy-tale details, values and even plots, since the seventeenth century, some things remain the same. The fairy-tale world remains one in which marriage and inheritance mark an end, not a beginning. Here we find one of the reasons why the tales have so consistently been associated with youth. The achievement of financial independence and a relationship with a desirable partner are the horizon for the vast majority of adolescents. For younger children, the horizon is even vaguer. Whether exposed to fairy tales or not, and however carefully their parents may attempt to free them from stereotyped gender prescriptions, preschool children repeatedly draw and play scenarios which involve a wedding (and perhaps babies) for girls and a career (preferably heroic and action-oriented) for boys. Young children recognize these "markers" of adulthood long before they know what they actually entail.

In their stylized, metaphorical way, the tales offer a similarly truncated, foreshortened view of the future for Everyboy and Everygirl. "Making one's fortune" or being granted "half the kingdom besides" is something that all children can wish for; nor do such wishes depend on being a powerless peasant. And to achieve these wishes requires us to leave home and to negotiate a different relationship with our own parents. But what follows success—the maintenance of power or wealth, the negotiation of a satisfactory relationship with our chosen partner and with our own children, the gaining of self-knowledge—these are the Matter of Adulthood, and play no part in fairy tales.

Happy endings have become an invariant feature of almost all the tales we have preserved today. Here, perhaps, the changes in the tales walk hand in hand with changes in our attitude to childhood. As late as the early modern era, says Lloyd de Mause in his 1974 collection *The History of Childhood*, children could still be regarded by adults with brutal neglect, or manipulated sexually for adult gratification; only over the last century or so have we seen the triumph of what he terms empathic childrearing, in which the adult's duty is conceived as being to understand the child's needs at a deep level and try to "make things right" for him or her. Fairy tales, as our children know them now, may still contain death, but it is not the death of the protagonist. Whether or not this makes the tales emotionally safe for very young children is a moot point. But at all events, unless they have known early loss and pain, most children *do* expect a happy future.

The fairy-tale world consistently proposes a division between "big" and "small," between "powerful" and "powerless." Middle-class child listeners at the beginning of the twenty-first century will most likely respond to this dichotomy at the level of their own experience—the distinction between powerless child and powerful, competent adult. They will be less likely to think of inequalities of political power and wealth. Tricksterism, which Darnton calls "a way of coping with a harsh society instead of a formula for overthrowing it," is also highly relevant to the concerns of modern children: the reality is that children do "bend the rules," fudge the truth and manipulate adults, in order to address their own felt disadvantage.

We have already seen, earlier in this essay, that there are good reasons for the association of children with fairy tales. Magical thought is natural to children in Piaget's pre-operational stage (between the ages of approximately two and five years). That, in itself, does not mean that three- and four-year-olds form a "natural" audience for fairy tales. In fact, four-year-olds may well ask rational questions when confronted with the irrational events of fairy tale (Paley; White) or express grief for the dead wolf rather than joy for Red Riding Hood's escape. But it does mean that the emotional logic of the tales is familiar to them. When the four-year-old assumes that 'Mummy's gone away because I was naughty', she is thinking in the same way as Jack when he assumes his right to steal from the giant at the top of the beanstalk—this kind of thinking is what Piaget describes as egocentric, meaning not "selfish" but "relating all external events to the self." When Carol White insisted after listening to "The Forsaken Merman" that "you know what happened later? The mermummy went back" (170), she was obeying the same deep need for strong closure and "happy ever after" that we associate with fairy tales in the modern canon. Modern preschool children can thus find fairy tales *both deeply disturbing and deeply satisfying* (Crago 1980; Paley 1981; Crago and Crago 1983; Wolf and Heath 1992) even though their ability to retell the events of a fairy story in logical sequence may not yet have developed fully (Applebee 1978). Indeed, the seemingly discontinuous narrative sequences of fairy tales may be more acceptable at this age than they will be later.

By around the age of seven, as André Favat demonstrated, the average child's mind is exquisitely matched with both the mentality and the narrative conventions of the fairy tale. It is as if, by attaining Piaget's concrete operational thought, children can delight in the overt triumphs of the tales' protagonists over ogres, ugly sisters and giants and, simultaneously, resonate with a primitive emotional logic which still lies not far beneath the surface of their own newly acquired sense of "how the world really works."

A convincing proof of Favat's thesis is provided by the fact that the narratives spontaneously evolved by children in the concrete operational stage are, exactly like folk tales, devoid of description, and do not seek to represent the passing of time "realistically." Typically, seven- to eleven-year-olds' stories are composed of sequences of rapid-fire actions, and embody characters who are mere ciphers with no interior life. Ten-year-olds "naturally" write like the tellers of fairy tales, even when dealing with the realities of their own lives (Steedman).

So What is a Fairy Tale?

Much of the argument about fairy tales and their meaning stems from a tendency to blur two levels. "Jack and the Beanstalk" may embody a *generalized* meaning (for society) about growing up and becoming a man; but there is also an *individual* meaning for each reader or listener, which cannot be predicted. "Jack" may be understood very differently by a child with a secure sense of self and belonging, and by another child who lacks those certainties. To the latter, the tale might constitute a justification for sociopathy; the former might be more likely to wonder why Jack takes such risks, while still enjoying his exploits. A child without a father might react differently to this tale, with its two exaggerated, symbolic substitute fathers, from the way a child with a known and loved father would react, and so on. The generalized (social) and the individual meanings do not contradict each other, or wipe each other out: they refer to different contexts.

The evidence (White 1954; Crago and Crago 1976; 1980; 1983; Wolf and Heath 1992) does, however, suggest that there are certain common denominators in the way that preschool children respond to fairy tales. We have seen that children prior to Piaget's concrete operational stage react strongly to some of the illogicalities of which Anne Wilson speaks, seeking insistently to "take them inside" themselves so as to resolve the puzzle or threat they seem to pose. The children do this taking-inside by repeatedly drawing, dramatizing, or talking about key incidents and scenes: the prince's courtship of Rapunzel by climbing her long braids, the Wicked Queen's attempts to kill her rival, Snow White, and the pricking of Sleeping Beauty's finger with the spindle, which sends her into enchanted sleep—all these motifs resonate with their young audience in a way that is somehow beyond conscious cognitive processing—exactly as Fromm and Bettelheim asserted.

Perhaps, after all, the cheerfully ignorant view of fairy tales with which we began this essay may turn out to contain some deeper truths. Fairy tales do belong to childhood, not because they are sweet, simple and uncomplicatedly gratifying but because their mode of thinking is a mode that young children share, and because what they deal with is the Matter of Youth.

Moreover, as the fairy-tale corpus has evolved into its modern form, details that relate to magic, mystery and poetry (which Darnton sees as more typical of Germanic tales and tellers than of their French equivalents) have been favoured at the expense of details that reflect a world of simple peasant life. In this sense, the tales our children hear today are indeed "about magic," and they do end with "happy ever after" (although some of them once did not).

A fairy tale is a narrative form which represents a society's collective concerns with some aspect of "growing up," and it explores these concerns at the level of magical thought. In the process of growing up, a child becomes an adult and (in traditional, patriarchal arrangements) succeeds to its father's authority. The child also becomes sexually mature and finds a partner, supplanting its opposite-sex parent. The process sets up painful conflicts for both child and parent, so painful in fact that they cannot be openly talked about. Clever triumphs over ogres or kings are emotionally safer for all of us than acknowledging aggressive feelings towards fathers, and wicked stepmothers are easier to come to terms with than mixed feelings of both love and hate towards the real women who mother us.

Sweeping changes in social and material life have ensured that the tales that remain in the canon after three hundred years will now, inevitably, be understood primarily on a symbolic and psychological level. In that sense Bettelheim is right, even though in matters of detail his prescriptive, dogmatic interpretations ignore differences between versions, and differences between the response of individual children. As we enter a new millennium, the tales that shaped the last thousand years are still with us, still a point of reference that most people recognize—but both their form and their function have altered to keep up with humanity in its most recent phase of development.

Now our children wander unprotected in the cyberforests of the Internet, where predatory wolves still roam; now it is divorce rather than death that brings us stepfathers and stepmothers, but children still resent the usurper; now our princes and princesses may be supermodels or pop stars, but we continue to dream of escaping from everyday toil into the life of luxury and pleasure we want to believe they lead. Fairy tales are neither good for us nor bad for us: they simply represent some very basic things about us—ambition, envy, hate, desire, greed—which we may feel uncomfortable about but which are unlikely ever to change.

Works Cited

Applebee, Arthur. *The Child's Concept of Story Ages: Two to Seventeen.* Chicago and London: U of Chicago P, 1978.
Ariès, Philippe. *Centuries of Childhood.* 1960. Harmondsworth: Penguin, 1962.
Bettelheim, Bruno. *The Uses of Enchantment: The Meaning and Importance of Fairy Tales.* New York: Knopf, 1976.
Byatt, A.S. "The Story of the Eldest Princess." *The Djinn in the Nightingale's Eye: Five Fairy Stories.* London: Chatto & Windus, 1994. 39-72.
Chomsky, Noam. *Syntactic Structures.* The Hague: Mouton, 1966.
Crago, Maureen. "Snow White: One Child's Response in a Natural Setting." *Signal* 31 (January 1980): 42-56.
Crago, Hugh and Maureen Crago. *Prelude to Literacy: A Preschool Child's Encounter with Picture and Story.* Carbondale IL: Southern Illinois UP, 1983.
——. "The Untrained Eye? A Preschool Child Explores Felix Hoffman's *Rapunzel.*" *Children's Literature in Education* 22 (Autumn 1976): 135-51.
Darnton, Robert. "Peasants Tell Tales: The Meaning of Mother Goose." *The Great Cat Massacre, and Other Episodes in French Cultural History.* New York: Basic Books, 1984. 9-72.
de Mause, Lloyd, ed. *The History of Childhood.* New York: Psychohistory P, 1974.
Ellis, John M. *One Fairy Story Too Many: The Brothers Grimm and Their Tales.* Chicago: U of Chicago P, 1983.
Favat, André. *Child and Tale: The Origins of Interest.* Urbana IL: NCTE, 1977.
Freud, Sigmund. *The Interpretation of Dreams.* 1905. Trans. by James Strachey. Penguin Freud Library, 1976.
Fromm, Erich. *The Forgotten Language: An Introduction to the Understanding of Dreams, Fairy Tales and Myths.* New York: Holt, Rinehart & Winston, 1951.

Paley, Vivien Gussin. *Wally's Stories*. Cambridge MA: Harvard UP, 1981.

Propp, Vladimir. *Morphology of the Folktale*. Trans. Laurence Scott. 2nd ed. rev. and ed. Louis A. Wagner. Austin and London: U of Texas P, 1968.

Pullman, Philip. *Puss in Boots*. Illus. by Ian Beck. London: Doubleday, 2000.

Sendak, Maurice. *The Juniper Tree and Other Tales from Grimm*. Trans. by Lore Segal and Randall Jarrell. New York: Farrar, Straus & Giroux, 1973.

Steedman, Carolyn. *The Tidy House: Little Girls Writing*. London: Virago, 1982.

Tatar, Maria, ed. *The Annotated Classic Fairy Tales*. New York and London: Norton, 2002.

Von Franz, Marie-Louise. *The Psychological Meaning of Redemption Motifs in Fairy Tales*. New York: Inner City Books, 1980.

Warner, Marina. *From the Beast to the Blonde: On Fairy Tales and Their Tellers*. London: Vintage, 1995.

White, Dorothy Neal. *Books Before Five*. London: Oxford UP, 1954. Rpt. Portsmouth NH: Heinemann Educational, 1984.

Wilson, Anne. *Magical Thought in Creative Writing: The Distinctive Roles of Fantasy and Imagination in Fiction*. Stroud, Glos.: Thimble Press, 1983.

——. "Magical Thought in Story." *Signal* 36 (September 1981): 138-51.

——. *Plots and Powers: Magical Structures in Medieval Narratives*. Gainsville: UP of Florida, 2001.

——. "What is Magic?" *Signal* 57 (September 1988): 170-80. Wolf, Shelby & Shirley Brice Heath. *The Braid of Literature: Children's Worlds of Reading*. Cambridge MA: Harvard UP, 1992.

Zipes, Jack. *Breaking the Magic Spell: Radical Theories of Folk and Fairytales*. London: Heinemann, 1979.

——. *Fairy Tales and the Art of Subversion: The Classical Genre for Children and the Process of Civilization*. New York: Wildman P, 1983.

——. *The Trials and Tribulations of Little Red Riding Hood*. South Hadley MA: Bergin & Garvey, 1983.

Zipes, Jack, ed. *The Oxford Companion to Fairy Tales*. London: Oxford UP, 2000.

Parody and Poesis in Feminist Fairy Tales (1994)

Anna E. Altmann

Two years ago I submitted to a scholarly journal a paper on Robin McKinley's *The Hero and the Crown*, in which I argued that McKinley had reclaimed the metaphor of the heroic quest for girls and women in a particularly significant way. One reviewer commented in rejecting the paper that I could more profitably have written about Patricia Wrede's *Dealing with Dragons*. The suggestion was that Wrede's was a more feminist book than McKinley's, probably because it is a parody of the masculine heroic quest. We seem largely to assume that parody is the most powerful feminist tool we have to change oppressive social practices and rules implicit in children's literature, especially in fairy tales. This assumption is worth questioning.

Parody certainly has a very sharp edge, useful for exposing the ideological positions that our most commonly known fairy tales reflect and perpetuate. But parody is metafiction, a criticism of established forms. Criticism produces insight, but it does not necessarily make new use of the forms, create new meaning: it is not always poesis. That is its greatest limitation as a tool for opening new horizons, peopling a new landscape. Parody has other limitations as a feminist agent for socializing children. To achieve its intended effects, parody depends on pre-existing literacy. Readers or listeners must know not only the usual literary codes, but also that what they are reading is a parody, and what the conventions are that are being parodied. This is a demanding prerequisite. Further, in recalling the conventions it plays with, parody to some extent reinforces them. And, what I find irritating and retrograde, is the simplest form of feminist parody, which works like a see-saw: it merely inverts or reverses feminine and masculine gender roles as its main joke, and leaves us still trapped in a hierarchical structure of power relations.

The distinction between parody and what I have chosen to call poesis is one that must be considered if we are to evaluate feminist fairy tales as agents for social change. Parody, as I have said, is metafiction, a critical commentary on an established form. Its most pronounced characteristic is self-conscious and pointed reference to established narrative conventions that are assumed to be known. If these established conventions are unfamiliar to the reader or listener, the primary storytelling tactic fails to have its anticipated effect. The reader may still make some sort of sense of the story, but it will not be the sense the writer intended. In feminist fairy tales that are straightforward parodies, the point, usually the main joke, is oversetting the readers' previously formed expectations, and in the process challenging the inevitability of those expectations. That is, parody looks back, plays with a particular genre or narrative form to comment on that form and on the meaning that has already been made with it.

Poesis, in contrast, looks forward, creates new meaning. The term poesis is not a tidy or commonly recognized antithesis to the term parody. It does not identify a genre, and the two terms are not mutually exclusive. But I need a word to set against "parody," to stand for what is not parody. The first meaning of the Greek word poesis is "a making: a forming, creating," and in that sense I juxtapose it to the critical nature of parody. Feminist fairy tales that are poesis rather than parody use the form of the fairy tale without commenting on it. Or, at least, commentary is not the main point, although such stories will undoubtedly revise readers' notions of fairy tale conventions.

Where the parodies foreground in order to undercut the currently conventional characters and events of fairy tales, the stories that are poesis offer a new and wider world of meaning through reconfigured events and characters directly. Both types of story have a role in opening the language of fairy tales so that it speaks with equal meaning to both girls and boys, women and men. But they have two different roles, and I would argue that poesis is more powerful, that it moves beyond parody and takes us further.

I would like to use several feminist fairy tales, two simply parodic, one more complexly parodic, and two that are not parodies at all, but rather poesis in order to explore what new visions these forms offer. The stories are Patricia Wrede's *Dealing with Dragons*, Robert Munsch's *The Paper Bag Princess*, Catherine Storr's stories of Polly and the wolf, Jane Yolen's "The Moon Ribbon," and Katherine Paterson's *The King's Equal.*

Patricia Wrede's *Dealing with Dragons* is an example of what Linda Hutcheon identifies as traditional parody in that it has a pragmatic ethos of ridicule (50). For 212 pages (in the paperback edition) the book cocks a thoroughgoing snoot at centuries of golden-haired princesses held captive by fierce dragons and rescued by brave knights and princes whom the princesses marry to live happily ever after. Wrede establishes her critical distance from the tales she imitates by means of reversals or inversions. Princess Cimorene, the protagonist, is a complete contrast to the obedient and boring princesses in various shades of blonde that are among the secondary characters. She has black hair, is too tall, and would rather learn fencing and magic and Latin and cooking and politics than the embroidery and dancing that are the appropriate curriculum for princesses in her world. The official heroes, all princes and knights, are sticklers for etiquette, and because their brave deeds are done for the sake of following the correct form, heroism as social convention, they are reduced to self-centred, unimaginative bunglers.

Wrede's chief inversion is making the fabulous determinedly ordinary. The dragons, rather than embodiments of a chaos that must be overcome because it threatens to rob one of being, are just another civilized species, very like people in their politics and fondness for chocolate mousse. Motifs from the tales that are Wrede's target are sprinkled about liberally in order to be debunked: "'I'd much rather have good teeth than have diamonds and roses drop out of my mouth whenever I said something,' Cimorene said. 'Think how uncomfortable it would be if you accidentally talked in your sleep! You'd wake up rolling around on thorns and rocks'" (69). The sense of wonder that fairy tales should induce is relentlessly dispelled (Zipes, "Changing Function" 11).

In its feminist program, *Dealing with Dragons* is both parody and satire. While the target of parody is always another text, satire mocks some aspect of society, and the two genres are often used together (Hutcheon 43). Wrede parodies fairy tales in order to attack through ridicule the patriarchal gender definitions of masculine as heroic, feminine as prize to be rescued. Perhaps the simplest way to change a pattern and to mark the difference with an obvious reference to the source pattern is to invert or reverse it. This is what Wrede has done both with the conventional gender roles of our society and with the fairy tales that have mirrored them back to us.

The problem with this tactic when it is used on the binary opposites of masculine and feminine gender roles as they have been constructed in our society is that simply inverting the binary does not displace it. The result is, rather, like the working of a see-saw: in order for one end to go up, the other must come down, and both ends are ineluctably separated but connected, whichever one is up. The see-saw is evident in Wrede's story. Every male character—prince, knight, dragon, or wizard, whether evil or well-intentioned—is in some way an ineffectual nuisance. Wrede does point out that gender roles are socially constructed rather than essential, through Cimorene herself and in a brief passage explaining that female dragons can be kings ("'King' is the name of the job. It doesn't matter who holds it" [85]). But the implication of the story as a whole is that a woman can be something other than a passive princess only if all men are ineffectual and most of them jerks. While this redefines gender roles to open new space for women, it does so at the cost of maintaining a hierarchical, and therefore oppressive, gender structure.

The feminism of Wrede's parody is also limited in that it opens new space only for the exceptional woman. For as Hutcheon points out, the paradox of parody is that "even in mocking, parody reinforces; in formal terms, it inscribes the mocked conventions onto itself, thereby guaranteeing their continued existence" (75). In *Dealing with Dragons* this is particularly obvious. One of the ways in which Wrede marks the difference of her story from the fairy tales that are her target is by surrounding the revolutionary princess Cimorene with doubly conventional princesses (conventional in social terms within the story and in terms of literary conventions). She thus inevitably holds up the passive feminine as social and literary norm.

Dealing with Dragons is a particularly extended traditional parody of the see-saw type. It is doubly satiric in that the parody is aimed against the power of fairy tales as well as against traditional gender roles. While it makes considerable demands on the pre-existing literacy and life experience of its readers, the teenaged audience that it anticipates undoubtedly has had enough exposure to parody, fairy tales, and feminist issues to get most of the joke, and therefore the point.[1]

Parody's dependence on the previous knowledge of its audience does, however, limit its effectiveness as a socializing agent when it is written for young children. A fair example of this can be seen in children's responses to Robert Munsch's picture book, *The Paper Bag Princess*. This book, another clearly feminist parody, has been enormously popular with the adults who buy picture books and read them to children. The soft cover edition has sold almost two million copies, and a 30-minute videocassette has recently been released by

Cinar. Adults are amused by the parodic inversion that has Princess Elizabeth rescue Prince Ronald from a dragon and then not marry him after all, and they applaud the feminist lesson. Four- and five-year-olds respond differently. They enjoy the fairy tale action of burning castles and forests and flying around the world. They laugh at Elizabeth's last line—"Ronald ... you look like a real prince, but you are a bum." But what they find funny is coming across a rude word in a book. (Indeed, after the book was first published, "bum" was temporarily changed to "jerk," and in the British edition it has been replaced by "toad," although this may be a question of idiom rather than propriety.) What young children are unlikely to get is the parody and its feminist point. Bronwyn Davies, in *Frogs and Snails and Feminist Tales*, a study that explores children's understanding of feminist stories, reports the reactions of a group of Australian pre-schoolers to *The Paper Bag Princess*. For Davies herself, "[Elizabeth's] foolishness in loving someone so patently unworthy as Ronald and her capacity in the end to recognize that and walk away are the salient features ..." (140). But "most children believed she should have cleaned herself up and then married the prince" (60).

The children who reject the humorous lesson of the twist at the end know the rules of fairy tales, but they either don't recognize parody or refuse to accept it as a legitimate alteration of what they know of stories or the world. "Parody is a sophisticated genre in the demands it makes on its practitioners and its interpreters. The encoder, then the decoder, must effect a structural superimposition of texts that incorporates the old into the new" (Hutcheon 33). While the parody in Munsch's book is not at all subtle, unfamiliarity with the genre makes it unlikely that young children will construct the meaning from it that adults do.

A review article (Foster) on politically correct children's literature published in *The Independent* in November 1992 gives further evidence that the feminist message of at least this particular parody was singularly ineffective in persuading young children to give up the fairy tale as they know it. Foster reports the story of an infant-school headteacher who read *The Paper Bag Princess* with her class. (In the article, the book is misattributed, by either Foster or the teacher, to Babette Cole: the parodies are apparently becoming as generic as the tales they play on.)

"We had long discussions about that story," the headteacher told me, "focusing on issues like aggression, the dangers of judging people by their appearance and the empowerment of girls. We even wrote a script to dramatise the story." It was when the children handed in their suggestions for costumes that the teacher realised what she was up against: "There was no sign of a paper bag; every single outfit for the princess was some version of a ball gown, with tiara, satin pumps, the lot!" (Foster 43).

The teacher may have been wrong to judge the impact of her lesson entirely by the exclusion of the paper bag from the costume list. After all, the children may not have looked on the dramatization as primarily an exercise in accurate reproduction of the story in the classroom, but rather as an opportunity for imaginative play.[2] However, it is noteworthy that the paper bag did not capture their imaginations, although it is featured in the title of the story and is the instrument that reveals Ronald's unworthiness. For adults who see fancy clothes as an uncomfortable restriction associated with social duty and a required display of status, the paper bag is a good joke. For the teacher, it was the price and symbol of Elizabeth's empowerment. (In the last picture in the book, after "They didn't get married after all," Elizabeth dances off into the sunset dressed only in her paper bag.) The children ignored the paper bag as both joke and symbol. Their refusal to give up satins and jewels for the utilitarian bag may be read as a refusal to exchange the extra-ordinary, the wonder of fairy tales, for a moral in a plain brown wrapper.

Further evidence of the shortcomings of *The Paper Bag Princess* as a feminist tale for young children is the effect on a young audience of the see-saw inversion of the gender roles. Like *Dealing with Dragons*, this book makes the princess the hero by discrediting the prince. Davies has documented that this confuses the children, and some of the boys refuse to make sense of the story in this way (63, 65). Carol Anne Wien noted in her review of the book in *Canadian Children's Literature* that her five-year-old son "could not bear to hear Ronald called a 'bum' and instructed the reader, 'Don't read that part; don't turn the page!'"(57). Elizabeth, like Cimorene, fails as a princess precisely because she succeeds as an individual. Ronald ultimately fails as a prince because he's a bum. On the feminist parodic see-saw, a girl who fails as a princess becomes a hero. But the prince just can't win: his failure as a hero makes him a laughing-stock. Small boys can find no acceptable role in such a story, and that is unfortunate. It seems to me a pity to visit the sins of the fathers on the heads of five-year-olds.[3]

The feminism of the two traditional parodies I have discussed is so easily recognizable, and so apparently powerful, because both are informed by the "negative evaluation" and "corrective intent" characteristic of satire (Hutcheon 54). However, as Hutcheon points out, parody need not ridicule, although ridicule is part of the common definitions of the genre. What Hutcheon calls modern parody respectfully works with or plays with the text it incorporates, and I would argue that feminism in such stories is considerably more productive, especially when the intended audience is younger children, than that which is grounded in mockery.

Catherine Storr's stories of clever Polly and the stupid wolf mark their difference from conventional fairy tales by bringing the conventions of the fairy tale into our every-day world. The wolf is a fairy tale wolf, whose role is to eat little girls, and who reads fairy tales for instructions on how to catch Polly for his next meal. Polly is a clever seven- or eight-year-old school-girl who saves herself from the wolf by using her wits. Although the parody is delightfully funny, the wolf is a real danger to Polly in the story because Storr plays with rather than debunks the tales she incorporates into her own. The joke is on this particular wolf, not on the fairy tales themselves. One example of Storr's understanding of what fairy tales are about, of what the wolf is in fairy tales, comes in "The Wolf at School" in *Last Stories of Polly and the Wolf.* Polly's class is putting on a play, Hansel and Gretel. The wolf says to Polly:

> "I know that story! They get lost in a wood, don't they? I'm sure there must have been a wolf in that wood. Woods in fairy stories always have wolves in them."
> "This one didn't. It had a witch who lived in a gingerbread house."
> "Why gingerbread? Nasty stuff. It makes my throat tickle."
> "To catch children who liked it. Then she cooked them and ate them."
> "That sounds like a good part. I shall be the witch." (8)

The wolf recognizes his role at once, as Storr does. He is the threat, the embodiment of the possibility of annihilation, whatever form it takes.

The feminist force of these stories is not, perhaps, obvious, because it is not a direct protest against the past. Polly is a hero in her own right, as Polly, rather than because she is an exception to a constricting convention. But Storr gives us an independent female hero whose competence is all the more persuasive because it is unexceptional, and she does so without closing out male readers. Such modern parodies have more of poesis in them because they are not so much concerned with kicking the stuffing out of the old as with making something new.

Two feminist fairy tales which are not parodies at all and are, as I read them, very good examples of feminist poesis, are Jane Yolen's "The Moon Ribbon" and Katherine Paterson's *The King's Equal.* "The Moon Ribbon," written for older readers, was published in 1976 in a collection of Yolen's stories to which it gives its name. The collection is now, regrettably, out of print, but this story is included in Jack Zipes's *Don't Bet on the Prince. The King's Equal* is a new picture book. Both stories use the structure and tone of a fairy tale, with no nudging or winking to mark their difference.

"The Moon Ribbon" is a Cinderella story without the ball, the slipper, and the prince, but with all the magic and high seriousness of the wonder tale. Sylva, the Cinderella figure, acts to save herself from the misery of life with her stepmother and stepsisters. Her courage comes from despair, but it is courage. Her helper, a numinous female figure whom Sylva is invited to claim as both mother and sister, teaches her that there is always a choice, and that the jewel of one's heart, oneself, can only be given with love, never under coercion. There are no men in this story, except for the father who dies on the first page "in order to have some peace" (81). It is a woman's tale of self-definition, but both women and men may choose to find meaning in it.

The King's Equal is also a serious story. Rosamund, a poor farmer's daughter, saves her people from oppression, and a cruel, grasping prince from his own arrogance, because she is kind and truly wise. She passes the prince's three tests with a little magical help and two shrewd insights of her own, and then refuses to marry him until he has passed *her* tests and is truly *her* equal. While the prince learns to know himself, Rosamund undoes all the evil he has done in the kingdom. The story ends in marriage, but Rosamund is not a prize for the prince, nor is he her salvation. Rather, she is his.

It seems to me that fairy tales like Paterson's and Yolen's are more deeply feminist than the ridiculing parodies. They are about what women can be and are, not about how women have been constructed in the past, and so they are far more immediately transformative than the parodies. Their challenge to constricting gender roles is made within the form of the fairy tale, by creating a new vision rather than contesting the old. They thus have all the power of the wonder tale to give them force, a power that is lost in ridiculing parodies. And because the expected form and tone are not altered, young readers or even younger listeners are not disrupted or confused by demands for critical reflection that they are not prepared to meet.

The ridiculing see-saw parodies seem to work from the premise that in fairy tales told straight the questing hero must inevitably be male, and the object of the quest, when it is a person, must inevitably be female. But these roles are not fundamentally male or female at the basic level of the narrative, although storytellers or readers, because of their own ideological positions, may see a particular function or relation to the events of the narrative as necessarily masculine or feminine (that is, as gendered).

I am suggesting that in considering feminist critiques of fairy tales it is important to observe the distinction narratologists make between fabula and story.[4] The material of the story, what I have called the basic level of the narrative, is the fabula. In Mieke Bal's definition, "A story is a fabula that is presented in a certain manner. A fabula is a series of logically and chronologically related events that are caused and experienced by actors" (Bal 5). At the level of the fabula, which is the material that is worked into a story, actors are not yet characters. They cause or experience events, and, as classes of actors determined by their relation to the events (actants), are distinguished only by their function as, for example, subject, object, sender, receiver, helper, or opponent. "An actor is a structural position, while a character is a complex semantic unit" (Bal 79). Neither sex nor gender (the behaviour that is deemed to be properly characteristic of one sex) is essential in the fabula. The distinct traits that transform the actors into characters are aspects of a specific story (Bal 7). The elements of the fabula—events, actors, time and location—are manipulated in their presentation as a story. "The fabula is 'treated,' and the reader is being manipulated by this treatment. *It is basically at this level that ideology is inscribed*" (emphasis added, Bal 50).

In my discussion of *The Hero and the Crown* I compared two quest-romances, McKinley's novel and Northrop Frye's epitomization of the stories of St. George and Perseus (Altmann 150). There are salient differences between the two at the level of the story, including the fact that McKinley's hero is a young woman, while St. George and Perseus, like the heroes of most traditional quest tales, are men. But at the level of the fabula, these differences disappear, and I argued that the sex of the hero is not one of the basic elements of the quest-romance. Maria Tatar makes a similar point in discussing the interpretation of fairy tales.

Once we realize that German female Cinderellas did not outnumber male Cinderellas until the eighteenth century, we look at the Grimms' version of the story with different eyes. The discovery of male Cinderellas and Snow Whites in modern Turkish folklore invites further meditations and investigations. That Russian folklore has a male Sleeping Beauty reminds us that we must show caution in drawing generalizations about female developmental patterns on the basis of that plot. And we are obliged to think twice about male hero patterns when we come across a collection of tales depicting heroines who carry out tasks normally put to male heroes alone or who denounce fathers too weak to protect them from evil-minded stepmothers (47).

Tatar confuses the issue somewhat by using the word "heroines" to refer to female heroes. She has just warned her readers that the actor who embodies the structural position of the hero at the level of the fabula is not always characterized as male at the level of the story. To label male heroes as "hero" and female heroes as "heroine" conflates actor and character, fabula and story. But in grouping Cinderellas and Snow Whites and Sleeping Beauties, Tatar is, in fact, making that distinction by recognizing similarities at the level of the fabula among different stories.

My point, then, is that at its basic level, the level of the fabula, the fairy tale does not promulgate or enforce gender roles of any type. That happens at the level of the story. Certainly, as Bal suggests, "The suspicion that the choice of a hero and of the features attributed to him or her betrays an ideological position is a reason not to ignore the problem but rather to study it" (93). But that study, and the protest or indictment that may follow from it, are properly aimed at particular stories and the societies in which they are told. For the actor becomes a character, and ideological positions are inscribed, at the level of the story, not the level of the fabula. Our images of rescuing princes and rescued princesses are formed from the fairy tales we have heard, or heard about. These stories are shaped by tellers, and, just as importantly, by listeners, in their own time and place, according to their way of understanding the world. Other fairy tales, new and old, use the same type of fabula differently.

When we are shocked into cooperative laughter by a grubby princess dressed in a paper bag or one who wants to live with dragons, it is because these characters challenge our preconceptions of what a princess in a fairy tale should be. It is important to understand that the challenge is really to our preconceptions, rather than to the material of fairy tale itself. There is no need to condemn fairy tales altogether because the ones we know seem to teach or reinforce gender roles that we have begun, for very good reasons, to question.

It is also important to understand that a feminist parody that ridicules fairy tales is not a feminist fairy tale. The intended response to a ridiculing parody is derisive laughter, rather than the wonder that a fairy tale evokes. Fairy tales aren't reclaimed or replaced by feminist see-saw parodies. Rather, they are discounted.

Certainly the critical distance of parody, particularly when it is satiric, can bring us to an awareness of the need for change, and clear the ground for it. As Stephen Jay Gould has written in another context, "We must have gadflies ... to remind us constantly that our usual preferences, channels, and biases are not inevitable modes of thought" (381). Criticism is useful because it exposes the structures that prevent us from realizing the wonder of our lives. But poesis, fairy tales like Yolen's and Paterson's, creates new images that deepen our understanding of what it is to be human and to live in the world.

Notes

1 Wrede's *Dealing with Dragons* has been a success with reviewers (it was a *Booklist* Editor's Choice, a *School Library Journal* Best Book of 1990, and a nominee for the Young Reader's Choice Award in 1993), and teachers and librarians report that it is popular with teenagers. I am not challenging these evaluations. The somewhat sophomoric humour of the extended joke is appropriate for its audience, and the writing is both competent and clever. My point is that to prefer it to *The Hero and the Crown* as a more feminist version of the same sort of tale is to confuse two genres. I do find the sequel, *Searching for Dragons*, more engaging: while it is also funny, it has more magic in it, and less of the see-saw.

2 It seems to me that any sensible child given the option will choose a ball gown over a paper bag for dressing up. A young friend of mine was dressed as the Paper Bag Princess, in a brown grocery bag, by her parents for Hallowe'en when she was two. Any doubt about the character she was impersonating, and about the authors of the impersonation, was settled by the caption written in large letters on the bag: "Our Paper Bag Princess." Now that my young friend is six, her own choice of dress-up clothing is a swirling, purple satin cape, a truly royal garment sent to her by a sensible (and feminist) aunt, and worn on every possible occasion.

3 Zipes, in his *Fairy Tales and the Art of Subversion*, acknowledges that children resist the changes in what he calls emancipatory fairy tales, but he argues that "The quality of emancipatory fairy tales cannot be judged by the manner in which

they are accepted by readers but by the unique ways they bring undesirable social relations into question and force readers to question themselves" (191). Perhaps their quality cannot be judged by the manner in which they are accepted, but I think their efficacy can. The responses that Davies, Foster, and Wien report show no signs of young readers questioning themselves, but rather simple avoidance or resistance.

4 My use and understanding of these terms relies on Mieke Bal's *Narratology: Introduction to the Theory of Narrative.*

Works Cited

Altmann, Anna E. "Welding Brass Tits on the Armor: An Examination of the Quest Metaphor in Robin McKinley's *The Hero and the Crown.*" *Children's Literature in Education* 23.3 (1992): 143-56.

Bal, Mieke. *Narratology: Introduction to the Theory of Narrative.* Toronto: U of Toronto P, 1985.

Davies, Bronwyn. *Frogs and Snails and Feminist Tales: Preschool Children and Gender.* Sydney: Allen & Unwin, 1989.

Foster, Aisling. "Narratively Challenged." *The Independent* 22 November 1992: 43-44.

Hutcheon, Linda. *A Theory of Parody: The Teachings of Twentieth-century Art Forms.* New York: Methuen, 1985.

Munsch, Robert N. *The Paper Bag Princess.* Illus. Michael Martchenko. Toronto: Annick, 1980.

Paterson, Katherine. *The King's Equal.* Illus. Vladimir Vagin. New York: HarperCollins, 1992.

Storr, Catherine. *Clever Polly and the Stupid Wolf.* Harmondsworth: Puffin, 1967.

——. *Last Stories of Polly and the Wolf.* London: Puffin, 1990.

Tatar, Maria. *The Hard Facts of the Grimms' Fairy Tales.* Princeton: Princeton UP, 1987.

Wien, Carol Anne. "Problem-solving Models for Children." *Canadian Children's Literature* 22 (1981): 56-61.

Wrede, Patricia. *Dealing with Dragons.* New York: Scholastic, 1992.

Yolen, Jane. "The Moon Ribbon." *Don't Bet on the Prince.* Ed. Jack Zipes. New York: Methuen, 1986. 81-87.

Zipes, Jack. "The Changing Function of the Fairy Tale." *The Lion and the Unicorn* 12.2 (1988): 7-29.

——. *Don't Bet on the Prince: Contemporary Feminist Fairy Tales in North America and England.* New York: Methuen, 1986.

——. *Fairy Tales and the Art of Subversion.* New York: Methuen, 1988.

Fantasy (1992)
C.W. Sullivan III

In a great many respects, fantasy literature is a nineteenth- and twentieth-century conception and creation. To some extent, publishers and booksellers have made it a category so that readers can go directly to the fantasy section of W.H. Smith's or Waldenbooks' shelves and make their selections. But fantasy literature, as an international genre, developed in response to realistic fiction, a genre only a century or so older than fantasy and itself a development of the seventeenth-century's interest in non-fiction prose—journalism, essay, history, and biography. Before the consciously realistic fiction of the eighteenth century, the *Beowulf* poet, the *Gawain* poet, Shakespeare, and Spenser (to name but the most prominent) could use what we would now call elements of the fantastic without anyone's remarking on them as such.

Lin Carter's argument, in *Imaginary Worlds*, that fantasy has been around since epic, saga, and myth suggests either a desperate attempt to provide a noble heritage for modern fantasy or a sincere misunderstanding of what modern fantasy actually is (5). Certainly, some of the elements of epic, saga, and myth—as well as legend and folktale—appear in modern fantasies, but the contemporary fantasy writer's borrowing of materials from medieval and ancient literatures for his modern text automatically makes those older narratives no more fantasy than it makes them modern. While we, as modern readers might consider *Beowulf* or *Sir Gawain and the Green Knight* pieces of fantastic literature, we have no way of knowing exactly how the original composers of or audiences for those poems felt about them.

Reality and fantasy are terms which we use today without much analytical thought, perhaps because, when we apply them to literature, we use them as labels more often than we use them as critical tools. Moreover, we have set them up as opposites when, following Kathryn Hume's lead in *Fantasy and Mimesis*, we might better see them as separate ends of a continuum. Hume suggests that:

> literature is the product of two impulses. These are *mimesis*, felt as the desire to imitate, to describe events, people, and objects with such verisimilitude that others can share your experience; and *fantasy*, the desire to change given and alter reality—out of boredom, play, vision, longing for something lacking, or need for metaphoric images that will bypass the audiences verbal defenses. (20)

All literature, then, is part mimetic and part fantastic, with what we call realistic fiction toward one end of the spectrum and what we call fantasy fiction at the other.

"*Fantasy*," Hume continues, "*is any departure from consensus reality*" (italics in original) (21). Consensus reality includes that which most of the population of a culture group believes to be or will accept as real.

Moreover, since the Renaissance and especially since the seventeenth century in England, which saw the promulgation of Francis Bacon's scientific method and the founding of the Royal Society, the real and the not-real (or fantastic) have been mutually exclusive terms, and western Europeans and Americans have been led to believe that they can know what is real and what is not. Therefore, fantasy must contain a large element of what is not real; fantasy must deal with the impossible.

In fact, "impossible" is a word which appears in a good many twentieth-century definitions of fantasy. In *An Experiment in Criticism*, C.S. Lewis defines fantasy as "any narrative that deals with impossibles and preternaturals" (50). S.C. Fredericks calls fantasy "the literature of the impossible" in "Problems of Fantasy" (37). Colin Manlove, in *Modern Fantasy: Five Studies*, suggests that "a substantial and irreducible element of supernatural or impossible worlds, beings, or objects" is essential to fantasy; and he explains "supernatural or impossible" as "of another order of reality from that in which we exist and form our notions of possibility" (3). And in *The Fantastic in Literature*, Eric Rabkin says of fantasy that "its polar opposite is Reality" (15). These definitions, and others, have led Gary K. Wolfe, in "The Encounter with Fantasy," to assert that the "criterion of the impossible ... may indeed be the first principle generally agreed upon for the study of fantasy" (1-2).

The writer cannot merely toss a few "impossible" characters, creatures, items, or events into a narrative and call it a fantasy, however; he or she must create a place in which the impossible can exist. J.R.R. Tolkien said it best in "On Fairy-Stories":

> What really happens is that the story-maker proves a successful "sub-creator." He makes a Secondary World which your mind can enter. Inside it, what he relates is "true": it accords with the laws of that world. You therefore believe it, while you are, as it were, inside. The moment disbelief arises, the spell is broken; the magic, or rather art, has failed. You are then out in the Primary World again, looking at the little abortive Secondary World from outside. (37)

Others have since made similar comments about the Secondary world. In *Touch Magic*, Jane Yolen remarks that the "amazing thing about fantasy is its absolute consistency" (77). Lloyd Alexander, in "Flat-Heeled Muse," says that the muse of fantasy writers wears "very sensible shoes" and bothers writers with questions about consistency (141-46). In *The Green and Burning Tree*, Eleanor Cameron says, "It is required of [the author] that he create an inner logic for his story and that he draw boundary lines outside of which his fantasy may now wander" (17). And Brian Attebery asserts that fantasy "needs consistency" in *The Fantasy Tradition in America: From Irving to Le Guin* (2). In light of such remarks, it might be argued (as I have in *Welsh Celtic Myth and Modern Fantasy*) that the logically-created Secondary World is the second principle generally agreed upon for the study of fantasy (94-96).

An important aspect of these two principles is that they are reader-oriented and, ultimately, dependent for their meanings upon readers who can distinguish between the possible and the impossible, the Primary World and the Secondary World. The audiences of *Beowulf* and *Sir Gawain and the Green Knight* lived in cultures whose worldview included a large component of the preternatural; their world was one of vast wilderness tracts in which anything might exist. Their world was one of magic and mystery. Modern western European/American readers live in a culture with a very small preternatural component; their world is largely explored, mapped and settled, with only a few spots in which a Bigfoot, Abominable Snowman, or Loch Ness Monster might exist. And contemporary consensus reality may, in fact, not include them either; the modern Western world is one of science and rationality.

For the modern reader, then, reality and fantasy have meanings which would not have been understood by the audience for *Beowulf* or *Sir Gawain and the Green Knight*. Although we cannot know how they might have reacted, it is doubtful that the people listening to the *Beowulf* poet would have said "Impossible!" the way modern readers of those poems would. The modern reader makes categorical distinctions between the possible (real) and the impossible (not-real) and between the Primary World and the Secondary World (and is quite comfortable doing so). Thus fantasy literature, which by these definitions and limitations is fiction set in a Secondary World where the fantastic (departures from consensus reality) occurs in believable ways, is a product of the nineteenth and twentieth centuries and should be approached as such.

* * *

It has become commonplace among social and literary historians that the Western cultural attitude toward or view of children and childhood changed early in the nineteenth century. Immediately prior to the Romantic movement, children were thought of as miniature adults, and their literature was, to a large extent, instructive without being particularly entertaining; but as the Romantic movement took hold and an emphasis on imagination, naturalness, and innocence developed, children, who were thought to possess these qualities in greater quantity and purer form than did adults, were assigned their own existence which, while still leading to adulthood, was significantly different from it.

Wordsworth's "Intimations of Immortality from Recollections of Early Childhood" separates and, at the same time, attempts to reconcile the two states of being, the child having a higher state of spiritual perception and the adult a greater capacity to know and appreciate. This focus on children as innocently and naturally perceptive has led a number of critics, especially Stephen Prickett in *Victorian Fantasy* and Humphrey Carpenter in *Secret Gardens*, to discuss fantasy in such a way as to emphasize its connection with children (and all of their literature) and de-emphasize fantasy's connection with adult literature.

Prickett concentrates on Lewis Carroll, Charles Dickens, Charles Kingsley, Rudyard Kipling, George MacDonald, and E. Nesbit. Carpenter looks closely at Charles Kingsley, Lewis Carroll, George MacDonald, and Louisa Alcott in the first section of his book and at Richard Jeffries, Kenneth Grahame, E. Nesbit, Beatrix Potter, J.M. Barrie, and A.A. Milne in the second. All of the writers and many of their books are important in the development of fantasy, and Prickett and Carpenter mention a number of others in passing; but they also leave out some important books which, if not written specifically for children, had an important formative effect on all fantasy, including children's fantasy. Four of these works, two discussed by both Prickett and Carpenter and two virtually ignored by them, are signposts in the development of fantasy in the nineteenth century.

The first is Mary Shelley's *Frankenstein*. In part, Shelley's book belongs to the horror literature tradition, and her immediate predecessors were the Gothic writers—Matthew "Monk" Lewis, Horace Walpole, Ann Radcliffe, William Beckford, and many others—of the late eighteenth and early nineteenth centuries. Like most of them, Shelley portrayed her contemporary world with something menacing added to it. In the Gothics, the menace was often, but not always, connected to the satanic or to ancient, non-Christian powers. *Frankenstein*, however, was also, if not primarily, a scientific fantasy or, more accurately, a scientific extrapolation. In his *Billion Year Spree*, Brian Aldiss credits Mary Shelley's *Frankenstein* as the first science fiction novel (20-37).

Instead of rejecting the emerging technological world, Shelley extrapolated on it. Dr Frankenstein uses the latest in medical skill and technology to create his monster, and Shelley used her extrapolation to suggest that technological capabilities were advancing more rapidly than the moral, ethical, or philosophical perceptions needed to interpret and control them. Her horror is not based on otherworldly or satanic powers using humans for evil, but on humans using their own powers with horrific results.

Rejected by his maker, the creature turns on Frankenstein and destroys everything, especially his family and his new bride, that he holds dear.

Mary Shelley's *Frankenstein* may have been the formative influence on the sub-generic category of fantasy called science fiction, but that influence was not felt in force until the twentieth century's increased interest in science and technology made science fiction a popular literature. The world may not have been quite ready for science fiction when Shelley wrote her novel, but in just half a century, her first great successor, Jules Verne, began publishing scientifically-based extrapolations featuring technological marvels, many of which actually came into being in the next century. Three decades later, H.G. Wells would begin publishing his five "scientific romances," novels which, more so than Verne's, used science fiction as a vehicle for social criticism. Ironically, Wells, like Shelley, is remembered much more for his monsters than his social criticism.

The next two books are closer to what one generally considers fantasy, and both are discussed by Prickett and Carpenter. The first is Charles Kingsley's *The Water Babies*. The main character, Tom escapes both from and to in this book. He escapes from the horrible life of a mid-nineteenth century child chimney-sweep, which Kingsley seems to have drawn in rather mimetically, and escapes into the river to become a water baby who, living in the river, discovers an essential kinship with the other river creatures. Prickett calls *The Water Babies* a "theological allegory" (51) and Carpenter remarks that it was "full ... of his personal convictions, his destructive hatred of the wrong-headedness of children's authors, and his obsession with maternal-sexual female figures and the purifying, regenerative power of cold water" (41). It is that, and more.

The Water Babies is a serious escape novel. According to Prickett, Kingsley, like many other Victorian fantasy writers, "makes use of 'another world,' but his underwater is essentially a part of this one and is ready-created for him" (156). It was this particular creation of another world that makes Kingsley's novel important here, for as Carpenter notes, Kingsley "was the first writer in England, perhaps the first in the world with the exception of Hans Andersen, to discover that a children's book can be the perfect vehicle for an adult's most personal and private concerns" (37). Explained another way, Kingsley synthesises the *story* component of literature for entertainment with the *thematic* content of the literature for instruction, successfully bringing the separate strands of late eighteenth- and early nineteenth-century children's literature together in a single novel.

The next book, George MacDonald's *The Princess and the Goblin*, is also a synthesis and, perhaps, a religious allegory. Prickett certainly thinks this way; he discusses MacDonald and Kingsley in the same chapter, "Adults in Allegory Land" (150-97). And while that interpretation has merit, Carpenter is more to the point in saying that *The Princess and the Goblin* "was in fact the first British children's book to make an utterly confident, fresh use of such traditional materials as an old fairy spinning in a tower, and a race of wicked dwarfs beneath a mountain—or, rather, beneath the castle itself" (83). MacDonald discovered that one can do more with the old tales than merely retell them; they can be a fresh source of materials with which to tell a story.

MacDonald's "confident use of traditional materials" opened the way for all manner of stories about elves, dwarfs, goblins, fairies, and the like; and it did more. It set both the *pattern* and the *style* for the fantasy novel. The pattern is that of the märchen, or magic tale, in which an ordinary mortal (who is to be the hero) is drawn into a magical adventure during which he or she is challenged and tested, through which he or she matures, and after which he or she returns "home" to dispense justice, marry, and live happily ever after (Dégh 63). Curdie and the Princess do all of this, even though they have children to carry on after they die. The style MacDonald sets is the serious and sometimes almost medieval prose style of High Fantasy which never makes fun of itself or in any way suggests that what happens in the novel is fanciful or inconsequential; it is a style appropriate to actions upon which the fate of the world may depend.

The nineteenth-century novel in which the full potential of High Fantasy was first realised was William Morris's *The Wood Beyond the World*. Prickett and Carpenter mention Morris only in passing, and that seems unfortunate. Morris's effect on fantasy was profound. *The Wood Beyond the World* synthesizes the best of what Kingsley and MacDonald contributed to the fantasy genre: style, theme, pattern, traditional materials, and the invented world. In fact, Lin Carter calls Morris's novel "the first great masterpiece of the imaginary-world tradition" (25). And it is the invented world that makes the difference.

When Golden Walter leaves Langton on Holm, he leaves the ordinary world for an imaginary medieval world, an impossible Secondary World of the sort Tolkien would not define for another four decades. Walking on the docks one day, Walter sees a ship that seems to beckon to him, and he decides to sail wherever she is going. More by instinct than plan, Walter arrives in a new land and becomes entangled with three persons he had seen several times before: a Maid, a hideous Dwarf who mistreats her, and an astoundingly beautiful woman called the Mistress who seems to control the other two. In the end, or course, Walter and the Maid marry, but the traditional adventures of the plot are carried out in a medieval world populated by characters from folktale and legend as well as from medieval history.

The Wood Beyond the World is also important as part of many nineteenth-century authors' reaction to the new emphasis on science and technology that was central to the Industrial Revolution. That reaction was founded, to some extent, by the Romantic poets, beginning with Blake's "dark Satanic mills" and continuing with the emphasis on nature and ruralness found in the poetry of Wordsworth *et al.* Even Shelley's *Frankenstein*, with its dire warnings about the possible dangers of misusing the "new knowledge" was a part of this concern. But where Shelley used the context and constructs of the new technology as a part of her fiction, Morris used the Secondary World of High Fantasy to pose an alternative, almost atechnological worldview.

These four nineteenth-century novels—*Frankenstein, The Water Babies, The Princess and the Goblin,* and *The Wood Beyond the World*—are important because they set standards for the two major branches of fantasy popular in the twentieth century: science fiction and High Fantasy. The science fiction of Robert Heinlein, Isaac Asimov, and Arthur C. Clarke is descended directly from Mary Shelley's novel; and the fantasies of Lord Dunsany, T.H. White, C.S. Lewis, and J.R.R. Tolkien are descended from the novels of Kingsley, MacDonald, and Morris. These novels establish the subject matter and the styles, the patterns and the themes, of the fantasy that is read today; and while there are more sub-genres of fantasy than the two mentioned here, they, too, have been affected by what these four authors created.

* * *

As the century turned, advances in book production were combining with advances in literacy to expand significantly the number of books and magazines available to an ever-increasing market. This market included not only a lot more books, but an even greater number of new magazines and, soon, a new kind of book, a book of smaller size, softer cover, and lower price—the paperback. Even though most children's fantasy continued to be published first (and often only) in hardback volumes, fantasy in general found its greater and more profitable home first in the magazines and later in the paperbacks.

This expanded fantasy audience has helped make children's fantasy more popular and, therefore, more possible. It has also increased the amount of fantasy being published so that there are now *categories* within which to discuss fantasy literature in the twentieth century. The following categories, and most of the books mentioned therein, are from Ruth Nadelman Lynn's *Fantasy Literature for Children and Young Adults: An Annotated Bibliography,* a most useful volume which not only categorizes and annotates but also cross references (as many fantasy books could legitimately be placed in more than one category) hundreds of fantasy books (155).

Several of Lynn's categories are relatively self-explanatory. "Allegorical Fantasy and Literary Fairy Tales" includes such examples as C.S. Lewis's Narnia books and all of Hans Christian Andersen's stories respectively. "Animal Fantasy" is split into two categories, "Beast Tales," serious and often didactic stories about animals trying to escape human evils as in Richard Adams's *The Plague Dogs* or Robert O'Brien's *Mrs Frisby and the Rats of NIMH,* and "Talking Animal Fantasy," lighter and anthropomorphic stories like Michael Bond's Paddington series or E.B. White's *Charlotte's Web.* "Magic Adventure Fantasy" includes those stories of lighter tone such as P.L. Travers's *Mary Poppins,* E. Nesbit's *The Five Children* (trilogy), and Chris Van Allsburg's *Jumanji* in which ordinary people gain special powers or otherwise come into contact with magical beings, objects, or events. A lighter tone is also present in the category of "Humorous Fantasy," examples of which are Joan Aiken's *The Wolves of Willoughby Chase* (and its sequels), Russell Hoban's *How*

Tom Beat Captain Najork and His Hired Sportsmen, and Daniel Pinkwater's *The Frankenbagel Monster*.

"Ghost Fantasy" includes Lucy Boston's Green Knowe books and Eleanor Cameron's *The Court of the Stone Children*; but Lynn saves the scarier stories for the "Witchcraft and Sorcery" category and includes John Bellairs's *The Face in the Frost*, Ray Bradbury's *Something Wicked This Way Comes*, and Diana Wynne Jones's *Fire and Hemlock* therein. "Time Travel Fantasy," which owes its greatest debt to H.G. Wells's *The Time Machine*, includes Janet Lunn's *The Root Cellar*, Jill Paton Walsh's *A Chance Child*, and Phillipa Pearce's *Tom's Midnight Garden*. "Toy Fantasy," as the name implies, focuses on fantasies whose main characters are toys (regardless, almost, of whatever else the fantasy contains) and include Margery Bianco's *The Velveteen Rabbit*, Carlo Collodi's *The Adventures of Pinocchio*, E.T.A. Hoffman's *The Nutcracker*, and A.A. Milne's *Winnie-the-Pooh*.

I mention these categories here to suggest the current scope of that which we call fantasy literature, literature which includes an element or elements of the impossible and which takes place in a Secondary World (which may only be this world with the added impossible). There is one other category in Lynn's book, indeed the largest category in the book by far, which includes those works which spring most readily to mind when one thinks of fantasy literature—works such as Ursula Le Guin's Earthsea trilogy, Lloyd Alexander's Prydain novels, Susan Cooper's "Dark is Rising" series, T.H. White's *Once and Future King*, L. Frank Baum's *The Wizard of Oz*, Lewis Carroll's Alice books, J.M. Barrie's *Peter Pan*, and perhaps the best and the brightest of all, J.R.R. Tolkien's *The Hobbit* and *The Lord of the Rings*. That category is High Fantasy.

Lynn uses the term High Fantasy for this category, and although she subdivides it into "Alternate Worlds/Histories," "Myth Fantasy," and "Travel to Other Worlds," she does not really define High Fantasy other than to say that such books "involve worlds other than our own" (155). In his generally excellent *Critical Terms for Fantasy and Science Fiction*, Gary Wolfe does little better, defining High Fantasy as "Fantasy set in a fully imagined Secondary World ... as opposed to Low Fantasy which concerns supernatural intrusions into the 'real' world" (52). These definitions may point in the right direction, but they are too broad to be of much use to someone who is not already familiar with the field of fantasy. For example, these definitions could allow a newcomer to include science fiction (travel to other worlds) in this category, even though more experienced readers and critics "know" that science fiction is quite another matter.

Lynn and Wolfe define only the location of the story; neither says anything about the style or the subject matter. Dainis Bisenieks comments, "There is no pretending, as in some modern novels, that inconsequence is the rule of life; tales of Faërie are of those who walk with destiny and must be careful what they are about" (617). As Ursula Le Guin has said:

I think "High Fantasy" a beautiful phrase. It summarizes, for me, what I value most in an imaginative work: the fact that the author takes absolutely seriously the world and the people which he has created, as seriously as Homer took the Trojan War, and Odysseus; that he plays his game with all his skill, and all his art, and all of his heart. When he does that, the fantasy game becomes one of the High Games men play. Otherwise, you might as well play Monopoly. (qtd. in Cameron, "High Fantasy" 130)

The first and perhaps most obvious indication of this seriousness lies in the writer's style. Le Guin argues, "The style, of course, *is* the book.... If you remove the style, all you have left is a synopsis of the plot" (84). Style is especially important in fantasy, Le Guin continues, because to "create what Tolkien calls a 'secondary universe' is to make a new world. A world where no voice has ever spoken before; where the act of speech is the act of creation. The only voice that speaks there is the creator's voice. And every word counts" (85).

The subject matter also makes the best High Fantasy a literature of consequence and places it in the company of the epic. As I have said elsewhere, High Fantasy implies a number of concepts which make it a particular type of fantasy: "seriousness of tone, importance of theme, characters of noble birth or lineage (secondary if not primary characters), emphasis on magic and mystery (and an almost total lack of technology and machinery as effective devices in the action), and a generally clear presentation of good and evil, right and wrong" (*Welsh* 106). And although it may be true of all High Fantasy, the High Fantasy written for children and young adults is, as Lloyd Alexander suggests, "about growing up" ("Substance" 6158) even if it does not feature a main character who ages chronologically.

More generally, High Fantasy derives much of its form and content from older literatures. The nobles knights and ladies, the magicians, the quests, the raw youth who is tested throughout before he becomes hero and king, the young girl (sometimes a princess) who will become the queen, the true companions of the hero, the villains and monsters (especially the dragons), the elves and dwarfs and goblins, the castles and caverns, and the noble ideals can be traced back through Medieval Romance, and especially the Arthurian romances, to the origins of western literature in myth, legend, and folktale. Lloyd Alexander, Alan Garner, and Kenneth Morris draw on the *Mabinogi*; Rosemary Sutcliff sets much of her fiction in very realistic ancient or Roman Britain; T.H. White bases his novel on Malory's rendition of the Arthurian materials; Mary Renault rewrites the Mediterranean stories; C.S. Lewis draws on Christian, Greek, and Norse materials for the Narnia stories; and there are many more. Even those who create their own worlds—Le Guin's Earthsea, Norton's Witch World, Tolkien's Middle Earth, and others—use characters, ideas, and constructs from myth, legend, and folktales to add depth and texture to their narratives.

Tolkien is, perhaps, the ultimate example. *The Hobbit* and, more to the point, *The Lord of the Rings* are novels in which the author creates a fully-imagined Secondary World, a world which Tolkien takes as seriously as Homer took the Trojan War, and a world in which the characters walk with destiny. The story of Frodo's attempt to return the One Ring to Mount Doom and destroy it is more than just the story of one Hobbit's quest: it is the account of a period of Middle Earth's history during which an evil power was thwarted, and the true king returned to his throne, and the fate of the known world decided for generations to come. External indications of the seriousness with which Tolkien took his narratives include the appendices to *The Lord of the Rings* as well as the whole mythology behind it later published as *The Silmarillion*. As material published since his death has shown, there was a creation of even larger than epic proportions from which *The Lord of the Rings* sprang. In many ways, Middle Earth was his life's work.

The creation of Middle Earth certainly drew heavily on Tolkien's academic life. The names of the Dwarfs in *The Hobbit* and *The Lord of the Rings* come from the Norse Eddas as do the Trolls and the Elves. Gandalf's name, from the same source, can be translated as "Sorcerer-Elf" (Sturluson 41). Beorn, the shape-changer, is a character from Scandinavian legend. Smaug, the dragon, is very similar to the dragon in *Beowulf*—right down to knowing his treasure hoard so well that he can tell when a cup is missing. Aragorn and Galadriel come from Arthurian romance. As Gandalf becomes more of a guide and a wizard, he grows to resemble Merlin. The idea of Hobbits living in caves inside hills may have come from Tolkien's knowledge of the Celtic *sidhe* dwellers. Tolkien's style, too, comes from these traditional narratives; it is the plain and direct language of the Greek epics, the Norse sagas, the *Mabinogi*, and the *Song of Roland*, valuable especially for its clarity and its flexibility (Le Guin 83).

Tolkien once intimated that *The Lord of the Rings* "contains, in the way of presentation that I find most natural, much of what I have personally received from the study of things Celtic" (1). That "way of presentation" and the borrowings I have already cited (a few of the many) have, unfortunately, left Tolkien, and the other High Fantasy writers who draw on older materials, open to the charge of being derivative. Such a charge might be true if Tolkien, or any other High Fantasy author, were trying to write a modern novel, but such is not the case. I believe that Tolkien was trying to write, in so far as such might be possible in the twentieth century, a Heroic Age narrative, perhaps an epic; and in doing so, he was following an ancient and honourable tradition (244-45). As Gerhard Herm states in *The Celts*, one of the areas of learning which the druids were to master included "all of the old stories circulating that the public invariably wished to hear again and again, in the same traditional form" (239). The ancient tellers were valued less for their creation of new stories than for their ability to tell an old story well. And judged by his performance, Tolkien is a pre-eminent storyteller.

In addition to its subject matter and style, High Fantasy also derives much of its power from the older materials it incorporates. The characters and archetypes from myth, legend, and folktale resonate with a power of their own (Hume 88). Tolkien, one example among many, uses Light to represent good and order and uses Dark to represent evil and chaos, and in doing so, he employs archetypes traceable to many ancient mythologies. But such materials must be used in ways consistent with their traditional intent or value. When the reader picks up an Arthurian fantasy, he or she has a number of expectations about what the narrative will contain. If the expectations are met, the whole narrative will be enhanced by the Arthurian inclusion; if the expectations are violated (should Arthur be cast as an evil character, for example), the reader may, reacting negatively to this use of the Arthurian materials, reject the whole book. The well-integrated narrative, then, has not only the power of the fantastic, but also the power of the traditional materials included therein.

The power of High Fantasy, Stephen Donaldson suggests, is the power to portray internal conflicts. "Put simply, fantasy is a form of fiction in which the internal crises or conflicts or processes of the characters are dramatized as if they were external individuals or events" (3-4). Ursula Le Guin says that fantasy "is a journey into the subconscious mind, just as psychoanalysis is. Like psychoanalysis, it can be dangerous; and *it will change you*" (italics in original) (84). And Lloyd Alexander asserts, "If the creator of fantasy has done his work well, we should be a little bit different at the end of the journey than we were at the beginning. Maybe just for the moment, maybe for a long while" ("Truth" 174). While these statements are true of much fantasy, they are especially true of High Fantasy; and if we understand the darker aspects of our own personalities better after Frodo's confrontation with Gollum in *The Lord of the Rings* or Ged's integration of his conscious Self with his Shadow in *A Wizard of Earthsea*, it is the result of the writer's ability to create High Fantasy and High Fantasy's power to tell us something about ourselves.

* * *

Regarded thus, fantasy is certainly not an escape literature. As Alexander notes, these fantasies "are written by adults living in an adult world, trying to cope with it and understand it, subjected to and responding to all the pressures and problems of real life. If the writer of fantasy is a serious creator, his work is going to reflect this" ("Truth" 170). *The Lord of the Rings* may, indeed, have been influenced by Tolkien's experiences in World War I, however well he kept them hidden (Brogan 353); and Grahame's *The Wind in the Willows* may, on one level, reflect a "Victorian paranoia about the mob" (Philip 313). If so, those novels are reflecting "the pressures and problems" with which Tolkien and Grahame had to deal. In this way, too, modern fantasy is a creation of the modern world.

Works Cited

Aldiss, Brian. *Billion Year Spree.* New York: Schocken Books, 1974.

Alexander, Lloyd. "Flat-Heeled Muse." *Hornbook* 41 (1965): 141-46.

——. "Substance and Fantasy." *Library Journal* 91 (1966): 6157-59.

——. "Truth About Fantasy." *Top of the News* 24 (1968): 168-74.

Attebery, Brian. *The Fantasy Tradition in America: From Irving to LeGuin.* Bloomington: Indiana UP, 1980.

Bisenieks, Dainis. "Tales from the 'Perilous Realm': Good News for the Modern Child." *Christian Century* 91.22 (1974): 617-20.

Brogan, Hugh. "Tolkien's Great War." *Children and Their Books.* Eds. Gillian Avery and Julia Briggs. Oxford: Clarendon Press, 1989. 351-67.

Cameron, Eleanor. *The Green and Burning Tree.* Boston: Little, Brown, 1962.

——. "High Fantasy: *A Wizard of Earthsea.*" *Hornbook* 47 (1971): 129-38.

Carpenter, Humphrey. *Secret Gardens.* Boston: Houghton Mifflin, 1985.

Carter, Lin. *Imaginary Worlds.* New York: Ballantine, 1973.

Dégh, Linda. "Folk Narrative." *Folklore and Folklife.* Ed. Richard Dorson. Chicago: U of Chicago P, 1972. 53-83.

Donaldson, Stephen. *Epic Fantasy in the Modern World.* Kent: Kent State University Libraries, 1986.

Fredericks, S.C. "Problems of Fantasy." *Science Fiction Studies* 5 (March 1978): 33-44.

Herm, Gerhard. *The Celts.* New York: St. Martin's, 1976.

Hume, Kathryn. *Fantasy and Mimesis.* New York: Methuen, 1984.

Le Guin, Ursula K. "From Elfland to Poughkeepsie." *The Language of the Night.* Ed. Susan Wood. New York: Berkley, 1982. 73-86.

Lewis, C.S. *An Experiment in Criticism.* Cambridge: Cambridge UP, 1965.

Lynn, Ruth Nadelman. *Fantasy Literature for Children and Young Adults: An Annotated Bibliography,* 3rd ed. New York: Bowker, 1989.

Manlove, C.N. *Modern Fantasy: Five Studies.* Cambridge: Cambridge UP, 1975.

Philip, Neil. "*The Wind in the Willows*: The Vitality of a Classic." *Children and Their Books.* Eds. Gillian Avery and Julia Briggs. Oxford: Clarendon, 1989. 299-316.

Prickett, Stephen. *Victorian Fantasy.* Hassocks: Harvester, 1979.

Rabkin, Eric. *The Fantastic in Literature.* Princeton: Princeton UP, 1976.

Sturluson, Snorri. *The Prose Edda.* Trans. J. Young. Berkeley: U of California P, 1966.

Sullivan C.W. "Name and Lineage Patterns: Aragorn and Beowulf." *Extrapolation* 25 (1984): 239-46.

——. *Welsh Celtic Myth in Modern Fantasy.* Westport: Greenwood, 1989.

Tolkien, J.R.R. "English and Welsh." *Angles and Britons.* Cardiff: U of Wales P, 1963.

——. "On Fairy-Stories." *The Tolkien Reader.* New York: Ballantine, 1966.

Wolfe, G.K. *Critical Terms for Fantasy and Science Fiction.* Westport: Greenwood, 1986.

——. "The Encounter with Fantasy." *The Aesthetics of Fantasy Literature and Art.* Ed. Roger C. Schlobin. Notre Dame: Notre Dame UP, 1982. 1-15.

Yolen, J. *Touch Magic.* New York: Philomel, 1981.

VI

Young Adult Literature

Part of the disagreement [about the term *young adult*] comes from the fact that people working with books and young readers have different training and different perspectives. Editors and authors commented that adolescent literature has "academic overtones"; English teachers said that juvenile fiction was "a publisher's term"; librarians said that "adolescent literature is what English teachers (or educators) use for young adult literature." One English teacher said she was trying to switch over to young adult literature while another one said she hesitated to use this "library term" because she wasn't sure of all the ramifications. (7)
—Kenneth Donelson and Alleen Pace Nilsen, *Literature for Today's Young Adults* (2nd ed., 1985)

[N]ovels of development and of initiation—and for that matter, children's literature—evolved during a romantic era when many authors explored individual psychology, but the YA novel, with its questioning of social institutions and how they construct individuals, was not possible until the postmodern era influenced authors to explore what it means if we define people as socially constructed subjects rather than as self-contained individuals bound by their identities. (2-3)
—Roberta Seelinger Trites, *Disturbing the Universe* (2000)

Another aspect of both the sentimentalisation of children and the sexualisation of them is that the end of childhood becomes an unwelcome event. If we value baby-smooth skin instead of unsmooth, or contoured skin, if we value flatness and small waists, hips, feet and minds it's not surprising that adolescence is seen as an unattractive development.... We have constructed childhood as a time of happiness and pure innocent joy. We have constructed adulthood as a time of anxiety, responsibility, fear of death....

It follows therefore that adolescence, being the bridge between these two opposed states, is constructed as stressful, truly a time of *sturm und drang*. In a matter of a few years—almost overnight really—the progression from joy to despair, innocence to guilt, purity to impurity, life to death, must be made. Small wonder then that the adolescent journey is so dangerous.

Some adults are not able to make the journey. They find all kinds of ways to avoid such a scary experience, notably, by staying child-like all their lives, retaining many of the characteristics of children. We can reasonably expect that part of the profile of such adults will be an idealization of childhood: an attitude that childhood is where it's at, not a real childhood of course, but a grossly distorted one, best defined by that useful word "nice." ...

We're very happy to accept the notion of a child within us. We're very unhappy at the idea of accepting the adults within our children. (paragraphs 44, 46-48, 52)

> —John Marsden, "Speech to the Sixth National Conference of the Children's Book Council of Australia, Perth, May 2002."

The chief characteristic that distinguishes adolescent literature from children's literature is the issue of how social power is deployed during the course of the narrative. In books that younger children read, such as *Peter Rabbit*, *Where the Wild Things Are*, *Alice in Wonderland*, *Winnie-the-Pooh*, *Charlotte's Web*, *Zeely*, or *Sarah Plain and Tall*, much of the action focuses on one child who learns to feel more secure in the confines of her or his immediate environment, usually represented by family and home. Children's literature often affirms the child's sense of Self and her or his personal power. But in the adolescent novel, protagonists must learn about the social forces that have made them what they are. They learn to negotiate the levels of power that exist in the myriad social institutions within which they must function, including family; school; the church; government; social constructions of sexuality, gender, race, class; and cultural mores surrounding death. (16)

> —Robert Seelinger Trites, *Disturbing the Universe* (2000)

The books that find their way into the hands of adolescents and young adults increasingly explore issues previously thought "too hot to handle" in schools: sex, drugs, alcohol, gambling, racism, abuse, and violence. Such "relevant" and "social issues" topics appear to dominate youth fiction being published at this time. As Wendy Parsons—adult reviewer and lecturer in children's literature— noted in our column, the age boundaries of reading are now very fluid, and what is obvious now is "the power of global marketing to stretch traditional categories of what will appeal to young people" (JAAL, October 2000, 188). We found that young people are aware of the practices of teachers, parents and publishers in matching books with people. They are aware of censorship: They are aware of the differences between books designed specifically for them (as an age group, a market) and those designed for adults or for younger children. Several 12-year-old reviewers who were very interested in the books they read nonetheless recommended that the books might perhaps be best given to slightly older readers than themselves. 12-year-old Kenna wrote of one book that "I would recommend [this book] for 13-17-year-olds." Of another book 12-year-old Cassandra wrote: "I think this book should have been given to high school students rather than primary school students, but some primary students like me would like it" (JAAL, December 2000/January 2001, 396). These young reviewers understood that they were complexly positioned in relation to such books. (58)

> —Helen Nixon and Barbara Comber, "Reviewing Literature for Adolescents and Young Adults: Critical Pedagogy in Action?" (2001)

Pigeonholing has always been tempting for teachers and librarians. It would be so easy if we could place students in neat categories but reality doesn't work that way. Teachers or librarians who force-feed a steady diet of either great literature or teenage books, or any other kind of book, down the gullets of young readers prove that they know nothing about them and care as little about finding out. (32)

—Kenneth Donelson and Alleen Pace Nilsen, *Literature for Today's Young Adults*
(3rd ed., 1989)

Introduction

Generally speaking, children's literature is more commonly accepted as a category than young adult literature, despite all the changes that have transpired since the rise of the latter category in the 1960s. Caroline Hunt's article "Young Adult Literature Evades the Theorists" presents the matter bluntly: "A picture-book scholar may or may not be an apologist for the nude Mickey of *In the Night Kitchen*; just about every teacher of young adult literature is an apologist for the material." Those who work in the field know full well how rich and diverse and relevant this literature is, but somehow the voices of those who haven't read widely or recently often seem to win out in school board decisions. In his "A Plea for Radical Children's Literature," Herbert Kohl argues:

The release of adolescent passion and intelligence, when validated, can explode into learning. It is a positive force that is too often repressed in schools. Young people who are silent, who sit with their heads down on the desk and pretend to be asleep, can be awakened by literature that speaks to their worries, validates their experience, and offers them a future less horrible than their present. (74)

Young adults, like children, need encouragement from courageous adults to help them through the sloughs of conformity their social environments often seek to enforce. Virginia Monseau's collaborative work with young adults of different ages and reading abilities and with adult readers ("Responding to Response") chronicles the potentiality of young adult literature that is supported by Helen Nixon and Barbara Comber's work on the *JAAL* [*Journal of Adolescent and Adult Literacy*]. Anne Scott Macleod ("The Journey Inward: Adolescent Literature in America, 1945-1995") and Caroline Hunt provide overviews of the development of the literature and the criticism respectively, from a primarily American perspective, as well as giving many useful references for further reading. Geralde Schmidt-Dumont's "Report from Germany" provides a European counterpoint to the seemingly inevitable polarity between the conservative forces that wish to scrub sex clean from reading for young adults and those that dare to "grow the mind one size larger" (Hearne 571). As Peter Hollindale argues in "The Adolescent Novel of Ideas," it is vitally important to recognize challenging young adult literature because it "speaks with particular directness to the young adult mind—the mind which is freshly mature and intellectually confident, mentally supple and relatively free of ideological harness" (86). This window of intellectual freedom is an opportunity that is soon closed off. By the time young adults enter university, many of them are relatively hampered by "ideological harness"—it takes considerable effort for them to untangle themselves from received ideas and constantly reinforced perspectives, particularly where children are concerned. Perhaps this rigidity regarding their views of children and teenagers comes from a desire to be responsible and protective of a younger generation; nevertheless, it is remarkable how quickly the frustrating restrictions on youth are forgotten (or repressed!) by many adults of all ages. Reading children's and young adult books can help to clear the window of intellectual freedom, and sometimes it opens views to forgotten passions.

Works Cited

Donelson, Kenneth and Alleen Pace Nilsen. *Literature for Today's Young Adults.* 2nd ed. Glenview, IL: Scott, Foresman, 1985. 7.

———. *Literature for Today's Young Adults.* 3rd ed. Glenview, IL: Scott, Foresman, 1989. 32.

Hearne, Betsy. "Hamilton, Virginia." *Twentieth-Century Children's Writers.* Ed. D.L. Kirkpatrick. New York: St. Martin's, 1978. 569-71.

Hollindale, Peter. "The Adolescent Novel of Ideas." *Children's Literature in Education.* 26.1 (1995): 83-95.

Kohl, Herbert. "A Plea for Radical Children's Literature." *Should We Burn Babar?: Essays on Children's Literature and the Power of Stories.* New York: The New Press, 1995. 57-93.

Marsden, John. "Speech to the Sixth National Conference of the Children's Book Council of Australia, Perth, May 2002." *John Marsden.* 18 January 2006. <http://www.panmacmillan.com.au/johnmarsden/jmscbc0205.txt.1>.

Nixon, Helen and Barbara Comber. "Reviewing Literature for Adolescents and Young Adults: Critical Pedagogy in Action?" *Papers: Explorations into Children's Literature* 11.2 (2001): 56-65.

Trites, Roberta Seelinger. *Disturbing the Universe: Power and Repression in Adolescent Literature.* Iowa City: U of Iowa P, 2000. 2-3.

The Journey Inward:
Adolescent Literature in America, 1945-1995 (1997)
Anne Scott Macleod

The end of the Second World War brought the United States a prosperity that for two decades reached nearly every level of American society. It also opened a half-century that would give adolescents greater freedom, greater economic power, and more adult attention, both approving and otherwise, than at any other time in American history. The juncture between adolescence and economics was not at all coincidental; puberty is biological, but the nature, length, burdens, and hazards of adolescent experience are shaped by economic and social realities. In the Depression and the war years, American youngsters moved quickly through adolescence into adult responsibilities. After 1945, as prosperity made the earnings of teenagers less necessary to their families, society could, and did, mandate a longer period of education. By 1960, high school attendance became nearly universal in the United States, stretching young adult dependency at least through four years of secondary school. The same period saw adolescents become a prime consumer market. Since many teenagers worked part-time, and since family incomes often allowed them to keep their wages, adolescents became avid consumers of carefully targeted leisure products, including films, recordings, magazines, and, of course, books.

Adolescent fiction has continued as a major subset of children's literature. The novels evolved over five decades as society, demographics, and a changing economy altered the experience and the expectations of the young. Stated broadly, and ignoring variations that inevitably exist in so large a literature, the path of American adolescent novels has been from outward to inward; from concern with the young adult's relationship to the larger community to a nearly exclusive emphasis on the adolescent's inner feelings. Over the same period, the social distance between adults and adolescents has diminished. The contemporary fictional adolescent is less firmly attached to traditional family structures, more autonomous, on more nearly equal terms with adults than were the fictional youngsters of earlier literature.

From 1945 to about 1965, adolescent novels sang of intact families, affection between parents and children, and an accepted hierarchy of adult over child. Apart from their contemporary language, the stories would have seemed quite familiar to readers of the nineteenth century, committed as they were to proving the rightness of home-taught values. Patricia Spack, in her study of adult fiction about adolescents, notes that eighteenth- and nineteenth-century moralistic texts offered fantasies of ideal adolescents who combined "the rationality of the adult with the compliance of the child" (25, 26). So, too, did the teen novels of the first two postwar decades. In the work of mainstream authors like Beverly Cleary, Lenore Weber, and Madeleine L'Engle, girls complied with conventional expectations and were rewarded with the affection of family and friends, and the attentions of a truly nice boy. Boys' stories taught similar lessons, though against tougher odds. Henry Felsen's stories about car-crazy high school boys rang with adult concern over the explosive mix of youth and gasoline. The stakes were high, and Felsen's instructive plots hit harder than the mild tales written for girls. In the end, however, even reckless boys learned to heed adult counsel and to conform to conventional social mores. While the postwar era had its share of anxiety over adolescents, the literature on the whole conveyed confidence that community values would prevail.

The social revolutions of the 1960s and 1970s, however, transformed literature for the young. The literary model for most teen novels became J.D. Salinger's *The Catcher in the Rye*, so much so that by the 1970s the first-person narratives of an alienated adolescent commenting on and rejecting the tainted mores of adult society were a cliché of adolescent fiction. *Catcher*, however, is neo-Romantic: the protagonist is idealistic and kind-hearted, a better person than any of the adults who fail and betray him. Adolescent literature adopted the alienation of the Salinger model, and the rejection of conventional values, but not the Romanticism that gilded its hero. Protagonists of the new teen novels were rarely romanticized; they were just lost and unhappy and remarkably passive in their distress. They were not idealistic but cynical. To these fictional adolescents, their alcoholic mothers and deserting fathers justified their scorn of adult values, but remarkably few of them thought about other, more satisfactory ways to live. In fact, they seldom envisioned a future in which they actually did anything other than survive.

While this literature was clearly shaped by social and political events, the books read less like social criticism than like private psychotherapy sessions. Authors said little directly about society's flaws, but much about adolescents as victims of society and especially of their families; they took a therapeutic approach to their protagonists, suggesting that they look inward for the emotional strength they needed, since the adult world could not—or would not—help them. They shifted the focus of adolescent development from adaptation to a larger world to contemplation of the inner self, a contemplation that was neither spiritual nor intellectual, but psychological. The task for adolescents in these books had less to do with finding a place in society than with achieving a tolerable level of emotional comfort. John Donovan's 1969 novel says a good deal in its title alone: *I'll Get There. It Better Be Worth the Trip*. "There" is undefined, but the implied goal here, as in most of the literature, is little more than simple survival—getting through the teen years to the equally undefined territory beyond.

The inwardness of these novels is striking; so is the nearly universal hostility toward adults in general and families in particular. The first-person voice offers no moderating commentary on the thesis—again all but universal in the fiction—that adults are unhappy, ineffectual beings who have nothing to teach the young. Few 1970s authors tried to defend either the family as an institution or the values of the adult society.

Since 1980, the bleakness of the literature has modified, but the basic landscape is in many respects unchanged. Fictional adolescents still struggle with a dysfunctional society, still deal with adults who are mostly unable to offer much help, and still contend with a staggering range of personal problems. Two differences stand out, however. First, fewer authors insist on the total isolation of their protagonists. Though some repeat the formulas of the 1970s, most 1980s and 1990s novels acknowledge that human beings need other human beings. Family, defined broadly as people who care about one another, whether related or not, is understood to be important. Second, fictional adolescents are less passive now than they were in the 1970s. They are still largely on their own, but in many novels they have the resources, in the form of friends, emotional maturity, and an occasional helpful adult, to deal with serious problems and even to arrive at an outlook that accommodates the pain of experience without blighting all hope.

One contemporary novelist brings together a number of the elements that seem to me to distinguish current adolescent literature from that of the 1970s. Chris Crutcher has published six novels since 1983, and while his work is not prototypical, his sense of the middle-class adolescent's world, and of the relations between adults and adolescents, has many echoes in contemporary young adult novels.

Crutcher's characters are high schoolers on the brink of adulthood. Unlike the adolescents of 1970s fiction, they are not isolated but living—not always peacefully—within a web of relationships with friends, teammates, coaches, teachers, and school life. Their lives are as riddled with problems as any in the sixties-seventies era: these teenagers contend with sexual and physical abuse, tragic death, crippling accidents—but the stories and the moral judgments are more complex.

What emerges from Crutcher's books is a general picture of adult-adolescent relationships in a new age. The affection and respect between generations, so taken for granted in the 1940s and 1950s and so thoroughly repudiated in the 1960s and 1970s, are reinstated, but with profound differences. Neither is automatic; they must be earned, as they are between adults. Parental authority, insofar as it exists, is influence, and is granted by the child. Crutcher's protagonists are on generally easy terms with their parents, though scarcely in the 1950s mode. They are casually knowledgeable about adult sexuality, even in connection with parents and teachers—unthinkable in the past but emblematic of the shrinking social distance between generations in adolescent fiction.

Yet teenagers are not adults, as they well know. A recurrent figure in Crutcher novels is a coach or a trainer who functions as a guru. He or she challenges students to stretch their physical limits, inducing the Zen experience of dissolving boundaries between action and actor, and—sooner or late—supplies tough-minded wisdom. It is to these gurus that protagonists turn when troubles pile up, and it is they, rather than parents, who voice the philosophy that Crutcher offers to the young.

The advice is therapeutic—personal and limited. There are no universal moral systems invoked, no absolute codes of behaviour, no comprehensive attempts at explaining the evil in the world (and there is evil in these books). Adolescents are counselled to accept what is, and to take responsibility for their own actions. Their attention is directed to their own behaviour, and to that alone, as one coach says:

> All you have in this world, really, are your responses to it. Responses to your feelings and responses to what comes in from outside.... That's all responsibility is, responding to the world, owning your responses. It isn't about taking blame or finding out if something's your fault.... You have no control over the world. You have no control over anyone except you. (Crutcher 122, 123)

This advice, like the trauma that brought it about, is a far cry from the mild dilemmas and comfortable messages of teen fiction in the 1950s. Today's adolescent literature reflects fundamental revisions in American social attitudes and in the structural arrangements of American families. Ironically, the revisions had their roots in the 1950s, though authors of adolescent novels, like most other Americans in that complacent era, hardly noticed. The agent of change was the same affluence that made Americans sure that they lived in the best of worlds. As prosperity extended adolescence, promoted consumerism, and gave adolescents unprecedented freedom via cars and spending money; as growing numbers of women began to work outside the home; as government assumed greater responsibility for the welfare of the old and the poor, family expectations, for parents and children alike, began to change. The reciprocal obligations of kinship diminished, and the autonomy of both adults and children increased.

The 1960s and 1970s are now synonymous with social upheavals, including the remaking of the family. Adolescent fiction responded not with an accurate picture of the new social landscape, but with the highly ambivalent adult reaction to it. It was an oddly unsympathetic literature. As harshly as authors criticized adult society for failing children, they rarely conveyed much warmth toward the alienated young who were its victims. Like most other adults, authors had mixed feelings about rebellious teenagers, and little counsel to offer. They understood no better than the young what had gone wrong or how it was to be mended. If fitting into the existing society and accepting its values was no longer the definition of growing up, it was not at all clear what was.

Nor is it now. Some Americans hope to restore 1950s calm by reconstructing the traditional family. But the realities of a postindustrial economy argue against such simplicities. In the 1990s, not affluence but a society with little need for unskilled labour dictates extended education and therefore years of semidependence for young adults. Together with high divorce rates, greater fluidity in working careers, and long life expectancy, the need to support children well past legal majority has altered the relations between men and women as well as between adults and children. It is hard to imagine families returning wholesale to the man-as-breadwinner, woman-at-home pattern of the past. The autonomy of today's young adults is not, as in the past, the independence of full-time workers. Autonomy now is emotional, not economic, a product of new family arrangements and of the earlier exposure of children to adult life, in reality and on television. In spite of political agitation, these developments are not likely to reverse.

Contemporary mainstream adolescent literature has absorbed most of these changes. The fiction as a whole accepts nontraditional models of family, concedes the sexual knowingness of the young, and acknowledges a more equal standing of adolescents with adults. The definition of maturity is still unclear, but where it comes through—as in Crutcher's work—it is personal rather than social. Very little in contemporary adolescent fiction suggests that maturity requires or even involves taking a stand on social needs, problems, prospects, or failures. There are many implied and explicit *values* in the literature—kindness, tolerance, antiracism—but little critique of a social system that often ignores these. It is even rare for modern protagonists to come to any conclusions about their future role in the world, as earlier fictional adolescents so often did. The late twentieth century has granted adolescents a level of personal freedom undreamed of in the 1940s, 1950s, and 1960s, yet the literature seldom suggests that adolescents can or even want to translate that freedom into the power to change a society that manifestly fails them.

Works Cited

Crutcher, Chris. *Chinese Handcuffs*. New York: Dell, 1983.
Donovan, John. *I'll Get There. It Better Be Worth the Trip*. New York: Harper & Row, 1969.
Salinger, J.D. *The Catcher in the Rye*. Boston: Little, Brown, 1951.
Spacks, Patricia Meyer. *The Adolescent Idea: Myths of Youth and the Adult Imagination*. New York: Basic Books, 1981.

From "Responding to Response" in *Responding to Young Adult Literature* (1996)
Virginia Monseau

> Every reader's response matters. Writers need readers to complete the work of the book. That's not something we're often taught in school.
>
> —Sandy Asher

As both a teacher and an interested reader, I can't resist making a few observations about what is documented in the chapters of this book and what I've seen in my research of the last two years. As I've watched and listened to readers interact with young adult novels in various circumstances, I've become more convinced than ever of the folly of labelling literature according to who should read it. Just a glance at what took place with the advanced placement students described in Chapter 3 ["Voight and Kafka; Crutcher and Camus: Responding to Young Adult Literature in the Advanced Placement Class"] and the adult readers in Chapter 6 ["What's Age Got to Do with It? Adults Respond to Young Adult Literature"] is enough to trigger regret that certain literature has limited exposure because it happens to focus on the lives of people between the ages of twelve and eighteen. I hope you'll compare the observations of mine that follow with your own and that my thoughts might initiate a dialogue about YA literature that will continue into the future.

Young Adult Literature across Learning Tracks

Engagement was the order of the day for most students, regardless of their academic ability, when they read Robert Cormier's *After the First Death*. Because they cared about and could identify with the characters, students entered the world of the book almost automatically—slipping into the bus seat next to Kate, sitting with Miro and Artkin in the restaurant, standing next to Ben on the bridge. No matter what their reading level, the students wondered about Artkin's use of "the fingers" to torture Ben; wanted to understand why General Marchand sacrificed his son Ben for "the cause"; and condemned Miro for killing Kate. And, interestingly enough, all the students focused on Miro more than any other character in their writing and discussion. Something about him put them in touch with their own loss of innocence, with a contradiction in themselves unconsciously suppressed.

Basic Ninth Graders

Perhaps the most surprising reaction came from the ninth graders in the basic class, who weren't expected to understand the novel—or even read it by themselves. Though there were probably several who lived up (or down) to this expectation, the students who did read and discuss the book showed remarkable insight for supposed nonreaders. The males in the class were most vocal—perhaps because of the book's subject matter—but one or two female students showed an active interest in Kate. I found it intriguing that those who took part in the discussion—Jason and Derek—were confident of their interpretations and seemed unaware that they were tackling the most difficult aspects of the book. I wonder what might have happened if their teacher hadn't led the book discussion with questions—whether the students would have talked more about their own reactions to the book, as they began to do in the collaborative activity "Hit Vids!".

As a result of my research I became particularly interested in Jason, who, as I noted in Chapter 1 ["Having Their Say: Responding to Young Adult Literature in the Basic English Class"], contradicted all my assumptions about reluctant readers. Through more investigation I learned that Jason was mostly a D student, and had received one B in a reading class in junior high. Raised by his grandparents, he fell into bad company early and had missed over forty days of school the previous year. While the missionary in me wanted to take Jason by the hand and lead him down the path of literacy, the realist in me said that the Jasons of the world are on their own—unless the system changes. And we teachers are, after all, part of the system. Somehow we have to find ways to plug the cracks that the Jasons keep falling through. We may be holding one of those plugs in our hands when we hold a young adult novel. YA literature isn't the answer to everything, but we have to start somewhere.

Advanced Ninth Graders

Just as I was pleased to see the confidence with which the basic ninth graders expressed their views in discussions, I was a little surprised at the tentativeness of the advanced students when they discussed *After the First Death* among themselves in small groups. They were just as curious about the novel's events as the other students were, but they felt more secure asking their teacher for the answers to difficult questions than they did developing those answers themselves. I attribute this to the students' conditioning and to their emphasis on getting the "right" answer, and I see a potential problem in the students' lack of confidence in their own interpretation skills. It's not my intention here to disparage the literary classics, but we can't ignore the way these more difficult pieces of literature may influence student confidence. If readers in advanced classes are accustomed to waiting to hear their teacher's interpretation of a work before they venture one of their own, they may think twice—especially if a grade is involved—before they make a definite statement about any work. In Chapter 2 ["More than an Easy Read: Responding to Young Adult Literature in the Honors Class"], for example, we saw the students who felt it necessary to ask Marcia whether or not Artkin was Miro's "first death." When, instead of giving a straight answer, Marcia tried to lead the students to come to their own conclusion, the group remained unsure. This is only one documented incident, of course, but in classroom observations over the years I've seen many similar occurrences. It seems to me that this is a matter worthy of more study.

Advanced Placement Twelfth Graders

Unlike the advanced ninth graders, the advanced placement seniors had no lack of confidence in expressing their interpretations. Perhaps this tells us that such insecurities go away as students mature, or perhaps it means that academically insecure ninth graders don't go on to advanced placement work. Whatever it means, the students I observed subjected the young adult literature they read to the same kind of scrutiny they gave other literary works. These particular students were in their second year of AP English, so they were well trained in the art of discussion. There *was* a difference in the level of intensity between the two classes I observed, just as there was a difference in the aspects of the novel they chose to discuss. The AP students were certainly more global in their concerns than were the ninth graders, and their discussions focused on the more sophisticated concepts of tragedy and existentialism.

As I sat in on classes with these students and read their writing, I sensed a real tension between what they thought was good reading and what they felt was good for them. As the transcripts in Chapter 3 ["Voigt and Kafka; Crutcher and Camus: Responding to Young Adult Literature in the Advanced Placement Class"] reveal, their talk was directed by teachers' questions about the nature of tragedy in *After the First Death* and the existential philosophy in *Running Loose*, though we do get some idea of their personal identification with the works— especially with *Running Loose*. The tension is more apparent, though, in the students' written answers to my questions about reading young adult literature in the AP class. Their comments give me the feeling that, on the one hand, they have an image to uphold—the image of the super smart kids who read and analyze only the most difficult literature; but, on the other hand, they want to understand the power of literature—the power felt when a book connects to their lives, moving them to anger, frustration, or tears. For these students, the difference seems to be between intellectual engagement and emotional engagement. While they were intellectually intrigued by Meursault's actions in *The Stranger*, for example, they were emotionally challenged by Louie Banks's moral courage in *Running Loose*. Such polarities created a conflict for them: How can an American novel about a seventeen-year-old protagonist, written only a few years ago by a relatively new author, compare with a French classic, written in 1942 by a man who later won the Nobel Prize for Literature? Though such a question smacks of literary snobbery, conflicts like this are of real concern to students trying to feel their way across the political landscape of academe.

The answer is that there's no answer. Different literature does different things for different readers. If students come into an AP English class assuming that they're going to read only the literary classics that will help them score well on the national AP exam, the mindset is already there—and the AP exam being what it is, that mindset is justified. (In fairness to the AP test makers, they do now say that students may use appropriate young adult literature to answer open-ended exam questions; however, most of the students I observed seemed unwilling to take the risk. It's going to take much more evidence from the College Board and from AP teachers that intellectual and emotional engagement are valued equally before students feel comfortable writing about contemporary works of young adult fiction.) For the most part, high school students—especially those in AP classes—think in terms of what reading literature does *for* them, not what it does *to* them, so their ambivalence about YA literature is not surprising. As they've made their way through school, students have learned that many literature scholars disdain works enjoyed by the general public, preferring esoteric works that are inaccessible to any but the "best" minds. The credo of these scholars might be, "If you can't understand it, it must be good literature." Unless attitudes change drastically—and I don't expect they will anytime soon—young adult literature will remain, at best, a welcome diversion that helps AP students better understand the classics, but that doesn't stand on its own as a component of the AP English curriculum. What YA literature does to these students as young adult readers is another matter entirely.

Collaboration through Young Adult Literature

When I first had the idea of bringing basic and advanced ninth graders together to work on a literature simulation in response to a young adult novel, I had misgivings. I worried that the students wouldn't talk to each other, wouldn't feel comfortable together. I fretted about the difficulty of the project—was I asking too much of them in a forty-five-minute class period? Most of all, I was concerned that the project would fail—that I would learn nothing of interest. As it turned out, I learned a great deal about how ninth graders read young adult literature, how they respond to the literature within certain constraints, and how they interact with each other in a collaborative situation.

More than ever, I'm convinced of the value of teachers and students reading and studying literature together. We have not employed collaborative study much in literature classes—even though we may see its value in teaching writing—and collaborative literature study across learning tracks is virtually unheard of. For the most part, students in literature classes read alone, answer study questions alone, and take tests alone. True, they do have the opportunity to participate in class discussion, but they are still alone with their thoughts about their reading and still alone when they venture an interpretation or a question about a work. The students who participated in the "Hit Vids!" simulation didn't have to worry about isolation. They could toss ideas at each other, reject some, accept others, and come up with a variety of responses to *After the First Death.* I'm sure the experience of planning and writing together resulted in learning that can't be observed or measured, learning that may surface at other times in the students' lives. Allowing students to collaborate on literature study—whether it's working through a simulation, generating questions about their reading, or answering questions they have about a work—removes the tension that often exists when students worry about having the right interpretation of a work. It offers fresh perspectives, nudging readers toward different ways of looking at a text. It encourages them to be student critics and to explore the aspects of a work that are meaningful to them, not just to perform superficial exercises designed by their teacher or a textbook. Students will become much more familiar with a work through this kind of study than they ever will by answering preconceived study questions.

My college students, many of whom are education majors, often ask me how they can study for a literature exam—particularly when they will have to answer essay questions. They are used to reading for the facts, listening to lectures, taking notes, and answering objective test questions. I tell them to study together—to talk through the literature, to review each work we've read, to ask each other questions about what puzzles them. Many of these students have commented that they learned much through this kind of study, and they invariably do well on essay questions. What I haven't yet done is give my students the opportunity to collaborate with one or two others on an exam—to write together about the works we've read, perhaps learning as they write. When I was a student this would have been called cheating. Answers were your own and not to be shared with others. You covered your paper as you wrote and turned it facedown when you were finished. The contest was to determine who was the smartest and who could remember the most. Learning didn't seem to have much to do with it. Of course, this attitude still exists in some classrooms, but more and more educators are becoming aware that true learning is an *experience,* not an exercise. The only cheating occurs when students are denied the chance to have such an experience.

Allowing students to study literature collaboratively has benefits for teachers, too. Our first thought might be, "Yes! A lighter paper load!" but there are even better reasons to encourage working together. We teachers do an incredible amount of preparation when we introduce a literary work. In addition to reading the work again and again to refresh our memories, we generate questions for students to answer, create activities and projects related to the literature, compose lecture material, and devise test questions. Then we must orchestrate discussions, field questions, and generally try to keep students interested in the literature. And we do this for each work we teach. No wonder we're exhausted. We're doing all the work. Why not spread it around a little? If we know our John Dewey, we should remember that students learn by doing (or as one of my cornier professors put it, "learn by Dewey-ing"), and this applies to literature study, too. Self-preservation aside, we must get our students involved in the reading and study of literature if we ever hope to make the works come alive for them.

Young adult literature is the perfect vehicle for encouraging this kind of involvement, since the works are so accessible to students. It might even be worthwhile to let students try their hand at teaching a short story or two to the class, in pairs or in small groups. I guarantee that they will know the work thoroughly by the time they finish.

Adults Reading Young Adults

One of the things I was most curious about when I began my research was what I might find when I looked systematically at the responses of adults to young adult literature. Aside from critical and pedagogical articles by teachers and scholars, little documentation of adult response is available outside of anecdotal evidence. Why is adult response important? Because one of the loudest criticisms of young adult literature is that its appeal is limited, and adult response can either support or refute that contention. It's no secret that many adults, even teachers, are condescending in their views of young adult literature. I suspect that their attitude stems in part from the literature they remember reading as adolescents—the series books, the formulaic romances, and the career books that were common in the 1940s and 1950s. Such condescension reveals a failure to keep abreast of the latest developments in literature, which is not a good excuse for criticizing what young people are reading today.

Another less understandable and far more dangerous reason that some adults shun young adult literature is the elitist belief that anything adolescents read and enjoy must somehow be inferior in quality to adult literature. While this reasoning is likely to be more prevalent in college English departments, it exists among the general public as well. The danger of this kind of thinking is the way it stigmatizes adolescents as being a sort of less-intelligent subspecies that's incapable of literary discrimination. Because adults who hold such a belief have never read the works of authors like Robert Cormier,

Cynthia Voigt, Bruce Brooks, and Kathryn Lasky, they make unwarranted assumptions based on their own uninformed biases. There is a third group also—though their number is happily decreasing. These are the adults who have never heard the term "young adult literature," even though they may have read books marketed in this category. These adults are perhaps the easiest to convince, since they come to the literature free of preconceived notions about its value.

The responses of the adults noted in Chapter 6 ["What's Age Got to Do with It?: Adults Respond to Young Adult Literature"] reveal an astonishing engagement with various works of young adult literature. Subjecting the novels to the scrutiny with which they read all literature, these adults found in the books universal elements that are sometimes missed by younger readers—evidence of the layering that characterizes all literature of quality. They approached each novel expecting the author to be skilful, thought-provoking, and entertaining. When their expectations weren't met, they attacked the aspects of the work that failed to measure up. But unlike the high school students and undergraduates who failed to see that disliking a book is often a reflection of the author's craft, these readers were quick to acknowledge the artistic skill of writers like Cormier and Myers while at the same time criticizing the writers' motivation and purpose. The charge of some critics that there is nothing to say about young adult literature is refuted in responses that identify *After the First Death* as a post-modernistic "systems novel" written in the manner of Don DeLillo's *White Noise*, and that compare the "angel warriors" in Myers' *Fallen Angels* to the fallen angels in Milton's *Paradise Lost*. Similarly, if a nonfiction work like Anson's *Best Intentions* can engender such a powerful response in a young mother of African American descent, it merits reading by other adults, for we are all responsible for a society that creates and destroys the Eddie Perrys of the world.

Not all of the adults' responses were positive. That's to be expected. But their engagement and insightful analysis should be enough to make sceptics take another look at this genre, which is producing some fine writing. Like literature classified as "adult," young adult literature does have its clunkers, but only the unfair and uninformed will judge all young adult works by the worst among them.

Works Cited

Anson, Robert Sam. *Best Intentions: The Education and Killing of Edmund Perry*. New York: Vintage, 1987.

Cormier, Robert. *After the First Death*. New York: Dell, 1979.

Crutcher, Chris. *Running Loose*. New York: Dell, 1983.

DeLillo, Don. *White Noise*. New York: Penguin, 1986.

Myers, Walter Dean. *Fallen Angels*. New York: Scholastic, 1988.

Poetic Encryption and "Sex Scrubbed Clean":
A Report from Germany (1994)
Geralde Schmidt-Dumont

One of the greatest challenges facing teenagers anywhere is the search for a personal identity, for one's "self." During this tumultuous process, young people must learn to cope with the physical changes their bodies are undergoing; explore and accept gender and societal roles; "test out" their ability to attract one another; and experience their first sexual encounters. Books that are read during this period are often selected in the hope that they will provide guidance, not just fun. In addition to the entertainment value of reading, young people are also looking for practical information to help them cope with their day-to-day existence, even in works of fiction. They seek information about sexuality, about conventional and alternative social norms and lifestyles, and help in developing their problem-solving and communication skills. Yet it is not only a reflection of their own realities that they are seeking, but also of their unfulfilled wishes, fears, fantasies, and possible futures.

Strategies of Avoidance and Intimation

In this quest for information and guidance, the foremost topic of interest for many adolescents, in Germany as elsewhere, is sex. Yet until the 1960s, sexuality was a taboo topic in books for children and young people. Though a natural part of human living and loving, it was simply ignored or left out. This was only one consequence of a pervasive speechlessness when it came to bodily functions in general. Authors simply talked around the topic or ignored it altogether. For those authors who dared to broach the subject, there was no generally accepted "language of sexuality" they could fall back on. Instead, they had to employ a language of concealment or vague intimation, a strategy which inevitably left a great deal to the fantasy of the reader. Ironically, these open spaces had a highly erotic effect: Scenes that had been deliberately left out by the author sparked in young readers a vivid imaginative response—far more vivid, perhaps, than would have been evoked by the explicit account. And so in the reader's mind, the scissors of censorship had quite the opposite effect of what their wielders had intended.

Over the years, other authors for young people have rescued themselves from the brink of transgression by using metaphor as a means of poetic encryption that does not refer overtly to sexuality, but instead captures in images what is experienced and felt by the characters. This strategy has led writers to distance themselves from customary language and conventional modes of expression, creating a certain semantic tension and, in the best cases, raising their stories to the level of the uncommon and poetic. Such texts throw readers off balance, surprise them, make them reflect on what actions and meanings underlie the metaphoric language. Noteworthy examples of this are Wolfgang Gabel's *Immer zusammen frühstücken* (1977; in English as *Breakfast Together for Always* [1980]), Wolf Spillner's *Die Wasseramsel* [The water-blackbird] (1984), and Doris Meißner-Johannknecht's more recent *Amor kam in Leinenschuhen* [Amor came in canvas shoes] (1993).

Writers for young people also use imagery and symbolism to "translate" harsh realities into a form that can be grasped on a non-intellectual level by young readers, especially useful when dealing with the topic of sexual abuse. Books tackling this difficult subject matter must proceed with caution and avoid potentially jarring directness. For example, in Ellen Howard's *Lilians Geheimnis* (1988; orig. *Gillyflower* [1986]), an abuse victim retreats with her fear, shame, and self-doubt to a hiding place under a rhododendron bush. There she escapes into the fairytale land of the beautiful princess Juliana, where the real-life situations she faces are carefully recast and interpreted through her fantasy stories about the princess. This strategy creates a poetic superstructure, giving form and expression to Lilian's temporarily split personality as she grapples with her feelings toward her father and her surroundings.

As long as certain behaviour—homosexuality, for example—was not officially sanctioned in children's literature, authors who nonetheless elected to write about it did so using a disingenuous language through which a character's actions could be interpreted by the reader in a variety of different ways. Homosexual conduct was alternately presented as if it were a socially recognized friendship, a case of adolescent excess, a temporary phase, an infatuation triggered by another's stronger charisma, or the search of young, lonely people for human closeness and security. The author's true intent, of course, was to find a literary vehicle for the expression of homoerotic drives, and savvy readers knew how to read between the lines. Several books in this vein come to mind: Herbert Günther's *Unter Freunden* [Among friends] (1976), John Donovan's *Du sagst ja, ich sag' nein* (1976; orig. *I'll Get There. It Better Be Worth the Trip* [1969]), Tilman Röhrig's *Langes Zwielicht* [Long twilight] (1974), Monika Seck-Agthe's *Morella* (1983), Deborah Hautzig's *Hallo, Englechen* (1984; orig. *Hey Dollface* [1978]), Hannelore Krollpfeiffer's *Die Zeit mit Marie* [The time with Marie] (1986), and Kirsten Holst's *Ganz nah und doch so fern* [So near and yet so far] (1992).

The Not-So-Revolutionary Sexual Revolution

The Woodstock generation of the late 1960s saw as its mission the "liberation" of the people and regarded openly expressed sexuality as a means to escape degradation and oppression. During this self-declared sexual revolution, previously subversive expressions of sexuality gained social acceptance, but were then, in turn, domesticated, scrubbed clean, commercialized, and even didacticized. Certainly there were anarchic outbursts from time to time, but the Woodstock generation actually had very rational and even quite traditional Enlightenment goals. "Emancipation," for example, meant that information should be available to all. In this specific instance, information about sexuality was to be made public, thus effectively ending adult control of sexual knowledge.

In those years, many books were published which presented sexuality couched in a sterilized, clinical, scientific language. Even works of fiction appeared with informational inserts and appendices with address lists. These were the so-called "problem books" or "problem novels." They were non-fiction books in disguise, whose purpose was to communicate socially relevant knowledge about such topics as clothes, make-up, parental conflict, friendship, falling in love, physical changes caused by puberty, menstruation, tampons, birth control pills, abortion, intercourse, rape, and homosexuality. Two books of this type are Marion Bloem's *Es muß aber geheim bleiben* [But keep it a secret] (1985; orig. *De geheime plek* [1980]) and Lutz van Dick's *Verdammt starke Liebe* [Damned strong love] (1991).[1]

Another language trend of recent years has been the greater use of psychological vocabulary. Some of the topics handled in this manner are homosexuality, as in Inger Edelfeldt's *Jim im Spiegel* [Jim in the mirror] (1985; orig. *Duktig Pojke!* [1983]); adolescent conflicts and the psychological processes accompanying them, as in Selma Noort's *Und dann schweigt Maris* [And then Maris is silent] (1990; orig. *Meer dan een zwijgen schoolkind* [1988]), abuse, as in Marc Talbert's *Das Messer aus Papier* (1989; orig. *The Paper Knife* [1988]); and rape, in Aase Foss Abrahamsen's *Wie ein endloser Schrei* [Like an endless scream] (1990; orig. *En dag med sol* [1987]) and Isolde Heyne's *Funny Fanny* (1987).

Few authors known to German readers have succeeded completely in leaving behind the cold neutrality of scientific language in favour of new and livelier idioms which render sexual longings and encounters with emotive color and aesthetic grace, linking poetry and feeling. A number of works stand out, for example *Und plötzlich willste mehr* [And suddenly you want more] (1979) by Helma Fehrmann and Peter Weismann, Myron Levoy's *Drei Freunde* (1986; orig. *Three Friends* [1984]), Gunnel Beckmann's *Drei Wochen über die Zeit* [Three weeks past due] (1974), and Annette Schlipper's *Ein Teil von mir* [A part of me] (1992).

The "Discovery" of Sexual Abuse

The women's movement of the early 1980s seemed to polarize authors into two camps, those encouraging women to pursue a career as the key to emancipation, and those who viewed the mother-child bond as the primary meaning of life for women. Also during the 1980s, increasing awareness of sexual abuse added a disturbing new dimension to the literary picture of the father and fuelled the conflict between feminism and male-dominated society. A number of books examined the viewpoints of women who are pressured to carry their pregnancies to term and bring unwanted children into the world: Elke Hermannsdörfer's *Mondmonat* [Lunar month] (1990), Elisabeth Schulz-Semrau's *Liane und ihr Baby* [Liane and her baby] (1988), and Christa Grasmeyer's *Friederike und ihr Kind* [Friederike and her child] (1988).

Women who have been sexually abused as children often write of their experiences in order to free themselves from the weight of ruined childhoods. In the "harmonized" versions of these experiences written for younger readers, the abused heroine often reconciles herself with the male world through a relationship with an understanding male friend of her own age group. This is the case in Brigitte Blobel's *Herzsprung* [Heartburst] (1990) and Hadley Irwin's *Liebste Abby* (1986; orig. *Abby, My Love* [1985]).

In the "harder" accounts for older readers, the lasting psychological and emotional effects of abuse doom all later attempts to form relationships with men. Instead of a happy ending, these books remain at best open-ended, leaving the reader to arrive at his or her own conclusions. But just as frequently, abused girls, with whom the reader has come to identify, fail to cope—and die. In both variants, these abused girls are damaged for life; their conflicts are simply not eradicable. There are many bleak variations in books read by German teenagers. Pregnant girls may be persecuted and driven to suicide, as in Ruth White's *Schlangenbrücke* (1992; orig. *Weeping Willow* [1992]). Or girls who cannot deal with the transition to womanhood starve themselves to death. In Maja Gerber Hess's *Reto, HIV-positiv* [Reto, HIV-positive] (1991) and Kirsten Holst's *Ganz nah und doch so fern*, characters die from AIDS-related illnesses. Earlier, publishers would not have dared to offer children's books with such depressing endings. Now, however, the adolescent novel frequently crosses this line and becomes indistinguishable from much writing for adults.

There appears to be a modern dichotomy between books with open endings and those with closed and decidedly negative ones, where the protagonist has no escape. Among the latter is Deborah Moggach's *Rot vor Scham* (1985; orig. *Porky* [1983]). In this book, Moggach charts the destruction of a human being with unflinching honesty. The narrator removes herself from her ordeal and seems to create an existence separate from her own experiences. The unhappy ending finds her incapable of positive feeling and emotional closeness to any other human being. In fact, she deliberately ruins her relationship with a man who has loved her despite her personal difficulties.

Through such books, modern children's literature builds on the great tradition of psychological fiction written in the first half of this century. In Germany, examples would be Hermann Hesse's *Unterm Rad* [Under the wheel] or Frank Wedekind's drama *Frühlingserwachen* [Spring's awakening], in which

young people are driven to their deaths through the ignorance and loveless-
ness of their surroundings.

Looking Ahead

In the postmodern age, norms seem to have lost much of their power to
oppress individuality. It often appears as if they have been overturned or elim-
inated entirely. Words or acts which once triggered an existential crisis are no
longer seen as a problem or a reason for conflict. Traditional roles seem to
be caught up in a process of dissolution. A new understanding of gender
roles, for example, has allowed lesbianism to be articulated openly in children's books for the first time, as in works by Bernheim, Pausacher, Faerber,
and Woodson. This new understanding also permits the exchange of gender
roles and even their reversal. Girls can now be the more active partner in a
relationship, and young men can be single parents, e.g. Gun Jacobson's *Peters
Baby* (1976; orig. *Peters baby* [1977]) or Norma Klein's *Madison und die Freiheit
der Jugend* (1990; orig. *No More Saturday Nights* [1988]). Characters may even
gather both heterosexual *and* homosexual experiences in order to develop a
clearer understanding of their orientation, as in Susanne Fülscher's *Vielleicht
wird es ein schoener Sommer* [Maybe it will be a nice summer] (1991) and Regina Faerber's *Der weite Horizont* [The broad horizon] (1992). In Peter Pohl's
Jan, mein Freund [Jan, my boyfriend] (1989; orig. *Janne min vän* [1985]), the
title character's actual gender has been left so totally unclear that some
reviewers have assumed that it is male, and others, with equal certainty,
female.

Looking back, the last 30 to 40 years have witnessed a variety of trends and
strategies used in the portrayal of sexuality in books read by German children. The last ten years have marked an especially significant turning point.
The spectre of AIDS, the increased awareness of sexual abuse, and a general
trend toward conservatism have motivated many authors to focus on the darker side of sexuality, linking it with suffering, violence, and death. If the message of the sexual "revolution" and "liberation" movement of the 1960s and
1970s was that one's sexuality was something to be enjoyed, the sombre message of the 1980s and 1990s is that sexual activity can hurt or even kill.

Geralde Schmidt-Dumont is a librarian who teaches at the Fachhochschule
für Sozialpädagogik in Hamburg. This article is a shortened version of a
paper presented at the conference "Hautnah" (October 30-November 2,
1993) in Remscheid, Germany, and published in German in *JuLit* 20.1
(1994): 19-36.

Translated from the German by Gregory Humpa.

Note

1 Van Dick's book is based on the true story of a Polish boy who falls in love with a German soldier during World War II. It is included here because the story contains a wealth of information about the life of homosexuals during the Weimar Republic and their subsequent persecution under Hitler.

Works Cited

Abrahamsen, Aase Foss. *Wie ein endloser Schrei* [Like an endless scream]. Würzburg: Benziger, 1990. Orig. *En dag med sol.* Oslo: Gyldendal, 1987.

Beckmann, Gunnel. *Drei Wochen über die Zeit* [Three weeks past due]. Würzburg: Arena, 1974.

Blobel, Brigitte. *Herzsprung* [Heartburst]. Solothurn: Aare, 1990.

Bloem, Marion. *Es muß aber geheim bleiben* [But keep it a secret]. Reinbek bei Hamburg: Rowohlt, 1985. Orig. *De geheime plek.* Baarn [Netherlands]: De Fontein, 1980.

Donovan, John. *Du sagst ja, ich sag' nein.* Cologne: Benziger, 1976. Orig. *I'll Get There. It Better Be Worth the Trip.* New York: Harper & Row, 1969.

Edelfeldt, Inger. *Jim im Spiegel* [Jim in the mirror]. Stuttgart: Spectrum, 1985. Orig. *Duktig Pojke!* Stockholm: Almqvist & Wiksell, 1983.

Faerber, Regina. *Der weite Horizont* [The broad horizon]. Bad Homburg: Riedel, 1992.

Fehrmann, Helma and Peter Weismann. *Und plötzlich willste mehr* [And suddenly you want more]. Munich: Weismann, 1979.

Fülscher, Susanne. *Vielleicht wird es ein schoener Sommer* [Maybe it will be a nice summer]. Reutlingen: Ensslin & Laiblin, 1991.

Gabel, Wolfgang. *Immer zusammen frühstücken.* Baden-Baden: Signal, 1977. Orig. *Breakfast Together for Always.* Trans. Anthea Bell. London: Macmillan, 1980.

Grasmeyer, Christa. *Friederike und ihr Kind* [Friederike and her child]. Berlin: Verlag Neues Leben, 1988.

Günther, Herbert. *Unter Freunden* [Among friends]. Recklinghausen: Bitter, 1976.

Hautzig, Deborah. *Hallo, Englechen.* Aarau/Frankfurt am Main: Sauerländer, 1984. Orig. *Hey Dollface.* New York: Greenwillow, 1978.

Hermannsdörfer, Elke. *Mondmonat* [Lunar month]. Bad Homburg: Riedel, 1990.

Hess, Myra Gerber. *Reto, HIV-positiv* [Reto, HIV-positive]. Lucerne/Stuttgart: Rex, 1991.

Heyne, Isolde. *Funny Fanny.* Berlin: Klopp, 1987.

Holst, Kirsten. *Ganz nah und doch so fern* [So near and yet so far]. Freiburg: Herder, 1992.

Howard, Ellen. *Lilians Geheimnis.* Vienna: Ueberreuter, 1988. Orig. *Gillyflower.* New York: Atheneum, 1986.

Irwin, Hadley. *Liebste Abby.* Weinheim: Beltz & Gelberg, 1986. Orig. *Abby, My Love.* New York: Atheneum, 1985.

Jacobson, Gun. *Peters Baby.* Munich:Bertelsmann, 1976. Orig. *Peters baby.* Stockholm: Bonnier, 1977.

Klein, Norma. *Madison und die Freiheit der Jugend.* Frankfurt am Main: Alibaba, 1990. Orig. *No More Saturday Nights.* New York: Knopf, 1988.

Krollpfeiffer, Hannelore. *Die Zeit mit Marie* [The time with Marie]. Berlin: Klopp, 1986.

Levoy, Myron. *Drei Freunde.* Munich: Deutscher Taschenbuchverlag, 1986. Orig. *Three Friends.* New York: Harper & Row, 1984.

Meißner-Johannknecht, Doris. *Amor kam in Leinenschuhen* [Amor came in canvas shoes]. Recklinghausen: Bitter, 1993.

Moggach, Deborah. *Rot vor Scham.* Reinbek bei Hamburg: Rowohlt, 1985. Orig. *Porky.* London: Cape, 1983.

Noort, Selma. *Und dann schweigt Maris* [And then Maris is silent]. Kevelaer: Anrich, 1990. Orig. *Meer dan een zwijgen schoolkind.* Amsterdam: Leopold, 1988.

Pohl, Peter. *Jan, mein Freund* [Jan, my boyfriend]. Ravensburg: Maier, 1989. Orig. *Janne min vän.* Stockholm: Almqvist & Wiksell, 1985.

Röhrig, Tilman. *Langes Zwielicht* [Long twilight]. Mülheim a. d. Ruhr: Anrich, 1974.

Schlipper, Annette. *Ein Teil von mir* [A part of me]. Düsseldorf: Patmos, 1992.

Schulz-Semrau, Elisabeth. *Liane und ihr Baby* [Liane and her baby]. Berlin: Kinderbuchverlag, 1988.

Seck-Agthe, Monika. *Morella.* Reinbek bei Hamburg: Rowohlt, 1983.

Spillner, Wolf. *Die Wasseramsel* [The water-blackbird]. Berlin: Kinderbuchverlag, 1984.

Talbert, Marc. *Das Messer aus Papier.* Kevelaer: Anrich, 1989. Orig. *The Paper Knife.* New York: Dial, 1988.

van Dick, Lutz. *Verdammt starke Liebe* [Damned strong love]. Reinbek bei Hamburg: Rotfuchs, 1991.

White, Ruth. *Schlangenbrücke.* Stuttgart: Verlag Freies Geistesleben, 1992. Orig. *Weeping Willow.* New York: Farrar, Straus and Giroux, 1992.

Young Adult Literature Evades the Theorists (1996)
Caroline Hunt

Adolescent literature has been "coming of age" for over a quarter of a century if you count from *The Pigman* and *The Outsiders*, more than half a century if you count from *Seventeenth Summer.* Beginning in 1992-93, this coming of age has been marked by quasi-official rites of passage—such as a widespread acceptance of the grown-up name "young adult"; commemorative issues of *English*

Journal and *Journal of Youth Services in Libraries*; and individual articles in other journals. As Richard Peck points out, young adult literature has become "a second-generation literature now for the children of our first readers" (19). Other acts of recognition range from the positive (increased speculation about whether a canon of young adult literature can, or does, exist) to the pessimistic, exemplified by Marc Aronson's "The YA Novel Is Dead and Other Fairly Stupid Tales." The field is mature in some ways—here I use the word "mature" as we might speak of a "mature economy"—but unstable or regressive in others.

As the literature has developed, so has the study of that literature. (In reviewing its history, I deal primarily with fiction because recent theory about children's literature centers on fiction.) I suggest that the study of "adolescent" literature has developed in a rather different way from that of children's literature in general, and that one result of its peculiar development has been a striking lack of theoretical criticism.

The first problem is that virtually no theoretical criticism attaches to young adult literature *as such*. Theorists in the wider field of children's literature often discuss young adult titles without distinguishing them as a separate group and without, therefore, indicating how theoretical issues in young adult literature might differ from those in literature for younger children. Important critical books of the 1980s take it for granted that young adult books and books for younger children are essentially alike. Jacqueline Rose's *The Case of Peter Pan; or The Impossibility of Children's Fiction* (1984) does not treat young adult titles as in any way unlike those for younger children, and neither does Juliet Dusinberre's *Alice to the Lighthouse: Children's Books and Radical Experiments in Art* (1987). Zohar Shavit, in *Poetics of Children's Literature* (1986), similarly considers juvenile literature as more or less unified and does not separate works for the upper age ranges.

Moving into the 1990s, one can see theorists noting some key distinctions; still, they do not, on the whole, address young adult books separately. Sometimes they do not address them at all. The concept of the child employed in Peter Hunt's *Criticism, Theory, and Children's Literature* (1991) clearly describes a preadolescent being; Hunt cites Nicholas Tucker's list of the characteristics of children, including "spontaneous play, receptivity to the prevailing culture, physiological constraints (children are generally smaller and weaker), *and sexual immaturity* (which implies that certain concepts are not immediately relevant to them)" (57, my italics). Accordingly, most of Hunt's examples are from the mid-range of children's books—for readers past the toddler years but not yet in their teens. This schema has the merit of consistency (and *implies* a distinction between children and adolescents) but appears to exclude any systematic examination of young adult books.

John Stephens, in *Language and Ideology in Children's Fiction* (1992), covers a broader age range, including a number of young adult texts: Jan Needle's *My Mate Shofiq*, Robert Cormier's *After the First Death*, and books by Rosemary Sutcliff, Ursula Le Guin, and Cynthia Voigt. Stephens shows his awareness of age differences in a brilliant account of ideological manipulation in picture books for younger readers; however, he pays specific attention to differences at the upper end of the age line only occasionally, as when he states that traditional values in Leon Garfield occur "in a context which renders them contingent.... especially ... in Garfield's novels *for older readers*" (230, my italics).

Perry Nodelman, too, lumps young adult books in with other children's books in the first edition of *The Pleasures of Children's Literature* (1992); the only section to address these books specifically deals with problem novels such as those of Judy Blume (200-02), and the bibliographical appendix lists a few young adult items as a subset of "Kinds of Children's Fiction" (243-44). Like Stephens, Nodelman shows elsewhere in the book, and especially in discussing picture books, that he is well aware of differences between age groups. Unlike the previous critics, Nodelman makes explicit his belief that, for theoretical purposes, there is no need to regard young adult books as a separate category; his revised edition (1996) confronts this problem directly, while allowing for the possibility that others may differ:

> Many people disagree with my contention ... that young adult fiction is merely a subgenre of children's literature. I've been told that I ought not to have even mentioned young adult literature in a book about children's literature. As a kind of writing intended for teenagers, a group of people quite different from younger children, young adult literature [appears to some people to be] a completely different kind of writing, with its own distinctive characteristics. (191-92)

Nodelman then suggests that readers compare several young adult novels to some with "similar characters or situations but intended for younger children" (192). Though ostensibly a textbook, *Pleasures* touches upon most of the issues that theorists are currently discussing.[1]

At the other end of the spectrum from Nodelman's approach, but agreeing about the essential unity of juvenile fiction, is a recent and controversial book by Karin Lesnik-Oberstein, *Children's Literature: Criticism and the Fictional Child* (1994). Picking up where Rose left off a decade earlier, Lesnik-Oberstein challenges not only the possibility of children's fiction but also the validity of children's-literature criticism. As Nodelman himself crisply summarizes the case on the electronic discussion group CHILD_LIT,

> because [she] has serious problems with the accuracy of critical representations of the child, she has serious problems with the criticism she perceives as being based upon it. And this is, according to her, all children's literature criticism—which therefore becomes a totally wrong-headed and counterproductive endeavor.

Lesnik-Oberstein's cited examples range from materials for the very young to those for what must surely be adolescent readers, although she mentions very few specific titles. Despite the strong correlation between her concept of childhood and that of children's books and their criticism, this theorist, too, moves effortlessly from the toddler to the teen with few distinctions along the way.

The only conclusion I am able to draw from examining this sample of influential critical texts, produced over the fifteen-year period from 1980 to 1995, is that not a *single major theorist in the field deals with young adult literature as something separate from literature for younger children*—though Stephens and Nodelman allow for differences of opinion on this separation and/or for differential treatment of specific texts.

Second, the relative youth of the young adult category compounds the problem; it takes a while for serious criticism to get started. (Consider the parallel case of science fiction, for instance.) Literature "for" children, in various senses, has been around for centuries. Many estimates start with John Newbery, two hundred years before *Seventeenth Summer*, others go back to James Janeway, or the Elizabethans, or the *Babees Boke*, and Gillian Adams pushes the date back to ancient times in "The Case for Sumer." But no one, as far as I know, seriously suggests that young adult literature as a separate category begins before World War II (*Seventeenth Summer*) or, alternatively, the late 1960s (*The Outsiders*). An important corollary is that adolescence, as a prolonged period of maturation, is itself a relatively recent concept and is much more firmly entrenched in North America and Europe than elsewhere. There is no way to push the origins of the young adult novel back to Sumer.

Both of the previous points are readily apparent, and both bear directly upon the relative scarcity of theory in the young adult field. Obviously, a literary subgenre that has existed for twenty-five to fifty years will accrue less commentary than an older one; typically, too, critics begin by considering a subgenre within its class and only gradually detach it for separate examination. A Modern Language Association volume titled *Teaching Children's Literature: Issues, Pedagogy, Resources* (1992), edited by Glenn Sadler, makes this latter point neatly. In his introduction to the survey of actual courses, Sadler observes that "as a subject for instruction, literature for children has passed through its adolescence" and is gaining acceptance; he further notes that "before the first [MLA] seminar on children's literature was held ... in 1969, courses in the field were being offered" (144). Note the date. In the year when the Modern Language Association began to have sessions on children's literature, 1969, very few of the books that we now call young adult had yet been written.

My next five topics—marketing, censorship, the canon, young adult literature courses, and the growth of young adult literature scholarship—are less obvious. Yet these questions matter too: where the books are sold, why people involved with these books spend so much time on the defensive, what books become "classics," how the books are presented in colleges and schools, and, last, who teaches and writes about these books (and how). The answers help to explain why this branch of juvenile writing has amassed less theoretical criticism than others.

The first point of major difference between young adult and children's literature concerns how books are publicized and sold—and, more important, how they are bought. Marketing poses a number of important issues. Children, especially younger ones, have books bought for them by parents, or perhaps select them with parents; young adults can select or even buy their own books. This power means that popularity reigns supreme, except perhaps for sales to libraries. A visit to any chain bookstore will reveal how this works. Many young adult titles are issued as original paperbacks—far more than in the children's section. Many belong to series. There may be few or no reviews, as the standard reviewing sources tend to concentrate on hardcover single titles. In addition, far fewer individual authors are represented in the young adult section than in the children's section (even allowing for the fact that the young adult section is much smaller to start with); instead there are likely to be multiple titles by a few well-established authors. In short, the young adult books being reviewed and written about are not on the bookstore shelves, and those on the bookstore shelves are not being written about or reviewed.[2]

A related issue is that the very evanescence of the teenage years causes young adult books to "date" more swiftly than their counterparts for younger children. A second-grader may enjoy *Charlotte's Web* (1952) as children have enjoyed it for decades, but her older sister will get little from Mary Stolz's *The Sea Gulls Woke Me*, published the year before E.B. White's classic. In this charming tale of an awkward young girl's summer away from home, the entire romantic "action" consists of a chaste kiss (during a dancing lesson) on page 161 followed by a slightly more ardent one on page 204. The social customs of Stolz's 1951 suburban world, in which the protagonist's apron-clad mother greets her after school with a silver pitcher of iced tea, then washes and buffs the pitcher and carefully stores it in a blue flannel bag, seem alien forty-odd years later. Indeed, some well-known young adult books of the late 1960s and the 1970s suffer from just the same kind of obsolescence: though frequently taught in young adult literature courses as "relevant," the older titles of Paul Zindel and some other groundbreakers seem like historical novels to many teenagers today. ("They talk like my mom," one student said revealingly of *My Darling, My Hamburger* [1969]; "she says stuff like 'groovy.'") Language, particularly dialogue, can date a young adult book faster than anything else. So, ironically, the more accurate the portrayal of adolescent speech patterns, the shorter will be the life span of that particular book's "relevance" to the present experience of teenaged readers.

Similarly, the evolution of taste in clothing, amusements, drugs, and so on will have more direct impact on young adult social realism than on children's. Clothing *matters* to teens as an outward symbol of their search for identity, and so clothes usually figure in young adult fiction to a greater extent than in children's books. Alas, characters in bell-bottoms may not appeal to the 1990s reader. Books in which a once-trendy drug appears may seem irrelevant to those using its "designer" equivalent ten or fifteen years later. Legal developments can affect teens more directly than their younger siblings; the legalization of abortion and the rise in the legal drinking age have made many young adult novels outdated. Because young adult literature is marketed as, essentially, a disposable record of a fleeting moment, the theory that accompanies it is more likely to focus on social issues than on literary theory. Critics, understandably, find it more feasible to study the phenomena than to analyze the books themselves, which are often read simply as documents of an ever-changing adolescent social scene.

Finally, the threat of censorship to young adult books has diverted the attention of many writers who might otherwise theorize the field. It is difficult for scholars in children's literature to understand why their colleagues in the young adult area focus on censorship so much. It is, after all, possible to design an entire children's-literature course, or write a book about children's literature, or edit an issue of a children's-literature journal, without mentioning censorship. This is simply not the case in the young adult book world. Every textbook in the young adult field has an extensive section on censorship; journals and newsletters in the field constantly report censorship updates; and many scholars of young adult literature spend time in court as expert witnesses, or prepare material to assist others in doing so. The Winter 1993 issue of *The ALAN Review* was devoted to articles on censorship, as was the Fall 1994 issue of *SIGNAL*. A steady stream of articles related to censorship continues to appear in *English Journal* and in other journals with a focus on young adult books.

Why should this be so, particularly when YA books are themselves, like children's books, censored by publishers, authors, and societal expectations? Many books that speak directly to the adolescent experience use language that some adults do not like, mention experiences (especially sexual experiences) that make some adults uncomfortable, and examine the possibility, at least, of serious challenges to authority. These characteristics are not *necessarily* found in the majority of books for younger children (even though these works may in fact be just as "subversive"). The children's books do not always involve *obvious* taboos, but the YA ones generally do. Nor are these taboos limited to "New Realism" titles: increasingly, parents object to fantasies as well. Most scholars in the young adult field like the books they teach and are willing to spend time and effort defending them. In these circumstances, it is not entirely surprising that the same scholars do not tend to concern themselves with theoretical approaches to the books whose very right to existence they are defending. To a general public that objects to the number of times body parts are mentioned in *The Chocolate War* (an actual instance), it is fruitless to offer a defence based on the ideas of Michel Foucault—interesting though this might be as a response. In other words, approaches to young adult books are, for many scholars, conditioned more by "outside" (non-academic) conditions than is the case in other areas of children's literature. A picture-book scholar may or may not be an apologist for the nude Mickey of *In the Night Kitchen*; just about every teacher of young adult literature is an apologist for the material.

Marketing and censorship, two external pressures on young adult literature, help to explain the lack of theory but do not entirely excuse it. The failure of young adult literature specialists to confront the canon is equally significant; after all, the existence of a canon gives students and critics something to focus on, and the more that is written on a relatively small number of books, the more likely it is that some theoretical criticism will emerge. In 1942 and 1967, the two frequently proposed birthdates for adolescent literature, no one talked much about a canon. As recently as 1976, when I entered the field, the study of adolescent literature did not centre on a canon; in fact, it might not even focus on adolescent literature. Instead, a course might deal primarily with methodology, or review classic works that had adolescent characters or were traditionally taught in high schools (*A Separate Peace* would fit both of these categories), and might sometimes—briefly—introduce what was called the "junior novel." The only widely available textbook, Stephen Dunning and Alan B. Howes's *Literature for Adolescents*, was significantly subtitled *Teaching Poems, Stories, Novels and Plays*; it contained one chapter (out of twenty) on the "junior book." Not that Dunning and Howes were ignorant of the field: Dunning had done a pioneering dissertation on junior novels as early as 1959, had edited a highly successful collection of poetry for adolescents, and remained active and influential. Rather, the educational system was, simply, geared to much older works. Apologists for "adolescent" literature usually felt themselves to be on the defensive—even in 1975, the date of the Dunning and Howes textbook. The canon, at that point, was widely seen to consist of "classics"; apologists for young adult books avoided the idea of a canon altogether, or were vaguely anti-canon, or, occasionally, suggested that the canon might be broadened to include a few young adult titles.

With the arrival of Kenneth Donelson and Aileen Pace Nilsen's *Literature for Today's Young Adults* (1980), all this changed. The new text covered a broad range of historical periods and subgenres; more important, it covered hundreds of young adult texts. In each edition, the textbook has printed an Honor Sampling of the best books for every year from 1967 to the cutoff date for that particular edition.[3] "Adolescent" literature, deliberately retitled

"Young Adult" by Donelson and Nilsen in an effort to reduce the supposed stigma of the word "adolescent," had come of age sufficiently to have its own classics. Meanwhile, high school and college teachers were constructing their own YA canon, one that tended to put more emphasis on fiction and, in particular, on a smaller number of very well-known authors than the eclectic Honor Sampling. The 1980s were the Age of the Canon, when just about everyone taught *The Pigman*, *The Chocolate War*, and so on.

Today YA specialists are constructing not one canon, but many. One college YA syllabus, or high school library collection, or book award list may stress readability; another, "classic" status; another, social implications; still others, a mixture. Even more than books for younger readers, YA books tend to have "multicultural" values. Most of us would now include in our canon some books not originally written for adolescents. This inclusion was harder to justify when we were still defensive about YA books; it then seemed to play into the hands of the argument that YA books as such were unnecessary. Now a book such as Olive Ann Burns's *Cold Sassy Tree* is included, without comment, on the Honor Sampling. Most of us, too, would now include more books from other lands, and indeed, today there are more adolescent books available to us from other countries than there used to be.

In its short official lifetime, YA literature has gone from having no acknowledged existence, to forming a generally recognized category with a central canon, to displaying a more fragmented, ever-changing multiplicity of canons. There are people who believe in a permanent "best" list (beginning with either *Huckleberry Finn* or *A Separate Peace* and ending somewhere around *The Pigman* or *A Day No Pigs Would Die*). There are moderates who believe in a canon that occasionally requires adjustments and combines the function of a "best" list with a record of changing tastes—for instance, Donelson and Nilsen's Honour Sampling. The books recognized for excellence in the 1990s are quite different from those of the early years. In some cases, books have been de-canonized and removed entirely from the Honor Sampling: Richard Peck's *Princess Ashley* (formerly included for 1987), Whitley Strieber's *Wolf of Shadows* (1985), Janine Boissard's *A Matter of Feeling* (1980), Vera and Bill Cleaver's *Trial Valley* and Don Bredt's *Hard Feelings* (1977), Jessamyn West's *Massacre at Fall Creek* (1975), and Erich Segal's *Love Story* (1970) are among the Third Edition honor books omitted from the Fourth Edition. Donelson and Nilsen say simply, "We've used our own judgment about deleting a few of the older books" (9). Without comment, the authors have also augmented the Honor Sampling for some of the early years. In retrospect, books may merit inclusion in the Honor Sampling that did not seem to meet the criteria earlier, and these titles have now been silently added: Robert Lipsyte's *The Contender* (for 1967); Barbara Wersba's *Run Softly, Go Fast* (1970); S.E. Hinton's *That Was Then, This Is Now* (1971); Paula Fox's *The Slave Dancer* and Bette Greene's *Summer of My German Soldier* (1973); Laurence Yep's *Dragonwings*

(1975); and Cormier's *I Am the Cheese*, M.E. Kerr's *I'll Love You When You're More Like Me*, and Robin Brancato's *Winning* (1977) did not appear in the original (1980) edition but are included in the Fourth Edition (1993).

Then there are the anarchists, such as myself, who question the validity of any YA canon. My student who identified the Zindel characters with her mother's generation illustrates this futility perfectly. Can we speak of any kind of permanent canon in a field where the "real" readers, the young adults themselves, value "now" to the virtual exclusion of whatever is not "now"? Here is where we have largely failed, until recently, to initiate a necessary element in our critical dialogue. Children's-literature critics generally agree upon the desirability of a canon; their disagreements are more in the details. YA critics, though, have barely begun to discuss the existence of a canon, or what standards should be applied, or whether it is possible for books to remain canonical after their readership has completely deserted them. Without any agreement about the nature (much less the content) of a YA canon, further theoretical discussion has, understandably, lagged.

The current debate about the canon seems to be taking two rather different tracks. Those who are interested both in children's literature and in the YA area have conducted a lively debate about the existence of a YA canon on the electronic discussion group CHILDLIT (reconstituted, during the middle of the canon discussion, as CHILD_LIT). Meanwhile, the YA "specialists," that is, those who do not work much or at all in the area of children's literature, have begun to appropriate the term "canon" to apply to what they have been talking about all along—the inclusion of "popular" (i.e., specifically YA-oriented) books in recommended reading lists and school curricula. Robert Carlsen has been active in this debate for decades; recent expositions have been seen at regular intervals in *English Journal* and other classroom-oriented publications. A clear statement of this position occurs in Chris Crowe's "Aiming the New Canon: Developing a Reader Friendly Curriculum":

> This new canon will be considerably more open, freed of its predecessor's established and moldy classics that taught students that reading is not only difficult, but something one does only under duress. It will be cosmopolitan and multi-ethnic. Instead of representing only the traditional aristocratic works, it will include a broad variety of literature, making it infinitely more accessible and approachable to students. (11)

In other words, one group of scholars (chiefly YA specialists concerned with high school curricula) is working on the inclusion of YA books in an existing canon of "classics," while another (people who teach in colleges, especially outside of the secondary-education area) is considering the existence of a canon composed entirely of YA books. Within the second group, some are interested in a permanent canon, while others envision one that is constantly changing.

Course development has proceeded in tandem with changes in the canon: from no courses, to fairly standardized ones, to a wide variety. In the 1970s another coming of age took place when many states began to require that education students take a course in YA literature in order to be certified for secondary school teaching. It was common for this course to be assigned to a junior member of staff—not because it was less desirable but because often no one on staff knew much about the subject. So, like many others, I said goodbye to the familiar authors of my own field, the seventeenth century, and moved hesitantly into the far stranger world of the Socs and Greasers, of Edna Shinglebox and Marsh Mellow, of Jerry Renault and Brother Leon and the rest. Colleagues and students participated in impromptu discussions: could a couple really conceive a baby underwater, as appears to happen in *He's My Baby, Now?* (We decided that Charles and Daisy must have climbed onto a convenient raft between sentences.) In *The Contender,* is it plausible for Alfred's employer, Mr. Epstein, to have boxed as "Lightning Lou"? (For the time period, yes.) Would a boy carry a raincoat to school to conceal possible erections as Tony does in *Then Again, Maybe I Won't?* (Opinions were divided.) One colleague in another department was willing to borrow books and comment on them—as long as I put them in his mailbox in a plain envelope. Thus the early teachers of YA literature in colleges, the people from whom one might expect the majority of YA criticism to emerge, spent much of their time learning the field as they went along and introducing and justifying it to other professionals. People who do not yet have a firm grip on their material, and who feel that other academics do not understand or value it, are unlikely to produce theoretically oriented criticism.

Those days are gone. Today we see a group of trained people—the older ones trained in the trenches but, at any rate, trained by now, the young ones trained in varied and challenging programs, either in English departments or in schools of education or library science. Some courses focus on classroom applications of YA literature, others on the criticism of this body of work as if it were, say, metaphysical poetry, others (including mine) on a variety of topics. Beginning in the mid-1980s there has been a choice of several textbooks, from the relatively literary Donelson and Nilsen to Arthea (Charlie) Reed's aptly named *Reaching Adolescents: The Young Adult Book and the School* (1985) to Jean E. Brown and Elaine C. Stephens's recent offering, also classroom-oriented, *Teaching Young Adult Literature: Sharing the Connection* (1995). Today's students come from a variety of disciplines, not just secondary education; few expect an easy grade. Today's teachers of YA courses have learned their field, have justified their existence, and can now go on toward theory if they wish.

The persistent connection between YA literature courses and high school certification, however, continues to exert a strong influence toward "applied" criticism, particularly with reference to the use of YA books in the high school classroom. Since the main rationale for the existence of YA courses (in terms of enrolment) usually rests upon secondary certification requirements, the mindset of a YA class—even if the instructor, like me, does not cover classroom applications—remains resolutely pragmatic. English department instructors of YA literature, too, tend to think that most theory, with the possible exception of psychological theory, is less relevant here than it is in other upper-level courses. In most cases, the mindset of the class affects the instructor outside the class also, and his or her criticism is thus influenced toward praxis, away from theory. In this regard, YA instructors are probably in the position of children's-literature instructors ten to twenty years ago.

The YA journals, however, have not remained unchanged in the last twenty years. In the mid-to late 1970s, a small band of dedicated scholars promoted adolescent literature in a few journals. Donelson's support for YA books in the *Arizona English Bulletin* included two special issues, one in 1972 and one in 1976, as well as numerous individual articles. Like the Arizona journal, a special issue of the *Texas Tech Journal of Education* in 1980 featured some of the most influential names in the field: Mike Angelotti, Dwight Burton, Theodore Hippie, Don Gallo, and others.

The two most important journals came from NCTE: the venerable *English Journal* and *The ALAN Review*. The founding of the latter marked still another coming of age for adolescent literature. In the journal's early days, many articles were either much-needed reviews, classroom applications, or aggressive advocacy, sometimes mixed with cries of agony. In the Fall 1979 issue of *The ALAN Review*, a fledgling journal that had not yet developed a cover and that at that time abbreviated itself inelegantly as *TAR*, two of the three lead articles are Angelotti's "Will There *Be* an Adolescent Literature in the 21st Century?" and Ellen Lewis's "Teachers in Adolescent Literature: Are We the Good Guys?"—both, in different ways, advocacy/agony pieces. (Angelotti's essay was perceived as being so well in tune with the editorial focus of the issue that the journal ran it as a guest editorial.) With the next issue came a geometrically patterned cover and a better pagination system; in the 1980s, most issues had fifty or more pages and featured substantive articles on a variety of topics. On entering the 1990s, the publication adopted a snappy new cover, an attractively redesigned format, and, at last, MLA-style documentation. Articles include both classroom-oriented and "scholarly" (including historical) topics. The journal also continues its advocacy of YA literature and its excellent clip-and-file reviews.

From the International Reading Association comes *SIGNAL*, the journal of the IRA's Special Interest Group on Literature for the Adolescent Reader. A recent (1995) issue on nonfiction illustrates the journal's emphasis on usable information about the real-world reading tastes of young adults. Pamela Sissi Carroll's "Acne and Tattoos, Skateboards and Hip-Hop: The Magazines That Adolescents Read for Information" should be required reading for all who have difficulty seeing beyond a narrow canon of YA "classics." (Articles in the "applied" journals serve, too, as useful reminders of how much of what YAs read is not fiction, or at least not book-length fiction. My exclusion of non-fiction from the discussion of theory does not mean that it is unimportant.) In the two cited NCTE journals, as well as in *SIGNAL*, critical articles normally stop short of the theoretical. Since the readership of these journals consists largely of high school teachers and those who train them, the emphasis on comprehensibility and practicality is logical.

While *English Journal* went its steady way and *The ALAN Review* grew under a series of exceptionally able editors, some important "mainstream" journals also gave more space to YA materials. The British-American journal *Children's Literature in Education* published a number of distinguished articles on YA authors, from the famous (Alan Garner) to the cultish (Richard Allen). *Horn Book* did the same, showcasing YA writer Bruce Brooks as early as 1987. The *Children's Literature Association Quarterly*, which once maintained a separate YA column, began printing articles on YA literature and themes alongside its other articles. *The Lion and the Unicorn* saw an increase in articles on YA literature; the issue for June 1988, for instance, entitled "The Dark Side of Nature in Children's Books," deals extensively with YA titles. Also in 1988, the prestigious annual *Children's Literature* carried an article by Frank Myszor analyzing Cormier's *After the First Death* in terms of French structuralist concepts. Perhaps the mixed readership of these journals affords more encouragement for theoretical approaches than do the classroom-oriented publications.

Today, then, scholars in the YA field are very like scholars in any other literary field. We have, it seems, successfully infiltrated. The first "normal" conference at which I delivered a YA paper (1980) was a comparative literature gathering, and my audience reacted as if hearing for the first time of books for and about a species from another galaxy. Today, that audience would probably have heard of, or even read, the texts under discussion. One result of this change is that papers and articles on YA literature must now be just as scholarly as any others; with novelty gone, quality becomes important. My 1980 paper probably would not be accepted today.

However, in terms of theory, YA scholarship lags behind its children's-literature counterpart. Partly, as I have suggested, this results from the perceived need for YA professionals to act as boosters, introducers, and defenders of a strange but valuable new product. Boosterism, though often necessary, does not produce much theorizing. Meanwhile, those who do deal in theory are perhaps discouraged from the use of YA texts by a lingering myth that such texts are beneath notice. Michael Cart quotes Aidan Chambers on the "lack of critical apparatus" in the YA field, stemming in his view from the "endless disparagement of the form, by people who, for whatever reasons, dismiss teenage books as beyond serious interest—a bastard and unwanted hybrid" (qtd. 154-55).[4] A related problem is that many YA scholars operate from a popular-culture approach, drawing conclusions from sometimes large numbers of rather ordinary (even "subliterary") books. Though valid, this approach does not lend itself to theorizing, at least not beyond historical-cultural contextualization. And, as I have also suggested, the emphasis on classroom applications found in some journals that welcome YA articles, while not precluding excellent scholarship, does not foster theoretical scholarship.

The growth of criticism has also been hampered by lack of communication among different segments of the YA critical community. The main groups are college professors in English departments, college professors in education departments, high school and middle school teachers, high school and middle school librarians, public library YA staff, and professors in MLS programs. Too often, even within a single discipline, those "in the field" (teachers and practicing librarians) may not communicate with those in academia. Though the same situation prevails in the children's section, I believe that it has more serious implications for YA practitioners. To begin with, the often-controversial nature of the books used by YA professionals makes lack of cooperation costly. We simply do not have time to waste gathering, in defence of challenged books, materials that someone else has already assembled. Second, the absence of an agreed-upon canon, the relatively small number of frequently discussed books, and the popular-culture tendencies of the YA field make a wide acquaintance with large numbers of YA texts essential. Experience suggests that this wide knowledge is often more common among librarians than among academics. Anyone who has ever served on a book award committee can attest to this. Although librarians may not always choose to become involved in theory, they have a broad grasp of the texts that we would do well to include in our academic discussions.[5]

Further, different professions publish in different journals, so this fragmentation may not be rectified in print. Academics usually read (and publish in) *The ALAN Review, Children's Literature, The Lion and the Unicorn,* the *Children's Literature Association Quarterly,* and *Children's Literature in Education,* or perhaps in *English Journal* or *Journal of Children's Literature* if their interests include classroom application. Except for *VOYA* (Voice of Youth Advocates) and *Horn Book,* however, most reviewing sources and marketplace publications go unread by academics—who are thus deprived of useful information from the *Bulletin of the Center for Children's Books, School Library Journal, Booklist, Publishers Weekly,* and the late lamented *Wilson Library Bulletin.* Similarly, the reading-oriented *SIGNAL, Bookbird,* and *Five Owls* have helpful articles often unknown to academics outside of library schools.

Not only the reviewing media, but the professional library journals, as well, contain wonderful materials that academics need to know about. For instance, in June 1994, Cart delivered a speech at the YALSA preconference in Miami. (YALSA, short for Young Adult Library Services Association, is a subgroup of the American Library Association.) Cart's speech, "Of Risk and Revolution: The Current State of Young Adult Literature," was published in the Winter 1995 issue of the *Journal of Youth Services in Libraries*, an ALA journal sponsored jointly by YALSA and the Association for Library Service to Children (ALSC). In it he assesses the field's publishing status, critical conditions, and relation to its young readership. Ranging over some fifty sources, from Italo Calvino to a singing group called the Disposable Heroes of Hiphoprisy, the piece is the most significant overview I have seen in several years. Sadly, however, few academics read *JOYS*; and, since it is indexed in *Library Literature, Library and Information Science Abstracts,* and *Current Index to Journals in Education* (*CIJE*), many MLA-oriented academics will not learn about the article through their normal search techniques either.[6] Conversely, that many of the library journals use either the thirteenth or the fourteenth edition of the *Chicago Manual of Style* for documentation may deter MLA-trained scholars from contributing to them, as it is time-consuming to change from one system to another.

Why does any of this matter? As I have argued, knowledge of numerous texts is especially important to YA scholars and librarians, and their journals can help to provide that knowledge. (And possibly, as a member of YALSA and ALSC and a referee for *JOYS*, I am biased.) Further, I suggest, theoretical criticism does not come out of nowhere. A good grasp of what is going on generally in a field makes the leap to theory possible. A wider angle of information is needed than that which most academic practitioners now enjoy.

Young adult practitioners in the United States have also been handicapped by a sort of myopic nationalism. Though several journals have steadfastly combated this tendency by publishing quality surveys of YA books from other countries—nearly every issue of *The ALAN Review* in 1979-80 contains one such article—there is a widespread assumption that YA literature is, somehow, peculiarly "American" (meaning from the United States, as some YA critics seem oddly unaware of the existence of Canada, not to mention Mexico and South America). Books from Britain are underrepresented, and the fact that Chambers, John Rowe Townsend, Josephine Kamm, and others were active in this field very early is not widely known.[7] Peter Hollindale, one of the pioneering academics who fought to make the study of children's and young adult literature acceptable in Britain, recently provided an overview of what he calls the "adolescent novel of ideas," a thoughtful account that balances texts from both sides of the Atlantic, highlighting those by Le Guin and Peter Dickinson. How many YA critics in the US would take a similarly balanced view? How many would have heard of one of Hollindale's examples, Kamm's *Young Mother*, which predates *The Outsiders* by two years?

I suspect that a high percentage of YA scholars received their training in American literature—or in "English Education," which is also strong in US texts. Many children's literature scholars whom I know, by contrast, come from backgrounds in British or comparative literature, especially in the Renaissance and Victorian periods. The geographic clustering of YA scholars in the US and the narrowly American basis that often marks their training, factors that can sometimes make YA professionals seem more provincial than their children's-literature counterparts, is beginning to close, thanks to the Internet. Discussion groups to which I belong include contributors from Australia and Finland, as well as the US, Canada, and Great Britain. This diversity will, surely, help to broaden the outlook of scholar and student alike. Until more people have access to online groups, though, some provincialism will persist.

Will the theoretical criticism of YA literature ever reach the standard already seen in children's-literature criticism? Perhaps not. It seems unlikely that this turbulent field will ever produce such criticism in quantity; its roots were formed in other soil. Individual exceptions, such as the Myszor article, will continue to appear. They will probably cluster around a few YA authors: Cormier, Garner, and so on. Excellent articles using the traditions of historical criticism, of popular culture, and of reader-response theory will also continue to appear—many of them very scholarly indeed, though not "theoretical" in the manner of Myszor. Theorists who cover the wider field of children's literature may well begin to consider the separate problems of YA books and address them directly; the increasingly sophisticated examination of picture books provides a recent analogy.

Reference books pertaining specifically to YA books and authors have already caught up to the high standard of their counterparts in children's literature, as signified by recent fine offerings from Beacham, Salem, and St. James. The fact that a standard reference book, *Twentieth-Century Children's Writers*, has now become two separate volumes—one for children's writers properly so called and the other for young adult writers—suggests the trend. Similarly, the long-lived *Critical Handbook of Children's Literature*, by Rebecca Lukens, now has a companion volume by Lukens and Ruth K.J. Cline, *A Critical Handbook of Young Adult Literature*. Cormier's introduction to the new *Twentieth-Century Young Adult Writers* expresses admirably the state of affairs in the 1990s: even though "YA literature continues to be neglected or misunderstood," he observes, still "the gains made in the field are truly astonishing, considering that ... the first major work to be labelled YA, [*The Outsiders*], was published ... less than thirty years ago" (ix). Cormier is right, I think. The gains are astonishing—not only in the quality and quantity of young adult books, but in the development of criticism as well. All in all, YA scholarship is healthy even if not, or not yet, particularly "theoretical."

Notes

1 A very different textbook, David Russell's *Literature for Children: A Short Introduction* (1991) follows the same grouping as Nodelman's: many young adult titles

are included with those for younger children, concentrated heavily in the chapter called "Realistic Fiction."

2 Richard Ammon's "Last Rites for the Young Adult Novel" connects the marketplace, the writing community, and the critical situation in a brief overview; most critics of young adult literature fail to make these connections unless they are talking about horror or romance series.

3 The Honor Sampling is compiled by a composite method: sources such as *Booklist, New York Times, Horn Book*, and the various ALA lists are compared, and titles that appear in at least three of these lists are ranked.

4 The original Chambers piece, "Alive and Flourishing," which appeared in *Booktalk* (Harper, 1985), is well worth reading in its entirety; several other articles in *Booktalk* also pertain directly to the young adult field, including some consideration of the differences between British and US books for this age group.

5 On a more optimistic note, intercommunication has begun to improve with the spread of electronic discussion groups. It is now common for professionals from different backgrounds to participate in several groups and to cross-post to several groups at once—for instance, to CHILD_LIT, KIDLIT, and PUBYAC. Most of the groups have participants in several countries, and the International Research Society for Children's Literature has recently begun a group (for members only). *The ALAN Review* and *JOYS* have home pages on the World Wide Web, and no doubt others will follow.

6 Editors' note: *Children's Literature Abstracts* lists *JOYS* and the other YA journals mentioned in this article, as does the *Quarterly* bibliography, though fewer citations can be included.

7 Readers who feel that they, of course, were well aware of this should ask themselves whether they noticed the omission of the groundbreaking British journal *Signal*, not to be confused with the unrelated US publication *SIGNAL*, from my account of journal developments. Though *Signal* probably carried more articles of genuine interest to YA enthusiasts than any parallel publication of the 1970s, it is seldom mentioned in US textbooks or referenced by US scholars.

Works Cited

Adams, Gillian. "First Children's Literature: The Case for Sumer." *Children's Literature* 14 (1986): 1-30.

Ammon, Richard. "Last Rites for the Young Adult Novel." *Journal of Children's Literature* 21.1 (1995): 61-62.

Angelotti, Michael. "Will There Be an Adolescent Literature in the 21st Century?" *The ALAN Review* 7.1 (1979): 2.

Aronson, Marc. "The YA Novel Is Dead and Other Fairly Stupid Tales." *School Library Journal* 41.1 (Jan. 1995): 36-37.

Brown, Jean E., and Elaine C. Stephens. *Teaching Young Adult Literature: Sharing the Connection*. Belmont: Wadsworth, 1995.

Carroll, Pamela Sissi. "Acne and Tattoos, Skateboards and Hip-Hop: The Magazines That Adolescents Read for Information." *SIGNAL* 19.2 (1995): 5-10.

Cart, Michael. "Of Risk and Revolution: The Current State of Young Adult Literature." *Journal of Youth Services in Libraries* 8.2 (1995): 151-64.

Cormier, Robert. Introduction. *Twentieth-Century Young Adult Writers.* Ed. Laura Standley Berger. Detroit: St. James, 1994. ix-xi.

Crowe, Chris. "Aiming the New Canon: Developing a Reader Friendly Curriculum." *SIGNAL* 19.3 (1995): 9-11.

Hollindale, Peter. "The Adolescent Novel of Ideas." *Children's Literature in Education* 26.1 (1995): 83-95.

Hunt, Peter. *Criticism, Theory, and Children's Literature.* Oxford: Blackwell, 1991.

Lewis, Ellen. "Teachers in Adolescent Literature: Are We the Good Guys?" *The ALAN Review* 7.1 (1979): 3, 8.

Myszor, Frank. "The See-Saw and the Bridge in Robert Cormier's *After the First Death.*" *Children's Literature* 16 (1988): 77-90.

Nilsen, Alleen Pace and Kenneth Donelson. *Literature for Today's Young Adults.* 4th ed. New York. HarperCollins, 1993.

Nodelman, Perry. "Lesnik-Oberstein's Thesis." 14 December 1995. Online posting. Children's Literature discussion group CHILD_LIT.

——. *The Pleasures of Children's Literature.* New York: Longman, 1992.

——. *The Pleasures of Children's Literature.* 2nd ed. New York: Longman, 1996.

Peck, Richard. "The Silver Anniversary of Young Adult Books." *Journal of Youth Services in Libraries* 7.1 (1993): 19-23.

Sadler, Glenn Edward, ed. *Teaching Children's Literature: Issues, Pedagogy, Resources.* New York: MLA, 1992.

Stephens, John. *Language and Ideology in Children's Fiction.* London: Longman, 1992.

VII

DRAMA AND THEATRE

Children's theatre is a vision of the future. It shows how playwrights, directors, and theatres want to shape their audiences as future spectators, as citizens, and as individuals. Contemplating this when you're sitting with a very young person at some saccharine, patronizing, smarmily produced play in which cute animals solve cute kids' self-esteem problems can be depressing. Things get even gloomier if, while you squirm, you also consider that stage work for children reflects a culture's adult theatre, and, finally, its social attitudes in general. Most American theatre for children is dreadful.

But not all. The work in this issue [of *Theater*]—American or not—starts from one basic perspective: children are full human beings though they haven't yet fully experienced being human, and their imagination, their reasoning, their ethical sense must be respected. Artists should resist the easy art of further socialization into a system that, after all, hasn't worked out benignly so far. Instead they should be presented with scenarios that encourage them to make their own arguments, articulate their particular ways of seeing, and exchange ideas and feelings with other children and the artists (who, of course, may be other children). Such engagement can be quiet, still, and introspective, needless to say. Whatever the form, it should be freeing. (1)

—Erica Munk, "Up Front" (2003)

Theatre for Young Audiences (TYA) in English Canada has grown consistently stronger over the last ten years. But the genre still suffers from an unfortunate stigma that delegates artists working in the form to second-class citizen status. The stereotypes ironically parallel many adults' preconceptions about children generally, who are perceived as irrelevant, irritating, and trivial. Given that sad state of affairs, it is no wonder that artists who work for children are held in low esteem....

Theatre for Young People sets out with the objective to reflect the concerns and reality of its audience with the hope that the play will give the spectators some tools to better cope with a complex and confusing world. The development of future audiences is not a concern because the present young audience is considered to be a valid, important entity in itself—whether or not they choose to go to the theatre when they grow up is up to them. The plays presented are often (though not always) realistic and contemporary with an emphasis on topical social issues addressed from the child's perspective. At its best, Theatre for Young People can be illuminating, moving and exciting; at its worst, this approach can also become didactic, simplistic and tedious. (253)

—Dennis Foon, "Theatre for Young Audiences in English Canada" (1985)

Introduction

As with books for children and youth, drama is often viewed for its pragmatic and didactic merits, rather than its artistic ones. The worlds of children's books and theatre for young audiences have a great deal in common, and yet often seem to exist on separate planes. This fact is perhaps due to the frequent division between critical and creative educational practices, and it is also partly because children's literature as a whole spans nearly as many divisions as literature in general, so the division is no more surprising here. The more relevant distinction when incorporating drama and theatre into children's and young people's experience has to do with where they live in the world, both geographically and socio-economically. Who is the audience? Who are the performers? What is the purpose of the play? How are children viewed by the society in which they live? These key questions might also be applied to books. All three articles in this chapter explore different perspectives on these questions; together, they provide some insight into the complexities of both local and global concerns. Plays are often political in nature, yet in the context of young people, the web of politicking gets stickier, depending on the relationship between the adults and children involved and the location in which they find themselves. Street theatre supporting social justice is worlds apart from British pantomimes celebrating the Christmas season, but both bring live performers and spectators together in a collective experience whose power has long been recognized. In "Theatre for Children in India," Sanjay Kumar provides a brief and poignant overview of how some of these questions are at work in that country in 1998. Jack Zipes's "Political Children's Theatre in the Age of Globalization" provides an in-depth comparative analysis of children's theatre in Germany and the United States of America, culminating in the description of an inter-neighbourhood school exchange program grounded in creative and critical literacy. Finally, Wolfgang Schneider's "'Rosy Cheeks and Shining Eyes' as Criteria in Children's Theatre Criticism" suggests that the adult critics' views of children's theatre have not changed in the decade since Dennis Foon pronounced the basic difficulties of working in the face of adult disdain. Schneider's comments, set in Germany, are pertinent for other parts of the world as well. The fact remains that the individual actors and directors who do this vital work rarely have funds or widespread support for their activities.

Works Cited

Foon, Dennis. "Theatre for Young Audiences in English Canada." *Contemporary Canadian Theatre: New World Visions: A Collection of Essays.* Ed. Anton Wagner. Toronto: Simon & Pierre, 1985. 253-61.

Munk, Erica. "Up Front." *Theater* 33.2 (2003): 1.

Theatre for Children in India:
An Instrument for Social Change? (1998)
Sanjay Kumar

A group of children was playing a game of make-believe called ghar-ghar (house-house). As they acted out the roles of parents, siblings, and servants, they were hardly self-conscious about stepping out of their class and gender roles. One boy took over the part of the mother, when the "mother" was called inside by her parents; and a girl played a male servant and a chauffeur in turn. Just as easily, the game changed to "school-school," and the same children were now asking questions, correcting assignments, and teaching math or history. Scenes like these are common in any neighbourhood in India. Whether adults call this child's play or children's drama, it is an attempt by children to relate to and understand their environment. They are, as in all collective play, developing social skills and learning the adult roles they will later assume in life. Their creativity enables them to question stereotypes and subvert through ridicule and exaggeration what they find reprehensible about the adult "roles." Theatre for children can fulfill this same function. Since adults are involved with theatre for children, before examining a particular manifestation of this art form one must first determine whether it is theatre for children or by children. At least three types of plays can be located in the contemporary Indian scenario: plays produced and directed by adults, meant for viewing by children; plays that are produced and directed by children; and plays emanating from drama workshops for children, where adults have the clear aim of promoting theatre among children. Each type has a potential for effecting social change.

Children's theatre is inevitably linked to the context within which it operates. As a developing, postcolonial country, India is riddled with economic, political, and social problems. The theatre exercise takes place in a larger cultural context and partakes of society's biases, where power and discourse are located with the upper class, upper caste, and upper sex. It is a society marked by unbridgeable and incomprehensible differences between rich and poor, urban and rural. It is a society whose children seek the meaning of their existence in paradigms taken from contexts hostile to their reality, and all want to be successful, with success often being defined in terms of who has more money. Neocolonial forces are stronger than ever in contemporary India— every boy who picks up a guitar wants to be a Michael Jackson; every girl who sings, a Madonna. Should children's theatre in India, then, uphold these "success myths," regardless of the fact that they are rooted in a Western context, or should drama exercise the didactic role of critiquing these paradigms?

In a third-world economy with limited resources, it is unclear whether priority should be given to the pedagogic or entertainment aspects of theatre for children. In a larger sense, all theatre teaches, with its special ability to make a dramatic impact. The tendency in most Indian schools is to see theatre as an extra-curricular activity. Most schools, especially those for upper class children, organize theatre workshops and invite professionals to direct school plays. At the same time, many theatre specialists in the educational system demand that theatre be included as an integral subject in the curriculum. The debate focuses around whether schools should teach the rudiments of theatre in order to prepare children for adult theatre, or whether theatre should compensate for the inadequacies of formal education by emphasizing personality development and providing opportunities for self-expression.

Children's theatre as entertainment is beset by two basic yet interrelated problems: the difficulty of obtaining funds and the tendency to regard children's theatre as nonproductive or at best an auxiliary activity. Hence, children's theatre in India remains largely an amateur activity. Even when the actors and staff are paid, the production is dependent for survival on sponsors and grants. The gate money seldom suffices to pay the rental charges of the auditorium. Theatre companies have to depend on government sources, donors, and the corporate sector to finance performances—and each donation comes with strings attached and an agenda to be pursued.

In the mainstream of contemporary children's theatre are the ubiquitous summer workshops and a theatre directed by adults that seeks to perpetuate the "success myths" of our time. It is a theatre that borrows its paradigms from the "moneyed" fairy tales of the West. This theatre is slick, well-produced, and thoroughly professional. The standards are high—after all, it represents a Broadway or Royal Albert Hall in India. In metropolitan cities, productions of *Aladdin, Evita, My Fair Lady,* and *West Side Story* are staged by diverse school groups. The problem with such theatre is that it presents inferior repetitions, without questioning the Western paradigms and without any modifications or adaptation. For instance, in the Cinderella story—popular fare in children's theatre—no attempt is ever made to revisit the story from the point of view of the stepmother or the stepsisters, who are actually the marginalized outsiders; there is no critique of the father, who for personal (sexual?) satisfaction has placed the four women in an undesirable situation; and there is no questioning whether the "dear prince," who throws his heart away after one dance and insists on marrying any girl who fits the shoe (common sense tells us that it could have fit more than one girl), is worth having at all. It is a theatre that titillates, creating fantasy worlds and presenting standards and stereotypes that emanate from a different cultural context.

At the other extreme is theatre that is often (and unfairly at that) called sarkari, or propaganda theatre. This theatre is often a part of governmental programs and seeks to create social awareness. The Saturday clubs and summer workshops held by the National School of Drama (NSD) are a case in point. Modeled on the Theatre in Education (TIE) concept that originated in the United Kingdom in the 1970s, NSD opened its first TIE company at the end of the 1980s. The experiments consist of an interaction between young graduates of the school and children between eight and fifteen years old. Workshops are run simultaneously in several locations in a city, and children are encouraged to express their ideas, often leading to an in-house production rather than a public performance.

Besides NSD, the Sahitya Kala Parishad and the National Bal Bhavan also offer opportunities for a less restricted and more innovative children's theatre. The adult director sees himself as one who imparts technical knowledge on the basics of theatre and acting, while the children build the production largely on their own. The director's greatest challenge is to retain the spontaneity of the child and spark creativity. Folk tales, nonsense stories, and rhymes form the subject matter of such dramatic experiences. Participants later broaden the scope of the program by diversifying and experimenting with other groups and sponsors. This theatre provides some of the better examples of children's theatre in India today.

To target the needs of children and serve as an agent of social change, the avant-garde groups stage plays that focus on themes and issues pertaining to children, voicing the problems children face in a space largely occupied by adults. Two such groups are Uttra (meaning "north" and "answer" in Hindi), which is composed mainly of seventeen year-olds, and Umang, which is managed by adults and has children as its audience. However, such groups are marginalized. Strapped for funds and beleaguered by organizational problems, they are unable to survive financially for long; often they regroup or appear under new names.

Before theatre in India can be an instrument of change by providing awareness of the socially important issues of gender, class, and race, the first step is to acknowledge that neither children nor theatre receive adequate prioritization.

Political Children's Theatre in the Age of Globalization (2003)
Jack Zipes

Thirty years ago I went to Germany to write about Peter Stein's Schaubühne am Halleschen Ufer and other experimental theatre groups sprouting in the aftermath of the 1960s student movement. While I was in Berlin, a friend told me that its most significant political theatre was not really the Schaubühne, but Grips, founded by the writer Volker Ludwig. Its members, who used to

245 Political Children's Theatre in the Age of Globalization

perform in a left-wing cabaret for adults, had recently turned their attention to developing unusual plays for children that incorporated rock music and Brechtian dramaturgical methods. Their work overwhelmed me. And unlike the spectacular Schaubühne and many other so-called political theatres of that time, Grips continues to challenge and provoke children and adults to change their lives, if not society as a whole.

The name Grips means something like "common sense" and implies using one's intelligence politically to understand the world; accordingly, Volker Ludwig, Grips's director and major writer, seeks to link theatre to emancipatory education. He has often remarked that Grips's plays are designed to show our condition as changeable and to reveal possibilities for social transformation and critical thinking: "Primarily this means that we want to encourage children to ask questions, to understand that criticism is their undeniable right, to enjoy creative thinking, and to gain pleasure from seeing alternatives" (Zipes, *Political Plays* 2). How does the Grips ensemble, which has constantly responded to changing political conditions, bring this about? Almost all of their plays are Brechtian Lehrstücke (learning plays) performed in a cabaret style. The adult actors do not try to mimic children or to act naturalistically. On the contrary, social conditions and events are explained and demonstrated from a child's point of view. The plays do not present solutions but show possible alternatives to conditions that are oppressive or self-defeating. The plays are not ends in themselves; they do not preach the right answers, nor should they be performed this way.

Each scene tends to be a social experiment, a testing of social conditions to see if perhaps some other form of organization might allow for more freedom of movement and development. Characters represent antagonistic principles, and as they are unmasked, the social relations underlying the principles become more visible, as in *Mannomann!* (1973), an early play about male chauvinism, in which a factory worker realizes that his violent behaviour is connected to his own exploitation; *Bella, Boss und Bulli* (1995), a drama about bullying, in which children grasp how their conflicts are tied to family issues; and *Melody's Ring* (2000), a musical that connects the behaviour of the homeless to business corruption and unemployment. Cabaret performance has been the dominant influence on the actors and the playwrights, because it is illusion-smashing, frank, quick, and jovial, yet serious. Grips's productions and techniques can be repetitive, but more than any children's theatre I know, Grips has resisted the forces of compromise and continues to demonstrate how theatre can address ordinary children's daily struggles with the authorities and institutions that govern their, and our, lives.

But this essay is not about Grips, which even in Berlin is special and unique.[1] Rather, it is an attempt to grasp why we need an alternative, not just to lily-white, run-of-the-mill, middle-class children's theatre but also to a youth entertainment industry whose spectacles make even the productions of

246 Drama and Theatre

middle-class children's theatre seem radical at times. First I want to hark back to Walter Benjamin's essays on children's literature and culture.[2] Then I want to say a few words about the state of children's culture in the United States and how it is organized—that is, homogenized—for them. Finally I want to discuss different kinds of "unspectacular" children's theatre that thrive in the nooks and crannies of public realms.

The Timeless Walter Benjamin

In 1928, Walter Benjamin, who had already expressed an interest in children's literature by collecting children's books, began to do radio commentary on children's culture. The same year he wrote a curious piece entitled "Program of a Proletarian Children's Theatre"—curious because Benjamin knew very little about children's theatre, which nobody then took notice of— a piece that forty years later, in the late 1960s and 1970s, shaped the way West German activists approached children's culture. Benjamin wrote "Program" for the Latvian director Asja Lacis, whose work he admired and with whom he was very much in love.[3] Benjamin met Lacis on the isle of Capri in 1923. A dedicated Communist, Lacis played a short but important role in developing a unique Russian children's theatre during the agitprop years of the Revolution. In 1928 she was sent to Berlin as a Communist cultural worker to do experimental drama with young people at the Liebknecht House. Benjamin proposed to assist her by writing a theoretical framework for a new political children's theatre. The result, based on their conversations, stressed spontaneity, collectivity, and autonomy in young people and focused on process, on integrating children's intuition into the work, and on raising the participants' awareness of social and economic differences.

In the 1920s, a period of cultural war in Weimar Germany, theatre became a battlefield and a realm for experiments ranging from the agitprop work of Erwin Piscator to the opulent productions of Max Reinhardt. All the major parties—Social Democratic, Communist, and Nazi—formed youth groups that made theatre into propaganda, a means to win the minds of children. Because this political aspect of theatre was less obvious in the mainstream middle-class *Luxustheatre*, which generally produced charming fairy-tale plays at Christmas and other appropriate times, Benjamin declared: "The theatre of the present-day bourgeoisie is economically determined by profit. Sociologically it is, above all, an instrument of sensation in front of and behind the curtains. It is different with the proletarian children's theatre. Just as the first firm grip of the Bolshevists was used to raise the red flag, so their first instinct was to organize the children.... From the viewpoint of the bourgeoisie, nothing is more dangerous for children than theatre" (81).

Neither Benjamin's use of such terms as *bourgeois* nor his strident tone should put us off. After all, he was writing for his "comrades" and for Lacis. He was trying to make a crucial class and experiential distinction that holds true even today: theatre that addresses the concerns of the majority of children—who, then as now, are poor and disadvantaged—fuses play and reality and allows children to become more conscious of how they can explore the forces that act upon them. This indeed makes theatre dangerous, but not just for today's corporate and professional elite groups. Theatre that prompts children to take charge of their actions is risky for all social classes. It upsets authorities and institutions. Freed to explore, children will cross all sorts of lines, often in politically incorrect ways, something even Benjamin did not grasp.

Or did he? Benjamin goes on to say that productions are not the real goal of the strenuous collective work accomplished in the children's clubs. Productions are incidental; "they come about by mistake, almost as a whim of the children.... More important are the tensions which are resolved in such productions. The tensions of the collective work are the educators" (81).

Such tensions between individuals and social conditions are explosive, demanding patience and comprehension on the part of the theatre's adult leaders and the young people themselves. Emphasizing the status of children as independent agents, Benjamin conceived of young people, especially between the ages of six and sixteen, as supremely qualified directors. They were *erdenfern und unverfroren*—that is, they were not yet fixed and bound to earth, but were fluid and malleable. They could take ordinary situations and turn them around to reflect their own tastes and needs.

Key ideas of Benjamin's "Program" and his essays on children's culture were in direct opposition to the pedagogical principles and discipline of his period, when formal German idealism and middle-class notions of what was appropriate for children regulated youthful enthusiasm and naive susceptibility. If I summarize some of his ideas, their subversiveness will become apparent.

• All books, toys, clothes, plays, films, and other products for children are created by socialization and by the prevailing means of production and reception. Class specific even when they do not appear to be so, they were and still are used for children's "own good." Their inescapable prescriptiveness can be suspended only by children who appropriate them on their own terms and use them to create their own world, one that functions according to relatively new rules.

• From the "bourgeois" perspective, the carefully designed and censored production of children's objects greatly determines their reception. Children are to be protected from reality and are to see, read, and buy only what adults believe is good for them. In other words, children are to be raised as passive and obedient spectators and readers.

- It has always been illusory to believe in predictable, positivist social conditioning. Children are not automatons. To develop their own identities, they read and play with what has been printed, produced, manufactured, and organized not only for them but also for adults.
- Only through play can children create an environment where they can pursue their own interests, which they intuit and need to articulate in a free space.
- A "true" childhood, in which the child functions as a player, a collector, and a producer of his or her identity, is impossible in the traditional public sphere, for there a child's life is narrowly prescribed and reflects the interests of hierarchical classes.
- By developing a "proletarian" public sphere, that is, a "proletarian" children's theatre, one creates the conditions for producing new plays, new books, new insights. At the heart of children's play is the re-formation of the world.

Today in the United States the old divisions between the proletariat, petite bourgeoisie, agrarian class, middle class, and upper class no longer function as cleanly as they did in Benjamin's Germany. The ideology of consumerism tends to erase or conceal differences. For anyone with sufficient money, class boundaries are easy to cross and transgress. Because the international conglomerates that produce books, toys, clothes, plays, videos, and so on seek the lowest common denominator, any boy or girl can subscribe momentarily to an illusive social group and feel wealthy, important, strong, or cool. The purpose of production is to conceal class.

Multiculturalism contributes to the concealment of class differences because it argues for inclusion in the "grand" middle class of America. But whatever is produced by America's underclasses and nonmainstream groups eventually is appropriated by the professional and corporate classes and marketed for everyone. Cultural homogenization makes it extremely difficult to demarcate a class-specific game, toy, film, or play. The discourse of the professional and corporate classes in the public sphere and in the cultural industry tends to foster a notion of one nation or one family under God, which can enjoy the fruits of American life if we all do our respective jobs and keep the economy working. Such occlusion of class differences makes it all the more important to find the differences that do exist.

For American children to have a "true childhood," in Benjamin's sense of the term, they must live and interact within both public and private spheres and be allowed to use their imaginations freely, to notice class differences, to grasp the ideology of consumerism, and to deal with imposed religions, ideologies, and pressures.[4] Accordingly, their adult leaders should not act just as observers who receive new impulses from the creative efforts and productions of the children; they should encourage and guide the children, fostering awareness of how consumerism works and how society's spectacles can conceal reality.

For the learning process to be effective, the adults must be honest with the children, and they must also learn how to learn from the children, who will appropriate everything that comes their way. As Benjamin writes in *Einbahnstraße*: "It is foolish to grumble pedantically about the production of objects appropriate for children—illustrative materials, toys, or books," because "the earth is full of the most incomparable objects that capture the attention of children who use them," especially "garbage and junk left over from building, gardening, housework, sewing, or carpentry." Using these "objects of junk" in play, they "form their world of things by themselves, a small world in the large one. One has to have an eye for the norms of this small world of things if one wants to create deliberately for children" and let oneself find a way to them (73). Now, in the age of consumerism and globalization, Benjamin's critique can help us understand how social conditions and contradictions limit our ability to let children play freely with "junk" to explore alternatives and discover their talents.

Children and Children's Culture Today

American children have become insatiable consumers of manufactured identities that falsely promise excitement and happiness. This creates a major dilemma for children's theatre: how to attract an audience while at the same time avoiding absorption into the culture industry, where it would be subjected to the forces of globalization, which turn everything into spectacle. Because the transformation of theatre into spectacle diminishes the "threat" of theatre to the dominant forces of power, it is important to understand the distinction between the two. In *The Society of the Spectacle*, written in the heyday of the student revolution in France, Guy Debord declared:

> By means of the spectacle the ruling order discourses endlessly upon itself in an uninterrupted monologue of self-praise. The spectacle is the self-portrait of power in the age of power's totalitarian rule over conditions of existence.... If the spectacle—understood in the limited sense of those "mass media" that are its most stultifying superficial manifestation—seems at times to be invading society in the shape of a mere apparatus, it should be remembered that this apparatus has nothing neutral about it, and that it answers precisely to the needs of the spectacle's internal dynamics. (19)[5]

There are many problems with Debord's overall analysis, such as his attribution of monolithic power to the state and his conviction that we are living in a totally administered society, a viewpoint that he shared with other eminent postwar critics, including Theodor Adorno, Max Horkheimer, Herbert Marcuse, and Louis Althusser. They were not entirely wrong, but they did not give enough credit to the resilience and sheer inventiveness of human beings: we create spaces for alternative lifestyles; we find ways to undermine the abuses of power and show the spectacle for what it really is.

Still, Debord's discussion helps us grasp that the spectacle, instead of revealing society, produces and reproduces power relations that maintain and reinforce the status quo. It is a social construct that reduces us to mere spectators, thus engendering alienation. Debord argues that the more the spectator watches, "the less he lives; the more readily he recognizes his own needs in the images of need proposed by the dominant system, the less he understands his own existence and his own desires. The spectacle's externality with respect to the acting subject is demonstrated by the fact that the individual's own gestures are no longer his own, but rather those of someone else who represents them to him. The spectator feels at home nowhere, for the spectacle is everywhere" (23).

We need only think of the staging of "authentic" emotions on TV talk shows to realize how people *perform* emotions and end up looking like replicas of themselves. It is not just this deep alienation of emotions that the spectacle fosters, however. It also generates modes of behaviour. Whether children actually will become what the culture industry presents as ideal is an open question. In fact, the culture industry does not care in the least what happens to children as long as they agree to consume, as long as they are disposed to become professionals who will maintain the system in some capacity. Benjamin was right when he talked about the profit motive of bourgeois theatre, but he underestimated the power of the culture industry.

Children's theatre as spectacle furthers the pauperization of children, if not their prostitution: material pauperization and pauperization of the mind, prostitution of the body, and prostitution of talent. Much of children's theatre today tries to prevent critical thinking by children even as it presents itself as moral, serious, patriotic, and God-fearing. Public spectacles are rampant, and children cannot escape their vamped-up ideologies. To be sure, they continue to play with junk, but even that won't help them form new meanings without guidance. They may become "shrubs"—wooden Howdy Doodies, funny, cute, adorable puppets who trip over their own strings. Although they are jerked constantly, they believe that they do not have strings attached to them. Shrubs are devoid of identity.

Globalization contributes to the devastation of everyone's identities, especially children's, but it does this in a very class-specific manner. In perhaps the most astute and concise analysis of globalization I have read, Zygmunt Bauman says,

> To put it in a nutshell: *rather than homogenizing the human condition, the technological annulment of temporal/spatial distances tends to polarize it. It* [global-

ization] emancipates certain humans from territorial constraints and renders certain community-generating meanings extraterritorial—while denuding the territory, to which other people go on being confined, of its meaning and its identity-endowing capacity. For some people it augurs an unprecedented freedom from physical obstacles and unheard-of ability to move and act from a distance. For others, it portends the impossibility of appropriating and domesticating the locality from which they have little chance of cutting themselves free in order to move elsewhere. With "distances no longer meaning anything," localities, separated by distances, also lose their meanings. This, however, augurs freedom of meaning-creation for some, but portends ascription to meaninglessness for others. Some can now move out of the locality—any locality—at will. Others watch helplessly the sole locality they inhabit moving away from under their feet. (18).

With the dissolution of public places, or public spheres, communities break down. One of the ironies of polarization is that it leaves loose bunches of people, who are no longer bound by community ties, open to homogenization and uniformity. They want to belong to some sort of meaning-producing group, be it a church, sports team, cult, choir, or fan club.

This is the paradox, I think, that evades Bauman. As he correctly remarks, globalization brings about polarization and fractures communities. Yet it also seeks to replace religious and social forms of community with a consumer ideology and to replace established forms of work and play with more organized forms that homogenize behaviour and limit the development of class and political consciousness.[6] Seemingly diverse and enclosed groups that seek to form distinct identities are actually more uniform and similar than they realize; all forms of interaction revolve around the same customary practices, which make activities into commercial undertakings and children into consumers.

Here are two brief examples: organized sports and school. The pressure to conform and celebrate uniformity begins, in American sports, before children turn five. They learn to perform according to adult expectations—how to play the game, which uniforms to purchase, what to expend energy on, what to feel. Only forty years ago, children organized themselves on streets and in backyards and playgrounds and developed their own games. Now the dominant forms of sports are associated with professionalization; the child is raised, educated, and groomed to think of selling his or her body for profit at some point. If that expectation cannot be fulfilled, there are others, such as perfecting one's body so that it looks like a machine, an exercise of self-denial instead of self-expression.

The most startling transformations in schooling are connected to the encroachment of business corporations into schools and the privatization of public schools.[7] The focus used to be on children and how they might be assisted in defining their identity; now it has shifted conclusively toward adult expectations of preparing their children for careers, and state expectations of maintaining the level of functional literacy needed for business and government to preserve themselves. Except at certain schools, such as those run according to the Montessori, Reggio Emilia, and Waldorf (Rudolf Steiner) philosophies, the child is now merely the object of experimentation.

Children's Theatre as the Unspectacular

Theatre cannot avoid spectacle. Most plays for children are produced for the play's sake, not for the children's; most pander to the entertainment industry's expectations and conceal power relations in the way Debord demonstrated. Traditional plays show off talent while concealing any connection to the daily struggles of children or their attempt to grasp how art can play a role in their immediate lives. While many performances deal with social issues, they divert attention from those mediations that bind children into the corporate interests of the public sphere. A good example of this perniciousness is *A Christmas Carol.* The Guthrie Theatre in Minneapolis, for one, reproduces a version every December—not to prompt children to think about capitalism, misers, poverty, and exploitation but to exhibit grandiose stage effects and fine acting. *A Christmas Carol* is performed to ease the conscience of the rich and to celebrate philanthropy without questioning it. The producers imagine that children cannot think for themselves.

Fortunately, work in the theatre can also endanger spectacle. Many forms of theatre are subversive. But theatre demands space for constant experimentation with the world of objects and for self-experimentation with one's body and mind. And unless children can appropriate the scripts, all plays—Broadway plays, classical dramas, adaptations of famous novels—have minimal value for their lives. To appropriate scripts, children must have the freedom of space and time to investigate the texts and see how they have been produced, received, and distributed. Any leftover signification forms the basis of the children's production.

I do not mean to dismiss the production of such traditional plays as *A Christmas Carol, Little Orphan Annie,* and *Peter Pan* in the professional children's theatre or in schools. I have often been struck by the excitement and pleasure children exude when they watch a live performance. Yet they are being introduced to prescribed ways of performance. Even question-and-answer sessions after a play or a tour of the stage do not lead to self-exploration or critical examination of their environment.

Benjamin insisted that plays not be performed for children. Rather, children should develop their own plays with the guidance of adults, who are also part of the learning process. All other theatrical forms he disregarded as "bourgeois" and discounted as spectacle, although he did not use that term.

This position, I think, is too narrow. No matter what children watch, they will cherish and cultivate some aspect of it in original ways. There is, however, no doubt in my mind that the most effective political theatre for children demands children's physical and intellectual immersion in a project of their own conception and undertaking.

Numerous Western theatrical groups formed of adults only or a mixture of adults and children are nonetheless managing to do unusual unspectacular work that can be considered politically subversive or threatening. Grips is the kind of theatre that produces plays written and performed by adults to provoke children and adults to question the political relations in their lives.

Antispectacular theatre conceived and performed by adults to animate children opens up fissures in the totalizing tendencies of global capitalism. No one model of political children's theatre exists, and perhaps even the term *political* fails to describe adequately some of the important experiments I have seen in the past ten years. I will use the term *political children's theatre* anyway, because the political nature of their work is what sustains the focus of the young spectators, enabling them to glimpse the power relations that distort their view of the world.

Reviewing the Unspectacular

What, then, is children's theatre? Is it theatre for the very young, aged three to ten, or for teenagers? Are some plays and performances age-specific? Should plays be censored for certain age groups? Why even make distinctions? Aren't the best plays and performances for children productions that appeal to people of all ages?

It would take a book to answer these questions, but certainly distinctions can be made with regard to children's reception of plays. While the best work is universal, many theatre groups create modes of production expressly designed for people of certain ages. Dockteatern Tittut (the Peek-a-Boo Puppet Theatre, Sweden), Mimika Theatre (England), Teater Terra (Netherlands), and the Catherine Wheels Theatre Company (Scotland) have all created plays that address very young audiences and use space and sound in unusual ways to address alienation, loneliness, and loss. The actors, directors, and designers invest care and thought in their productions. This adult investment in animating children to ponder complex existential problems is, I think, what is of value in political children's theatre.

I saw two plays, *Langel and the Horse Named Blue* and *Wanna Be Wolf*, performed by the Dockteatern Tittut in Minneapolis, and what struck me was the manner in which they used puppets, dolls, and scenery to tell simple narratives with poetry, humour, and poignancy. *Langel and the Horse Named Blue* is about a boy who has a best friend named Gudmar; a blue horse comes between them, and jealousy almost ends their friendship. *Wanna Be Wolf*, based on a book by Ulf Stark, is a shadow-puppet play about a wolf with whom nobody wants to play because she is so zany and wild and a rabbit who is scared of his own shadow. They meet, exchange identities, play together, and in the end become good friends.

All the plays created and produced by Dockteatern are intended for children between the ages of two and six, and the audience is generally limited to thirty or forty spectators at most. The atmosphere of intimacy and the stage music are soothing, and the brevity of the plays (approximately thirty minutes) enables the children to relax and concentrate. The dialogue, sounds, rhymes, and songs demonstrate how language and relationships can be played with and transformed, recalling how children interact with one another in their own play. The puppets are almost like the found objects that children invent stories for. There is nothing overtly political about Dockteatern's plots or dramatic style, but the unpretentious acting is exactly the opposite of spectacle theatre. The actors talk to the children before and after the performance and invite them to touch and look at the sets and puppets. These interactions show respect for the children's intelligence. There is nothing sweet about Dockteatern. The language is idiomatic, and although the characters and colors are marvellous, the problems depicted are real ones that the very young confront in their everyday lives.

The struggles of daily life also shape Mimika Theatre's production *Landscapes*, which I saw at the 2002 International Children's Festival at the Ordway Center for the Performing Arts in St. Paul. Like the Dockteatern actors, Mimika's two puppeteers limited the audience to twenty children, taking them two at a time into a dimly lit canvas tent filled with music based on sounds from nature. Once the play started, the audience was taken on a journey through a desert, a tropical rain forest, the sea, and Antarctica. The scenery kept changing, and the animals in each landscape preyed on, as well as played with, one another. There was a sense of survival of the fittest, but with the twinkle of an eye, for the smaller creatures managed to escape the predators. Here, too, the puppeteers were often visible, and after the play came to a close, they talked with the children and showed them how they worked the puppets and scenery. Although the magic of the performance was thereby dispelled, the art was passed on, and the children may later experiment in much the same way the actors themselves did.

The unselfish dedication of the actors to educating children through their experimental art always comes through in the best of the small groups I have seen, as does a persistent attempt to link the personal to the social and political. At the 2001 Ordway festival, the Dutch troupe Teater Terra performed *Swan's Down*, about a child's confrontation with death. Simon, a small boy played by a large puppet, lives with his father near the sea. The boy's mother recently drowned, but thanks to a friendship the boy develops with a mother swan, he begins to take joy in life again. When a nasty neighbour kills another swan, the boy empathizes with the mother swan and comes to terms with the loss of his own mother. Performed by three actors on a proscenium stage with no change of scenery, this play moved slowly yet had a poetic flow: the actors did not waste a gesture or word, nor did they seek to create a melodrama. Rather, the reserved, somewhat blunt acting style and the spare scenery captured a mood of loss that was gradually overcome by the puppet/boy, who shared his feelings with the young spectators without trying to overwhelm them.

The Catherine Wheels Theatre Company performed a drama entitled *Martha* at the 2002 Ordway festival. A grumpy woman of that name lives in a shack by the sea. She has tacked a sign on her shack that reads: "Don't knock. Just go away!" Most people are scared of her, and even the mailman, who tries to befriend her, is driven away. Then a stray white goose shows up at her shack and begins to pester and play with her. When the goose gets sick, Martha brings him into her home, where she nurses him back to health. They form a friendship, and Martha becomes an agreeable and joyful person. When the goose disappears overnight to join his flock, Martha realizes why the goose had to leave. She joins the mailman on an outing and appears to have overcome her loneliness. Performed by two actors, the play had no young characters, unless one considers the goose a kind of wild child. The goose was a rod puppet, and the setting was spare. Once again, the actors took a simple situation—the outcast condition of a disgruntled older woman—and turned it into a poignant drama about the possibility for change and friendship.

The didactic elements of these unspectacular dramas for the youngest spectators were not emphasized by any of the groups I have discussed. Adult actors used metaphors and puppets to tell a simple, fantastic story as realistically as possible. This style was in stark contrast to that in two productions for teenagers I witnessed at the International Festivals of 2001 and 2002. Both plays were highly realistic, involved violence, and were intended to create postperformance discussions about particular incidents.

The Stones, by Australia's Zeal Theatre, is based on an event that took place in Melbourne. Two boys kicked rocks from a freeway overpass for fun, accidentally causing a driver's death, and were charged with manslaughter. The verdict was "not guilty." But here, ultimately, the audience is called upon to deliver the verdict, for the play ends with one of the boys realizing how reckless he had been and the other just relieved that he was "getting off." Two actors play all the roles—the boys, officers, attorneys—in a small space with a minimum change of costume. They never "identify" with their characters, but in good Brechtian fashion demonstrate how small acts of vandalism can lead to tragedy. Going beyond pure documentary, the play calls upon the spectators to reveal what they have learned and to make judgments.

The work of the Teatergruppen Mariehønen of Denmark is also based on the Brechtian *Lehrstück* methodology. Here the set, which can easily be transported into schools or open spaces, acts as a metaphor of life. An equilateral triangle surrounds a box that contains large boxing gloves; a lighting rig at each point of the triangle is the designated space for each character. The spectators are ushered in as if they are going to witness a boxing match. The characters, all in their early teens, are Poul; Stevens, a bully, who makes life hell for Poul; Norman, who has an alcoholic father who beats him and his mother; and Henrietta, whose parents are going through a divorce. The play begins at the end of the school year. Stevens beats Poul up and makes him promise that on the first day of school in the fall he will wear girl's clothing to indicate that he is a "sissy." Poul spends the summer with his friends Norman and Henrietta learning how to box so he can defend himself in the fall. Stevens frequently interferes with the friends, as do their conflicts at home. All their personal problems emerge as they engage in the boxing ring of life. In the end they find a way to stop the turmoil and violence of bullying, confronting it inside and outside their homes.

The actors do not mimic teenagers. Instead, they illustrate the dramatic situations in which teenagers may find themselves. Making full use of the boxing metaphor, they reveal the shifting sides of the different combats that the characters are obliged to enter. What becomes clear is that there are many ways to defend oneself and that solidarity is essential when one is confronted by tyranny.

There are hundreds of tiny groups like Teatergruppen Mariehønen and Zeal Theatre in the Western world, formed by adults with a message for children. Their work varies according to their grasp of the power relations of their social world. Characteristically their best work is unspectacular, enabling their audiences to unravel some of the forces that control their lives. When children and adults play together and learn how to cooperate against these forces, they form unspectacular theatre that is dangerous to the theatre of the spectacle.

It is crucial to support the kind of educational children's theatre that generally takes place unseen in thousands of schools in the Western world. In the United States this comes closest to what Benjamin envisioned as proletarian children's theatre. If we don't support it, the unspectacular will not thrive as a subversive force—and I think that is our only hope for it. Fortunately (or, some might say, unfortunately), the society of the spectacle, like the theatre of the spectacle itself, feeds off the unspectacular. Both need its life force to make themselves appear interesting as well as interested in their spectators. I will close with a summary of the work that I do with the Children's Theatre Company of Minneapolis. This large, wealthy organization exemplifies how a traditional middle-class theatre, while creating spectacles, can transcend itself through subversive unspectacular work.

Neighborhood Bridges

Neighborhood Bridges, originally sponsored by a generous grant from the Open Foundation in New York, is now entirely funded by the Children's Theatre Company of Minneapolis. The syllabus is based on my book *Creative Storytelling: Building Community, Changing Lives* (1995). The aim was to set up a year-round program in two inner-city elementary schools in Minneapolis, with storytellers meeting with one class in each school for two hours a week. The children in these schools are mainly African American, Hmong, Somalian, and Native American, with a sprinkling of whites. The two classes were to contact each other during the course of the year, and in May, after exploring different genres of storytelling, writing, drawing, and improvisation, they each would present a play they had created for their own school and parents. They would perform this play for the partner school and then, finally, join the other class in a festival at the Children's Theatre. In other words, productions would create bridges within the school, the community, and the theatre.

In the spring and summer of 1998, I trained eight actors and taught an intensive summer seminar for teachers and storytellers to prepare them for the first year. Our success in developing the talents and skills of more than one hundred students during the first two years enabled us to obtain more support from other foundations and to expand; by the fall of 2002, Neighborhood Bridges had effective programs in six inner-city schools in Minneapolis. More actor-educators have been trained in summer seminars taught in collaboration with the Perpich Center for the Arts and Hamline University. The program, now with thirteen classes of more than three hundred students, involves extensive collaboration with teachers in all the schools, as well as with the Book Arts Center and the College of Education at the University of Minnesota. The children become pen pals with their friends at other schools and meet at the Children's Theatre to see performances and learn about the production of plays. To celebrate their work during the school year, they perform their own plays in school festivals in May.

Neighborhood Bridges has three guiding principles:

1. We believe that much harm has been done to children by the mass media in all its forms, and our creative work is in part a means to offset and question this influence. We do not, however, dismiss or denigrate popular culture. We try to expose contradictions instead. For instance, we discuss how wonderful superheroes are as they fight for the disadvantaged, but we prompt the students to ask why the superheroes earn so much money by getting children to buy consumer articles while they, the children, remain poor. Why don't superheroes change the conditions of the children's lives? How can any of us change our lives? Do we need heroes? The actor-educators of Neighborhood

Bridges offer not solutions or resolutions but alternative ways of thinking and acting.

2. We know that we cannot fully change children's lives, and we do not want to play the role of therapist. But we do want to engage teachers and children, to animate them, to set them on a path of self-discovery, to provide skills, to strengthen self-confidence. In the process, we learn as much about ourselves and our capabilities as they do about theirs.

3. Our work is not limited to a specific grade level or school. We focus on storytelling as a means to enable people to become storytellers of their lives, a technique that can be used from preschools to universities and elsewhere. We do not believe in one-time workshops, seminars, or performances. Primarily we seek to build community, which means that our work is long-term and that we want to involve not just children but also parents, teachers, administrators, actor-educators, and friends. At times the creative process may even test the conception and self-conception of the institutions within which we work.

To keep ourselves from imposing our method and ideas, we borrowed a slogan from Brecht: Make yourself dispensable, especially when it comes to sharing knowledge. To this end, we make contact with all the schools, teachers, and administrators, hand out a printed syllabus, offer a summer workshop for teachers, hold preparatory meetings each week with the teachers, and hold three meetings a year with teachers from all the schools in our program. Ironically, there is one major problem that we actually hope arises and that we seek to resolve through collaboration: teachers have found that our work makes the writing, reading, and learning that the children do more pleasurable and even more effective than the official programs.

Outside the schools themselves, our collaboration involves the staff at the Children's Theatre Company, parents, and university students and professors at certain stages of our work, and in the spring, each class also has the opportunity to bring in musicians, set designers, costume makers, or dancers to help the children learn about different arts and crafts. In short, our May celebration of nine months' work with the children is a collaborative effort in which the entire community expresses and articulates how the children see and imagine themselves in the world around them.

The children in May are not the same children that we met in September. Obviously, they have grown because of all sorts of biological, psychological, and social factors. Viewed in light of our program, we can note additional individual and collective changes. We encourage and foster transformation in two primary ways: (1) by constantly changing the classroom environment and introducing the children to new environments and (2) by improvising to alter rules and regulations and to shift their expectations, and the audience's. For instance, we begin by playing a game called the fantastic binominal, which is varied throughout the year. It begins with the actor-educator writing prepositions called linking words on the board and asking the class for any two nouns, which she or he also writes on the board. After asking the students to choose a linking word, the actor-educator improvises a story based on the three words (perhaps "bear on ice cream," or "ice cream on the bear"). After that story is done, the actor-educator asks for two volunteers to write two more nouns on the board. The words are to stimulate the students to write and illustrate very short stories. Three or four volunteers read their stories aloud after reading the stories to themselves to make sure they understand what has been written. These stories can serve as the basis for further work during the week, with the teacher helping the students hone their stories and draw pictures. They also serve as scripts for plays that the students develop.

After the children write and perform their stories for the other children, we push the chairs and tables to the side to create a free space. The children, recognizing that the classroom can be changed to their liking, turn found objects—"junk"—into props, people, scenery—things other than they are—just as the children themselves will become other than they think they are. Environmental change leads to personal change. Our initial game with the fantastic binominal animates the children to conceive stories in which two haphazard elements are brought together to form a story, their story. In the same way, movement and taking over terrain in the classroom for storytelling, discussion, and performance can lead to an understanding of how appropriation can work.

We want to suggest to the children (and the teachers) that appropriation can enable them to express their desires and needs. We model change. We tell fairy tales, legends, fables, tall tales, myths, and then similar tales that question the traditional versions. For instance, we tell "Little Red Riding Hood" as a tale of rape in which the girl is blamed for her own violation, and we counter it with Catherine Storr's "Little Polly Riding Hood and the Stupid Wolf" to show how girls can trick and escape predators. We develop plays that contrast heroes like John Henry or Kate Crackernuts with the superheroes of comics and popular films and animate the students to create their own heroes or question heroism. We act these stories out with the students and push them with our suggestions to take over all the tales told during the two hours we are with them. We show that we are not afraid to take risks even when we may make blunders. We adapt to constantly changing conditions in the classroom and in the school. We try to show how change may be linked to tolerance. By forming within the classroom three groups of children that stay together throughout the year, we hope the children will build their own little community and cooperate with one another. We try to foster respect and understanding among the three groups. In the end, they will join together and be changed into one large community to produce a play for other classes and schools.

We have seen shy children step into spaces they had never entered before. We have seen previously uncooperative children join in freely. We have seen children conceive projects that represent changes they have been undergoing and discoveries they are making. In the May 2002 festival of Crossing Bridges, one class turned "The Magic Table, the Gold Donkey, and the Club" into a play about drug dealing. Another class created a story about a soldier bringing peace to an ethnically divided neighbourhood through a song contest.

Finally, in all our work, we note changes in the teachers and ourselves—how we become more sensitive to children's needs and our own and how we use conversation to solve problems and to create projects that build on our social awareness and creative designs.

Creative and Critical Literacy

Neighborhood Bridges is an explicit critique of functional literacy and how schools and politicians hinder learning by testing rote skills. Until the end of the nineteenth century, most people did not know how to read and write, yet they were able to solve problems and build great things. The oral form of transmitting and sharing knowledge was sufficient and, in many cases, still is sufficient to spark imagination and inspire people to think critically about their circumstances. On the other hand, reading and writing are important skills in our advanced technological society, and they can enable children to gain meaningful pleasure out of life and to structure their existence in manifold ways. So we do help children learn how to read and write. Without the requisite oral, literary, and dramatic skills, it is difficult for them to project themselves into the world and to narrate their own lives.

A remark by the psychologist Jerome Bruner encapsulates our approach:

> I conceive of schools and preschools as serving a renewed function within our changing societies. This entails building school cultures that operate as mutual communities of learners, involved jointly in solving problems with all contributing to the process of educating one another. Such groups provide not only a locus for instruction, but a focus for identity and mutual work. Let these schools be a place for the praxis (rather than the proclamation) of cultural mutuality—which means an increase in the awareness that children have of what they are doing, how they are doing it, and why. The balance between individuality and group effectiveness gets worked out within the culture of the group; so too the balancing of ethnic or racial identities and the sense of the larger community of which they are part. (81-82)

Bruner calls for mutual learning that depends on cooperation and participation because it also enables individuals to develop their talents more fully.

The stories and plays that the children create from mutual learning in the Neighborhood Bridges program make the ordinary seem strange, and the strange and fantastic images and words reveal their hopes for a better future. The stories and plays demand close reading, just as each child calls for close reading.

In becoming stimulating and demanding storytellers, the children become risk takers. Their willingness to cross bridges and spread what they have learned, that is, to apply their learning to the world, brings us back to one of the key notions in Benjamin's "Program": "Children who have played theatre in this way have become free in such productions. Through play they have fulfilled their childhood."

Certainly, it is impossible to speak about his "Program" today without revising and expanding it. History has changed childhood. But children still play and labour to define themselves; they still struggle against oppression in the family, school, and community; they still seek to articulate their needs. Benjamin saw a specific "proletarian" theatre as a way for children (the most oppressed group in society) to come to terms with conditions that were not of their own making. He demanded, perhaps too rigidly, a theatre in which children could voice their wants and develop projects that spoke to their needs. This type of theatre work is still possible, but it is a theatre work that must cut across all social classes in schools and communities, and it should include the unspectacular theatre productions of adults. Such unspectacular work by children's theatres and other groups must continue to confront the society of the spectacle if theatre's vital, dangerous impulse is to be kept alive.

Notes

1 For information on Grips, see Zipes, *Political Plays for Children*, a translation of three plays with an introduction about the history of the Grips Theatre. Gerhard Fischer has just published an excellent social history of Grips: *Grips: Geschichte eines populären Theatres (1966-2000)* (2002).

2 His essays, including "Programm eines proletarischen Kindertheatres," can be found in Walter Benjamin, *Über Kinder, Jugend und Erziehung* (1970). All the page citations in the text are taken from this volume. For a translation of "Programm," see Susan Buck-Morss. I have not used Buck-Morss's translation because there are problems with it. To begin with, the title is wrong. Benjamin did not write a program for a proletarian theatre; he wrote a program of or about it. In fact, he was writing about the work that Lacis had already accomplished. I consulted Buck-Morss's translation, but all the translated passages in this article are mine.

3 For information about their relationship, see Jack Zipes, "Building a Children's Theatre, 2: Documents: Asja Lacis/Walter Benjamin."

4 For excellent critiques of consumerism, see Charles McGovern, Susan Strasser, and Mattias Judt, eds., *Getting and Spending: European and American Consumer Societies in the Twentieth Century* (1998); Charles McGovern, *Sold American: Inventing the Consumer, 1890-1945* (2002); and Gary Cross, *An All-Consuming Century: Why Consumerism Won in Modern America* (2000).
5 Debord, who died in 1994, wrote a preface for the third French edition of 1992, included in the American edition.
6 I have amply discussed homogenization tendencies in my book *Sticks and Stones: The Troublesome Success of Children's Literature from Slovenly Peter to Harry Potter* (2001).
7 See Alex Molnar, *Giving Kids the Business: The Commercialization of America's Schools* (1996).

Works Cited

Bauman, Zygmunt. *Globalization: The Human Consequences.* New York: Columbia UP, 1998.
Benjamin, Walter. *Über Kinder, Jugend und Erziehung.* Frankfurt am Main: Suhrkamp, 1970.
Bruner, Jerome. *The Culture of Education.* Cambridge: Harvard UP, 1996.
Buck-Morss, Susan, trans. "Program for a Proletarian Children's Theatre." *Performance* 1 (March-April 1973): 28-32.
Cross, Gary. *An All-Consuming Century: Why Consumerism Won in Modern America.* New York: Columbia UP, 2000.
Debord, Guy. *The Society of the Spectacle.* Trans. Donald Nicholson-Smith. New York: Zone Books, 1995. Trans. of *La société du spectacle.* Paris: Buchet-Chastel, 1967.
Fischer, Gerhard. *Grips: Geschichte eines populären Theatres (1966-2000).* Munich: Iudicium, 2002.
McGovern, Charles. *Sold American: Inventing the Consumer, 1890-1945.* Chapel Hill: U of North Carolina P, 2002.
McGovern, Charles, Susan Strasser, and Mattias Judt, eds., *Getting and Spending: European and American Consumer Societies in the Twentieth Century.* Cambridge: Cambridge UP, 1998.
Molnar, Alex. *Giving Kids the Business: The Commercialization of America's Schools.* Boulder, CO: Westview, 1996.
Zipes, Jack. "Building a Children's Theatre, 2: Documents: Asja Lacis/Walter Benjamin," *Performance* 1 (March-April 1973): 22-27.
———. *Sticks and Stones: The Troublesome Success of Children's Literature from Slovenly Peter to Harry Potter.* New York: Routledge, 2001.
Zipes, Jack, ed. *Political Plays for Children: The Grips Theatre of Berlin.* St. Louis: Telos, 1976.

"Rosy Cheeks" and "Shining Eyes" as Criteria in Children's Theatre Criticism (1995)
Wolfgang Schneider

"There are three types of readers: one who appreciates without criticizing, another who criticizes without appreciation, and the intermediate one who appreciatively criticizes and critically appreciates; this latter one essentially reproduces a work of art again." Even Johann Wolfgang von Goethe concerned himself with the criticism of criticism when he sent the above lines to Friedrich Rochlitz, the musical author from Leipzig, on June 13, 1819. Therefore the question must be permitted whether theatre critics, for example, have taken their bearings from this perspective. The answer is that this is hardly so! Instead of providing their own assessments, instead of showing theatre in its aesthetic and social dimensions, in its relationships to other arts and spheres of life, instead of assessing a performance, its structures, forms, and means, critics furnish descriptions that remain on the surface. An analysis of theatre criticism in newspapers and magazines in the Federal Republic of Germany confirms this. In 1981, the *Theatre-Zeitschrift* of West Berlin asserted the crisis of theatre criticism: "To the critic, theatre only provides a set piece for concealing himself fashionably behind the actual object by playing on words or codes, at the same time using the press as a stage for flaunting himself and to put himself in the limelight." This calamitous situation becomes even more apparent if one turns to the manifestations of the theatre that established themselves in the Federal Republic of Germany as a result of the cultural and sociopolitical awakening of 1968, particularly as an outgrowth of the student movement. In particular, this is the case with the theatre for children and young people, which brought forth plays and productions that were biased on behalf of the children, combative for children's rights, and hedonistic in appealing to children's emotions. While a lot has changed in production practice, this assessment can only be applied to theatre criticism with difficulty. In large measure, theatre criticism disregards, even despises children's theatre.

On the Economic Basis for Children's Theatre Criticism

A first question: Where are reviews of children's theatre published? In spite of the concentration of the ownership of the press, the media scene in the Federal Republic of Germany is varied. Most periodicals have a so-called cultural section. However, the major daily papers often do not include critiques of children's theatre. Reviews of individual performances are mainly placed in the local sections, where the provincial papers sometimes even include detailed reports. The most popular form of reference to children's theatre appears to be the publication of a photograph with a caption. Weekly papers and magazines comment on special theatrical events for children, such as a children's theatre festival, no more than once, if at all. Although specialized magazines occasionally also review performances of children's theatres, the selection is accidental, arbitrary, or does not show any continuity whatsoever. This also applies to the so-called alternative press, which, however, gives more space to children's theatre than bourgeois papers generally do.

What is particularly remarkable is the large number of reviews of children's theatre performances on the radio where local events are reported in the program sections of the Culture and Topical Items departments. These also publicize reports of a more general nature, for instance on the situation of a children's theatre or the children's theatre scene. There are no reviews of children's theatre on television.

A second question: Who writes children's theatre reviews? The few children's theatre reviews that are published are mostly not written by those working full-time for the editor of the cultural section. This job is often relegated to trainees and free-lance writers. Thus reviews of children's theatre also serve as a transition stage in the career of a critic, a woeful phenomenon that is also manifested in other working spheres of the children's theatre, for example, among actors, directors, and authors, all of whom consider children's theatre to constitute an opportunity for launching their careers.

Regrettably, children's theatre criticism thus increasingly deteriorates into a playground for beginners, and children's theatre criticism often shows a lack of competence. Renowned critics leave children's theatre reviews to the unskilled workers of the writing profession.

A third question: Who actually reads children's theatre reviews? Children's theatre criticism occupies a special position in that the recipients of the performances and the consumers of the review are not the same. This problem is to be found in all children's media. Thus the trustees of children's literature, like those of children's films, can identify with the criticism of the practice of criticism. The particular nature of the target group automatically causes problems in children's theatre criticism because children hardly read literary journals or magazines and because critics hardly write for children. Even children's and young people's magazines and review programs on radio and television, which at least mention books and films, lack children's theatre reviews. The theatre is too volatile a medium and cannot be received everywhere, let alone simultaneously, and can thus only address a minority. Aspects of the market economy, which in our country mostly take precedence over cultural considerations, are also documented here.

However, critique always requires the ability to criticize. Critical discourse, however, is not exactly pronounced among the sensitive producers of children's theatre. There is not a great deal of courage for self-criticism in evidence. Yet criticism of children's theatre is vital to the survival of children's theatre, if only to prevent periodicals from polemicizing against poor performances in adult theatre by using children's theatre as a dirty word. However, the aesthetic debate is often set aside locally because the local children's theatre requires political protection. Yet it would be fatal to assume that quality can be assured in the long run by audience numbers and by favourable audience reactions. Although the consideration of children's reactions, which are, after all, not exactly irrelevant, represents a part of criticism of children's theatre, this has to involve both sensitive perception and critical analysis. Neither applause and approval, nor boos and restlessness, should be the sole criteria of criticism.

On the Present Form of Children's Theatre Criticism

Children's Theatre Criticism as a Rumination Upon Events in the Theatre

For the most part, reviews dealing with children's theatre show obvious shortcomings. Inferior language seems to be spreading, and the resources of journalists appear to be limited to such simple forms as word games with assonance and alliteration. More often than not, nothing new lies behind the review. This is because, all too frequently, reviews of children's theatre are merely descriptions of the performance. Approximately two-thirds of reviews describe the content or repeat the story told in the play. How it was told, with what sorts of pictures, in which sequence of scenes, and with which means of language and dramatic art—these things are kept from the reader of children's theatre reviews. Perhaps the names of some individuals are mentioned, packaged into rather biased sentences, but the part that these persons played in the performance, on stage or behind the scenes, is usually not mentioned.

The criticism of children's theatre to be found most frequently does not deserve that name because it does not criticize, neither in the positive nor in the negative sense. Which critic of children's theatre reads the text of the play before the performance? That which can be taken for granted in the review of a Shakespeare play is by no means common practice in children's theatre reviewing.

The Criticism of Children's Theatre as a Guideline for Educators

To the extent that children's theatre is reviewed, it is mostly done with a view to its educational-ideological objective and effect. The visit to the theatre is not considered to be a cultural event but rather an opportunity to learn. Theatre becomes a place of learning. The critic's glance, however, is not directed at the artistic product in this case, but at the spectators, the target audience. While adult audiences are considered to be mature observers of the theatre, children are presumed to be immature. Admittedly this also has something to do with the prevailing attitude among the theatre producers who primarily select their plays according to educational considerations. As a consequence, some reviews of children's theatre are reminiscent of brief reports on socioeducational matters. Proof of this attitude can be found in examples of the critic watching the "test child" and drawing conclusions based on that child's behaviour during the performance. In any case, critics always seem to be convinced that they know how and what children feel.

Criticism of Children's Theatre as a Tribute to Idyllic Childhood

I quote from some reviews of children's theatre of recent years that appeared in the press in the Federal Republic of Germany:

> While the last of the snowflakes slowly melted in the children's hair and the delight of the first snow gave way to curiosity about the fairy tale theatre, the teachers attempted to dampen the resounding children's voices in the foyer, struggling to push their pupils together in rows of two.

> What was shown was superb: salient scenes, sparkling actors, gorgeous scenery, characters punning. And what about the children? Were they sitting before the wonder-world of "theatre" with glowing cheeks?

> Not even the so-called emancipatory children's theatre can take away the shining of their eyes.

> Imagination is trump: the play, a feast for the eyes, fulfilled the sensual experience of imagination; at least in their heads the children were able to be full of abandon.

> Pantomime, light, music, sounds and props merge into a wonderful whole.

> All in all, the merry group of actors around the director excelled with perfect acts. And the author, too, is ever-present in the play, though it is questionable whether the message is conveyed.

There is only one thing which I regret; that I was not able to experience this play as a child.

Children's theatre reviews seem to inspire the adult critic to rediscover the child in himself or herself. The critic develops romanticizing reminiscences of an intact world of people who are unspoiled because they are young. Sometimes "rosy cheeks" and "shining eyes" are thus the only criteria used to review children's theatre. And that, in turn, has something to do with the ancient tradition of the so-called "Christmas fairy tales," which has freely dominated the repertories in Germany since the middle of the nineteenth century. Numerous theatres only remember their children's audiences around the 24th of December of each year, and respond by producing fairy tales. With a great deal of to-do, sharp theatre people make eyes shine and heat up the atmosphere to fight the cold season, an effort that is gratefully received with rosy cheeks.

On the Social Relevance of Children's Theatre Criticism

In a society that does not accept, respect, and promote its children and their culture on an equal level, criticism of children's theatre can take on relevant tasks. The society that deliberately overlooks children's theatre has debased itself to the service of profit. It turns the social acceptance of a whole line of theatre into the measure of its value! Criticism of children's theatre should, therefore, seek to accomplish the following tasks:

1. Criticism of children's theatre ought to assume the responsibility of standing in a position of substituting for its aesthetically inexperienced recipients.
2. Criticism of children's theatre must take up the fight against the low regard in which children's theatre is held by educators.
3. Criticism of children's theatre has the task of promoting the awareness of substance and aesthetics among authors, directors, dramatic advisors, set designers, and actors.

Formulated into a clear thesis, this could be condensed to read: It is, in fact, primarily in the children's theatre that theatre criticism in general has an important role to play if it seeks social relevance, for this is where criticism needs to struggle for great art. Because the so-called adult theatre has a well-established existence, theatre criticism needs to direct its efforts primarily toward children's theatre, where forcefulness, expert knowledge of art, and public acceptance are still lacking. After all, good children's theatre is always interesting theatre for everyone!

Goethe's demand, quoted earlier, for appreciative criticism and critical appreciation applies here. However, what also applies is the invitation to theatre critics issued by the Swedish manager of a children's theatre, Suzanne Osten: "What we theatre people expect is the desire to watch us, to describe us, and to experience us. If people know more about our work, they will find a language for it."

VIII

FILM ADAPTATIONS

Approaching the production [of *Lord of the Rings*], the filmmakers faced a huge, flawed, but complex and arguably great novel that was aimed at adults while read by children (whereas *The Hobbit*—and the Harry Potter series—were children's books read by adults). Unlike most fantasies, *LOTR* was admired not just by young fans but by older adults, including many academics, who had read and reread the books for decades. The filmmakers would have difficulty turning *LOTR* into a prestige franchise with broad appeal unless they convinced a substantial part of the public that the integrity of the original would be maintained.... Their first task was to transform a literary work primarily oriented toward adults into a movie for teenagers without that fact being obvious. Both fantasy films and franchises traditionally have been scorned as teenage fodder by older audiences, and that perception could not be reinforced. Second, in order to extract the full value of the original book, much of the core fan base had to be reassured and made devotees of the film as well. Once the filmmakers accomplished these two things, the other advantages of fantasy franchises would follow. (46-47)

—Kristin Thompson, "Fantasy, Franchises, and Frodo Baggins:
The Lord of the Rings and Modern Hollywood" (2003)

Children's reactions [to films based on Astrid Lindgren's books] have, in contrast [to the critics], consistently been positive, varying primarily by age and to a lesser degree by gender. The 1950s detective films unleashed an epidemic of play, replete with a secret language. In the 1980s, Margareta Rönnberg found many day care-age children pretending to be Pippi and Emil, basing their imitations on the 1970s Hellbom films; my young relatives still do so today. Costumes are, after all, easily in reach—for Pippi, unmatched stockings, big shoes, red yarn braids; for Emil, a wooden stick for a gun, a cap, and black clogs. Key to the films' *cum* television episodes' popularity, of course, are their clearly delimited, familiar settings, easily interpreted daily dramas, catchy songs, and tag lines delivered by little heroines and heroes who speak Swedish. In my own mid-1990s interviews with ten older (nine to thirteen) children, everyone told me she or he liked Ronia best because she is "active, funny, and lively"; the adventure-filled *Lionheart Brothers* was their next favourite. The girls thought Madicken sweet and they loved Pippi, but the nine- and ten-year-old boys could not imagine pretending to be Pippi "because she dresses too bizarrely," and insisted they would *never* want to be Madicken because she is too "girlish." The two oldest boys, both thirteen, however, remembered hopping and climbing "like Pippi" when they were little.

One volunteered that he liked the times when Ronia's father cried "because that's realistic": his parents were on the verge of divorce. (17)

                                    —Christine Holmund, "Pippi and her Pals" (2003)

The Ozification of films such as *The Blue Bird, Alice in Wonderland,* and *Jumanji* seems proof of the apparent Hollywood adage that if a film is successful, just remake it, again and again. To paraphrase MGM's Dorothy Gale, "If I ever go looking for a movie plot, I won't look any farther than my own backyard." Unfortunately, in these films, reinterpreting Oz appears to require wresting power away from strong child protagonists, especially girls, and suggesting that all problems may best be solved by retreating to one's home. What the producers of these films fail to realize is that one children's fantasy is not interchangeable with another. In addition to creating lackluster movies, they do *The Wizard of Oz* a disservice by reducing it to a neat little formula that can be replayed again and again. (18)

              —Joel Chaston, "The 'Ozification' of American Children's Fantasy Films:
                     The Blue Bird, Alice in Wonderland, and *Jumanji*" (1997)

Introduction

The link between children's literature and film has existed since the beginnings of commercial film production. Baum's *The Wonderful Wizard of Oz* (1900) was first produced as a film in 1910, and the connection has continued to this day. Two common threads in discussions of children's films are, first, the way in which filmed versions of children's literary classics often serve to obliterate the written works and, second, the predominance of economic concerns in marketing the films themselves and in selling other consumer products based on the film. The use of the terms *film* and *movie* raises the same debate between artistic expression and commercial entertainment that forms one of the pivots in every chapter of this book, and for which there are no absolute boundaries.

The underlying question behind the "television versus reading" debates begun in the 1950s and 1960s—that is, whether watching television or films is more or less active than reading—also informs the consideration of how and why literature is transformed into film. As should be clear from various claims made in this book about the different kinds of reading, every medium has its share of "rubbish" that invites passive retreat, as well as its finer works crafted to encourage active and critical thinking in those who enjoy that sort of thing. Thus, there is much in children's film that one can object to as lacking in content, theme, or structure, but there is also much that is thought provoking, as well as entertaining.

The articles in this chapter discuss one of the issues that has preoccupied most critics of children's film over the past 30 or so years: what the process of comparing film and literary versions of texts can tell us about culture and conceptions of childhood. Comparing the film text to its original print publication, be it a novel, picturebook, comic book, or another story form, can lead to all sorts of insights regarding socio-historical or cultural trends in filmic storytelling, conceptions of audience, and other ideological matters. As with picturebooks and dramatic adaptations or performances, style, medium, and attitude toward the audience determine whether the end product of a film adaptation is designed for spectacular and commercial success à la Disney or is created out of a genuine artistic regard for both the original and the adaptation, such as in John Clark Matthews's claymation videos based on Arnold Lobel's Frog and Toad stories or *The Animated Shakespeare* produced by the BBC. Keith Mehlinger's "Literature Resists Film" provides an important basis for understanding some of the basic differences between book and film narratives. A. Waller Hastings's "Moral Simplification in Disney's *The Little Mermaid*" explores the remarkable variation in story between originals and their adaptations, and the resulting political implications. Finally, Shaul Bassi's "Traffic in the Jungle" examines the ways in which adaptations change according to the social climate.

Works Cited

Chaston, Joel. "The 'Ozification' of American Children's Fantasy Films: *The Blue Bird, Alice in Wonderland,* and *Jumanji.*" *Children's Literature Association Quarterly* 22.1 (1997): 13-20.
Holmund, Christine. "Pippi and her Pals." *Cinema Journal* 42.2 (2003): 3-24.
Thompson, Kristin. "Fantasy, Franchises, and Frodo Baggins: *The Lord of the Rings* and Modern Hollywood." *The Velvet Light Trap* 52 (2003): 45-63.

Literature Resists Film: A Case Study of
The Planet of Junior Brown (2000)
Keith Mehlinger

Virginia Hamilton can claim many firsts: the first Black writer to win the Newbery, the first author to win both the National Book Award and the Newbery Medal for the same book (*M.C. Higgins The Great*), and the first writer for children to receive a MacArthur Fellowship. She is recognized as a master storyteller and one of the most prolific and influential authors of children's books today. Her 1971 Newbery Honor book, *The Planet of Junior Brown*, tells the story of Junior Brown, an obese piano prodigy who becomes emotionally disturbed as he retreats into a fantasy world to escape the manipulations of his overprotective mother, the rejection of his absent father, and the abuse of his music teacher. Only Junior's best friend, Buddy Clark, an orphaned street kid, prevents him from losing his grip on sanity by assuming adult responsibility for him. The book transcends the social realism of its urban genre through explorations of the challenges, rewards, and sacrifices of friendship and unconditional love.

The recent film adaptation of *The Planet of Junior Brown* (released in the United States as *Junior's Groove,* no doubt as a marketing angle to increase its attraction for young adults), the second book by Virginia Hamilton to be adapted for the screen, illuminates the challenges and difficulties filmmakers face when bringing literature to the screen. Produced by Film Works Limited, in association with the Canadian Broadcasting Corporation, the film won Best Picture out of seventy international and independent film entrants at the Urban World International Film Festival in 1998. Clement Virgo, the internationally acclaimed Black Canadian director of *The Planet of Junior Brown,* shows that remaining true to literature in film cannot be judged by the word-for-word duplication of stanzas and passages, because film is so infinitely different from literature that it demands a reinterpretation of the original material. By no means a conventional filmmaker, Virgo admits that he "find[s] it very hard to tell a straight story" (Kirkland). He wanted to capture *The Planet of Junior Brown* on film because of its honest depiction of Junior's story, and its lack of cynicism, sentimentality, and melodrama.

Literature into Film

The truest path to preserving the authenticity of literature on film is to capture the emotional intent and spirit of the book. To achieve this goal, a filmmaker must approach literature with the license of an original storyteller, creating, reshaping, and purging characters, events, settings, and dialogue to transform the tale into a visual medium. This may mean that the literary version is unrecognizable, except that its spirit is conveyed through the feel—the mood and theme—or the meaning one is left with after the film credits roll.

Whereas the novel can bask in the subjective intimacy of language, engaging the reader's intellect with digressions from the story line, or gaining depth by meandering through the minds of characters, the motion picture adheres to a direct course that is more objective, for its immediacy requires viewers to perceive story as action under distinct limitations of time. Filmmakers attempting adaptation must ultimately rely on their story instincts for finding in the literary text an action line—the series of events that represents the major movements of the story and forms its "spine" Anything off the spine that does not advance the story or expand the characters is considered irrelevant. William Goldman, a novelist and Academy Award-winning screenwriter, tells writers, "When I say that screenplay is structure, it's simply making the spine. And you must protect that spine. There can be wonderful scenes if they're off the spine, [but if] you see them in a movie, they will simply die" (qtd. Hunter 88). Taking his cue from Goldman, Lew Hunter adds, "If screenplays are structure, 'spine' is the soul of structure. The soul of the screenplay" (Hunter 89).

Director Virgo and his cowriter, Cameron Bailey, capture the "soul" of Hamilton's book while transferring the locale, condensing the material, cutting or combining characters, and adding a love story. This type of creative license is required by screenwriters to succeed in adapting literature to dramatic form and structure. They move the story from 1970s Harlem in New York City to present-day Toronto, Canada. The advantages of this decision were to avoid the costs of re-creating a bygone era and designing period sets and costumes. Moreover, production costs are considerably lower in Canada than in New York City. Virgo also wanted to work on familiar ground—he was raised in Toronto after moving from Jamaica at the age of eleven. Hence Virgo transports the themes, characters, mood, and subtext of the book to a city he knows first-hand.

The success of a film adaptation stems partly from the ability of the original materials to resonate with issues and themes that are relevant to the viewing audience. Early in her book, Hamilton frames the main characters of her story as people "out of our time" (1). With New York City and Harlem as the setting, Hamilton's portrayal of a unique friendship between a homeless street kid and a disturbed 300-pound piano prodigy remains a compelling story of "outsiders." Almost prophetically, the problems of adolescence and broken families appear more urgent today—especially in the wake of increased teen violence in American schools—than they did in the 1970s.

The story also contrasts the rootless isolation of the homeless with the more devastating isolation within a dysfunctional family. It explores the need for friendship as a basis for virtual families held together not by blood and heritage but by trust, love, and kindness, as well as other values of traditional families. Hamilton is successful in making us care for these characters through a well-developed narrative that unfolds over a period of seven days (from one Friday to the next), when Junior and his best friend, Buddy, will face their darkest fears and overcome obstacles to affirm their brotherly bond and need for one another. The psychological and social realism of the book transcends time and reflects the spirit of contemporary issues of alienation and family fragmentation.

Virgo successfully mines the themes of *The Planet of Junior Brown*—isolation, self-esteem, love of family, self-determination, liberation, and independence—to give depth and meaning to the film. Likewise, in determining the structure of the film, he found Hamilton's novel to be uniquely suited to dramatic form—although generally the screenwriter cannot rely upon the structure of the novel. As Aristotle stated in *The Poetics*, dramatic form relates events through cause and effect, thereby requiring a strong story line that connects the story like a single action. Each scene or event of the drama advances the story and expands its characters in a chronology of rising action and conflict that includes unpredictable twists and turns. This economical structure leaves no room for the reflective grandeur of literature. Robert McKee, a prominent Hollywood story consultant, says that one of the reasons why pure literature fails on-screen is because of "aesthetic impossibility. Image is prelinguistic; no cinematic equivalences or even approximations exist for conflicts buried in the extravagant language of master novelists and playwrights" (367). Although both use dialogue, literature is not drama; yet, by reinventing literature as drama, screenwriters are able to reach the deep meanings of literature through cinematic form. Douglas Street observes that the screenwriter's initial step is to "take the novel and return its multifaceted nature to the basic elements from which the novelist's ultimate creation blossomed" (89). This procedure of reaching the "seed" of an original work requires repeated readings and analyses. Only by capturing the emotion and thought in the book can a filmmaker transform language into action.

As a well-plotted story with a conventional narrative structure, *The Planet of Junior Brown* lends itself to the Aristotelian three-act structure that most American films follow. An inciting incident brings chaos to order, triggering a hero's journey in the first act (the beginning). The protagonist or hero will spend most of the second act (the middle) of the film overcoming increasing obstacles to achieve a goal that will return order to life. The quest often becomes a metaphor for the deep-seated internal problems that the hero must reach and conquer through external action by the third act (the ending), which features a climax (the highest point of action), followed by the resolution of the drama.

The short period of time of a week over which *The Planet of Junior Brown* occurs was an advantage for Virgo's film adaptation. Hamilton's story comes with a built-in "time lock," a structural device often used in films that predetermines how long the hero has to overcome obstacles to reach his objective. Junior and Buddy (as the dual protagonists in the film) essentially have seven days to wrest control of Junior's life from those who are destroying him. Films that string out their drama over long periods of time—that is, weeks, months, or years—have a tendency to lose intensity unless their dramatic situations and characters are extremely compelling.

Virgo chose to anchor his film adaptation on character and theme, while departing significantly in some instances from the book's plot. Plot lines that do not serve Virgo's vision of the story have been dropped, re-created, or refocused. In creating a character-driven adaptation, Virgo has also determined the episodic structure of his film, choosing a "vertical" or character focused drama instead of a more linear or plotdriven narrative. This does not mean that Virgo has discarded a story line for the screenplay, but it explains the nonlinear nature of his film. Despite its episodic nature, the film's unfolding events of disconnected sequences have a unifying force in the three Aristotelian unities of time, place, and theme. As long as the audience cannot predict what will happen next to Junior and Buddy, the spectators' attention will be undivided in their desire to see how the characters overcome obstacles. William Froug notes that "episodic storytelling usually guarantees surprises, whereas cause-and-effect storytelling has a certain built-in predictability factor that can be difficult to overcome" (134). Episodic or not, the drama still has a duty to its audience, a duty that demands escalating tension by placing unrelenting and ever larger obstacles before protagonists. The resulting crisis for the protagonists will lead to decisions that culminate in the climax. The major scenes or pivotal events of the action line—the story spine—are the soul of the screenplay. Linda Seger, a well-known studio script consultant, says, "A good scene in a film advances the action, reveals character, explores the theme, and builds an image. In a novel, one scene or an entire chapter may concentrate on only one of those areas" (16).

Virgo and Bailey invent new characters whose interactions with Junior and Buddy add further dimensions to the film: Butter, a street urchin and prostitute, as Buddy's romantic interest; Mr. Tanaka, the stern owner of a piano shop with a showcased baby grand that Junior covets; and Sandra Tanaka, Mr. Tanaka's daughter, as Junior's love interest for still another romantic twist. Another character created by the writers is Derrick, the piano salesman, who expresses empathy for Junior and is the character most representative of Doum Malach, Buddy's sympathetic newsstand boss featured in the book. Virgo and Bailey eliminate Malach and the newsstand to intensify conflict for the characters, making Mr. Tanaka a central authority figure standing between Junior and the baby grand, as well as his daughter.

As in the book, Mr. Pool remains the eccentric self-appointed guardian angel of Junior and Buddy. Miss Peebs and Mr. Rountree are cast as White instead of Black, perhaps to reflect the multiethnic composition of Toronto. Instead of an asthmatic requiring an oxygen mask as in the book, Junella Brown (Junior's mother) is portrayed as a diabetic who almost seductively beckons her son to administer the insulin syringe for which she must partially disrobe, giving the ritual domination of her son a sexual connotation. Although this is a spin on the book, it effectively raises the stakes and adds another level of conflict that will inevitably rise between Junior and his mother. Franklin and Nightman, two street-savvy boys, are replaced by Doug and Lesley, two innocent street waifs who are threatened with corruption from the streets. Virgo and Bailey create the character Duckie as a composite of Hamilton's Tomorrow Billys, the symbolic guardians of street kids. Duckie is of

Jamaican descent, and his character reflects a meaner, crueller big brother of the streets than Hamilton created. Although Buddy displays a propensity for cunning in the book, he is still portrayed as a surrogate father living by a code and doing what he had to do to feed kids. The film conveys the harsher reality of today's world by portraying Duckie as a predator who will live by a code while taking what he wants for himself, including innocents like Lesley.

The writers reinvent the histories of Junior and Buddy to give their characters greater dimension for film. These details are not revealed through language; instead, they appear ever so briefly as flashbacks—that is, as fragmented memories that converge to a dramatic epiphany. These flashbacks reveal that Buddy carries the profound responsibility for his sister's tragic death in a house fire, and that Junior is tormented by his father's broken promises and his mother's cruelty. The film gives depth to Janelle through a brief flashback that reveals Junior's father as a married man caught between the responsibility for Junior (out of wedlock with Janelle) and for his real family. This scene, which lasts only a few seconds, balances Junella's cruelty with empathy, because she expects her son to suffer for attention and love as she has.

Cinematic Techniques

The fundamental difference between a movie and a book is that one "shows" while the other "tells." What in a novel might require several pages or an entire chapter to convey, and only in sequential fashion, is presented much faster in a film, because "[i]t builds up its details through images. The camera can look at a three-dimensional object and, in a matter of seconds, get across details that would take pages in the novel. Film can give us story information, character information, ideas and images and style all in the same moment" (Seger 16). Guided by his instinct for what is essential to advance the story and expand its characters, Virgo successfully adds filmic dimension to Hamilton's creation. Richard Walter, professor and screenwriting faculty chairman at the UCLA Film School, asserts that there are two kinds of information in a film, "sight and sound," and that "all aspects of a screenplay—story, character, action, setting, and everything else—derive from what an audience sees and hears" (115). The limitations of the format require that a screenwriter express action only as sight and sound. Walter reminds us "that the screenwriter never writes what a character 'thinks,' 'realizes,' 'recalls,' or 'remembers,' nor what he 'figures' or 'calculates' for these are in their nature internal, mental processes, which in screenplays are communicated by sight and sound alone" (116). Thoughts also fall into this realm of sight and sound, challenging the screenwriter to transform the mental into the physical—in other words, into behaviour—while the novelist can simply "blurt out" what is on a character's mind (Armer 166).

In adapting Hamilton's book, Virgo and Bailey immediately faced the problem of "condensation" and the difficult choices a screen adapter must make in deciding what to eliminate from the original to work into a 120-page dramatic format (Portnoy 95). Films demand an economy not imposed upon literature—its generous use of language to describe a character or setting in a script must be reduced from several pages, or even a chapter, into concise paragraphs and sentences. Screenwriters use "color words"—pumped up adjectives—to provide an embellished visual and auditory sense of the action in scene descriptions. With average screen times of two hours or 120 minutes, that translate into approximately a page a minute (110-20 pages for a finished screenplay), the screenwriter is faced with compressing, combining, or even eliminating events from a novel, and sometimes entire chapters, to meet the requirements of screen form.

Using cinematic techniques, Virgo transforms Buddy's planet from the hovel of the book into what almost appears to be a candle-lit art loft. With a bed of choral music, the warm light of the loft gives Buddy's lair a sanctimonious feel instead of the ice-cold dankness so effectively described in the novel. The director's vision of the planet is more exotic than inappropriate, getting us to buy into a world that is anything but Hamilton's setting of abandoned buildings and back alleys of Harlem. Mr. Pool's homemade solar system is turned into planet art appropriate for a Soho gallery: the glazed glass spheres, with their multicoloured topography, glow warmly and revolve in wonderfully complex paths in relation to a crystal sun. The result is visually stunning, more like a planetarium with its backdrop of shimmering stars than the home-strung translucent plastic spheres with lighted Christmas bulbs described in the book. Virgo gives Buddy's loft a metaphorical connection by creating interesting segues from Mr. Pool's creation to Junior's subconscious view of his fantasy planet, transitions that are depicted through special-effects space sequences worthy of Star Trek movies. It comes as no surprise that Virgo first thought of the planets when searching for the "seed" to transform the book into the film. "I think I structured the film unconsciously. I started with the idea of planets, then introduced all the characters. The story begins to unfold and then it stops and we start again. It all revolves around the idea of planets, solar system and mortality" (Amsden). Revolving in their orbits around the sun, these planets become a recurring visual metaphor for identity and individualism, while the solar system and its interrelated life support becomes symbolic of community and friendship. Virgo even uses film technique—montage, camera movement, and dissolves—to create a visual relationship between Junior's roundness and his planet namesake, thereby reinforcing the metaphor of the planets and the solar system.

Faced with the challenge of handling the layered themes and inner thoughts of Hamilton's characters, Virgo successfully turns the mental into the physical. He reinvents Hamilton's story to accommodate the embodiment of fear that

Hamilton so lavishly tracks through Junior's mind. Virgo turns the fear into a Freddy Kruger-like claw grotesquely wrapped in piano wire. A faceless trench-coated man stalks Miss Peebs's hallway like a monster, swaying his heavy arm with the claw-like appendage. Virgo succeeds in materializing Junior's deep fears as a flesh-and-blood manifestation of his subconscious that does not appear in the book. He also cinematically tackles Hamilton's vivid descriptions of Junior's obsession with the red canvas on which he depicts the world of his subconscious. The flush of the color red codes Junior's flashbacks to a painful inner landscape inhabited by his domineering mother complaining about the racket from the piano. It is the color red that also codes Junior's climactic flash-back to his mother sliding his fingers between the blades of a pair of shears. The memory triggers the subconscious connection between Junella's shears and the piano claw that Junior conjures as the hand of a monster.

The tone, style, and shadings that Virgo brings to the film through cine-matic language include choices of dialogue, camera angles, pacing, camera movement, lighting, and color. The film with its languid European feel is bursting with warm colors that defy the feel of Hamilton's original story, which seemed to evoke dark, cold spaces. Complaints that the film is not true to the book are more often a reflection of an obstacle of form than purpose-ful rejection of original material. The impressive look of the film does not betray Hamilton's themes because Virgo successfully mines the "seed" of her book and gets strong performances from an excellent cast. Virgo achieves the screenwriter's primary mission to capture the spirit and themes of the novel through characterization and action, and to remain true to the emotional intent of the original work.

Works Cited

Amsden, Cynthia. "Brave New Planet." *SEE Magazine.* 27 Nov. 1997.
  <http://www.seemagazine.com/Issues/1997/971127/screen2.html>.
Armer, Alan. *Writing the Screenplay.* 2nd. ed. Belmont, CA: Wadsworth, 1993.
Froug, William. *Zen and the Art of Screenwriting: Insights and Interviews.* Los Angeles: Sillman-James Press, 1996.
Hamilton, Virginia. *The Planet of Junior Brown.* New York: Macmillan, 1971.
Hunter, Lew. *Lew Hunter's Screenwriting 434.* New York: Perigee, 1993.
Kirkland, Bruce. "Gravitational Pull of Friendship; Virgo and Bailey Come Together to Make *The Planet of Junior Brown.*" *Toronto Sun* 5 Sept. 1997.
  <http://www.clive.canoe.ca/JamMoviesArtistsV/virgoclement>.
McKee, Robert. *Story: Substance, Structure, Style, and Principles of Screenwriting.* New York: Regan Books/HarperCollins, 1997.
Portnoy, Kenneth. *Screen Adaptation: A Scriptwriting Handbook.* 2nd. ed. Boston: Focal, 1998.

Seger, Linda. *The Art of Adaptation: Turning Fact and Fiction into Film.* New York: Henry Holt, 1992.

Street, Douglas. *Novels and the Movies.* New York: F. Ungar, 1983.

Walter, Richard. *Screenwriting: The Art, Craft and Business of Film and Television Writing.* New York: Plume, 1988.

Moral Simplification in Disney's *The Little Mermaid* (1993)

A. Waller Hastings

While generally praising Walt Disney's technical contributions to animated film, critics have been troubled by the studio's treatment of classic children's literature and fairy tales. In a famous attack over 25 years ago, Sayers blasted Disney for showing "scant respect for the integrity of the original creations of authors" and treating folk texts "without regard for [their] anthropological, spiritual, or psychological truths. Every story is sacrificed to the 'gimmick' [of animation]" (602). Her complaint specifically addressed a tendency to "dummy down" source material by eliminating psychological conflict: "Disney falsifies life by pretending that everything is so sweet, so saccharine, so without any conflict except the obvious conflict of violence" (609).

More recently, this pattern, which Schickel calls "Disneyfication" (225),[1] has been criticized on ideological grounds for reinforcing and/or contributing to dominant patriarchal and capitalist systems. For instance, Stone charges that Disney's adaptations of *Snow White* and other "classic" fairy tales "amplify ... the stereotype of good versus bad women" already present in the source material, offering heroines who "seem barely alive" and villains who are invariably female (44). Dorfman observes a neocolonial plundering of folklore and children's literature in the service of Disney's "average North American image" (24). So pervasive is Disneyfication that, as Zipes has noted, the Disney method has become the prototype for most film adaptations of fairy tales (and one might extend this to children's literature in general) made by other studios, all mass-mediated vehicles which co-opt fairy tales' subversive potential and convert it to the service of corporate capitalism (113-14).

Much Disneyfication, at least in the era of Walt himself, was evidently conscious; the filmmaker admitted that he sought out simple stories and simplified them further to create "nice" children's films. In *Pinocchio*, for instance, Disney intentionally narrowed the story to create a more cohesive plot and altered Pinocchio's character from that of a delinquent to "a well-meaning boy who was consistently led astray by conniving characters" (Thomas 26);

this sanitized hero was judged more acceptable for children. Disney himself acknowledged his preference for the morally simple over the complex:

> I look for a story with heart.... It should be a simple story with characters the audience can really care about. They've got to have a rooting interest.
>   That was the trouble with *Alice*. There we had a classic we couldn't tamper with; I resolved never to do another one. The picture was filled with weird characters you couldn't get with. (Thomas 22)

The conscious effort to produce children's movies with no alarming moral ambiguities contributed to such well-known Disney signatures as the ubiquitous cute animals, either as adjuncts to the film's main characters (*Snow White, Cinderella*) or as anthropomorphized protagonists (*Robin Hood, Oliver!*). Less noted signature traits of Disneyfication include the use of dogs and cats as moral compasses[2] and the imposition of generational conflict, absent from the original, which is always satisfactorily resolved, restoring family order (*Sleeping Beauty*).

Walt Disney is dead but his successors have followed and magnified the pattern he created for animated film. All of the characteristics described above are present in the studio's adaptation of *The Little Mermaid*; as one film critic noted, "we have seen before ... funny animal friends, a handsome prince, a grotesque villainess and her less funny animal friends" (Lloyd). Peter Schneider, Disney animation chief during the production of *The Little Mermaid*, says that "people have been trying to figure out what Walt would have done and to hold on to his tradition" (Solomon 273), and in *Mermaid*, as successful a commercial product as any of Disney's early triumphs, the studio appears to have identified "what Walt would have done." Schneider attempts to argue that Disney tradition was to innovate constantly; in effect, he denies any sameness to Disney products under Walt. But a Disney studio style for animated features was noted as early as *Dumbo* in 1941 (McReynolds 788) and Disney animator Ron Clements, who originated the Little Mermaid project in 1985, acknowledged that he tried to make the melancholy original more upbeat (Flower 177), just as Disney himself had done.

Disney's *Little Mermaid* thus appears to be a classic example of the corporate appropriation of an originally creative work of art. According to Zipes, the culture industry transforms works of imagination into "commodities within a capitalist social-economic system ... [so that] cultural objects appear to possess a life of their own beyond the control of the actual creators" (96-97). This co-opting of image and narrative is not value-neutral, but encodes ideological messages that may create a false picture of reality (Zipes 102).[3] It is thus advisable to consider the ideological basis and effect of alterations made between Andersen's tale and the Disney film.

In the Disney adaptation, the elements of the fairy tale remain recognizable, but superimposed are typical elements of Disneyfication and a happy ending that contravenes the moral intention of the original tale. McReynolds, faulting Disney for playing a Pollyanna-ish "glad game," has argued that the typical ending of a Disney film denies evil's reality: all wicked characters are banished, leaving a world "in which kindness and sympathy always prevail" (787-88). However, Disney's animated films do not so much deny the reality of evil as present a Manichean world of moral absolutes in eternal warfare, from which—in the Disney version—good always emerges triumphant. This is especially true of *The Little Mermaid.*

Andersen's mermaid is driven to the surface world by two complementary but separable impulses: a romantic/erotic desire for the handsome prince whom she rescues from drowning in a shipwreck and a moral desire, privileged in Andersen's telling, to attain a soul with the promise of an afterlife. Romantic desire is frustrated when the prince marries a human whom he wrongly believes to have been his saviour, but the mermaid has a chance to resume her original form if she will abandon both erotic and moral quests and slay the prince. She rejects this opportunity, however, throwing the knife with which she was to stab the prince into the sea as the sun, which will bring her death, rises. Rather than dying, the little mermaid miraculously becomes an ethereal spirit and is told by fellow spirits:

> "If for three hundred years we earnestly try to do what is good, we obtain an immortal soul and can take part in the eternal happiness of man. You, little mermaid, have tried with all your heart to do the same. You have suffered and borne your suffering bravely; and that is why you are now among us, the spirits of the air." (76)

Her willingness to sacrifice the happiness she has pursued through excruciating pain and very real dangers provides a second chance at immorality. Even though the romantic/erotic narrative is frustrated, the "higher" narrative of moral progress remains a possibility—is, in fact, enhanced by the mermaid's refusal to destroy another life.

Andersen, too, has been accused of saccharine sentimentality, as this synopsis of the fairy tale's Christian moral may suggest. But the Disney version accentuates the most sentimental and romantic aspects of the story at the expense of its moral and psychological complexity. Like previous Disney adaptations, *The Little Mermaid* provides wish fulfillment without true sacrifice and neatly encapsulates all "bad" desires within a figure of female evil.[4]

The Manichean world view requires an active principle—in the original heresy, Satan—who is responsible for all evil effects. In Disney's film, this principle is embodied in the sea witch Ursula, a repulsive half-woman/half-octopus who parodies the adult sexuality denied to Ariel herself. Ursula's character allows a streamlining of plot and characterization such as commonly occurs when texts are converted into film, defensible on the basis of generic convention. This defence, however, ignores the manner in which the character absolves Ariel of all responsibility for her own actions, simplifying the psychological and moral problem of desire and reconfirming the pattern of female stereotyping that Stone observed in early Disney products.

Ursula's ancestor, the sea hag, appears only once in Andersen's fairy tale; while she is undeniably evil, she acts only upon direct petition. His mermaid, having conceived her dual desires for human form, seeks transformation on her own volition; the sea hag grants it, "for it will bring ... misery" but warns her that it will involve great pain:

> "Your tail will divide and shrink, until it becomes what human beings call 'pretty legs.' It will hurt; it win feel as if a sword were going through your body ... [E]very time your foot touches the ground it will feel as though you were walking on knives so sharp that your blood must flow. If you are willing to suffer all this, then I can help you." (68)

The other conditions of transformation also involve suffering. In becoming human, Andersen's little mermaid takes an irrevocable step; whatever the outcome of her romantic quest, she cannot return to the sea and her family. If she fails to win the prince's love, she will die, thereby failing also to gain a human soul, which can only be received through that love. Her death will then be permanent. Finally, she must give up her voice to the sea hag by having her tongue cut out.

The Disney version purges these elements of pain. There is no physical pain associated with Ariel's transformation, as there is in Andersen; she experiences momentary hesitation at leaving her father and sisters, but separation anxiety is quickly overcome when Ursula conjures the image of handsome Prince Erik. While the price of transformation remains the loss of her voice, Ariel does not suffer physical mutilation; the voice is transferred to a shell from which it can later be released and returned to its rightful owner.

The most marked change, however, comes through a reversal of the active centre of the mermaid's relationship to the sea hag. Andersen's mermaid conceives of the transformation herself and must pass through deadly obstacles to reach the sea hag; the hag tells her of all the drawbacks to the scheme, then—at the mermaid's insistence—gives her a potion to be taken only when safely on land. The dangers and pain are all generated by the mermaid's own desire; the sea hag assists, but does not actively plan for evil to befall the mermaid.

Ariel's desire in the Disney film is more innocent, in itself carrying little risk. Ursula's plotting brings on everything. The sea witch is introduced as she observes Ariel watching the human world and plots how to use the mermaid's fascination with humans to revenge herself on Triton. Ariel only comes to

Ursula at the instigation of the witch's servants, the moray eels Flotsam and Jetsam, and it is Ursula who proposes that she win her prince by becoming human. Ariel lives in a fantasy land that ignores the incompatibility between species; not until the sea witch plants the idea in her head does she imagine a literalization of her girlish infatuation. Ariel, not the witch, brings up the separation from family that will accompany the transformation, and Ursula's temptation is needed to overcome her hesitation. They sign a contract that is clearly reminiscent of a pact with the devil, a comparison driven home by Ursula's display of her collection of damned souls, each one shrunken into misery after failing to fulfill his or her bargain with her.

If Andersen's sea hag is evil, she also sticks by a bargain. She leaves it to the mermaid to win her prince or to fail in the attempt. While Andersen's mermaid undergoes transformation when she has safely reached shore, Disney's Ursula effects Ariel's transformation while the mermaid is still at the bottom of the sea, putting her at risk of a drowning that would quickly negate the deal—immediate evidence that the sea witch has been bargaining in bad faith. A quick end to the mermaid's quest is only prevented when Ariel's sidekicks Flounder and Sebastian rush her to the surface.

Andersen's prince never imagines that he has been rescued by the mysterious, mute girl who appears soon after he escapes the shipwreck. In the film, Erik immediately suspects Ariel's identity and is thrown off track only by her inability to speak, which means she cannot be the one who sang so beautifully after pulling him from the sea. Nevertheless, Erik seems about to fall for Ariel and is prevented from bestowing the magic kiss only by Ursula's eels, who overturn the boat in which the prince and the mermaid are sitting. When Erik is about to abandon his imaginary saviour for life with Ariel, the sea witch again intervenes, disguising herself as a beautiful woman and using Ariel's stolen voice to convince the prince that she is his destined lover. Despite her evident beauty and the conclusive evidence of the voice, Ursula must hypnotize Erik to keep him from Ariel, so strong is the former mermaid's attraction.

Contrast this to Andersen's tale, in which the mermaid's erotic prospects never have a chance of fulfillment and the prince weds a mortal woman. The romantic failure of Andersen's mermaid may be seen as the inevitable heartache of human love, a heartache Andersen knew firsthand: she is destined not simply to be rejected, but to be ignored by the object of her desire. In Andersen's tale, there is no external agent to blame; the mermaid seems, before her final transfiguration, to be the tragic victim only of her own desires.

Ariel never has to face the consequences of her choices. As in Disney's *Sleeping Beauty*, even the conflict between parent and child proves illusory; order is restored through the discovery that parent's and child's wishes are the same. Triton himself makes Ariel human so that she may marry Erik, who has destroyed the sea witch, the source of her real troubles.[5] The marriage takes place aboard a ship, an intermediate locale that negotiates between the land world of humans and the undersea world of the merfolk; father and daughter are not really separated, as the newlyweds sail off under Triton's rainbow, escorted by merfolk. The evil principle has been purged through the joint courage of human and merfolk.

One might ask, "What is wrong with Disney's transformation?" It could be argued that Andersen's subtle moral tale is too complex to be grasped by most children, that children in fact need the reassurance of the conventional happy ending that Disney imposes. Niels and Faith Ingwersen have argued that the film's focus on the conflict between good and evil, while sacrificing the transcendent theme of the original, is "nevertheless truer to the folktale struggle between good and evil than Andersen's tale is" (415). They do, however, find the introduction of a strongly evil female power "troubling" and note a shift from a predominantly matriarchal world in Andersen's tale to a strong patriarchy in the film. Cravens, whose difficulties with the Disney film in some ways parallel mine, describes how she was "troubled" by aspects of the original tale when she first encountered it at age four or five. But this was counteracted by a sense of connection:

> even though her trials seemed intolerable, I felt as though the deepest part of my nature were being addressed by a sincere friend, and I was satisfied and uplifted by the ending without understanding the reason. (638)

This dimly understood sense of connection, I submit, is what the Disneyfied story, with its insistence on a "happily ever after" marriage plot, inevitably sacrifices.

Disney's conclusion certainly offers a more conventional happy ending than Andersen's original, reflecting a narrative and psychological urge to create apparent harmony that Bausinger has named "*Märchendenken*" or "fairy-tale thinking" (17). As an individual tendency of mind, *Märchendenken* has certain risks, but it also serves the useful psychological purpose of instilling hope. When embodied in the mass-mediated Disney form, however, the *Märchendenken* of *The Little Mermaid* poses social hazards.

Disney's manipulation of original material is a matter of special concern because of the studio's marketing machine, which enables Disney product to command consumer attention through interlocking movie, TV, book, record, and toy products.[6] Thus Disney versions of "standard" fairy tales tend to usurp the originals. The version of Cinderella most familiar to adults of my generation is Disney's adaptation of Perrault;[7] the image of Snow White is likely to be Disney's cartoon heroine. As "classic" texts are Disneyfied, more of children's literary legacy becomes endangered. In popular consciousness, *Alice in Wonderland* is a Disney creation, (though Disney himself thought the film a creative failure). In toy stores today, you can find many teddy bears that look like Disney's *Winnie-the-Pooh* but will search fruitlessly for one resembling the original Shepard illustrations for Milne's books.

The merchandisers' work on *The Little Mermaid* should be self-evident to anyone who has visited a toy store recently. The film itself grossed $76 million in its initial release, at the time establishing a record for an animated film (Flower 229). In an unprecedented move for Disney, *The Little Mermaid* was released on videotape within a year of its theatrical release, as the company's increasingly savvy marketing people responded to comments of those leaving the theatre after seeing the film (Flowers 292). Even after the releases of *Beauty and the Beast* and *Aladdin,* which promise to eclipse the earlier film in profits and spin-offs, shelves remain filled with Little Mermaid dolls, clothing, books, tapes, records, bath toys, etc. Product spin-offs continue to be introduced to an as-yet-unsaturated market.

The ideological content of children's films, like that of children's literature in general, should have a particular interest for us because it both reflects the pervasive world view of its producers and contributes to the formation of its viewers' own world view more strongly than does adult literature, thus influencing the ideology of the next generation. It is the perception of this ideologic influence that accounts for so much of didacticism that pervades children's literature.

Faced with the near-certainty that the Disney derivative will replace the Andersen tale in popular consciousness, then it is important to understand the moral ideology that shapes the film. The elimination of moral complexities reflects both Walt Disney's original moral vision, formed in the Depression and World War II and continued today by successors who imbibed "the Disney version" in their own childhood, and the conservative American ideology of the 1980s, when *The Little Mermaid* was developed and released. The film encourages a pervasive world view that sees malignant evil, not human fallibility, as the chief source of conflict; a similar world view can be seen in former President Reagan's characterization of the (pre-*glasnost*) Soviet Union as the "Evil Empire" or President Bush's more recent transformation of the Gulf War from a geopolitical conflict into a crusade against the person of Saddam Hussein.

In a Manichean world, one party to any conflict must always be "bad," the other "good"; insofar as we are conditioned to see ourselves as good, this perspective encourages conflict, since we can always justify our own actions, however terrible they may seem when deprived of the moral conviction that ends justify means. Those who oppose us become figures of evil, each "another Hitler," rather than normal human beings who, like us, pursue national or personal self-interests. In this Disneyfied world, there is no reason for diplomacy; the proper way to deal with an Ursula is to destroy her, not to negotiate.

As my brief discussion of *The Little Mermaid* should indicate, Disneyfication not only homogenizes individual creations into a simplistic narrative sameness, but eliminates the moral complexities of the original text. The child who reads Andersen's fairy tale has experienced a world in which desires have consequences that may be painful, where wanting something badly enough to suffer for it need not make it happen; the child who views the Disney film experiences a world in which bad things only happen because of bad people, where desire is always fulfilled. Such moral simplification increases the likelihood that these children will become adults who find the causes of their unhappiness in personalized, "evil" antagonists—a sure formula for continued conflict.

Notes

1   However, Schickel warns of "the folly of overinterpreting essentially innocent popular culture material in the light of any ideology—political, psychological, religious, or even literary" (166). Such criticism will rebound on the critic and leave the popular culture unaffected. Forewarned of my folly, I will yet proceed.

2   I am not aware that this aspect has been observed before, but almost inevitably, "good" characters in Disney cartoons are either dogs or dog-lovers. Cats, on the other hand, tend to be vicious, and cat-lovers are evil or morally obtuse, like the aunt in *Lady and the Tramp* who locks Lady outside and fails to recognize when Tramp saves the baby. There are some exceptions to this latter characteristic (*The Aristocats*, the eponymous hero of *Oliver!*), but none that I can think of for this positive moral value of dogs. Ursula's villainy in *The Little Mermaid* includes kicking Prince Erik's loyal dog, and Erik's goodness is shown when he risks his life to rescue the dog.

3   In my analysis of *The Little Mermaid*, I am probably guilty of what Rollin calls "the classic elitist position: a distrust of anything mass marketed for children and a confidence that one's educated personal judgment can decide what is best for others" (91). But she acknowledges that much of the Left's critique of Disney is on target, calling Disney's fairy tales "opiates ... that tell us just what we want to hear"; the elitism lies in deciding this is wrong, she says (91).

4   "It's a film about sacrifice in which nobody has to sacrifice anything they weren't all ready to. All misfortune finally accrues to the villainess.... Ariel herself remains absolutely static except for having changed her place of residence. She leaves the film the same wacky, wilful kid as when she entered. Nobody learns a thing" (Lloyd).

5   Note that while the resolution of Andersen's tale requires that the Little Mermaid refrain from the taking of life, Disney's version can only reach closure through the violent deaths of Ursula and her henchmen, the eels. In Andersen's

story, the sea hag disappears from the tale after her transformative function has been accomplished.

6   "As capitalism, it is a work of genius; as culture, it is mostly a horror" (Schickel 18).

7   An illustration: I recently used Anne Sexton's "Cinderella," which is based on the Grimms' version of the story, in my introduction to literature class and asked students to identify changes the poet had made in the fairy tale. All of the students pointed to details like the stepsisters' cutting off parts of their feet and the birds' pecking the stepsisters' eyes out as authorial inventions, even though these details appear in Grimm. Their conception of the true Cinderella corresponded exactly to the Disney version.

Works Cited

Andersen, Hans Christian. "The Little Mermaid." *The Complete Fairy Tales and Stories.* Trans. Erik Christian Haugaard. Garden City: Doubleday, 1974. 57-76.

Bausinger, Hermann. "Möglichkeiten des Märchens in der Gegenwart." *Märchen, Mythos, Dichtung: Festschrift zum 90. Geburtstag Friedrich von der Levens am 19. August 1963.* Ed. Hugo Kuhn and Kurt Schier. Munich: Verlag C.H. Beck, 1963. 15-30.

Cravens, Gwyneth. "Past Present." *The Nation* 11 May 1992. 638-40.

Dorfman, Ariel. *The Emperor's Old Clothes: What the Lone Ranger, Babar, and Other Innocent Heroes Do to Our Minds.* New York: Pantheon. 1983.

Flower, Joe. *Prince of the Magic Kingdom: Michael Eisner and the Re-Making of Disney.* New York: Wiley, 1991.

Ingwersen, Niels and Faith Ingwersen. "A Folktale/Disney Approach." *Scandinavian Studies* 62 (1990): 412-15.

Lloyd, Robert. "Trouble in Toontown." *American Film* 15 (December 1989): 17.

McReynolds, William. "Disney Plays 'The Glad Game.'" *Journal of Popular Culture* 7 (1974): 787-96.

Rollin, Lucy. "Fear of Faerie: Disney and the Elitist Critics." *Children's Literature Association Quarterly* 12 (1987): 90-93.

Sayers, Frances Clarke. "Walt Disney Accused." *Horn Book* 41 (1965): 602-11.

Schickel, Richard. *The Disney Version: The Life, Times, Art and Commerce of Walt Disney.* Rev. ed. New York: Simon and Schuster/Touchstone, 1985.

Solomon. Charles. *Enchanted Drawings: The History of Animation.* New York: Knopf, 1989.

Stone, Kay. "Things Walt Disney Never Told Us." *Women and Folklore.* Ed. Claire R. Farrer. Austin: U of Texas P, 1975. 42-50.

Thomas. Bob. *Walt Disney: The Art of Animation.* New York: Simon/Disney, 1958.

Zipes, Jack. "The Instrumentalization of Fantasy: Fairy Tales, the Culture Industry, and the Mass Media." *Breaking the Magic Spell: Radical Theories of Folk and Fairy Tales.* New York: Methuen, 1979. 93-128.

Postscript (2005)

This article began as a conference paper. Having watched the Disney film incessantly with my young daughter, I popped off an abstract based solely on a detailed comparison of the film to Hans Christian Andersen's story, with no preliminary research. The abstract ended up longer than the finished speaking text, even with the addition of secondary research to the latter.

In time, my paper was published in *The Lion and the Unicorn*. At that time, there were a few scholarly articles on Disney scattered across several decades and even fewer books, but within a few years, scholarly research on Disney was booming. Perhaps as a result of increased interest in the topic, "Moral Simplification in Disney's *Little Mermaid*" has been cited far and away more than anything else I've written.

Much of the subsequent work has adopted a negative attitude toward Disney products, as indeed this article does. As I have followed the field, too often it appears to me that the writers have begun as anti-Disney and sought evidence (sometimes pretty slight) to support their conclusions, rather than beginning with the film text and following where it leads. Revisiting my little piece from the vantage of a dozen or so years on (can it actually be that long?), it seems to me to continue to hold up because it remains rooted in a thorough exploration of the film, rather than a pre-existing ideological stance. That's a principle I still like to teach my students.

Traffic in the Jungle: Teachers, Lawyers, Doctors, and Animals in Three Kipling Films (2001)
Shaul Bassi[1]

This essay on Rudyard Kipling's *The Jungle Book* and its filmic adaptations rests on three bitter truths.

The first, well-known, bitter truth is that Rudyard Kipling was not a politically correct writer, and even his seemingly innocent animal stories are not immune from his imperialist ideology.

The second one is that children's literary classics are often made into films, which often overshadow their literary sources or, at best, heavily interfere with them. As early as 1972 Gillian Avery remarked that Kipling's "popularity appears to have declined.... The first *Jungle Book* is borrowed by Wolf Cubs, or by those who have seen the Disney film, but is usually returned without enthusiasm" (Seymour-Smith 235).

The third bitter truth, a less obvious one, is that the jungle that Kipling had envisioned as a rough but felicitous place, where little Mowgli could freely roam without annoying adults around him, has become congested with human traffic. The modern adaptations of the books have filled that jungle with teachers, lawyers, boy scouts, but also soldiers, economists, doctors, and priests.

I would like to offer a postcolonial reading of such traffic in three films based on the Mowgli stories: *The Jungle Book,* directed by Zoltan Korda in 1942; the Walt Disney cartoon *The Jungle Book,* directed by Wolfgang Reitherman in 1967; and the recent *Rudyard Kipling's The Jungle Book* by Stephen Sommers, 1994.

My purpose is to show how a powerful colonialist subtext can be inscribed in what was described by its author as "a children's beast tale" (Ricketts 205), and re-inscribed in widely popular films, travelling and transforming itself from age to age, and from page to screen. Moreover, on account of the apparent discrepancy between the genre of the animal story and the question of imperialism, I argue that the material under scrutiny may represent, from a pedagogical perspective, a useful case study to introduce the cultural dynamics of colonialism.

By postcolonial reading I mean an assessment of the impact of colonialism on Western culture and imaginary, an irreversible impact whose consequences have lingered well beyond the political end of the British Empire. It is important to emphasize that colonialism is a two-way process, which profoundly affects both the colonized and the colonizer (even though not symmetrically): if Indian culture has radically changed under British colonization, at the same time India has struck back to the centre, carving a secure space for itself in our culture, from high-brow literature down to pop music and cinema.

It may not be superfluous to add that a postcolonial reading is not about pulling down literary monuments. If Kipling were just a bad and dead white imperialist male writer, we would not bother with him. To bring a postcolonial perspective to him means reading him against his grain, much in the spirit of Salman Rushdie, who has written: "I have never been able to read Kipling calmly. Anger and delight are incompatible emotions, yet [his] early stories do indeed have the power to infuriate or to entrance" (74).

As a final preliminary remark, I have appropriated the trope of traffic—often employed by Kipling himself—from Parata Roy's recent study (1998), where she demonstrates that colonial India has been constituted as a sort of social laboratory where new identities are constantly negotiated across different cultures. A process that we will see at work both in *The Jungle Book* and in its films.

We can approach Kipling's text from a postcolonial perspective by way of a definition by John McBratney: "*The Jungle Book,* part fantasy, part fable, and part adventure story, provides a powerful analogy for the British imperial subject caught between individual desire and social restraint" (278). In other words Mowgli embodies the unconscious fantasy of the British colonizer to be loved by the natives and at the same time to control them (Sullivan 1, 2). It is precisely because the two *Jungle Books* are part fantasy, part fable, part adventure and because their protagonist is a child that this fantasy can be fully played out. As a result of that, the colonialist overtones of these texts are more complex and nuanced than in Kipling's notorious imperialist manifestos, such as "The White Man's Burden" or "The Ballad of East & West."

In many respects, Mowgli is indeed the ideal colonizer. He arrives in the Jungle as the weakest creature (Kipling, *Jungle* 9), in tune with that rhetoric of innocence whereby the British represented themselves as the victims rather than the aggressors, guided by Providence to accomplish a mission which was "above politics, beyond interest and self-interest" (Mohanty 337). And like the British, Mowgli is bound to become the "overlord" of the Jungle (Kipling, *Jungle* 241).

As Satya Mohanty points out, the myth of the child who has a gift for living and moving around in a hostile environment, easily communicating with its inhabitants, fantasizes the need for the colonizer to tame a dangerous territory by mapping and controlling it (326). In her words, the imaginary of the colonial ruler is based on "the ability to command respect and fear in the subject race, on the one hand, and on the other, the ability to blend in, to be no different from the colonized and their society" (315).

Mowgli, whose name in Hindi means "frog," is an amphibian creature, torn between the animal and the human world, between nature and culture, India and Britain. He is respected by other animals and has the power to stare them down. Childhood is the dimension which allows the subject to remain suspended between realms which are considered incompatible in the colonial space. But there is also a dark side to this hybrid condition. When Mohanty claims that Kipling's Indian narratives embody "an insistent desire to remain vaguely defined" (338), she overlooks the various instances in which Mowgli's split identity, his awareness that he belongs neither with animals nor with men, is also the source of deep anxiety and anguish. Mowgli is repeatedly abandoned by both animals and men, becoming, in the words of a Kipling biographer, a "super-orphan" (Ricketts 206). A condition reminiscent of Kipling's own predicament as a child, a *mlech*, or foreigner—falling by definition outside the caste system—in his native India (McBratney 282) and later traumatically removed from his country and family.

Whether we consider Mowgli as the perfect colonizer or prefer to interpret him as a dangerous experiment with the forbidden colonial fantasy of going native, there is no doubt that he is eventually reabsorbed in the colonial system. In "In the Rukh," which is the final Mowgli story but also the one that Kipling wrote first, the grown-up Mowgli enters the service of the British Government as a forest-guard. All the animal adventures were thus written by Kipling in view of a happy colonial ending.

If Mowgli is a covert colonizer, who are the colonized? The answer is provided by the wise bear:

> I have taught thee all the Law of the Jungle for all the peoples of the jungle—except the Monkey-Folk who live in the trees. They have no law. They are outcasts. They have no speech of their own, but use the stolen words which they overhear when they listen, and peep, and wait up above in the branches. Their way is not our way. They are without leaders. They have no remembrance. They boast and chatter and pretend that they are a great people about to do great affairs in the jungle, but the falling of a nut turns their mind to laughter and all is forgotten. We of the jungle have no dealings with them. We do not drink where the monkeys drink; we do not go where the monkeys go; we do not hunt where they hunt; we do not die where they die.... The Monkey-People are forbidden, ... forbidden to the Jungle-People. Remember. (*Jungle* 51-52)

This description recapitulates the main stereotypes that the British ascribed to the Indians in order to justify their *mission civilizatrice*. Like the monkeys, Indians were supposed to have no law, no leaders, no history and whatever culture they had, it belonged to a remote past (Cohn 1996; Nandy 1983). The Bandar Log inhabit a majestic city which now lies deserted in the jungle, with its ruined palaces and hidden treasures, a memorial to that ideal of an Aryan, manly race, much idealized by Kipling. That civilization gone, the current inhabitants are unworthy of their ancestors, anarchic and incapable of socializing as they are, a true community of untouchables. Their kidnapping of Mowgli in the hope that he will bring them the secrets of technology, embodies a well-known argument of the British: the Indians need us because they are unable to rule themselves and to make any progress towards modernity (a superiority complex that has been analyzed and deconstructed by Goody).

Finally, the monkeys want to be like men, they ape and mimic them, and one is tempted here to read a projection of the British desire that the Indian should become like them, as in Lord Macaulay's project of social engineering expounded in his *Minute on Indian Education*, which prescribed the creation of a class "Indian in blood and colour, but English in taste, in opinions, in morals, and in intellect" (Ashcroft 430).

* * *

The fifty years that separate Kipling's text from its earliest spinoffs witness, among other things, the vanishing of Victorian moralism and its replacement with more surreptitious ideological elements which lurk behind the promise of entertainment.

Hungarian director Zoltan Korda's film is quite a faithful adaptation of

Kipling's plot, but it revolves almost entirely on Mowgli's adventures among men rather than animals, possibly because of the technical limitations of the 1940s.

Here the colonial presence is inscribed only in the frame of the story, which, as shown in the opening scene, is narrated by an old Indian storyteller to a British memsahib to whom he promises that "she will hold the whole of India in her photograph" (one is reminded of Dr. Aziz in Forster's *A Passage to India* who thinks that the tourist's "pose of 'seeing' India was only a form of ruling India"). This storyteller is none other than Buldeo, the villain of the story and his presence here suggests that the colonial intervention has been ultimately able to restore order in the territory where the bad, unruly Indians of the tale had produced chaos and destruction.

Buldeo starts off with a motto: life is a struggle of man against nature, the struggle of the village against the jungle. Yet the events he narrates seem to suggest a different conflict: on the one hand we have Mowgli, his mother, and Buldeo's daughter, representative of a benign society, on the other hand the evil hunter Buldeo and his associates, whose only purpose is to lay their hands on the treasure of the deserted city. Buldeo does not only represent human greed; he is also identified with superstition. He persecutes Mowgli and his mother accusing them of witchcraft, and his association with the brahmin makes clear that superstition is Hindu. Interestingly enough a different religious symbol appears in the film: when Mowgli's mother saves him from the angry crowd and convinces them that he is only an innocent child, the rescue takes place on the background of an imposing statue of the Buddha. This historical incongruity seems rather a way of pitting a good, motherly, feminine, and pacifist Buddhism against a superstitious, aggressive, and rapacious Hinduism.

Another theme developed in the film is the corruptive power of money. Where Kipling had written almost incidentally that Mowgli "had to learn about money which he did not in the least understand" (*Jungle* 95), Korda creates a scene in which the child is given some coins by his mother and marvels at the importance of a piece of metal which cannot be eaten or used for heating. But he will use that money to buy the knife with which he'll kill Shere Kahn. And a single coin taken from the deserted city will lead Buldeo and his two friends on the tracks of the hidden treasure and cause the death of two of them. Money is thus the cause of the final destruction of the village.

It is at the end of the story though, that Korda departs more radically from Kipling. In the film the village is not destroyed by Mowgli, but by Buldeo. Mowgli's protest against the world of humans is expressed in a different way: he goes back to the jungle out of his disappointment for the silly destructiveness demonstrated by humans. The date of the film is 1942, and we wonder if that burning village cannot be read as an implicit reference to Korda's native Europe, devastated by World War II.

* * *

If Korda's film is a veiled anti-capitalist and pacifist allegory, Walt Disney's 1967 classic cartoon is a more problematic celebration of capitalism and racialism. At the opposite pole of Korda, its graphic medium makes possible for the story to be almost completely based on animals. Yet, the least human of all the jungle films, offers a wide range of ethnic stereotypes, thinly disguised under the animals and ingeniously expressed through their voices and gestures. Kaa, the snake, hisses in an Oriental style; the vultures look and speak like the Beatles, Hathi the Elephant is a caricatural British fellow, and Baloo a streetwise Yankee.

The contrast between Hathi and Baloo marks the transition from Kipling's Indian-British jungle to an American Jungle. Hathi appears as an old-fashioned British officer who leads his troop of elephants in exhausting and pointless marches through the Jungle. Mowgli is initially attracted by such a drill, and he joins the march. But soon the absurdity of this colonial discipline drives him away and makes him turn to Baloo, who is no longer, as in Kipling, a stern law professor but an Epicurean bear who, much to the chagrin of Bagheera, teaches Mowgli how to box and fight.

This transition from the Indian-British jungle to the American Jungle is nowhere clearer than in the change of economic setting. In Kipling Mowgli had to work hard to earn a living in the jungle, toiling in the prehistorical tasks of hunting and gathering. In the cartoon he receives from Baloo a different economic theory, exposed in the song "The Bare Necessities." For Baloo the "bare necessities" are in fact a profusion of fruits and edible insects that the jungle ceaselessly supplies. It is enough to shake a tree to find a bunch of bananas or a juicy cocoanut in your hands. Disney's Jungle is an open-air super-market where all items are on display, credit cards are superfluous, and the bare necessities coincide with excess itself.

The most disturbing ethnic stereotype concerns once again the monkeys, the Bandar Log, surreptitiously associated with Indian in Kipling, blatantly likened to African Americans in Disney. Their king, an Ourang-Utan—a species which does not live in India—sings and dances a Jazz song, a performance which stages a modern version of the age-old connection between Blacks and monkeys. The monkeys represent the squatters of consumer society, the inhabitants of a civilization that they don't understand even as they continue to get great benefits from it.

The conclusion of the film calls the children to the responsibility of growing up. When he sees a sweet little Indian girl, Mowgli immediately realizes that he will have to leave the jungle of endless playing and all-you-can-eat supplies. Yet one cannot ignore that this passage from the realm of children's omnipotence to that of adult responsibility, from the pleasure principle to the reality principle which curbs the consumerist fantasy of the "bare necessities," has strong racial overtones. "Will you marry a panther?" asks Bagheera to Mowgli, to warn him against the absurdity of interracial marriage. The good and orderly society, the film seems to suggest, is that where men and women are happy to work and ethnic groups stay where they belong, that is separately.

* * *

Stephen Sommers's 1994 film, is the most recent, and yet—or maybe because of this—is the most colonialist in its outlook. There are two crucial novelties in the film: Mowgli appears as post-puberal character, as a second Lord Greystoke who can be involved in a love story. Secondly, the Raj, which was a marginal—if structurally indispensable—presence in Kipling's text, looms large in the story.

At the beginning, Mowgli appears as the little son of an Indian servant of Brydon, the British officer who is leading an expedition whose mission is to garrison a remote site inside the jungle.

This officer has a daughter, Kitty, at whom the little Mowgli peeps from behind a curtain while she dances a waltz and whom he tries in vain to kiss. When the tiger Shere Kahn wreaks havoc over the caravan and Mowgli is thought dead, he is already a grown, speaking child, integrated in the colonial system.

This emplotment dismantles one of the key assumptions of Kipling's narrative. Mowgli is no longer a wild boy whom animals have kidnapped from civilization. On the other hand, his precocious relationship with Kitty subverts in a comical key one of the nightmares of colonialism, the sexual contamination of the British by inferior races. One of the cornerstones of colonialism was that it was not an aggressive enterprise but a defensive move against the sexual assault of "black" men at white women (Young 1995). The alleged rape attempt of Ms. Quested by Dr. Aziz in Forster's *A Passage to India* is the emblem of two civilizations which are not made for each other.

In a certain way Sommers's film seems to debunk other colonial stereotypes. Ethnic and social barriers collapse: there are good and bad Indians, as well as good and bad British. Kitty's father and Dr. Plumford are contrasted to the greedy soldier Wilkins and his accomplices, who harass Kitty, torture Mowgli, and exploit him in order to reach the treasure. Above all, in the end Kitty, daughter of an English officer, marries down and out, as it were, choosing Mowgli, the son of an Indian servant. Kipling would hardly have approved of that. Yet these progressive messages can hardly be taken at face value. Their final kiss by the waterfall hides the fact that the real context that makes this marriage possible is not the benign nature of the jungle but the integration of the two young lovers into the colonial order represented by Kitty's father. A social order which has its bad apples, of course, but which is fundamentally beneficial and benevolent, as it is further demonstrated by Mowgli's education.

Education is a prominent topic in the film. In Kipling Mowgli learns human speech from his mother, and human wisdom from Baloo. In Sommers

Mowgli has already learned as a child but has unlearned as a wild boy in the jungle. When he returns as a young man, he becomes malleable matter for Kitty and Dr. Plumford. This funny character, played by John Cleese, is the quintessential Victorian scientist, who surveys the colonial territory, mapping methodically its flora and fauna while he is made fun of by his pupils. But he is also the tender-hearted doctor who will help Kitty to rescue Mowgli and will heal Baloo, who has been wounded by the wicked soldiers, showing how colonial science is thus firmly on the side of good. Gone are the days of the savage parody of colonialism in The Monty Python's *The Meaning of Life*, where the irresistible Cleese played a British officer who shaves impassibly while, a few inches from him, his troops are engaging in a bloody battle against the Zulu.

When Mowgli returns to the society of humans, Kitty and the doctor administer him sheer lessons in civilization, teaching him how to bathe, to dress, to shave and, above all, to speak. He is first shown letters written on gigantic flashcards, to learn the phonetics of English, then they proceed to words and finally slides, that expose him to the wonders of technology and the semantics of Empire, whose emblem is a picture of Prince Albert, the Viceroy of India. The Indian Mowgli is the passive recipient of a British education.

The ultimate symbol of cultural colonialism is the music which Kitty and Mowgli first dance as children and later crown their reunion as adults: Strauss' waltz *The Blue Danube*. They dance it during a party held in a magnificent Indian palace, where this quintessentially European music is played by an Indian orchestra. The allegory is manifest: India may provide a beautiful setting and skilled manpower, but real culture, be it in London, Vienna or in the midst of the Indian jungle, remains an essentially Western prerogative.

The growing traffic in Kipling's jungle shows how little space seems to be left in the society of the spectacle even to imagine ourselves in a different, free world; and it testifies to the longevity of the colonial imaginary, which lingers on in contemporary popular culture as the countermodel of an intelligent multicultural education.

Note

1   I wish to thank Sema Postacioglu Banon and Laura Tosi for their precious contribution to this essay.

Works Cited

Ashcroft, Bill, Gareth Griffiths, and Helen Tiffin, eds. *The Post-Colonial Studies Reader.* London: Routledge, 1995.

Cohn, Bernard S. *Colonialism and Its Forms of Knowledge: The British in India.* Princeton: Princeton UP, 1996.

Goody, Jack. *The East in the West.* Cambridge: Cambridge UP, 1995.

Kipling, Rudyard. *The Jungle Book.* 1894. London: Macmillan, 1965.

——. *The Second Jungle Book.* 1895. London: Macmillan, 1962.

McBratney, John. "Imperial Subjects, Imperial Space in Kipling's *Jungle Book.*" *Victorian Studies* 35.3 (1992): 277-93.

Mohanty, Satya. "Drawing the Color Line: Kipling and the Culture of Colonial Rule." *The Bounds of Race: Perspectives on Hegemony and Resistance.* Ed. Dominick LaCapra. Ithaca: Cornell UP, 1991.

Nandy, Ashis. *The Intimate Enemy: Loss and Recovery of Self under Colonialism.* Delhi: Oxford UP, 1983.

Ricketts, Harry. *The Unforgiving Minute: A Life of Rudyard Kipling.* London: Pimlico, 2000.

Roy, Parata. *Indian Traffic: Identities in Question in Colonial and Postcolonial India.* Berkeley: U of California P, 1998.

Rushdie, Salman. *Imaginary Homelands: Essays and Criticism, 1981-1991.* London: Granta, 1991.

Seymour-Smith, Martin. *Rudyard Kipling.* London: Queen Anne Press, 1989.

Sullivan, Zohreh T. *Narratives of Empire: The Fictions of Rudyard Kipling.* Cambridge: Cambridge UP, 1993.

Young, Robert J.C. *Colonial Desire: Hybridity in Theory, Culture and Race.* London: Routledge, 1995.

THEORETICAL EXPLORATIONS AND PRACTICAL ISSUES

In the late-nineteenth and early-twentieth centuries, children's books and writing about children provided the soil from which *Sons and Lovers*, *A la recherche du temps perdu*, *A Portrait of the Artist as a Young Man*, Willa Cather's *O Pioneers!* and *My Antonia*, *The Voyage Out*, *To the Lighthouse*, and *The Waves* all sprang. To name these novels is perhaps misleading, for the argument is not that children's books created books about children, but that cultural change was both reflected and pioneered in the books which children read. Radical experiments in the arts in the early modern period began in the books which Lewis Carroll and his successors wrote for children. (5)

—Juliet Duisenberre, *Alice to the Lighthouse:*
Children's Books and Radical Experiments in Art (1987)

The ability of very young readers to enter into a dynamic interaction between text and reader has been documented by both "book" and "child" people, yet it is difficult to find a theorist acknowledging the early experience of text. Neither Culler and his "literary competences" nor Stanley Fish and the notion of the "interpretive community" [see Stanley Fish, *Is There a Text in the Class?*] refers to the earliest experiences with text, though constructions based on literary convention and expectation are learned during childhood. *It is the expectations that these early experiences set up, particularly in terms of the structures, codes, etc.*, inviting an active, *authoritative* role for the reader, that influence the ways in which any reader reads a text. (2)

—Deborah Thacker, "Disdain or Ignorance:
Literary Theory and the Absence of Children's Literature" (2000)

What I have tried to do ... is to set out this impossible subject: children's literature. I have no doubt that the various constituencies of this elusive discourse will continue to deal with and speak about children's books in their specialized and professional ways. And this is fine. On the other hand, as traditional literary criticism and the other disciplines interested in children's books become more and more comfortable with their young sibling, cultural studies, those who practice these specialized disciplines might find they have more in common than perhaps they thought they did. For those in these various disciplines who have a genuine interest in the children whose books they study, the most obvious concern they should have is with the ability of these children to read fully and self-consciously. The self-conscious reader is a reader conscious of the self as acted upon and yet capable of acting. The best reading is a form of action; the worst is a form of absorption. When we encourage—and model in ourselves—active reading, we give our child readers the opportunity of becoming informed critical readers who have powers of judgment that will serve them as citizens of truly democratic states. In this sense, all reading is political. And a truly political reading will make impossible things possible, and our delight will be no less intense for all that. (207-08)

> —Rod McGillis, "The Delights of Impossibility: No Children, No Books,
> Only Theory" (1998-99)

The deep-read is when you get gut-hooked and dragged overboard down and down through the maze of print and find, to your amazement, you can breathe down there after all and there's a whole other world. I'm talking about the kind of reading when you realize that books are indeed interactive.... I'm talking about the kind of deep-read where it isn't just the plot or the characters that matter, but the words and the way they fit together and the meandering evanescent thoughts you think between the lines: the kind of reading where you are fleetingly aware of your own mind at work. (165-66)

> —Tim Wynne-Jones, "The Survival of the Book" (1998)

Introduction

The connections between children's literature and the adult world are the concern of this final chapter of *Considering Children's Literature*. The articles collected here pick up on the issues and ideas introduced in the first chapter and throughout the collection—expanding the discussion—but they also show the ways in which the larger worlds of economic concerns, literary studies, and technological developments are important in the study of children's literature. In the past 30 or so years, that field of study has been growing, both in numbers of scholars studying it and in ways in which it is studied. Areas such as education, library sciences, history of publishing, and marketing have important things to say about the production and discussion of children's and young adult's literature, and thus we have included essays that present some of the practicalities of dealing in it. Wendy Lamb's "Strange Business" discusses publishing constraints, and Margaret Mahy explores the experience of being a writer in a country that does not have a large population but does have a distinct identity in "The Writer in New Zealand." The impact of literary theories developed during the twentieth century is apparent in the study of children's literature, and in "Fear of Children's Literature," Perry Nodelman discusses how literary theory can inform our perspective of the field. Finally, the ways in which our understanding of an audience's interaction with stories is being reconfigured by television and the Internet is considered by Margaret Mackey in "Playing the Phase Space." The chapter moves from cash flow to phase space, and as with every chapter in this collection, the articles cover only a fraction of the debates, but their Works Cited point the way to more in-depth reading and discussion.

Works Cited

Duisenberre, Juliet. *Alice to the Lighthouse: Children's Books and Radical Experiments in Art.* 1987. New York: St. Martin's, 1999. 5.

McGillis, Rod. "The Delights of Impossibility: No Children, No Books, Only Theory." *Children's Literature Association Quarterly* 23.4 (Winter 1998-99): 202-08.

Thacker, Deborah. "Disdain or Ignorance: Literary Theory and the Absence of Children's Literature." *The Lion and the Unicorn* 20.1 (2000): 1-17.

Wynne-Jones, Tim. "The Survival of the Book." *Signal* 87 (Sept. 1998): 160-66.

Strange Business: The Publishing Point of View (1998)
Wendy Lamb

I'm here today to tell you about the business side of publishing for children, and a strange business it is indeed. But let me begin with a few observations about the publishing industry as a whole. It's an industry unlike any other, and it is wildly unpredictable. Aside from celebrity books and big-ticket fiction and nonfiction by established writers, one source of energy for the business is the fact that many people in this country feel they can write a book— why, gosh, they *know* they can write a book better than anything they've ever read—and they are working away on one at this very minute. This work is done on speculation, for free, and it is sent to publishers and agents who read unsolicited manuscripts, or "slush," for free. In this sense, publishing is a high-tech, billion-dollar business partly fuelled by a universal dream. And those writers are not wrong to dream, because a certain percentage are truly talented and they are writing good books that will succeed.

Whether a manuscript is unsolicited or comes from an agent, editors invest a great deal of time in searching for material. In my first job I spent ten months reading "slush" at Harper Junior Books. I never found anything publishable, though we wrote encouraging letters to many people. Today at Bantam Doubleday Dell we have two competitions that enable us to keep the door open to unsolicited writers, one for a young adult novel and one for a middle-grade novel. We get about 700 manuscripts in those competitions, and some years we don't find a winner. Even when a manuscript is terrible, you can feel the writer's energy in the work and how he or she sent the package off with great hopes. Clearly, the story will out. This seemingly inextinguishable energy reminds me of a line I found in a ghastly manuscript about a ghastlier subject, lamprey eels: *the urge to spawn is too hard to resist.*

Another unique aspect of this business is the way books are sold. Unlike other products, such as food or clothing, when a book is shipped that sale is not final. A bookseller can return books for a certain period—usually six months—and it takes quite a while to know how many books the publisher has actually sold.

Publishing for Children: An Even Stranger Business

First of all, it's done by adults who spend their time trying to think like a two-year-old or a ten-year-old or an eighteen-year-old. Second, we are creating a product for one audience, children, but for the most part we must sell it to adults. Picture books, middle-grade novels and young adult hardcovers are generally purchased by teachers, librarians and parents. Young readers tend to buy paperbacks—series titles, celebrity books (such as recent ones about Leonardo DiCaprio, or the skater Tara Lipinski) and young adult novels.

And Who is Our Audience?

We are trying to create a product for an audience that is ever-changing: developing physically, emotionally and in terms of their literacy skills. I can't assume that I can edit a book for the kind of child I was at the age of seven, or ten, or fourteen; my childhood was quite different from the life of a young reader in the 1990s. Publishers must constantly study what is going on in family life, in schools, in the media, in entertainment. Because our maturing audience is seen as vulnerable, in need of protection, we face censorship issues and conflicts about what kind of materials a child is ready to read, and what kinds of books a child should have access to without parental supervision. These conflicts are part of the challenge of selling to the American market, an area full of special interests and labels: political correctness, religious right, conservative, liberal, activist, fundamentalist, parental rights, community standards, First Amendment issues, and so on.

My department is known for publishing very sophisticated, often controversial, books for the older young adult, such as the recent *Tenderness* by Robert Cormier, about a serial killer, or *Blood and Chocolate* by Annette Curtis Klause, an erotically charged novel about a girl who is a werewolf. Both are beautifully written and were named as "Best Books for Young Adults" by the

American Library Association. But these books would probably not be purchased in a conservative community.

Because our audience is learning to read, publishers are affected by educational trends and controversies, such as the recent conflict about phonics, the traditional method, versus the whole-language approach. The whole-language approach uses a literature-based curriculum, meaning storybooks and chapter books, as opposed to basal readers created by textbook publishers. Whole-language has been a boon to publishers, of course, for it has sold millions of books to school systems.

Books Must be Timely, and Timeless

Certainly, we want to create books with the eternal appeal of a good story and wonderful art, books that have the high quality of the classics we grew up with, books whose appeal endures over generations. We also want to create a different kind of book, ones that capture a fad or trend, such as Ninja Turtles, books based on TV shows, toys, Star Wars, a rock band or the passion for a sport like gymnastics. We must have the right book in the stores when readers want it most, in a format they like and can afford. As you can see in the following statistics, this is a growing market with enormous spending potential.

Sales figures provided from *The Bowker Annual* (a database of information about the publishing industry) by the Children's Book Council:

	Number of Books Published	Total Sales
1920	420	No financial figures available
1970	2,640	$111,000,000
1985	2,938	$336,200,000
1990	5,056	$1,041,100,000 (Hardcover: $781,500,000; Paperback: $259,600,000)
1996	4,734	$1,479,200,000 (Hardcover: $909,100,000; Paperback: $570,100,000)

An article in *The New York Times*, 23 February 1998, projects that the teenage population of America, 38.2 million in 1997, will soar to 42 million by 2010. Their present spending power is approximately 80 billion dollars.

Quality Control and Keeping Books in Print

The success of a book is generally review-driven rather than publicity-driven, for children's books cannot overcome bad reviews the way an adult book can and still sell. Children set a high standard—no ad or gimmick will make them keep reading something that doesn't hold their interest.

It costs more to publish an adult book in terms of marketing and publicity budget, and an adult book has a shorter shelf life. The lower cost of children's books once helped to keep them in print despite low sales. However, a recent change in tax laws means that publishers can no longer write off inventory, so it costs more to keep books in a warehouse. This is one reason for the alarming new trend of putting children's books out of print in hardcover at almost the same rate as adult books. The paperback, however, does tend to stay in print longer than the hardcover, usually due to school sales.

Eighty per cent of our sales of "literary" books is institutional, to schools and libraries. Marketing is focused on getting the book to teachers and giving them teachers' guides and other materials to help them use it in the classroom, and we post them on our web site on the Internet. We look for books that have curriculum value and sometimes add maps, historical notes and other materials to enlarge on the facts behind the fiction.

Publishers

I'm sure you have read about how independent publishers are being merged and swallowed up by multinational corporations which are run by "money people" rather than "book people." I work in the Books for Young Readers department of Bantam Doubleday Dell, three publishers owned and merged by the media giant Bertelsmann, a German company which has recently purchased Random House. The whole Bertelsmann US publishing group is now known as Random House, Inc. Another conglomerate is Viacom, which owns Paramount, which bought Simon and Schuster and Macmillan, which owned Atheneum, Scribner's, Four Winds and Bradbury. These new combinations have meant that distinguished imprints have disappeared, staff and lists have been cut. Not all of the cuts were wrong, since there are always too many bad books being published, but they have created a general feeling of insecurity for publishing professionals and authors. Each publishing group within one of these companies is under pressure to produce profits and to satisfy the stockholders who have invested in the company.

Editorial departments are caught between the pressure to produce faster profits and higher sales and the fact that publishing for children, aside from fads, is a slow business. A good novel, written with love, needs time. Publishers must allow writers and artists room to experiment, to fail, and to develop.

With a picture-book text, it can take a long time to find the right illustrator, who may have other commitments, so you must wait. And creative people often miss deadlines!

The pressure for faster profit can lead to internal censorship and market consciousness. Right now some houses are cashing in on the popularity of famous books by doing spin-offs from classics. HarperCollins has created picture books and chapter books based on the stories in the *Little House* series by Laura Ingalls Wilder and *The Chronicles of Narnia* by C.S. Lewis. Bantam Doubleday Dell and Avon have done a series of books based on the sisters in *Little Women*. Advocates say these books will introduce new readers at a simpler level and prepare them for the actual book. Critics call it "dumbing down." In YA, the declining market means that some publishers are not taking on "riskier" books.

Bookstores

We are all concerned about the fact that the rise of the chain bookstores such as Barnes and Noble and bookselling on the Internet are putting small independent bookstores out of business. In a world of shrinking outlets, the power of the chains has a big impact on children's books. For example, chains tend not to stock many young adult novels, and when they do they usually order paperback, not hardcover.

Diversity

We know that the future of America will be multicultural; by 2050 the United States will be predominantly Hispanic. Children's books departments have been way ahead of adult departments in developing diverse books for all age levels by African-American, Hispanic, and Asian-American writers. The publishing staffs, however, are hardly multicultural. This year, City College of New York began a Certificate in Publishing Program which is designed to bring minorities into the field.

The Electronic Age

We now have a generation of computer-literate children who represent the effects of a technological revolution that is as profound as the invention of movable type five hundred years ago. What kind of books will make children want to keep reading in an electronic age?

Eliza Dresang, associate professor of library science at Florida State University, and Kate McClelland, a librarian, have done some very interesting work in this area. A book to be published this year [1998], *Radical Change* by Dresang, reflects their research and speculates about the future. In an article in *Book Links*, Dresang and McClelland see a present trend toward "transformed books," which appeal to young readers immersed in a "point and click culture," readers who are accustomed to multi-levelled, varied ways of receiving text. These books will tell stories in a non-linear way and will employ and combine techniques such as multiple narratives and interactive and collaborative design that merges art and text. Nonfiction will use personal accounts of historic events and multiple points of view to give a "you are there" sense of immediacy and simultaneity. Sophisticated picture books will appeal to adults as well as kids.

Grimmer than Grimm?

The recent media explosion of the Internet and cable television and video also means that children are being exposed earlier and earlier to harsh truths and darker aspects of our culture. Young adult novels are becoming more mature or, simply, grimmer, dealing with problems created by the disintegrating structures of family, religion, public education and the economy. Young people are coming of age sexually in the shadow of AIDS. Children caught in toxic families struggle with the inability or refusal of adults to be parents and with the general insecurity of family life today. Despite this darkness, Dresang and McClelland are optimistic, seeing a generation of enthusiastic, empowered readers fluent in a new world where a preschooler can use a CD-ROM and master technology that is difficult for many adults.

Finally—There's Hope

When Jack Zipes spoke to me about participating in this panel, he asked me to address the "present crisis" in the world of children's book publishing. Well, children's books have always been in a state of crisis! There has always been conflict between what is "good" for kids and what kids *like*. From the days of the penny dreadfuls of the nineteenth century to the advent of television, to today's media explosion and pressure for profit, everyone has worried that this means the end of reading and the end of books. But I am full of hope. For one thing, the book is an object that has had great meaning to humanity for hundreds of years, and I don't think it will disappear any time soon. A child can love the book itself, can share it and give it, can control how he or she receives the story by turning the page backwards and forwards. In picture books the pacing of illustration and text from page to page is a high art. So far there is no technology that satisfies us the way a book does.

I find great hope in the way that children ask for a sequel to a demanding, literary book. Wanting a sequel has nothing to do with whether or not the story holds out the possibility of more to come. Children want to stay in the world of the book. Some authors receive thousands of letters asking for a new book just like the favourite one, and many letters suggest elaborate plots. Readers want the experience of the book to continue because they enjoyed it, of course, but also because they have invested time and effort in reading this book, and they are caught up in questions and feelings that are so rich and so interesting that they continue after the book is finished.

Investment—doesn't that mean you have excess capital to put away so it will increase? As long as a child feels that he or she has more to give to the reading experience, and as long as reading a fine book enriches the child, I don't think there's a crisis in the strange and wonderful business of publishing children's books.

Works Cited

Dresang, Eliza T. *Radical Change: Literature For the Young in an Electronic Age.* New York: H.W. Wilson, 1998.

Dresang, Eliza T. and Kate McClelland. "Radical Changes." *Book Links* 40.6 (July 1996): 40-46.

Weinraub, Bernard. "Who's Lining Up at the Box Office? Lots and Lots of Girls." *The New York Times* 23 Feb 1998: E1.

The Writer in New Zealand:
Building Bridges through Children's Books (1996)
Margaret Mahy (Lyttelton)

The following remarks on postcolonial children's literature in New Zealand are taken from the banquet address presented at the IBBY Regional Conference "The World at Our Doorstep," organized by USBBY in October 1995 in Callaway Gardens.—[*Bookbird*] Ed.

Building bridges of understanding seems to have a curiously symbolic function where my own life is concerned, both in my writing life—my true life—

and in my day-to-day life—my *real* life—a narrow differentiation that should
not be taken too seriously. I begin in an unashamedly egotistical fashion with
the opening paragraph from "The Bridge Builder" (in *The Door in the Air*,
1988), a story that I wrote some years ago.

> My father was a bridge builder. That was his business—crossing chasms,
> joining one side of the river with the other. When I was small, bridges
> brought us bread and books, Christmas crackers and coloured pencils—
> one-span bridges over creeks, two-span bridges over streams, three-span
> bridges over wide rivers. Bridges sprang from my father's dreams, thread-
> ing roads together—girder bridges, arched bridges, suspension bridges,
> bridges of wood, bridges of iron or concrete. Like a sort of hero my father
> would drive piles and piers through sand and mud to the rocky bones of
> the world. His bridges became visible parts of the world's hidden skele-
> ton.... Slowly as we children watched and played a bridge would appear,
> and people would cross over. (21)

Though my father did not build quite the variety of bridges the text suggests, he really was a bridge builder, and the shingle and sand, the steel and
cement are an intimate part of my childhood memories. I did watch bridges
appear and people cross over. The country in which I watched these bridges
being built was New Zealand. Curiously enough when I am in the USA I am
always much more confident as a writer of children's stories than as a New
Zealander. I have been so colonized by stories, and even more by popular film
and song, that America often feels like a place I have actually lived in. I walk
through airports muttering and singing under my breath because seeing
place names like Chicago, Tulsa, Galveston, Kalamazoo, Seattle, New York,
and San Francisco sends songs running through me with their own sort of
electricity. But the recognition isn't mutual. If I get into a taxi in New York,
perceptive taxi drivers, those that speak English reasonably well, detecting an
accent that is obviously not domestic, ask me if I am English, a question that
my mother would have found flattering in its implications. However, occasionally, some highly tuned and sensitive taxi driver will ask me if I am Australian, and it is a postcolonial irony that my mother would have found this
much less flattering, for the Britain of my childhood was my mother's idea of
what a country should be. No New York taxi driver has ever asked me if I am
a New Zealander.

Australia and New Zealand share an approximately similar history and geo-
graphical situation: they are Pacific countries in which an indigenous population was displaced and marginalized by Western, largely British, incursions.
In a curious way, the colonizers marginalized themselves as well. Australians,
Canadians, and New Zealanders consider with wonder the imaginative dislo-
cations implicit in colonialism, for a full imaginative relationship with the

place in which one finds oneself does not come about automatically. There is an inside room as well as an outside landscape, and the stories of childhood not only move children out into the world but also furnish that inside room and open windows and doors onto views that are not always those the future adult would select.

New Zealand Children's Literature

The first New Zealanders, the Maori, had an extensive oral tradition, a mythology, a folklore, and a view of family and tribe based on memory. The British tradition of stories in books, of memory printed, bound, and placed in a library rather than being contained in a wise human head, has, until recently, obscured the Polynesian voice. One of our great Maori writers, Patricia Grace, says that because of the distortions imposed by the dominant educational culture, she grew up believing her own life and experiences were not a true subject for fiction. Time had to pass before New Zealand publishers and writers began to believe in the importance of their own indigenous stories, before there was any prospect of profit in them, or before the Maori imagination had representation in print and illustration.

In a less alarming way, this was my experience, too. I began writing stories intended for children when I was eighteen or nineteen, at a time when my own childhood was behind me and before I had children of my own. I had already discovered that when I tried to write stories specifically about New Zealand, I just did not believe them. Perhaps this was because the stories I had heard and read in my childhood disconnected me from my surroundings. For instance, I had climbed pohutukawa trees for many years, but, once included in my stories, pohutukawas seemed to have no extension beyond the page. If I wrote of a pine or a willow, there was an imaginative resonance. Not only were pines and willows all around me, expensively planted by industrious colonizers, but they were in the stories too—mentioned by A.A. Milne or Kenneth Grahame, to choose two classic examples. The word *pohutukawa*, however, sat self consciously on the page and could go no further. There was no country in which I could satisfactorily use such language.

It was not that New Zealand children were totally without any sort of local books and tales. There have been children's stories written about New Zealand since the 1830s, and from the 1890s onward children's books began to appear quite regularly: one book in 1894, another in 1896, two in 1898. By the 1920s New Zealand had enthusiastic and even prolific writers for children—women who wrote at least one book a year. Some of them wrote like English writers uneasily displaced, but at least one of them, Edith Howes, has a true New Zealand feel about her stories. There were 11 books published in 1930—6 of them actually published within New Zealand—and 15 in 1944. But because of the difficulties of distribution beyond the cities and my mother's suspicions (shared by many other reading middle-class people) that cultural quality in local product was necessarily inferior, and because those suspicions were often justified and the local product was often rough, clumsy, or naive, I saw comparatively few of the New Zealand books that were available.

In 1969, 22 books that could fairly be called New Zealand children's books appeared. Five of them by me, and published in the USA. "The great thing about your books," my New York publisher said to me, "is no one could tell they were written in New Zealand!" It wasn't quite the compliment she thought she was paying, but I am the daughter of a tradesman, a man who built bridges *for money*, and I was glad of anything that might give me an edge in a competitive world.

It is surprisingly hard to get exact information as to the current situation, but in 1994, 169 books were submitted for the New Zealand Library Association awards (NZLA), which is something of a triumph and reflects an increasingly high public image for children's books. New Zealand is now officially proud of its children's literature and offers at least two annual awards, one involving money as well as honour. The Whole Book method of teaching reading has resulted in a large number of short books being published in New Zealand, an increased possibility for authors and illustrators to make a living, and a greatly increased chance for children generally to make contact with stories that reflect and confirm their own environment.

Entering the Magic Circle

Of course books imply publishing, which has always been a capitalistic venture. By now we have a number of publishers who have international—most frequently British—parent companies. One of our biggest and most successful publishers for children is Ashton Scholastic in both the USA and Australia. We also have a number of lively small presses. Mallison Rendall has had a huge success with the Hairy McLary books by Lynley Dodd, which do well in the UK and in Australia, although the originating publisher has a small way of doing business—local, personal, and dedicated. Of course, all our publishers dream of publishing internationally, of selling the book to publishers in the UK or the USA, which they do, but at a cost. Holding hands, for some in the magic circle, limits the ways they can wiggle their fingers.

The current New Zealand demand, a popular demand by now in families as well as in libraries and schools, is for books that tell our children about their own society. But New Zealand writers may still have stories turned down by New Zealand publishers because the associated Australian or American company does not see the story as having as much relevance to readers in Sydney or Los Angeles. And it is hard for a book with a Kiwi idiom to find a place in Britain, which produces 7,000 children's books a year, many of which are probably not as good as the best that New Zealand has to offer but have the advantage of local voices and local reference. Consideration of local idiom certainly affects the stories writers are encouraged to submit as trade books or for inclusion in the educational reading series. While New Zealand *needs* stories with local content and idiom to help its children become New Zealanders, local content may disadvantage the story when international sales are explored. New Zealanders are great bridge crossers. They have had to be. The food has often been on the other side of the bridge. Publishers, however, are cautious bridge builders, for, given the choice, many people do not want to cross over. Publishers need the international sales, and so do authors and illustrators if they are to buy the time it takes to produce the next book.

No doubt you have heard other antipodeans expand with varying degrees of indignation on the intransigence of publishers in the USA. Why shouldn't our voices be heard, we howl. Why is *our* language and vernacular edited out or translated into the idiom of some other country? Haven't *our* children adapted to books from the USA and the UK for years and years? Haven't *we* had to cross over? The fact is a big market does not *have* to adapt to a small one no matter how fair and reasonable the demand, and no matter what theoretical advantages may accrue from standing on the other bank of the river and looking back over your shoulder. Yet some publishers are adventurous and innovative, and sometimes in unexpected circumstances. For instance, Joy Cowley's story *Old Tuatara* (Wellington: Department of Education, 1983) is published as *Old Lizard* just over the Tasman in Australia, regardless of the fact that a tuatara, though a reptile, is not a lizard. But in the USA the enlightened publisher Richard Owens has allowed it to appear as *Old Tuatara.* "Who knows?" he says philosophically. "Someone may actually learn something."

Illustrators as Bridge Builders

Among the many trade books I have written are numerous picture books, all of which have been illustrated overseas by illustrators who have never visited my country and have never seen the landscapes I have seen. Some bridges spring simultaneously from both banks of the river or harbour, and work their way toward a meeting in the middle when the two pieces become one bridge. My own picture books are like that. Inevitably, there are occasions when I have been astonished at the pictures produced to go with my stories, not because the pictures are necessarily wrong, but because they are so different from the pictures in my head. And there have been times when I have been enchanted and intrigued by the difference. Steven Kellogg's illustrations for *The Boy Who Was Followed Home* (1975), for instance, invented a landscape in which the story can take place, and interestingly enough it is the landscape of many of my stories, even those he has not illustrated. The school and the house sit in a wide empty country, through which parents drive in long gracious cars that suggest a royal progress of Bentleys and Rolls Royces until they tangle with the proliferating hippos that follow the hero Robert to and from school. It isn't Britain, in spite of those cars, or New Zealand, and it isn't the US, either. It is simply the country of story, which is where I set it in the first place.

The situation with *The Rattlebang Picnic* (1994), also illustrated by Steven, is rather different, however. New Zealand is not mentioned. No volcanic eruption is in progress when the family in my story idyllically picnic on the mountainside and bathe in the hot springs as Steven shows, with the smoking cone rising ominously above them. However volcanoes are features of my New Zealand view. I live in the crater of an extinct volcano; an active one was visible on the horizon of my childhood. I originally called the mountain Volcano Mountain, but Steven suggested the more ambivalent Mount Fogg. He is now the one who gives the significant information.

Steven's pictures once again suggest a figurative landscape, the language of story with its own oddities. Two car dealerships—one palatial, the other filled with junk—exist in an otherwise empty countryside, which bears an accidental resemblance to what we call the High Country—the largely bare, folded slopes that rise toward and melt into the Southern Alps. We have no vultures in New Zealand, but vultures, like lions, are images that extend beyond their national boundaries. Steven's landscape has vultures circling around the apparently doomed family. Steven has set *his* story, his illustrator's story, at an angle to mine, but an angle I find harmonious. As a citizen of the country of story, that strange but familiar place, I don't mind this at all.

Shortly before the scheduled launch of this book, the publishers contacted me with a problem: the story ended with a plan to picnic the following week at Earthquake Valley. The bookseller's conference at which the book was to make its debut was to be held in Los Angeles that particular year, and Los Angeles had suffered a damaging earthquake in the recent past. Children's books are always subject to a singularly intent scrutiny by people anxious to detect insensitivity on the part of the author, and it was felt that joking about earthquakes might be seen as unduly callous. The publishers wondered if I would consider changing my reference to Earthquake Valley to Tornado Valley. I agreed, not so much because I was anxious about disadvantaging the book from the point of view of sales but because I was filled with anxiety on behalf of those who had suffered a really terrible earthquake. Anyhow, the alteration of this single word changed the story, more than Steven's pictures, from being a New Zealand story to being a story set once again in nowhere. When I tell it or read it aloud I find I still have to say Earthquake Valley, or the story is not what it was supposed to be.

Does this matter? The answer is both yes and no. By now New Zealand has a firmly established children's literature that is all its own. New Zealand books are separately displayed in bookshops, where once they used to be hidden or marginalized. I have seen many other writers emerge, people who are published and who are illustrated in New Zealand, and the development of a whole rank of illustrators, almost without exception anxious to sell their books overseas.

New Zealand is not the idyllic country that travel brochures try to suggest. It is part of the world and the damage of the world. Along with its wonderful patches of forest and South Island mountains, and its North Island beaches and its programs for saving endangered birds, it has its share of racial problems—sometimes bitter ones—of crime, broken families, youth suicide. It has its bullies, its abused and ruined people. Its writers describe the beauty, but they want to acknowledge its contentious areas, too. In the background of my own book *Underrunners* (1992) is a damaged landscape. The question of how much truth we tell children and young people, how much we acknowledge, is as lively in New Zealand as anywhere else, along with the question of whether it is the children we are trying to protect or our own secure view of what childhood should be. These days, we may be concerned with what it is to be a New Zealander, but we are part of the world, the Western world and the Polynesian world, too. We are all world citizens because of books, pictures, film and popular music. We have something to receive and something to offer.

At the end of my own story "The Bridge Builder," the child narrator, now grown up, says a magical word to the father, who actually *becomes* a bridge, becomes the essence of his own construction. The narrator finishes the story by saying, "Some day perhaps some child of mine may say my word back to me—the words I said to my father—but I won't turn into a bridge. I shall become a journey winding over hills, across cities, along seashores through shrouded forests, crossing my father's bridges and the bridges of other men too as well as the infinitely dividing roads and splintered pathways that lie between them" (34-35).

Works Cited

Cowley, Joy. *Old Tuatara*. Wellington: Department of Education, 1983.
Mahy, Margaret. *The Boy Who Was Followed Home*. Illus. Steven Kellogg. New York: Dial Books for Young Readers, 1975.
——. *The Door in the Air*. London: J.M. Dent, 1988.
——. *The Rattlebang Picnic*. Illus. Steven Kellogg. New York: Dial Books for Young Readers, 1994.
——. *Underrunners*. London: Hamish Hamilton, 1992.

Postscript (2005)

Re-reading this article I think it would be true to say that, after approximately six years, it is still largely relevant. The writers and illustrators, named in the article are still working, though of course there are new writers too ... writers like Vicky Jones who reveals that New Zealand writers are confidently moving into areas of fantasy without betraying that inherent responsibility to present New Zealand identity.

Nothing stands still in this world, and this applies to the production of children's books. Mary Hoffman quotes the number of children's books produced in the UK as ten thousand a year—more than are needed, with the result that many are quickly discounted or go out of print. Published today *The Wind in the Willows*, which was not an immediate best-seller in its own time, would not remain in print long enough to become the classic that it is today. The UK apparently publishes more children's books than the USA. Australia produces a wide range of books, including controversial young adult books and picture books aimed at readers well above the traditional elementary school level. Even in New Zealand a recent picture book (*Clubs* by Kate deGoldi) is a book for readers between 8 and 10 years old. At the same time, though the historical domination of UK books is inevitably modified, the Harry Potter books (surely the most successful children's books ever published) are powerfully displayed in New Zealand book shops. Let's read on and write on too. The flow of story may shift and change, but luckily it is endless.

Fear of Children's Literature:
What's Left (or Right) After Theory? (1997)
Perry Nodelman

The year is 1944. As war rages in Europe and elsewhere, Americans can open a newly published book and read these words:

> Children and grownups belong to different worlds.... How far removed is the world of childhood! Its inhabitants seem of another species.... Reason does not curb them, for they have not yet learned its restraints. Happy beings, they live in the clouds, playing light-heartedly without a care. (1-2)

Not surprisingly, such beings require their own special kind of stories: "those that offer children an intuitive and direct way of knowledge, a simple beauty capable of being perceived immediately, arousing in their souls a vibration which will endure all their lives" (42).

The book expressing these convictions was *Books, Children, and Men*, a translation into English of *Les livres, les enfants, et les hommes*, first published in France in the early 1930s by Paul Hazard. From the viewpoint of 1995, it's hard to imagine that children could ever have been so innocent, or that children's books could ever have been so innocent—or, above all, that an adult could ever have been so innocent as to believe so wholeheartedly in that childhood innocence. It's especially hard not to remember that, as Americans read these words, children were starving and dying and otherwise being abused, not only in European concentration camps but also in many of the poorer parts of the United States—and that they continue to be so treated now, all these decades later.

But Hazard wasn't alone in his views. They represent ideas about children and literature that most people took for granted for many decades. I bought my own copy of *Books, Children, and Men* in the late 1970s, as a newcomer to children's literature wishing to find out what the respected authorities had to say about my newly chosen subject. I knew the book was respected because it was still in print, more than thirty years after its first American publication, and it remained in print for some years after that. Furthermore, it wouldn't take more than a quick browse through journals that publish reviews of or articles about children's books to find comments similar to the ones by Hazard with which I began. A lot of people still share these views.

Yet much has happened since 1944. There has been half a century more of news about the astonishing persistence and prevalence of child abuse in all its despicable forms. There has also been half a century of developments in our theoretical understanding both of child psychology and of literature. Nowadays, it's pretty difficult for people to maintain the conviction that childhood is ever as innocent as Hazard wanted to imagine it always was. More significantly for those of us professionally interested in this subject, it's almost impossible to maintain that literature for children could ever be as simple, as direct, or even as wise as Hazard claims.

If anything, what we have come to know—and how we have come to think five decades later as a result of that knowledge—can encourage only one clear response in us to children's literature, perhaps to all literature. That response is, quite simply, fear. After having learned what theory has to tell us about the nature of childhood and the nature of literature, we can logically conclude only that literature in each and all of its forms and manifestations is very, very bad for children and other human beings.

And indeed, many people do reach that conclusion—or get uncomfortably close to it.

Most obviously, there are the censors: those people of every political stripe who are convinced that literature representing values other than the ones they themselves know to be right and true is incredibly dangerous and exceedingly powerful, and inevitably will pervert young readers' minds. If this logic is ever correct, then surely it is always correct. All children's literature is at least suspicious, if not downright horrifying.

But even those of us who are committed to freedom of speech and who know that children almost always grow up with a deep belief in their parents' or peers' values, no matter what books they read—even *we* aren't free from our fears about literature. Some of us believe that children who read too much of what we consider to be inferior or tasteless literature will themselves remain inferior and without taste, and so we deeply fear popular series like the Babysitters Club or Goosebumps. And some of us, deeply learned in our knowledge of theory and ineffably wise, have even deeper and more all-encompassing fears. We see literature, all literature, as a means of enmeshing children in repressive ideology. In an article I wrote a few years ago, in which I explored the similarities between the intellectual basis of the European colonial project, as described by Edward Said in *Orientalism,* and our common assumptions about childhood, I concluded that children's literature is best understood as a means by which adults claim power over children and force them to accept our repressive versions of who they really are. Scary stuff, that children's literature—very dangerous indeed. Maybe the only way to protect children from being ruined for life is to keep them illiterate—that, and drown all the TV sets.

In 1994, I gave a paper at a children's literature conference in the United States about a series of picture books by the American writer and illustrator David Wiesner. While Wiesner's books claim to be celebrations of the freed imagination, I argued that even they were profoundly manipulative and repressive. After the talk was over, a member of the audience, my friend Lois Kuznets—a critic who has done fine work of revealing repressive ideologies in apparently harmless texts—asked this question: "Is nothing safe anymore? Is it *all* dangerous?"

My immediate, automatic answer was, "Yes, Lois, of course, it is all dangerous." But I surprised myself by saying it, and I've been wondering about Lois's question ever since she asked it. It's a good question, and a very important one. Is there anything left worth salvaging after theory gets through with literature? Is the whole enterprise of adults providing texts for children ever anything but oppressive and repressive? *Can* it be?

I'd like to explore those questions here—and then try to find some answers to them.

Let me begin once more with Paul Hazard. When I was asked to talk about what's happened to our theoretical understanding of children's literature since 1945, my first thought was to reread his book—it seemed like an easy way to recall where we'd all come from. As I browsed through *Books, Children and Men* for the first time in almost twenty years, I found myself noticing things in it I didn't remember having noticed in 1977, and that I suspect no adult interested in children's literature in 1944 would be likely to have noticed at all. My knowledge of theories of various sorts was making the book seem different than I remembered it.

My strongest response was to Hazard's faith that some texts might "offer to children an intuitive and direct way of knowledge, a simple beauty capable of being perceived immediately, arousing in their souls a vibration which will endure all their lives" (42). This now bothers me on two accounts: what it says about children's literature, and what it says about children.

About literature: literary theories of many kinds, from reception theory to gender studies, has encouraged me to understand that texts, all texts, exist within a complex network of ideas and images and cultural values—and that includes apparently simple texts written for children. I can no longer believe that any text is ever direct or simple, and I've come to mistrust critics like Hazard who claim that some are. Hazard takes all of his own knowledge of French life and culture for granted when he assumes that young children will automatically read Charles Perrault's fairy tales as he does.

I also find myself noticing how strangely contradictory it is that Hazard offers detailed analyses of a number of the books he claims speak so perfectly and so directly to children, from Perrault's fairy tales to *Robinson Crusoe*. If they are so simple and so direct, why do they need to be explained?

Which takes me to what Hazard says about children. What children understand so intuitively needs to be explained to adults like me because, Hazard asserts, we adults have lost the ability to think like children. That's a doubly dangerous generalization. First, it *is* a generalization: surely not all children are alike in any way whatsoever, except in being young. Second, it assumes the shared likeness is a deficiency in relation to adults: if nothing else, it's surely a little insulting for us to assume that children, any children, are closer to nature than we are, less sophisticated, and therefore, presumably, less evolved.

As I read Hazard's descriptions of children and their reading, I found myself doing an act of translation. He might well be right, but not, I told myself, about actual children who might actually be reading books—for the real children I know are nothing like that, and they are not freaks. Rather, these might be accurate descriptions of what reader-response theorists call *implied* readers: the imaginary constructs of ideal audiences that writers had in their minds when they wrote, and therefore implied in the contents of their texts, and that actual readers might need to transform themselves into, in order to make best sense of the texts. In other words, Hazard may have confused the cart and the horse. In order to celebrate a certain kind of text, he had to pretend there already existed an audience, now defined as essentially childlike, exactly suited to respond to it. But in point of fact, the text precedes, and might even help to create, the audience.

Obviously, my act of translation changes what was apparently harmless in Hazard's text into something deeply suspicious. If a text invites and requires a real child to become the ideal reader—the ideal child—it implies, then the text is manipulative. And if that ideal child represents an ideal I don't myself share, then I have no choice but to see the manipulation as dangerous—something to fear.

I certainly fear Hazard's view of childhood—and recognize it as a very popular one even now. In insisting that children are exactly opposite to adults, an alien species who belong in a different and presumably better world, proponents of this idea force me either to share their views and despise adults for not being childlike, or to disagree with them and despise children for not being fully evolved humans. Both positions insist that children are more significantly different from adults of their own species than similar to them. As Hazard suggests in the first sentence of his that I quoted, "Children and grownups belong to different worlds."

As I consider that sentence, I can't help but notice the parallel between Hazard's view of children as an alien species and the kind of thinking that led too many human beings to believe for too many centuries that, for instance, women and men belong to different species, that white Europeans and black Africans belong to different species, that Englishmen and Frenchmen belong to different species. In this kind of thinking, the species are not only different but opposite in every way. If men are reasonable, women are intuitive, and if Europeans are pragmatic, then Africans live only for the day. The Other is always and inevitably the opposite—and Hazard's children are clearly opposite to adults in every important way: imaginative where adults have lost the ability to imagine, playful where adults insist on serious purposes even in their play. Childhood, says Hazard, "remains healthy because it has not yet reached the age for analysing the soul's emotions" (167).

Or to put it another way, adults are all sick—including the adult who wrote these words. For Hazard makes this comment in the midst of a carefully organized and presumably rational analysis. Thus we have to conclude that he, himself an analytical adult, is sick also—a sick being envying the health of those in a category so opposite to himself that he could not possibly enter it. For an adult cannot become a child, just as a white cannot become black or, except through extreme and still relatively rare measures, a man cannot become a woman. Thus, another thing Hazard's view of childhood shares with certain forms of racism or sexism is praise of those qualities that mark the other and opposite to oneself as a stick with which to beat oneself and one's kind.

Always, in this kind of thinking, there is more than a hint that what is being celebrated is, exactly, inadequacy, inhumanity, incapacity—the state of being less than completely human. Women are wonderful because they aren't restricted by the narrow confines of truth or rational logic, blacks are full of the joy of life because they don't have the corruptly sophisticated white sense of how the world really works, children are blissfully innocent because they're just too dumb (or, in this logic, too smart) to know any better—lucky things. As James Kincaid says in his remarkable book *Child Loving: The Erotic Child and Victorian Culture*, we see being childlike as "a kind of purity, an absence and an incapacity, an inability to do.... Unencumbered by any necessary traits, the emptiness called a child can be constructed any way we like" (70-71).

And so Hazard, I see, constructed it to his taste—which was, mostly, to privilege and celebrate its emptiness. "It is sweet, sometimes," he says, "to see the world again with a child's eyes." He goes on to say, "It is true that they lure us away from the feast of ideas, taking no pleasure there themselves. They place small value on the abstractions that are so useful to our grown-up pastimes." But it's clear that what he presents here supposedly as a qualification is exactly the reason why he wants to think like a child: "Let us admit that they have no skill in handling ideas. What they have is enough for them" (166). It would be enough for him, too, it seems, if only he weren't cursed with his awful adult superiority—the terrible knowledge of how very bad knowledge is. Thus he has it both ways: he is superior, and he knows how bad it is to be superior enough to hate it—which presumably makes him even more superior than the rest of us adults. This kind of thinking is still surprisingly common in children's literature criticism, in which sophisticated adults often celebrate the wonderful innocence of childhood.

If I fear this sort of thinking, and I find it so blatantly present in Hazard, then what am I to make of the children's books he prefers—that the many adult experts who still share his basic principles prefer? They are ones that celebrate the childlike as something directly antithetical to what we might normally see as mature or thoughtful or responsible. Their wisdom is to deny that most of what we usually consider to be true is wise. If children did indeed learn what it means to be childlike from these books as Hazard understands them, they would be learning to be proud of their immaturity, thoughtlessness, and irresponsibility. They would learn that it is good to be self-indulgent and egocentric and careless of the feelings or needs of others. I find myself asking why this should be seen as a good thing.

Hazard's own answer to that question is a little strange, I think, and once more suggests a profound degree of self-hatred. He says he admires books that provide children "with pictures, the kind that they like.... enchanting pictures that bring release and joy, happiness gained before reality closes in upon them, insurance against the time, all too soon, when there will be nothing but realities" (42). Children must be childlike, unreal, or else there is nothing but the brute horror of the bare truth, despicable and unbearable reality itself. I can't imagine anything more pessimistic or more life-denying. Hazard's paean of praise for the jolly, happy childhood he has imagined and tries so desperately to impose on children disguises an exceedingly negative and very ugly view of the world he knows as an adult. In teaching me how to see this aspect of Hazard, theory has taught me to fear all forms of praise for the delights of childhood—and that means just about all children's literature.

At this point, I'm reminded again of theorists like James Kincaid and Jacqueline Rose, who talk about how and why we adults attempt to persuade children that our imaginary visions of childhood are true. Rose believes that the actual nature of childhood—she focuses particularly on children's confused experience of sexual desire—frightens adults. We protect ourselves from knowledge of the chaotic confusion children really experience by constructing images of childhood that eliminate everything threatening, leaving only what Kincaid described as "a kind of purity, an absence and an incapacity, an inability to do" (70). We then present the images we have constructed to children in their literature, in order to persuade them that their lives actually are as we imagine them to be. If children's fiction builds an image of the child inside the book," says Rose, "it does so in order to secure the child who is outside the book, the one who does not come so easily within its grasp" (2).

Children's literature, then, represents a massive effort by adults to make children believe that they ought to be the way adults would like them to be, and to make them feel guilty about or downplay the significance of all the aspects of their selves that inevitably don't fit the adult model.

It's all too frighteningly easy to read Hazard from this point of view. He insists both that children are inherently and always imaginative, and also that they need help from adults in being imaginative—need the right kinds of books to feed their imaginations and the right kind of adults, supposedly childlike ones, to write those books. So it is adults who must write children's books. But as we've already seen, all adults are afflicted by reality, and cannot see as children see. Only one conclusion is possible: adults no longer childlike must imagine—invent, contrive, create, make up—how children *should* see, and then impose what they imagine upon children, lest children see the actual ugly truth and therefore force adults to acknowledge that it is in fact the only truth. Let us create a lie of childhood and then force children to believe in it.

Hazard gets very angry at most writers for children: "Entirely pleased with themselves, they offered the child books that represented themselves, with all their attributes thrown in" (3). Yet the books that he himself recommends, he admires exactly because they represent himself and his ideas of wisdom. He is himself one of the people he attacks.

From this point of view, obviously, the books Hazard admires are exceedingly dangerous ones—greatly to be feared. And yet, of course, the danger is unavoidable. For there is one other thing theory has taught me: the aspects of children's books I've been describing—that Hazard takes for granted as good and true, and that I fear as bad and dangerous—are always and inevitably present. There would be no children's books if we didn't believe children were different enough from adults to need their own special kinds of books; and of course it is adults—the ones with the ideas about just how it is that children differ—who write those books. All children's books always represent adult ideas of childhood—and inevitably, therefore, work to impose adult ideas about childhood on children.

Furthermore, the process works. Children do become what we believe they are; assumptions about childhood, like those of Hazard, have the potential to become self-fulfilling prophecies. If we believe, as many adults do, that children are limited in various ways, then we deprive them of experiences that might make them less limited. If we believe that children have short attention spans, we won't expose them to long books. If we believe they cannot understand complicated language, we will give them only books with limited vocabularies. If we believe they are susceptible, we will keep them away from interesting books that may contain potentially dangerous ideas or attitudes. And if we believe they like only certain kinds of books, we won't give them access to other kinds. Deprived of the experience of anything more than the little we believe them capable of, children often learn to be inflexible, intolerant of the complex and the unconventional.

And clearly, children's literature plays an important part in this process. As a wide range of ideological theorists like Antonio Gramsci and Louis Althusser and Raymond Williams have suggested, and as John Stephens in particular has so persuasively pointed out in *Language and Ideology in Children's Fiction*, whatever else literary texts are, and whatever pleasure they may afford us, they are also expressions of the values and assumptions of a culture and a significant way of embedding readers in those values and assumptions—persuading them that they are in fact the readers that the texts imply.

The reader whom Hazard suggests good children's books imply is one who luxuriates in a supposedly childlike freedom. Paradoxically, therefore, he implies the unsettling truth that good children's literature is that which constrains and represses children in the process of pretending to liberate them. To believe oneself childlike in this supposedly freeing way is to accept limited and limiting adult ideas—to be childlike rather than mature, simple rather than sophisticated, intuitive rather than reasonable, empty rather than full.

Writing before theory, then, Hazard neatly reveals all the ways in which theory has taught us to be suspicious of our assumptions about children and children's literature—why we might fear them. Too neatly, perhaps—you might well wonder why I have spent so much time attacking such an obvious target. I have done it simply because so much of what I read in Hazard could still appear in adult discussion of children's literature today—still does appear, albeit, perhaps, in less poetic and more scientific language, influenced by brands of developmental psychology and pedagogical theory whose unspoken and uncontested myths of origin are very much like the ideas and assumptions that Hazard expresses so boldly.

And they appear for a good reason. I find it hard to imagine a third position in addition to the one Hazard presents and the one that shows me the dangers of the one Hazard presents. Theory tells me to fear Hazard; logic tells me that as long as children's literature exists as an endeavour of adults, it will always emerge from adult representations of childhood, and therefore, will always be in some way what Hazard describes it as being. To attack Hazard and to learn to fear him is, in some fundamental way, to learn to fear the entire project of children's literature, its very existence.

Is there then any third way possible? That's what I'd like to consider next.

My first step beyond fear comes, I realize, as I think about whom or what I fear for. If I talk about embedding children or constructing their subjectivity as misrepresentation or oppression or limitation of their full potential, I'm assuming the existence of a child larger than, outside of, and complete beyond the construction—a whole, unified, coherent being whose unity and completeness I am fearing for. To be repressed is to be forced to be less than this whole.

But another kind of theory has taught me that such a child could exist only outside of human consciousness—beyond human life as we know it and could ever possibly be aware of it.

Before what the psychoanalytical theorist Jacques Lacan calls the mirror stage, that moment in infancy in which a child identifies itself with its image in a mirror, Lacan imagines that the child lives in a posited but in actual fact unknowable and utterly seamless universe, and makes no distinction between itself and other things—it is whole, complete, unified in the most absolute of senses. This pre-oedipal stage sounds very much like Hazard's vision of childhood: a prelapsarian paradise before knowledge of distinctions and divisions intervenes. What's interesting is that for Lacan it occurs early in infancy, at the very moment when self-consciousness first develops; what Hazard views as characteristically childlike actually disappears for Lacan at the moment when a child becomes conscious of itself as a child—or, more exactly, as just a human being. What Hazard calls childlike, Lacan might well define as not yet quite human.

In the mirror stage, the child develops an ego, a sense of self, and does so by realizing that there are things outside it, such as the space around its image in the mirror. It perceives that it exists as a separate being only inside a context that is larger than itself, and that makes the child feel small in relation to it. Once we identify ourselves with the smaller versions of ourselves we see in the mirror, therefore, we are always conscious of ourselves as diminished, lacking a wholeness we once had, eternally striving for and never achieving it, as Hazard strives for but never achieves what he perceives as the blissful delights of childhood. The mirror image, then, constrains and constricts us—as I believe the images of children that appear in children's literature work to constrict the children they attempt to embed in their images of the suitably childlike—and as, perhaps paradoxically, Hazard's idea of child-hood as prelapsarian bliss constricts less blissful real children. For prelapsar-ian wholeness is hard to imagine as anything but empty—a state less confus-ing and less complex than maturity. And it isn't much of a leap to conclude that children who are successfully embedded in the limited or empty images of the childlike offered in so many children's books might well feel dimin-ished by them—defined as being *less*, as lacking.

Inevitably, furthermore, to be conscious of oneself in terms of the imagery of mirrors is to be divided. Lacan speaks of the "bipolar nature of all subjec-tivity" (10). A self is both that which thinks or views, the separate, detached consciousness, and that which is being viewed or thought about. I am *that* which *sees* myself as *this*: in demanding and therefore confirming this rela-tionship—a reader sees himself or herself as a character or an implied read-er—literary texts for children play their part in establishing what Lacan calls "an alienating identity" built on what is only an "illusion of autonomy" (4, 6). We are both what the books have encouraged us to believe we are *and* the reader thus encouraged, a separate being who thinks about and acknowl-edges the truth of that representation. To identify is to see oneself as some-thing else in two senses—as being the thing seen *and* as being the one who does the seeing.

If Lacan is at all right, then this divided subjectivity is inevitable—is in fact, and exactly, human consciousness as humans of any age past early infancy always know it. To rail against it, to fear the ways in which books help to cre-ate it, is to rail against life itself—to hate the human condition.

I can put that in another, and much simpler, way. To fear texts because they embed children in ideology is to fear all of the social and communal aspects of human existence—and all the pleasures they offer.

To be embedded is to learn to understand oneself as a social being—in terms of the obligations and responsibilities one has toward others, and also in terms of the kinds of behaviour acceptable to others that will allow indi-viduals to survive and prosper as members of groups. To embed children is to encourage them to think of themselves as the kinds of people who can live and interact with and take pleasure from other people in the human com-munity as currently constructed around them.

There can be no question about the fact that the demands of community can—indeed, inevitably do—repress individual freedoms and limit individual potential. But they are also and inevitably necessary as the medium of our mind-expanding and deeply pleasurable exchanges with each other. *All* soci-etal interactions occur in a language of gestures and behaviours that allow us to express our private selves in the very act of replacing, and therefore repressing, those private selves. These social conventions are like any other language, and as repressive of choice as any language. In order to communi-cate within them, we must agree to use the signs and structures shared by others. If we choose to invent our own signs and structures, we will be both total-ly free and totally unable to communicate with anybody else. I conclude, then, that children who did somehow manage to escape the apparently fear-ful process of being embedded in ideology might indeed retain their free-dom to be whole—but they would do so only at the cost of being involved in any way at all with other people. That's more fearful than losing a little free-dom. What seems like the fearful repressive tendency of children's literature from one point of view is, from another point of view, its rich ability to pro-vide children with a means of making enriching connections with other human beings.

There is still, of course, the danger of the mask becoming the face. It is pos-sible, as I suggested earlier, that children encouraged by an adult world to see themselves as being childlike in a particular way might well *become* childlike in exactly that way. Furthermore, it's unquestionably true that some of the most popular ways of being childlike, as conveyed by literature and the mass media, are decidedly repressive and exceedingly limiting. And it's also unquestionably true that powerful forces in mainstream culture work hard to impose these repressive and limiting ideas of themselves upon children. Wit-ness, as just one example, the ways in which Disney films continue to confirm decidedly dangerous ideas about what desirable girls' and women's bodies should look like. Girls who accept these images, most often unthinkingly, as the one and only way to be attractive and powerful work very hard to conform themselves to these supposed ideals, at great expense and often at great dan-ger to their health. In fact, then, the real danger is *not* that literature might work to fragment childhood sensibility and provide children with a divided and incoherent view of themselves. It's just the opposite of that. It might per-suade children that one particular and partial representation is the complete and only truth.

Theory, which has helped me to perceive and understand this problem, also suggests a possible solution to it: knowledge of theory.

Representations possess the fearful potential to repress and envelop us without our being aware of it only to the degree to which we are unconscious of the fact that they *are* representations—and therefore accept them as the way things naturally and obviously are. Althusser says:

> It is indeed a peculiarity of ideology that it imposes (without appearing to do so, since these are "obviousnesses") obviousnesses as obviousnesses, which we cannot *fail to recognize* and before which we have the inevitable and natural reaction of crying out (loud or in the "still small voice of con-science"): "That's obvious! That's right! That's true." (245)

The potential for freedom, then, comes in realizing that the obvious may *not* be true—may just be a representation, just one possible way of being out of a vast spectrum of other possible ways of being that one might consider, try on, adopt. In the matter of ways of being human, one has a choice only at the point at which one realizes one has a choice.

Theory taught me that. If it worked for me, then why can't it work for children?

I believe that it can. I believe, indeed, that we adults must do everything we possibly can to make children aware of the "obviousnesses" that texts work to impose on them and to give them the means to weigh and consider the implications of the subject positions that texts offer. If we are not to fear for what texts might do to them, in other words, we must teach them to be divided subjects in their reading and in their lives—to be involved as both implied readers of texts and critical observers of what texts demand of them in that process. The texts I refer to here include literature—and also all the physical and social representations and gestures and conventions that make up our life in society.

To read the world in this way is to *be* this way—divided, fragmented, always aware of how the faces one puts on are merely masks, how there is always more to us than whatever particular way we've decided to represent our selves to others (and therefore, presumably, to ourselves) at any particular moment. This is not I that you see standing here talking to you—it is the I that I have chosen to represent myself as today.

In discussing how we perceive ourselves in terms of gender, Judith Butler argues that it is always a question of performance—that we become male or female by enacting in our minds and bodies our culture's ideas about maleness or femaleness. What's true of gender, an aspect of our self-perception, seems to me to be generally true of all aspects of our self-understanding. As representations, personalities are roles we put on and perform—and, perhaps, nothing more. We are, in fact, fragmentary, collections of roles or representations, each of which is merely partial, not unified at all. Rather than fear that fact and work toward some illusory utopia of unity and wholeness, we might instead celebrate the fragmentary. We might simply revel in and rejoice in the playful possibilities of the various masks and roles we can choose to put on, and the various beings we can inconsistently, at various points, choose to become.

In the end, then, theory teaches me that a foolish consistency is indeed the hobgoblin of little minds—minds that foolishly choose to perceive themselves as littler than they actually are. There is really no such thing as a complete or whole or coherent individual—and that's something to celebrate, not something to fear.

If we can learn to celebrate it, and teach children to celebrate it, then children's literature can be a source of much more than fear. It can, in its various manifestations, offer children a vast repertoire of ways of being human to choose from, to play with, to celebrate.

All we adults have to do, then, is not to fear—to fear neither children nor books. Not to fear children means to trust their ability to make wise decisions and enjoy playful possibilities once equipped with the strategies for doing so—the knowledge of theory I've just talked about. Not to fear literature is to not eliminate from children's experience books whose representations personally distress us, but instead to allow children access to as wide a range of representations as possible, in books of all sorts from places of all sorts by people of all sorts.

If we can be that fearless, then children will indeed learn to belong to a different world than our current repressed and limiting world of grown-ups. But then we grown-ups will belong to that different world, too.

Works Cited

Althusser, Louis. "Ideology and Ideological State Apparatuses." Trans. Ben Brewster. *Critical Theory Since 1965*. Ed. Hazard Adams and Leroy Searle. Tallahassee: UP of Florida and Florida State UP, 1986.

Butler, Judith. *Gender Trouble: Feminism and the Subversion of Identity*. New York and London: Routledge, 1990.

Hazard, Paul. *Books, Children, and Men*. Trans. Marguerite Mitchell. Boston: Horn Book, 1944.

Kincaid, James. *Child-Loving: The Erotic Child and Victorian Culture*. New York and London: Routledge, 1992.

Lacan, Jacques. *Écrits: A Selection*. Trans. Alan Sheridan. New York and London: Norton, 1977.

Nodelman, Perry. "The Other: Orientalism, Colonialism, and Children's Literature." *Children's Literature Association Quarterly* 17.1 (Spring 1992): 29-35.

Rose, Jacqueline. *The Case of Peter Pan; or, The Impossibility of Children's Fiction*. London: Macmillan, 1984.

Stephens, John. *Language and Ideology in Children's Fiction*. London and New York: Longman, 1992.

Playing in the Phase Space:
Contemporary Forms of Fictional Pleasure (1999)
Margaret Mackey

Storytelling has always been an important part of any society, and the forms and techniques of story adapt to the possibilities and pressures of different social arrangements. In our contemporary era of major technological change, we can see stories shifting and altering their borders even as the world of make-believe expands beyond anything our ancestors might have imagined. Television provides instant access to fiction day and night in an unceasing flow; video games offer extended hours of highly concentrated immersion; collaborative online fictional sites open the doors to co-operatively mandated and organized forms of storytelling where no one narrator is completely in charge. The commercial world supplies numerous prosthetics to fictional engagement in the form of toys and games and various "lifestyle" accoutrements. An entire magazine industry feeds on back-up information about television and film stars, special effects and computer graphics, and the whole elaborate decision-making process involved in the creation of screened fiction.

Contemporary citizens of most societies, not just the Western or most prosperous ones, will recognize all or part of this picture, yet the vocabulary for describing new hybrid forms of story that cross media boundaries and variously impinge on our daily lives is surprisingly limited. A fiction describes a possible world, but the boundaries of that world may seem nebulous when it can exist, more or less recognizably, in print, film, CD-ROM, audio, and website form, to name just the most obvious. The death of the author may or may not be finally established, but the issue of what is "authorized" is one that affects stories in many ways, commercial as well as intellectual. How far can a story be attenuated through sequels and spin-offs before its original power is diffused through dilution and/or over-exposure? It is commonplace to see many transmutations of a single story: a picture book is made into an animation and turned back into a newly reworked picture book that then becomes a board book, to take a single and highly representative example. How many generations does it take before the sense of what made the story matter in the first place is rendered indecipherable, replaced by a generic impression that plurality and reproduction are the key elements of storytelling?

The Limits of a Fictional Universe

It is relatively easy for those invested in the culture of literariness to ignore such manifestations, to dismiss them as the epiphenomena of a corrupt commercial enterprise that ensnares too many of our children but need not affect those in the elite who still care for and look after the interests of print literature. Yet the impact of technology is not confined to the slick and heavily funded world of popular culture, although some of its most radical effects may be felt there. Questions about the powers and limits of a fictional universe arise in more strictly literary worlds as well.

One great storyteller of the 1980s and 1990s is Philip Pullman. He is the author of the *Dark Materials* fantasy trilogy that is captivating already avid readers and creating many new ones; he is also the creator of a number of other stories including a handful of graphic novels. Pullman both gives us an example of textual play that challenges our thinking about literary practice at the end of the twentieth century and offers useful critical vocabulary for discussing these matters.

The first novel of *His Dark Materials* is published in North America as *The Golden Compass*, although its original British title is *Northern Lights*. The second novel appears as *The Subtle Knife* in both jurisdictions, and the third is still being written.[1] The underlying themes of the trilogy arise from Milton's *Paradise Lost*, which is the source of the titles and which informs many of the major structures of the story. There is no doubt that these books represent a serious literary enterprise in the best sense of the words.

At present, both books are available in hardback and paperback, and there is an abridged audio version of *The Golden Compass*. There is some talk of a film contract, but so far the world of *His Dark Materials* exists verbally, apart from some appealing cover art.[2] Both books have garnered rave reviews and *Northern Lights* won most of the awards going in 1995; sales figures to both children and adults are astonishing, and the impatience with which the third volume is awaited is a minor literary phenomenon in itself.

So far this description might just represent a consoling indication that the world of print fiction is still alive and well. The phenomenon of *His Dark Materials* is not floated on the back of tie-ins and commodities and television animations and advertisements. It represents the triumph of an intriguing and important words-only story, well told and compelling.

Yet even in this entirely verbal fictional world, there are some words that both do and do not belong to the published book. They appear on the lavish and fascinating website sponsored by Random House, the American publishers of the trilogy (*His Dark Materials*). Each book has its own site, and each site offers background information about the story world that does not appear in the novels but manifestly applies to them. *The Golden Compass* site offers a detailed history and symbol glossary of the alethiometer, the truth-telling compass of the American title. On *The Subtle Knife* site, there is information about the *Liber Angelorum*, the book of the angels, which now, we are told, survives only in the form of evocative "scraps" saved after a fire in the Torre degli Angeli.

Here is an example of the kind of information offered from the *Liber Angelorum*:

Envy   The angels envy us our solidity. Death, they think, would be a price worth paying for the power and brilliance of our senses. If an angel were to see with our eyes, or hear with our ears, he would be dazzled and stunned by the force with which we perceive the physical world. With gifts like this, he would think, why do these creatures not spend their lives in exploration of the physical universe that they are so well equipped to understand? Why are they not consumed with intellectual bliss? This is a mystery to angels. ("The Liber Angelorum")

This passage recognizably comes from the narrative voice of *The Subtle Knife*, dealing with substantive issues in a vigorous and lively manner. Yet it does not appear in the novel and the information does not really affect the story in any immediate way. What it does affect is the thematic underpinning that links *His Dark Materials* to its Miltonian predecessor; both poets and scholars can appreciate the extra layering and complexity such material adds to the story—and so, without a doubt, can many less credentialed readers who happen to find the website.

So we have an example of a kind of fictional add-on, an appendage that does and does not belong to the world of the novel. In the advertising world the name for this kind of material would be the back-story, the infilling fictional detail that sets up the parameters of play with advertised toys. For example, Stephen Kline describes a back-story (in this case, Barbie's) as "a narrative that established her personality profile within an imaginary but familiar universe" (170).

The "scraps" from the *Liber Angelorum* manifestly belong to the "imaginary but familiar universe" of *His Dark Materials*, but it is inappropriate and unsatisfactory to think of this vivid and poetic fragment as akin to the manipulative world of what Kline calls the "passive dictation" of the advertising back-story that is designed to place narrative constraints on children's imaginative engagement with toys like Barbie. Fortunately Pullman himself has supplied a more generous critical terminology that offers an opportunity to clarify some elements of contemporary story-making.

The Phase Space

In November 1997 Pullman delivered the Patrick Hardy Lecture to the Children's Book Circle in London. In this talk, he discussed some "rules" of storytelling, and introduced the concept of phase space, a scientific term that he explored as a metaphor for discussing the artistic potential of story-making. With a certain generosity of interpretive licence, it also serves as a useful metaphor for exploring many different aspects of contemporary culture.

As I understand it, phase space is a term from dynamics, and it refers to the untrackable complexity of changing systems. It's the notional space which contains not just the actual consequences of the present moment, but all the possible consequences. The phase space of a game of noughts and crosses, for instance, would contain every possible outcome of every possible initial move, and the actual course of a game could be represented by a path starting from the one move that was actually made first—a path winding past numbers of choices not made. Robert Frost:

> Two roads diverged in a wood, and I—
> I took the one less travelled by,
> And that has made all the difference.

Of course, it does make all the difference. And we do have to choose: we can't go both ways. I am surely not the only writer who has the distinct sense that every sentence I write is surrounded by the ghosts of the sentences I could have written at that point, but didn't.... So the opening of your story brings with it a phase space. (1998, 47)

Pullman goes on to make a number of interesting points about this phase space, but perhaps the most pertinent at this point is the metaphor of the path through the phase space:

> It has to do with phase space again, with the path through the wood. And a path is a path *to*: it has a destination.
>   For every story has to have an ending. Sometimes you know what the ending is before you begin. Well and good. Sometimes you don't, and then you have to wander about through the events until you manage to see the natural destination. But once you know where it is, you must make for it, and then go back and clear the path and make sure that every twist and turn is there because you want it to be: because this one shows a better view of the landscape to come, or that one illustrates the fate of someone analogous to our protagonist, or another because it reveals a deep romantic chasm just at the moment when you need to introduce a note of sublimity ... And all of them because they lead to the end. In other words you must design the path so that it leads to the destination most surely, and with the maximum effect. (50-51; ellipsis in original)

Pullman here is undoubtedly describing the steady hand of the confident storyteller, working a crafted line through all the potential elements that might be realized in a particular story world. And yet in that background territory of the phase space, it seems to me we see something that is also relevant to many forms of contemporary storytelling. What is the information on *The Subtle Knife* website but data from the phase space—information that might have been in the book but is not because it does not lead to the end of the story? Pullman is very definite that the direction of a story must always be towards its ending: "If a scene does not advance the story, it will get in the way," he says on one occasion ("About Philip Pullman") and on another, "Whatever doesn't add, subtracts" (1998, 50).

This clear-cut and even ruthless approach to storytelling has its own substantial satisfactions, but it seems evident that there is much productive potential left in the phase space of a story: things that might have happened in the plot but did not, aspects of characters or incidents that are known to the author or that can be imagined by readers but that are not laid down in the novel itself. The website of *The Golden Compass* and *The Subtle Knife* seem to have offered Pullman one venue for a different kind of play in the phase space he created for the world of the trilogy—imaginative, engaged, but not strictly narrative in the sense of driving to the ending. The author is a privileged player in this specialized game, of course, but in fact many school assignments invite students to explore the phase space. They are exhorted to write a "missing" chapter including a scene that occurs offstage from the main action of the novel, or to supply school report cards or news bulletins relating to characters or incidents of a book. The imaginative and imaginary hinterland of a story, it would seem, is often perceived as fair game to its readers as well as to its original creator.

One important point to remember about a phase space is how necessarily it relates to its originating story. A set of all possible noughts-and-crosses moves might be very large but each member of the set would recognizably be a playable nought or cross. Some news bulletins or report cards are simply not admissible to the phase space of a particular story. The phase space may be large and bristling with possibilities but it is also consistent and identifiable, coherent as part of the world of a particular story.

A second point to keep in mind is how many contemporary texts for both children and adults make specific and often parodic use of the phase space. Pullman, with his one crafted path through the phase space towards the ending of the story, is describing a particular kind of storytelling technique. Many stories play with that very decision-making process he describes, along the lines of, "Yes, but what if a different choice were made at this point?" Hence we have books like *The Three Little Wolves and the Big Bad Pig* by Eugene Trivizas and Helen Oxenbury and many different titles by the Ahlbergs. We have books like *The Stinky Cheese Man and other Fairly Stupid Tales* where the play in the phase space becomes part of the story. This example of "Cinderella," or "Cinderumpelstiltskin" as it is called in the version by Scieska and Smith, is a recognizable phase-space game:

> One day the local prince announced that he was holding a fabulous ball at his castle. Everyone was invited.
>
> The stepmother and stepsisters got all dressed up to go. But, as usual, they made Cinderella clean the house, so she didn't have time to get ready. After the stepmother and stepsisters left for the ball, Cinderella sat down and began to cry.
>
> Just then a little man appeared.
>
> "Please don't cry," he said. "I can help you spin straw into gold."

"I don't think that will do me much good," said Cinderella. "I need a fancy dress, glass slippers, and a coach."

"Would you like to try to guess my name?" said the clever little man. Cinderella looked at him. "No. Not really."

"Come on. Do you think it's 'Chester'?"

"If you don't have a dress, it doesn't really matter."

Clearly, in this as in many other such stories, part of the joke is knowing that the story is switching phase spaces as different characters speak. Very young children are expected to get the joke, and all the evidence suggests that they have little problem with what might seem a sophisticated task.

Meanwhile in another part of the culture, we have comic books re-working some of the basic decisions affecting Superman's career, killing him off and bringing him back to life. When Sherlock Holmes went through such a process at the turn of the century, the fans went wild; the nonchalance with which such a trick is greeted today may well reflect the degree to which contemporary readers are at home with the whole idea of fictional life in the phase space. Some of this familiarity is a feature of constant, even relentless, exposure to "quick and dirty" storytelling on television soaps and sitcoms (American television is particularly specialized in this regard): the evil twin has amnesia; no, she was just pretending in order to get the handsome and stupid hero to the altar; no, really it was all a plot by the mother-in-law who was hoping to find a route to make contact with her third-last ex-husband. Some of the contemporary nonchalance about living with alternative possibilities is an effect of living with multiple personalities attached to single proper nouns: Winnie-the-Pooh is the saccharine-with-an-edge creation of A.A. Milne as well as being the saccharine-with-extra-sugar creation of Walt Disney.

The enormous success of *The Dark Materials* trilogy testifies to our pleasure in the kind of storytelling Pullman describes, but there are many other kinds of fiction in contemporary culture that substitute a meander round the world of potentials for a decisive path-clearing operation that strikes out for the ending. And even in many stories where plot more or less drives the engine of the story, there is often back-up material that returns us to the phase space; the handbooks and maps and websites that accompany the elaborate fantasy of Terry Pratchett's *Discworld* books provide one good example of this phenomenon.

Adaptations and Misreadings

To a degree, any adaptation or retelling makes use of the world created by a story, not just the actual elements laid out in order on the page. Phyllis Bixler, discussing a musical made from *The Secret Garden* suggests that "narratives contain many secrets for a reader to discover—or buried seeds of many other stories which a reader's imagination can coax into bloom" (114). Bixler talks about the creative forces of "misreading" an original text to produce an adaptation that has "an energy of its own" (102). To some extent, what we judge when we view a movie developed from a familiar book is the degree to which we find the adaptation drawing successfully on the same phase space. We may not know what all the options in that phase space might be, but we certainly know what does not belong, and it makes us uncomfortable or angry when the film plays false. On the other hand, one of the true pleasures of a successful adaptation—and after all these years the television example of *The Jewel in the Crown* is still one of the best—is that it sheds light on the whole phase space of the original story, rendering it deeper and fuller and more intriguing. No matter how simplistic aspects of this particular story may appear to post-colonial eyes, the fictional phase space of both book and television series is undoubtedly rich and coherent in its own terms and the two different versions of the story are mutually illuminating. (Whether a story and its adaptation always share a common or identical phase space is an intriguing point. One image could be of overlapping phase spaces, another of separate spotlights into a single phase space. Whatever the image, there must be a sense that both versions are drawing on the same set of contingencies.)

What makes a fictional universe recognizable has implications for many forms of contemporary culture. In a survey of texts revolving around a single narrative starting point, the movie *Men in Black*, I turned up well over sixty examples in print alone, not counting television programmes and Internet sites that deal with various aspects of the phase space of that story. Some of these texts played with the boundaries of the phase space, another familiar contemporary game. At what point does actor Will Smith step out of his persona as Jay, the rookie alien hunter of *Men in Black*, and become his own self? Can he ever be completely dissociated from his specific embodiment of this fictional character? Such questions take on additional force when re-makes of films substitute new actors in the roles of familiar characters. It may even be that certain actors bring their own phase space to a part: the background shadings of Will Smith's persona probably affect his reception as Jay. Viewers of the film *Titanic* may well go one step further and associate the character of Jack with the Valentino-esque potential of Leonardo di Caprio rather than the other way around.

The various forms of retelling that are associated with most commercial productions of films these days also play in the phase space. Some, such as the printed screenplay of the movie, stick strictly to reproducing the original path, though it is remarkable how often such a reproductive text also includes an essay about the making of the movie, unpicking all the decisions that were eventually made to show how they might have been made otherwise.[3] Other approaches take the world of the movie and play around with it—literally in the cases of the many action movies that are turned into computer games, or in the case of children's films that act as source material for the production of toys. In a culture that values many forms of postmodern play with options and alternatives it might be argued that it is Pullman's steadfast pursuit of the single (though complex) path to the ending that is distinctive. Yet many (though not all) stories in contemporary popular culture feature a similar narrative drive, and it is often the surrounding galaxy of spin-off texts and toys that opens up the phase space.

Online Narrative

The concept of phase space makes room for a productive consideration of hypertext narrative and the kinds of "stories" developed in MUDs and MOOs, fictional online sites where each participant creates part of the scenario, typing in settings and characters that affect the larger picture.

Hypertext involves a computer text where readers follow different links from one paragraph, or lexia, to another. Sometimes it is possible for them to establish their own links but in most forms of hypertext fiction the links are developed by the author, and the reader simply makes choices between a varying number of pre-established options. At one level, readers read from the same text but in tracing different paths through the story their reading experiences are exceedingly diverse. In a very literal fashion, hypertext makes it possible for the writer to include all those sentences Pullman describes as ghosts, "the sentences I could have written at that point but didn't." This may not be the best or most constructive way to create a hypertext narrative either, but it now becomes possible to contemplate such an option in a realistic and material manner; indeed, it may well be that the format inveigles writers who would be terse and direct in standard print to opt for the recursive and meandering route when composing in this medium.

Jorge Luis Borges' story "The Garden of Forking Paths" describes the fabulous Chinese novel of the same title as "a shapeless mass of contradictory rough drafts" (96). Stuart Moulthrop, who converted the story into a hypertext version, quotes this line and comments, "As it happens, this is precisely what a hypertext fiction looks like when reduced to the printed page" (274). Moulthrop describes the universe created by Borges in print and himself in hypertext as "a cosmology of multiple universes containing all the plenary possibilities of selection," a phrase that could stand as an alternative definition of a phase space.

It is certainly clear that readers of hypertext narrative must assume they are taking only one of many possible paths through the phase space; pleasure in the phase space itself must form a major part of their engagement with the story. As Jane Yellowlees Douglas succinctly expresses it, hypertext "propels us from the straitened 'either/or' world that print has come to represent and into a universe where the 'and/and/and' is always possible" (155).

Janet H. Murray describes some of the appeal of nonlinear stories in congruent terms:

> In discussing labyrinths we distinguish between those that are coherent and those that are purposely more tangled. The coherent labyrinths are like the one Theseus discovered or the ones in English gardens: they have a single solution, a path in and a path out. They can be solved ... Other labyrinths, like the ones created by users of the Storyspace authoring system like Michael Joyce and Stuart Moulthrop are weblike in structure, multi-threaded, and have no single path. The pleasure here is not in solving but in dwelling in a seemingly inexhaustible resonant environment, luxuriating in a prolonged state of enticement and disorientation. (137)

Pleasure in the indwelling, in the phase space itself, is part of the appeal for participants in stories created online by groups of anonymous contributors to MUDs and MOOs (the rather obscure acronyms stand for Multi-User Domain and for Multi-User Domain, Object-Oriented). Sherry Turkle explains these complex fictions as follows:

> MUDs put you in virtual spaces in which you are able to navigate, converse, and build. You join a MUD through a command that links your computer to the computer on which the MUD program resides. Making the connection is not difficult; it requires no particular technical sophistication. The basic commands may seem awkward at first but soon become familiar. For example, if I am playing a character named ST on Lambda MOO, any words I type after the command "say" will appear on all players' screens as "ST says." Any actions I type after the command "emote" will appear after my name just as I type them, as in "ST waves hi" or "ST laughs uncontrollably." I can "whisper" to a designated character and only that character will be able to see my words.
>
>   MUDs are a new kind of virtual parlour game and a new form of community. In addition, text-based MUDs are a new form of collaboratively written literature. MUD players are MUD authors, the creators as well as consumers of media content. In this, participating in a MUD has much in common with script writing, performance art, street theatre, improvisational theatre—or even commedia dell'arte. (11-12)

MUD makers often create elaborate settings, describing their virtual worlds with detailed enthusiasm. The very act of creating this alternative universe constitutes much of the appeal of the process.

Like Murray talking about hypertext fiction, Turkle describes two kinds of storytelling in the online communal narrative domains of MUDs and MOOs.

> Two basic types of MUDs can now be accessed on the Internet. The adventure type, most reminiscent of the games' Dungeons and Dragons heritage, is built around a medieval fantasy landscape. In these, affectionately known by their participants as "hack and slay," the object of the game is to gain experience points by killing monsters and dragons and finding gold coins, amulets, and other treasure. Experience points translate into increased power. A second type consists of relatively open spaces in which you can play at whatever captures your imagination. In these MUDs, usually called social MUDs, the point is to interact with other players and, on some MUDs, to help build the virtual world by creating one's own objects and architecture. "Building" on MUDs is something of a hybrid between computer programming and writing fiction. One describes a hot tub and deck in a MUD with words, but some formal coded description is required for the deck to exist in the MUD as an extension of the adjacent living room and for characters to be able to "turn the hot tub on" by pushing a specially marked button. In some MUDs, all players are allowed to build; sometimes the privilege is reserved to master players, or wizards. Building is made particularly easy on a class of MUDs known as "MOOs" (MUDs of the Object Oriented variety). (182)

The phase space *is* the pleasure for many of the players in these fictional universes. In the social MUDs, the option of finding the single best path to the end is simply not available and indeed might be seen as arbitrarily short-circuiting the appeal of the whole process. We are in territory where very different rules of story-making apply.

Many commercially marketed computer games operate in a similar kind of fictional zone. The setting, the world of various options and alternatives, is the chief character in such games. Some, such as *Myst* and its sequel *Riven,* emphasize the lavish visual world on the screen but still offer a challenge to find the "right" path through the story. Others, along the lines of *SimCity* and its successors, civic simulation games, appeal to their many players by virtue of the world-building powers they offer; what actually occurs in these worlds is open-ended, and in many ways unimportant. Still others, such as *Virtual Springfield,* a CD-ROM tour of the home town of television's Simpson family, offer what might be described as one version of the phase space of the more narratively organized animated stories. Playing the game amounts to little more than moving in and out of different Springfield buildings, opening cupboards and drawers, and developing an intimacy (carefully fabricated) with all the hidden corners of the town.

In a slightly different form, Mindscape's computer game *Creatures* sets up a phase space in which the human player hatches and then rears digital babies

("Warning: Digital DNA enclosed," says the box).The renowned evolutionary biologist Richard Dawkins is quoted on the box as saying, "This is the most impressive example of artificial life I have seen." What is also impressive is the elaborate, even baroque play-space set up for the relatively uncomplicated "plot" developments in which the little creatures grow, succeed or fail in learning to talk, mate, reproduce, age, and die, with their actions developed through their digital make-up and also through the care and education offered to them by the game's players. The sense that much of what happens is utterly arbitrary, that it could at any given stage happen otherwise if the digits lined up in a slightly different formation, is part of the appeal of this eerie game. That this primal (though digital) crap-shoot occurs in the kind of cute kitschy environment so familiar to young people from numerous cartoons and plastic toy universes may help to make this particular phase space recognizable and even cosy to young people reared with television. That children seem rather less uneasy about the "life" created for and by these creatures than the adults watching over their shoulders may also partly reflect their life-long exposure to a culture full of many different kinds of phase space. A comparison of this game with more stilted adaptations of print stories in CD-ROM format[4] demonstrates that *Creatures* is predicated on a new kind of narrative development that can only be described as digitally organic. The strength of its long-term appeal is yet to be established but the sense of new fictional territory opening up is very powerful.

There are many ways in which our culture encourages engagement in the world of the story rather than the story itself. A few examples may give some idea of the range: a lavish book of *Little Women* offers many background pictures and notes supplying information about the social, cultural and historical matrix from which the book was developed (Alcott; Mackey); a CD-ROM of the Pulitzer-Prize-winning comic novel *Maus: A Survivor's Story* offers access to the background tapes that were used to develop the story and provides clips of the book's creator discussing why he made one decision rather than another (Spiegelman); the composite artform of the pop-up music video provides commentary in boxes on the screen describing scenes that were originally meant for the video but ultimately dropped.[5]

Many forms of literary tourism explicitly welcome you to the universe in which a story was set. The Prince Edward Island home of L.M. Montgomery, now turned into a living museum celebrating *Anne of Green Gables*, is highly seductive, for example. As a teenager I found myself straining to look through "Anne's" window to see if I could spot her friend Diana's bedroom light. I felt remarkably foolish when I realized what I had done, yet of course I was merely answering the invitation of the setting. Theme parks celebrating, for example, the doings of Asterix provide another similar invitation: step into the phase space; participate in the matrix from which aesthetic decisions arise. The symbiosis between Beatrix Potter and the National Trust encourages a temptation to look on all the Lake District as a Potter park, full of living incarnations of the tiny stories she chose to tell.

Why Does It Matter?

In many ways, what I am describing here is familiar stuff. Children have probably always known about the phase space in its loosest definition, playing numerous pretend games in the virtual hinterland of their favourite stories. As a child of the 1950s I took many of my games from television and books, playing cowboys with my brothers on some occasions, and on others marking out territory in the field behind my house to be my own stately home and ruined abbey, in an imagined recreation of the desirable universe of the Abbey Girls books by Elsie Oxenham. In each case, the domain of the story was far more important to me than particular details of the plot.

The concept may not be entirely new but there has been a vast increase in the quantity and variety of contemporary texts that are undeniably fiction but not quite narrative, at least not in the straightforward sense we have understood it in the past and that Pullman's description still enticingly represents in the present. It seems fairly clear that the idea of following the narrative thread from beginning to end of the story is now perceived very broadly as just one option for engaging with a fiction. Young people will sit through a film in the decreed linear fashion but once that movie is out on video their viewing becomes far more recursive, dwelling longer in the good bits, skipping other parts, circling and repeating, adding information about story, actors, and special effects from other sources (for example, Wood, 189-91). Much of their leisure-time engagement with texts in one medium or another is spent in fictional settings where a leisurely exploration of the details of the what-if is the most important part of the encounter.

If such experience is an important part of young people's out-of-school encounters with fiction, it is very likely to show up in their own writing, and may also affect how they respond to the writing of other people. The impact of nonlinear story world-building may be even more striking when they are given the opportunity to work in multimedia. Geri Gay explored the responses of young people to an interactive second-language program that allows students of Spanish to create stories about travellers on an aeroplane. Her account of their creations has a familiar ring, in the light of some of the ideas discussed above; the connections are not conclusive but they seem suggestive:

> The analysis of the records revealed qualitative differences in the way students explored the program's content. Some students seemed to move from one segment to another in one direction only. Employing a weaving metaphor, Mazur ... called this group Spinners, because although they were

constructing meaning, the result was but a literal interpretation or description of events in the order in which they were viewed. Others' use was characterized by a back and forth movement among scenes accomplished by use of the video controllers and the program's navigation features. This group was labelled the Weavers.

The "weaving" style of use also correlated to the kind of final stories the students wrote. The students who moved through the program in a linear way wrote stories primarily conveying actions, while students who displayed the nonlinear weaving pattern of program use wrote final stories which focused on the motivations or psychology of the characters. The Weavers' stories were more inventive, embellishing content by drawing connections between visual content viewed in particular scenes. (181)

There is not enough information about what really happens in English classes to develop any true sense of the degree to which the teachers of today's young people acknowledge and make room for the possible impact of new kinds of fictional experience and grounding. It seems likely that many, possibly still most of the texts used in English classrooms continue to represent the linear narrative drive. A survey of texts used in Grade 10 classes in Edmonton, in western Canada, established that the vast majority of authors being taught to fifteen-year-olds were born between 1900 and 1940, well before the advent of the new kinds of story-making I have been describing (Altmann et al. 214-15). It would be reckless to suggest that this survey speaks for a wider world, but it would also be foolish to ignore the fact that English syllabuses around the English-speaking world tend to reproduce the same favourite titles and authors. (In Edmonton, for example, the most taught novel in Grade 10 is *To Kill a Mockingbird*; the most popular play is *Romeo and Juliet*. Both titles will obviously resonate with teachers of fifteen-year-olds elsewhere.)

Students who enter their secondary classrooms knowledgeable about the back-stories of many movies, familiar with the leisurely, nonlinear appeal of *The Simpsons'* universe courtesy of handbooks and CD-ROMs, at ease with the circular and repetitive attraction of many different online forms of fiction, will often find that their expertise is little valued in the academic forum. If they are truly unlucky, they will be taught about "the" plot diagram and trained to think that there is only one way to write a valid story. Even in more enlightened classrooms, they may regularly wonder why their "fit" with linear school stories is often so uneasy.

Similarly, teachers, reading the writing of students who operate from many experiences of what we might loosely describe as the phase-set school of story construction, may well perceive the kinds of works submitted to them as undisciplined and prolix, rather than recognizing amateur representatives of a different kind of discipline. Pullman himself, in a fascinating article written for *Signal* a decade ago, highlighted the kinds of writing done by young people who grew up in a world where the picture was an important part of the storytelling process, and provided a useful new lens through which teachers could look at their students' written productions (1989, 181-86). Ten years of technological change have broadened the potential for divergent storytelling repertoires, and contemporary students writing out of a background of extensive experience with different forms of popular culture may well be more sophisticated than their teachers recognize.

There are some signs of a new pedagogy being developed to address new kinds of narrative challenge. Nancy Welch, writing recently in *College English*, contrasts the linear implications of foreshadowing with a more open and plural approach to texts that she calls "sideshadowing." Her description of the contrast between the two seems to describe a form of phase space:

> Thus while foreshadowing doubles our sense of time—what is, what will be—sideshadowing works to triple, to quadruple. What is and what will be are joined by what else this present moment may suggest, what else the future could hold. Events no longer exist as points on a straight timeline but instead within fields of other potential actions that vie for our attention too.
>
> By shifting our attention back to the present moment and the field of potential actions that moment exists within, sideshadowing doesn't supplant the practice of foreshadowing. Instead it opens up that view to other realities, along with a glimpse of the consequences for each. Too often ... we commit ourselves to a particular course of action without realizing that in the present moment there are other courses to be taken. Sideshadowing seeks out those might-have-beens and still-might-bes—other actions and outcomes, other interpretations and their implications ... [I]t can teach us that understanding any given moment—including any moment in a student's draft—means understanding the field of possibility that moment exists within. (383)

As Welch describes the process of sideshadowing, drawing substantially on the insights of Bakhtin and his intellectual descendants, the concept seems almost to offer the relevant verb to accompany the noun "phase space." Her article suggests fruitful avenues for exploring of the issue for teaching both writing and reading in different media.

Conclusions

Philip Pullman may well not recognize the free-and-easy use I have of his concept of the phase space (never mind what a mathematician would make of such a cavalier takeover!). Obviously not one of my examples deals with a complete phase space for any given fiction; there is still no way to create or describe the complete world of *all* fictional possibilities relating to a single story, even a simple one. The texts I have described, the CD-ROM cities and islands, the online MUDs and MOOs, the reworkings and adaptations of given stories—all these complex representations still provide only samplings from any given phase space. My point is that contemporary culture leads us to be at home with plural possibilities. The old question, "How many children had Lady Macbeth?" is askable again because our culture is now much happier to settle for an answer of *x*; Lady Macbeth might have had one child, or two children, or many, and all of these potential answers co-exist in the phase space of *Macbeth.* The fact that no one single answer is possible does not mean that the question should not be asked nor that the answer is somehow outside of any kind of literary purview. Plural and speculative answers are now part of the imaginative landscape.

Today, even very young children manifest a new ease with *not knowing,* a comfort with juxtaposed alternatives all of which are equally plausible. Such a response is part of the culture that nurtures them. Adults, particularly those who engage with young people's reading and writing, can also benefit from exploring, extending, sometimes resisting and sometimes celebrating the enticements of the phase space. New forms of fiction resonate within the recreational lives of many young people today; the adults in their lives also need to start paying attention to these new narrative playgrounds.

Notes

1 Editors' note: *The Amber Spyglass* (UK/USA) was published in 2000. See *His Dark Materials* <http://www.randomhouse.com/features/pullman>.
2 Editors' note: The trilogy has been adapted for stage and performed by the National Theatre, London, in December 2003 and November 2004. For more information, see *His Dark Materials: BridgetotheStars* <http://www.bridgetothestars.net>.
3 The screenplay of *Men in Black* follows this format, and so does Kenneth Branagh's book about the making of the movie of *Hamlet.* Numerous other examples demonstrate that this approach is not confined to high or popular culture exclusively.
4 See, for example, the CD-ROM game of *My Teacher is an Alien* where plot developments are relatively laborious involving much trial and error.
5 The pop-up video format involves the insertion of printed captions over the top of previously made music videos; these captions offer all kinds of relevant and irrelevant information, often including references to decisions made, alternative scenes dropped, and other background insights into the original creation of the video.

Works Cited

"About Philip Pullman." *Author Spotlight.* 29 Jan. 2006.
<http://www.randomhouse.com/author/results.pperl?authorid=24658&view=sml_
sptlght >.
Ahlberg, Allan. *Ten in a Bed.* Illus. André Amstutz. London: Granada, 1983.
Ahlberg, Janet and Allan Ahlberg. *It Was a Dark and Stormy Night.* London: Viking,
1993.
——. *The Jolly Postman or Other People's Letters.* Oxford: Heinemann, 1986.
Alcott, Louisa May. *Little Women.* Illus. James Prunier. London: Viking, 1997.
Altmann, Anna, Ingrid Johnston, and Margaret Mackey. "Curriculum Decisions
About Literature in Contemporary Classrooms: A Preliminary Analysis of a Survey
of Materials Used in Edmonton Grade 10 English Courses." *Alberta Journal of Educational Research* XLIV.2 (Summer 1998): 208-20.
Bixler, Phyllis. "*The Secret Garden* 'Misread': The Broadway Musical as Creative Interpretation." *Children's Literature* 22 (1994): 101-23.
Borges, Luis. "The Garden of Forking Paths." *Ficciones.* Ed. and Trans. Anthony Kerrigan. New York: Grove, 1962. 89-101.
Creatures. CyberLife Technology. CD-ROM. Novato, CA: Mindscape Entertainment,
1996-97.
Cyan. *Myst.* CD-ROM. San Francisco: Broderbund Software, 1993-94.
——. *Riven.* CD-ROM. San Francisco: Broderbund Software, 1997.
Douglas, Jane Yellowlees. "Will the Most Reflexive Relativist Please Stand Up: Hypertext, Argument and Relativism." *Page to Screen: Taking Literacy into the Electronic Era.*
Ed. Ilana Snyder. New York: Routledge, 1998. 144-62.
Gay, Geri. "Issues in Accessing and Constructing Multimedia Documents." *Contextual
Media: Multimedia and Interpretation.* Ed. Edward Barrett & Marie Redmond. Cambridge: MIT Press, 1997. 175-88.
His Dark Materials. 2000. 29 Jan. 2006.
<http://www.randomhouse.com/features/pullman/goldencompass/index.html>.
Kline, Stephen. *Out of the Garden: Toys and Children's Culture in the Age of TV Marketing.*
Aurora, Ontario: Garamond, 1993.
"The Liber Angelorum."*His Dark Materials.* 29 Jan. 2006.
<http://www.randomhouse.com/features/pullman/subtleknife/liber.html>.
Mackey, Margaret. "*Little Women* Go to Market: Shifting Texts and Changing Readers." *Children's Literature in Education* 29.3 (Sept. 1998): 153-73.
Moulthrop, Stuart. "No War Machine." *Reading Matters: Narratives in the New Media
Ecology.* Ed. Joseph Tabbi & Michael Wutz. Ithaca: Cornell UP, 1997. 269-92.
Murray, Janet H. "The Pedagogy of Cyberfiction: Teaching a Course on Reading and
Writing Interactive Narrative." *Contextual Media: Multimedia and Interpretation.* Ed.
Edward Barrett & Marie Redmond. Cambridge: MIT Press, 1997. 129-62.
My Teacher is an Alien, based on the series by Bruce Colville. CD-ROM. New York:
Byron Preiss Multimedia, 1997.

Pullman, Philip. *The Golden Compass.* Alfred A. Knopf, 1995.
——. *The Golden Compass.* New York: Scholastic, 1995.
——. "Invisible Pictures." *Signal* 60 (Sept 1989): 160-86.
——. "Let's Write It in Red: The Patrick Hardy Lecture." *Signal* 85 (Jan 1998): 44-62.
——. *The Subtle Knife.* New York: Scholastic, 1997.
Scieska, Jon. *The Stinky Cheese Man and other Fairly Stupid Tales.* Illus. Lane Smith. London: Viking, 1992.
SimCity Classic. CD-ROM. Np: Maxis, 1989.
Spiegelman, Art. *The Complete Maus.* CD-ROM, New York: Voyager, n.d.
Trivizas, Eugene. *The Three Little Wolves and the Big Bad Pig.* Illus. Helen Oxenbury. Oxford: Heinemann, 1993.
Turkle, Sherry. *Life on the Screen: Identity in the Age of the Internet.* New York: Simon and Schuster, 1995.
Welch, Nancy. "Sideshadowing Teacher Response." *College English* 60.4 (April 1998): 374-95.
Wood, Julian. "Repeatable Pleasures: Notes on Young People's Use of Video." *Reading Audiences: Young People and the Media.* Ed. David Buckingham. Manchester: Manchester UP, 1993. 184-201.

Postscript (2005)

"Playing in the Phase Space" was an article that took a long time to germinate and a short time to write. For more than a year, I collected samples of material that had "phase space" potential and mulled over the implications of the concept. The writing was a pleasure because the thinking was ripe by the time I began the real work of getting my ideas down on paper.

To have the article published in *Signal* was a great honour. Before long, however, I began to feel the collector's twinge again. Materials that demonstrated phase space potential or hinted at expansions to the theory began to attract my attention once more, and I re-established my collector's box in the office. In the first article, I looked briefly at some of the implications of the phase space concerning reading behaviours; with my new collection of materials, I began to consider issues of reading more closely. I was interested in the many ways in which readers step into and move outside of the story world, and curious to explore whether contemporary western culture particularly favours texts that foster such movement across the boundaries of the narrative.

By the time I had written "At Play on the Borders of the Diegetic: Story Boundaries and Narrative Interpretation," *Signal* was moving into its final phase, so it was not possible to publish this sequel article in that journal. Instead, I turned to the *Journal of Literacy Research*, the organ of the National Reading Conference, and the article appeared in 35.1 (2003): 591-632.

Further Readings

We urge readers to peruse the Works Cited for each of the articles to find additional further resources.

Encyclopedias and Companions

Carpenter, Humphrey and Mari Prichard. *The Oxford Companion to Children's Literature.* Oxford: Oxford UP, 1984.

Hunt, Peter, ed. *International Companion Encyclopedia of Children's Literature.* 2 vols. London: Routledge, 2004.

Jones, Raymond E. and Jon C. Stott. *Canadian Children's Books: A Critical Guide to Authors and Illustrators.* Don Mills, ON: Oxford UP, 2000.

Lees, Stella and Pam Macintyre, eds. *The Oxford Companion to Australian Children's Literature.* Melbourne, New York: Oxford UP, 1993.

Silvey, Anita, ed. *Children's Books and Their Creators.* Boston: Houghton Mifflin, 1995.

Watson, Victor, ed. *The Cambridge Guide to Children's Books in English.* Cambridge: Cambridge UP, 2001.

Reference Series

Children's Literature Review. Detroit: Gale Research, 1976-present.

Dictionary of Literary Biography. Detroit: Gale Research, 1978-present.

Something About the Author. Detroit: Gale Research, 1971-present.

Journals

Bookbird (IBBY; Online 2004-).

CCL/LCJ [*Canadian Children's Literature/Littérature canadienne pour la jeunesse*] (University of Winnipeg).

Children's Literature (Johns Hopkins UP; Online 2003-).

Children's Literature Association Quarterly (Johns Hopkins UP; Online 2005-).

Children's Literature in Education (SpringerLink; Online 1997-).

The Horn Book (Boston: Horn Book; Online 1990-).

The Lion and the Unicorn (Johns Hopkins UP; Online 1995-).

Papers: Explorations into Children's Literature (Australia: Magpies; Online 2004-).
Signal (Thimble Press, issues 1-100, 1969-2003; annotations Online 1994-2003).

Indexes

Children's Literature Abstracts. International Federation of Library Associates. 1993-1999.
Hendrickson, Linnea. *Children's Literature: A Guide to the Criticism.* 1987. Boston: G.K. Hall, 1987. 7 Feb 2006. <http://www.unm.edu/~lhendr/>.
MLA International Bibliography. New York: MLA, 1969-present. (Print and electronic).
Rahn, Suzanne. *Children's Literature: An Annotated Bibliography of the History and the Criticism.* New York: Garland, 1981.

Books, Special Issues, and Articles

Bingham, Jane and Grayce Scholt. *Fifteen Centuries of Children's Literature: An Annotated Chronology of British and American Works in Historical Context.* Westport, CT: Greenwood, 1980.
Egoff, Sheila. *Thursday's Child: Trends and Patterns in Contemporary Children's Literature.* Chicago: ALA, 1981.
Eisner, Will. *Comics and Sequential Art.* Tamarac, FL: Poorhouse Press, 1985.
Haviland, Virginia. *Children and Literature: Views and Reviews.* Glenview, IL: Scott, Foresman, 1973.
Hunt, Peter. *An Introduction to Children's Literature.* Oxford: Oxford UP, 1994.
Kiefer, Barbara. *The Potential of Picturebooks: From Visual Literacy to Aesthetic Understanding.* New York: Prentice Hall, 1995.
Lukens, Rebecca J. *A Critical Handbook of Children's Literature.* 7th ed. Boston: Allyn and Bacon, 2003.
——. *The Nimble Reader: Literary Theory and Children's Literature.* New York: Twayne, 1996.
Meek, Margaret, et al., eds. *The Cool Web: The Pattern of Children's Reading.* London: The Bodley Head, 1977.
——. *Information & Book Learning.* Stroud: Thimble P, 1996.
Mosaic 34.2 (2001). (Children's literature special issue).
Nodelman, Perry and Mavis Reimer. *The Pleasures of Children's Literature.* 3rd ed. Boston: Allyn and Bacon, 2003.
Poetics Today 13.1 (1992). (Children's literature special issue).
Sloan, Glenna. *Give Them Poetry!: A Guide for Sharing Poetry with Children K-8.* New York: NCTE, 2003.

Tatar, Maria. *Off with Their Heads!: Fairy Tales and the Culture of Childhood.* Princeton: Princeton UP, 1992.

Zipes, Jack. *Oxford Companion to Fairy Tales.* New York and Oxford: Oxford UP, 2000.

———. *Sticks and Stones: The Troublesome Success of Children's Literature from Slovenly Peter to Harry Potter.* New York, London: Routledge, 2001.

Websites

Bibliography of Children's Literature Criticism to Accompany Perry Nodelman and Mavis Reimer's Pleasures of Children's Literature, 3rd. ed. Compiled by Perry Nodelman. 7 Feb. 2006.
<http://io.uwinnipeg.ca/~nodelman/resources/allbib.htm>.

The Children's Literature Web Guide. 7 Feb. 2006.
<http://www.ucalgary.ca/~dkbrown/>.

Kay E. Vandergrift's Special Interest Page. 7 Feb. 2005.
<http://www.scils.rutgers.edu/~kvander/>.

SOURCES

Permission for the opening quotations from Margaret Meek in Chapter I (page 2) reprinted by permission from Thimble Press. Permission for the opening quotation from John Marsden in Chapter VI (pages 201-02) reprinted with permission from the author.

Chapter I

"Happy Endings? Of Course, and Also Joy" was first published in *The New York Times Book Review*, November 8, 1970. Reprinted by permission of Natalie Babbitt.

Chambers, Aidan. "Axes for Frozen Seas." *Booktalk: Occasional Writing on Literature & Children* (1985), reissued Stroud, Glos.: Thimble Press, 1995.

Rochman, Hazel. "Introduction: Beyond Political Correctness" in *Against Borders: Promoting Books for a Multicultural World.* Chicago: ALA Books, 1993. Reprinted with permission from the American Library Association.

Yusefi, Naser. "Good Books, Bad Books—and Who Decides Why" (Tehran). *Bookbird* 33.3-4 (1995): 48-49. Permission to reprint has been granted by Bookbird, Inc.

Chapter II

Adams, Gillian. "Medieval Children's Literature: Its possibility and Actuality." *Children's Literature* 26 (1998): 1-24. Published by Yale University Press, Copyright © 1998.

Hunt, Peter. "Passing on the Past: The Problem of Books that Are for Children and that Were for Children." *Children's Literature Association Quarterly* 21.4 (1996): 200-02. Reprinted by permission of the Children's Literature Association.

Gannon, Susan R. "Report from Limbo: Reading Historical Children's Literature Today." *Signal* 85 (1998): 63-74. Reprinted with permission of Thimble Press.

Chapter III

Brown, Marcia. "Distinction in Picture Books." *Illustrators of Children's Books 1946-1956*. Ruth Hill Viguers, Marcia Dalphin, Bertha Mahony Miller, eds. Boston: The Horn Book, 1958. 2-12. Reprinted with permission of Marcia Brown.

Deborah Stevenson. "Narrative in Picture Books or, The Paper that Should Have Had Slides" in *STORY: From Fireplace to Cyberspace: Connecting Children and Narrative*. Betsy Hearne, Janice M. Del Negro, Christine Jenkins, Deborah Stevenson, eds. Reprinted with permission from the Publications Office of Graduate School of Library and Information Studies, University of Illinois at Champaign, IL. Copyright © 1998 The Board of Trustees of the University of Illinois.

Chambers, Aidan. *Tell Me: Children's Reading and Talk*. Stroud, Glos.: Thimble P, 1993. 48-49, 94-97. Reprinted with permission of Thimble Press.

Copyright © 1993, 1994 by Scott McCloud. Reprinted by permission of HarperCollins Publishers.

O'Sullivan, Emer. "Translating Pictures" *Signal 99* (1999): 167-75. Reprinted with permission of Thimble Press.

Chapter IV

Nodelman, Perry. "The Nursery Rhymes of Mother Goose: A World without Glasses." *Touchstones: Reflections on the Best in Children's Literature*. Vol. 2. Ed. Perry Nodelman. West Lafayette: ChLA, 1987. 183-201. Reprinted by permission of the Children's Literature Association.

Styles, Morag, "'From the Best Poets'?: How the Canon of Poetry for Children is Constructed" Chapter 9 in *From the Garden to the Street: An Introduction to 300 years of Poetry for Children*. London: Cassell, 1998. 186-96. Copyright © Morag Styles, 1998. Reprinted with permission of the publisher, The Continuum International Publishing Group.

Chapter V

Crago, Hugh. "What is a Fairy Tale?" *Signal* 100 (2003): 8-26. Reprinted with permission of Thimble Press.

Altmann, Anna. "Parody and Poesis in Feminist Fairy Tales" *CCL/LCJ* 73 (1994): 22-31. Reprinted with permission of *Canadian Children's Literature/Littérature canadienne pour la jeunesse*.

Sullivan, C.W. "Fantasy" in Dennis Butts, editor, *Stories and Society: Children's Literature in its Social Context*, 1992, © Dennis Butts and Editorial Board,

Lumière (Co-operative) Press Ltd., reproduced with permission of Palgrave Macmillan.

Chapter VI

Macleod, Anne Scott. "The Journey Inward: Adolescent Literature in America, 1945-1995," in *Reflections of Change: Children's Literature Since 1945*, Edited by Sandra Beckett, Copyright © 1997 by International Research Society for Children's Literature. Reproduced with permission of Greenwood Publishing Group, Inc. Westport, CT.
Reprinted by permission from *Responding to Young Adult Literature* by Virginia Monseau. Copyright © 1996 by Virginia Monseau. Published by Heinemann, a division of Reed Elsevier, Inc., Portsmouth, NH. All rights reserved.
Schmidt-Dumont, Geralde. "Poetic Encryption and Sex Scrubbed Clean: A Report from Germany" *Bookbird* 32.2 (1994): 10-15. Permission to reprint has been granted by Bookbird, Inc.
Hunt, Carol. "Young Adult Literature Evades the Theorists" *ChLA Quarterly* 21.1 (1996): 4-11. Reprinted by permission of the Children's Literature Association.

Chapter VII

Kumar, Sanjay. "Theatre for Children in India: An Instrument for Social Change?" *Bookbird* 36.4 (1998): 30-32. Permission to reprint has been granted by Bookbird, Inc.
Zipes, Jack. "Political Children's Theatre in the Age of Globalization" *Theater* 33.2 (2003): 48-61. Reprinted with permission of Jack Zipes.
Schneider, Wolfgang. "'Rosy Cheeks and Shining Eyes' as Criteria in Children's Theatre Criticism." *The Lion and the Unicorn* 19.1 (1995): 71-76. © The Johns Hopkins University Press. Reprinted with permission of The Johns Hopkins University Press.

Chapter VIII

Mehlinger, Keith. "Literature Resists Film: A Case Study of *The Planet of Junior Brown*." *Bookbird* 38.1 (2000): 12-18. Permission to reprint has been granted by Bookbird, Inc.
Hastings, A. Waller. "Moral Simplification in Disney's *The Little Mermaid*." *The Lion and the Unicorn* 17 (1993): 83-92. © The Johns Hopkins Universi-

ty Press. Reprinted with permission of The Johns Hopkins University Press.

Bassi, Shaul. "Traffic in the Jungle: Teachers, Lawyers, Doctors, and Animals in Three Kipling Films." *Heart of Lightness: The Magic of Children's Literature.* Laura Tosi, ed. Venice: Cafoscarina, 2001. 175-85. Reprinted with permission of Libreria Editrice Cafoscarina.

Chapter IX

Lamb, Wendy. "Strange Business: The Publishing Point of View." *Signal* 87 (1998): 167-73. Reprinted with permission of Thimble Press.

Mahy (Lyttelton), Margaret. "The Writer in New Zealand: Building Bridges Through Children's Books." *Bookbird* 34.4 (1996): 6-11. Permission to reprint has been granted by Bookbird, Inc.

Nodelman, Perry. "Fear of Children's Literature: What's Left (or Right) After Theory?" *Reflections of Change: Children's Literature Since 1945.* Edited by Sandra Beckett, Copyright © 1997 by International Research Society for Children's Literature. Reproduced with permission of Greenwood Publishing Group, Inc. Westport, CT.

Mackey, Margaret. "Playing in the Phase Space: Contemporary Forms of Fictional Pleasure." *Signal* 88 (Jan. 1999): 16-33. Reprinted with permission of Thimble Press.

INDEX

Dresang, Eliza 303
  Radical Change 304
drugs 202
druids 198
Du sagst ja, ich sag' nein (Donovan) 218
Duktig Pojke! (Edelfeldt) 219
"dumbing down" 303
Dunning, Stephen
  Literature for Adolescents: Teaching Poems, Stories,
    Novels and Plays 229
Dunsany, Lord 195
Dusinberre, Juliet 75, 98, 295, 297
dwarfs 193, 197, 198
Dyer's Hand, The (Auden) 13

Each Peach Pear Plum (Ahlberg) 23
early modern
  period 58n4, 60n11
  texts 61n19
Earthsea trilogy (Le Guin) 196, 197
Easter 60n14
Easter Bunny That Overslept, The
  (Friedrich/Adams) 96
ebonics 59n9
Ecbasis Captiviti, The 52, 56, 60n14
Eclogues (Theodolus) 51
economics 205
economy
  post-industrial 208
  third-world 243
Edelfeldt, Inger
  Duktig Pojke! 219
  Jim im Spiegel 219
Edelstein, Der (Boner) 58n4
Edgeworth(s) 73
  Maria 76
editor(s) 1, 4, 29, 149, 151, 152, 154-57,
  201
Edmonton (Canada) 337
education 42, 48, 68, 70, 94, 165, 205, 209, 229,
  232, 243, 245, 265, 266, 294, 307
  departments 235
  history 75
  majors 214
  multicultural 295
  secondary 231, 232
  See also academia; classroom; curriculum;
    teachers
"Eena meena mina mo" 131
Egbert of Liège
  Fecunda ratis 53
Egoff, Sheila 1
Ehlert, Lois
  Circus 95
eighteenth century
  as beginning of modern childhood 44, 45
  as beginning of period of formalizing pre-
    existing ideas of childhood 74
  child-centred teaching methods in 73
  children's literature as a separate branch of
    literature 41, 58n4

female Cinderellas outnumber male
  Cinderellas in the 186
  marketing nursery rhymes in the 150
  rise of realistic fiction in 189
  See also Romanticism
Ein Teil von mir (Schlipper) 219
Einbahnstrae (Benjamin) 249
electronic discussion groups 231, 237, 238n5. *See*
  also CHILD_LIT; KIDLIT; PUBYAC
electronic text 98. *See also* hypertext
electronic technology 170
elementary school 128
Elephant and the Bad Baby, The (Vipont/Briggs)
  108
Elizabethans 226
Ellerbee, Linda 99
"Elsie Marley is grown so fine" 137
elves 193, 197, 198
emblem book 93
Emilia, Reggio 252
empowerment of girls 182, 183
enchanted sleep 176
End of the Rainbow, The (Reuter) 98
endings
  closed vs. open 220
  happy 7, 8, 171, 174, 175, 176, 180, 194, 220
  unhappy 220
England. *See* Britain English departments (col-
  lege) 68, 215, 232, 235
English Journal 223-24, 228, 231, 233, 234, 235
Enlightenment 219
epic 189, 197, 198
Erasmus
  Sermon of the Chylde Jesus 47
Es muß aber geheim bleiben (Bloem) 219
escape literature 193, 199
Essay on the Archaeology of Popular Phrases and
  Nursery Rhymes (Ker) 135
etching 86
euphemisms 25, 26
Europe 46, 48, 60n11, 160, 226
  Eastern 37
  Western 190
  medieval 46, 55
  YA literature in 203
  See also Britain; France; Germany; Italy
European Children's Literature Symposium
  125
Everett, Gwen
  Li'l Sis and Uncle Willie 102
Everyboy and Everygirl 174
Everyman 5
evil(s) 192, 197, 198, 199, 208
  human 195
Ewing, Juliana 76
exaggeration 141
existentialism 212, 221, 253
experimental art 254
Eyerly, Jeannette
  He's My Baby, Now? 232